Beyond Consensus

Beyond Consensus

Improving Collaborative Planning and Management

Richard D. Margerum

The MIT Press
Cambridge, Massachusetts
London, England

For information about special quantity discounts, please email <special_sales@mitpress.mit.edu>

This book was set in Sabon by Toppan Best-set Premedia Limited. Printed and bound in the United States of America.

Library of Congress Cataloging-in-Publication Data

Margerum, Richard D., 1965–
Beyond consensus : improving collaborative planning and management / Richard D. Margerum.
  p. cm.
Includes bibliographical references and index.
ISBN 978-0-262-01581-3 (hardcover : alk. paper)—ISBN 978-0-262-51621-1 (pbk. : alk. paper)
1. Environmental management. 2. Conservation of natural resources—Planning. 3. Land use—Planning. I. Title.
GE300.M368 2011
333.72—dc22
                                                        2010049666

10 9 8 7 6 5 4 3 2 1

For Sonya, Aidan, and Corey

Contents

Preface

This book is based on over fifteen years of research on collaboration in natural resources, land use planning, social services, and transportation planning. Much of this work is drawn from case study research, because I believe that theories for guiding practice need to take into account the complexities of real-world settings (Yin 2009). I have found it particularly valuable to compare across the rich diversity of cases in several countries, supplementing this research with narrower studies of specific issues through large-sample surveys.

The case studies span over sixty examples in two countries (see table 0.1), and I conducted the research both independently and with research partners. These case study investigations included site visits, interviews with participants, and the collection of written documents. During my years of research on collaboration, I also interviewed many individual participants involved in cases not listed in the table. For several of the studies I was involved in, we used surveys to assess phenomena from a broader perspective.

The lessons from one or even forty cases are not necessarily transferable to every setting. Nevertheless, having researched collaboration in many different places, I believe that we can all learn some common lessons from this to improve the effectiveness of collaboration. A more detailed description of the research methods for these various cases is contained in the appendix. Throughout this book, I use quotes recorded in surveys, on audiotapes, and in research notebooks. I have kept the sources confidential, except where I had permission to use their quotes.

In addition to my research, I have also been involved in several collaboration efforts. I worked for the Wisconsin Department of Natural Resources (DNR) and its Water Integration Team to develop policies for integrating water management activities across the agency. For four years, I was on the steering committee of the Long Tom Watershed Council in Eugene, Oregon, including roles as chair and vice chair. I continue to serve on the Southern Willamette Valley Groundwater Management Area Committee. Finally, I have facilitated a number of groups—some as a volunteer but others in a paid capacity. I call on a number of these firsthand

Table 0.1
Case study data

Case study	Location	Interviews	Observation	Other data	Dates of study
Black Earth Creek	Wisconsin	4	No	Reports, survey[1]	1993
Starkweather Creek	Wisconsin	7	No	Reports, survey[1]	1993
Lower Wisconsin River	Wisconsin	11	No	Reports, survey[1]	1993, 1997
Upper Wisconsin River	Wisconsin	11	No	Reports, survey[1]	1993
Milwaukee River	Wisconsin	20	No	Reports, survey[1]	1993
Lake Winnebago	Wisconsin	11	No	Reports, survey[1]	1993, 1997
Upper Mississippi River	Iowa, Wisconsin, Minnesota	14	No	Reports, survey[1]	1993
Lake Tahoe	California, Nevada	4	No	Reports	1993
San Francisco Estuary	California	5	No	Reports	1997
Chicamauga-Nickajack River	Tennessee	5	Yes	Reports	1997
North West	New South Wales	6	Multiple	Reports, survey[1]	1995
Illawarra	New South Wales	4	Yes	Reports, survey[1]	1995, 1998
Clarence River	New South Wales	5	Multiple	Reports, survey[1]	1995
Georges River	New South Wales	11	Yes	Reports, survey[1]	1995, 1997
Hacking River	New South Wales	9	Yes	Reports, survey[1]	1995
Berowra Creek	New South Wales	4	No	Reports	1998
Illawarra Integration Team	New South Wales	5	No	Reports	1998
Murray Darling Basin	Multistate	5	No	Reports, studies	1995, 2008
Goulburn-Broken	Victoria	5	No	Reports, survey[1]	1995

Table 0.1
(continued)

Case study	Location	Interviews	Observation	Other data	Dates of study
Corangamite	Victoria	3	No	Reports, survey[1]	1995
Mount Lofty Ranges	South Australia	2	No	Reports	1995
Lockyer Valley	Queensland	4	Yes	Reports, studies, survey[1]	1995, 1997
Condamine River	Queensland	5	Yes	Reports, survey[1]	1995
Mary River	Queensland	7	Multiple	Reports, survey[1]	1995, 1997
Pioneer River	Queensland	4	Yes	Reports, survey[1]	1995
Johnstone River	Queensland	9	Yes	Reports, survey,[1] minutes[2]	1995
Trinity Inlet	Queensland	10	No	Reports, minutes[2]	1995, 1998
Tully River	Queensland	4	No	Reports	1998
Herbert River	Queensland	3	No	Reports, survey[1]	1995
South East Queensland 2001	Queensland	12	No	Reports, survey[1]	1999
Denver Metro Vision 2020	Colorado	25	No	Reports, survey,[1] news[3]	2001, 2010
Long Tom Watershed	Oregon	3	Multiple	Reports, participation[4]	2001–2005
Southern Willamette Valley Groundwater Management Area Commission	Oregon	0	Multiple	Participation[4]	2003–present
Umpqua Watershed	Oregon	2	No	Reports	2001
Salem Area Councils	Oregon	2	No	Reports	2001
Johnson Creek Watershed	Oregon	1	No	Reports	2001

Table 0.1
(continued)

Case study	Location	Interviews	Observation	Other data	Dates of study
Rogue Coordinating Committee	Oregon	9	Yes	Reports, minutes[2]	2002
Mackay Whitsunday Natural Resource Management Group	Queensland	7	No	Reports, interviews	2007
Port Phillip and Westernport Catchment Management Authority	Victoria	5	No	Reports, interviews	2007
Multnomah County	Oregon	24	No	Reports, interviews, survey[1]	2005
Area Commissions on Transportation	Oregon	48	Yes	Reports, interviews survey[1]	2008–2009
San Diego Association of Governments	California	10	Yes	Reports, interviews survey[1]	2010

Notes:
1. For details of the survey methods and response rates, see the appendix.
2. The case studies included an analysis of all available meeting minutes.
3. The case studies included an analysis of all newspaper articles during the planning process.
4. The author is or was a stakeholder representative on the group.

experiences in this book, because I find that working with a group on an ongoing basis often provides insights into the nuances of collaboration that are not revealed through short-term observations or interviews.

Partly because of my involvement in collaboration efforts, I recognize that researching collaboration is complex because it involves so many issues and perspectives. This complexity requires considerable interpretation, distillation, and analysis by the researcher to draw out the issues, themes, or theories. Therefore, whenever possible my research has been verified with the participants to ensure it is an accurate reflection of the events that have occurred. Multiple sources of information have been used to explore different issues and questions as well. My goal has been to eliminate any factual errors, but there are likely to be differences in interpretation and conclusions.

In presenting this analysis, I have also made extensive use of the literature, including published articles and books, reports, theses, and other documents. I believe that this kind of comparison is essential to further test the findings, and compare my findings to those of other researchers and analysts.

Acknowledgments

There are many people to thank for their help over the many years of my research on collaboration. I deeply appreciate the mentorship of Dr. Stephen Born early in my research career. Steve first got me interested in complex interjurisdictional problems, stressed the politics of environmental management, and was a stickler for careful research and writing. He instructed me to never take a job with the word coordinator in the title, and although I ignored the advice several times, I was always reminded of it when dealing with the frustrations of the position.

I also want to acknowledge my research collaborators. Dr. Bruce Hooper welcomed me during my sabbatical in Australia and introduced me to the issues facing rural Australian communities. Dr. Geoff McDonald always offered insightful and critical perspectives on Australian natural resources management. He also hosted a series of informal research forums in Brisbane in the late 1990s that brought together a range of researchers working on collaboration issues, creating a rich environment in which to discuss nascent ideas and work in progress. Dr. Debra Whitall (U.S. Forest Service) and I collaborated on my research on the Rogue Basin, and she provided an invaluable insider-outsider standpoint. Dr. Cathy Robinson with the Commonwealth Scientific and Industrial Research Organization (CSIRO) reviewed all the early chapters of this book during my sabbatical in Australia. Her insights and ongoing cooperation on large-scale collaboration efforts continue to lead to interesting conversations and good debates. I also appreciate my discussions and collaboration with the other researchers at CSIRO, particularly Dr. Marcus Lane and Bruce Taylor. My recent work with Susan Brody and Bob Parker on collaboration in transportation and land use planning has also allowed for interesting comparative perspectives.

Another group of people I have appreciated over the years has been the doctoral and master's students who have worked with me. While I provided early guidance on their research projects and supported their efforts, in the end I learned as much from them as they did from me. In particular, I want to thank Dr. Stacy Rosenberg and Kate (Bodane) Parker, whose research was important for this book. I also want to thank Rachael Holland, Melanie Mintz, Sam Fox, and Chu Chen, all of whom worked on my research projects or helped collect data as part of their thesis work. Furthermore, I appreciate all of the students who have taken my collaboration class over the years; I often used them as a sounding board to float ideas, present hypotheses, and debate different views of collaboration.

I would also like to acknowledge the hundreds of practitioners, community members, and elected officials who agreed to be interviewed and observed over the years. Many of them took time out of their busy schedules to offer their insights, frequently extending their interview time long past my estimated duration. Many of these interviews were confidential to allow people to speak their minds about their experiences, so I don't list the interviewees individually. Yet I thank all of the named and unnamed sources for their wisdom.

Last but not least, I want to thank my family. My career and interests have really been a synthesis of my father's career as a scientific researcher and my mother's career as a politician. I am grateful to them for their love, inspiration, and support. Most of all, I would like to thank my wife, Sonya, and my sons, Aidan and Corey. All of this would not have been possible without their support. They endured long periods of time when I was away collecting data or holed up in my office writing. They came along on lengthy road trips to remote places while I gathered data and conducted interviews, including several thousand-mile journeys across Australia. Thank you for your love and understanding.

I

Introduction

1

What Is Collaboration?

There are places that you can easily fall in love with. Aimlessly floating down the Lower Wisconsin River past sandy beaches, you find yourself gazing up at the thickly forested hillsides. Your trance is only interrupted when your fellow canoeists find another sandy beach to stop at for a swim. But you are not the only one. Each year about four hundred thousand people spend a day on the river swimming, boating, fishing, hunting, picnicking, and visiting attractions such as Frank Lloyd Wright's Taliesin school.[1] Located within a few hours' drive of Chicago, Minneapolis, Madison, and Milwaukee, the area is popular for recreation. People come there to camp, or to stay at hotels and resorts, and some of them build cabins and second homes. It is a place that could easily become loved to death.

On the opposite side of the globe, in a dramatically different climate, millions of tourists flock to Cairns, Australia, each year to enjoy the tropical climate, hotels and seafood, and of course, Great Barrier Reef. They come from Asia, the United States, and Europe, and even a short package tour of Australia will usually include Cairns on the itinerary. At some point during their visit, almost all of these tourists will get on a boat and head out through the Trinity Inlet to the reef. As you leave the harbor, the city of Cairns fades into the lush green tropical rain forest on the hills surrounding the inlet and the water turns a deep, dark blue. These trips require boats, harbors, and navigation channels. The tourists want hotels, restaurants, and shops, and an array of other recreation activities during their stay. All of this affects the ecology of the Trinity Inlet, including impacts to water quality, fish, and habitat. Like the Lower Wisconsin River valley, it is a place in danger of being loved to death.

As different as these two spots are, they have several things in common. They are both places where natural amenities are at risk of being harmed by human use. They are both places where local control is fiercely defended, and state or federal involvement is looked at with suspicion. And they are both places where collaboration has had a significant impact on recreation, natural resources management, and land use planning. I chose to start with these two areas because they highlight the intersection of collaboration with politics and the public. They also illuminate the challenges, strengths, and weaknesses of translating consensus into results.

Collaboration involves a diverse set of autonomous stakeholders working to build consensus to produce results. The consensus-building process often does not produce complete agreement, but there are many examples where it spans ideology and deep-seated differences. The Lower Wisconsin and Trinity Inlet cases are not simply glowing accounts, however; they are also stories about the challenges and failures of translating consensus into an ongoing approach to delivering results. The important question posed in this book is not just how to build consensus but how the consensus achieved through collaboration can be translated into effective results. The issue I address is how to go "beyond consensus" in both a literal and figurative sense. Literally, this book concentrates on the factors for assessing collaboration, and helping groups produce agreements and create the products and networks necessary for implementation. Figuratively, the goal is to help shift the focus of research from consensus building to implementation.

The Cases

The story of the Lower Wisconsin River valley starts in the late 1980s, when the Wisconsin Department of Natural Resources (DNR) set up discussions concerning how the valley should be managed. Few people expected local efforts to succeed, because previous state and federal initiatives had already failed. The isolation of the hill and valley communities in the region supports strong feelings of independence and resistance to outside interference. In sum, the Lower Wisconsin River valley is an unlikely spot to expect collaboration to work. Yet recreation pressures were leading to user conflict and ecological damage, and the development of second homes and resorts was detracting from the valley's natural beauty. Several counties in the valley did not have any zoning laws, so initiatives to plan and manage the region were not met with open arms. State legislators from the area told DNR staff that any legislation to protect the valley would pass "over their dead bodies."[2]

Several years later, after months of deliberation by a twenty-six-member stakeholder group, thousands of mailed newsletters, and over four hundred hours of meetings, public forums, and open houses, the Wisconsin legislature passed the Lower Wisconsin Riverway Bill, sponsored by the same local legislators who vowed to oppose the initiative. This process, though, produced more than just legislation. It generated consensus on a plan for managing recreation along the river, agreement on the management of state lands in the valley, and a regional riverway board that administers performance standards to protect the scenic and ecological assets of the river valley. When the legislation passed, some of the counties in the valley still did not have any zoning regulations, but the region had visual performance standards that regulated the color, visibility, and screening of structures.

The story of the Trinity Inlet begins at a similar time, with a similar history of contention. Like the Lower Wisconsin River valley, there had been no regional plan for the inlet, and decisions by developers, the cities, and state government were leading to the inlet's deterioration. In 1987, the state of Queensland, local governments, and the Port Authority initiated a planning process to address the management of the inlet, bringing together technical experts, a range of stakeholders, community members, and Aboriginal representatives. The public input was not nearly as extensive as in the Wisconsin case, but the stakeholders all agreed to a management plan. The Port Authority, local governments, and state government also contributed funds to create the Trinity Inlet Management Program (TIMP) and hire staff.

A coordinator employed by TIMP worked with the participating organizations to administer the plan, produce a shared database, coordinate data collection, and establish a joint review process for activities and developments affecting the inlet. For the review process, managers from state government, local government, and the Port Authority agreed to jointly assess usage proposals. They reviewed marina plans, housing developments, and an array of tourism development proposals such as parasailing, jet boat operations, and canoe trails. TIMP itself had no new authority. It relied on the joint management plan and the shared decision-making authority of the participants. Representatives from each organization examined the proposals, reviewed information, identified concerns, and came to a consensus on recommendations; each organization then issued its own formal response.

Just as crucial to this story, in 1997 this carefully crafted structure began to dissolve, and TIMP and the joint review process no longer exist. Participants cited a number of reasons for the dissolution, including personality conflicts, a perception by some that it was no longer necessary, and concerns about sharing decision-making power. In particular, participants noted resistance to agency loss of autonomy along with tensions from underlying political differences between prodevelopment and proenvironment interests. The final blow to this integrated structure ironically came from the new Queensland Integrated Planning Act, which greatly reduced the time allowed to review development proposals and made the joint review committee structure unworkable.

These cases illustrate the potential and difficulties of collaboration. For one, they demonstrate that building consensus is time-consuming and difficult, but it can happen even in the most contentious settings. They also underscore how collaboration is often necessary because the complexity of a problem does not permit simple solutions, and many problems cannot be solved by one organization. Moreover, they show that collaboration is not just about developing a strategy but also about creating and sustaining arrangements to collaboratively implement it. The cases also emphasize that collaboration involves substantial transaction costs of time and money, and that such efforts are precarious given the need to share decision-making power. Finally, the cases illustrate the changing nature of many public policy and planning approaches today—changing because single-issue, narrowly focused approaches have addressed many of the more straightforward problems, and we are now left with the more difficult, contentious, and diffuse problems. These are the "wicked problems" (Rittel and Webber 1973) that collaboration frequently emerges to address.

Defining Collaboration

Collaboration is based on the concept that problems—whether defined by physical, political, socioeconomic, or other boundaries—need to be managed holistically. Over the years, these concepts have been captured by several different terms, including integrated environmental management, ecosystem management, place-based natural resources management, grassroots environmental management, watershed management, collaborative governance, and collaborative planning. I use the term collaboration in this book to refer to the collective set of ideas and principles encompassed by these other terms. Similarly, a wide variety of terms is used to refer to the groups that carry out collaboration, including stakeholder groups, consensus groups, councils, committees, and community-based collaboratives. Because I am interested in a range of collaborative enterprises, which includes groups operating at several different types of decision levels and scales, I have chosen to use the term collaborative to refer to these groups.

There are many different definitions of collaboration. Barbara Gray proposed one of the earliest and most succinct versions in her book *Collaborating*. She defined collaboration as a process through which "parties who see different aspects of a problem can constructively explore their differences and search for solutions that go beyond their own limited vision of what is possible" (Gray 1989, 5). The working definition that I have developed for this book focuses on both solutions and implementation:

Collaboration is an approach to solving complex problems in which a diverse group of autonomous stakeholders deliberates to build consensus and develop networks for translating consensus into results.

There are several other important terms encompassed in this definition. It is an *approach* to planning and public policy rather than just a process. People interact (or collaborate) all the time to share information or resolve differences, thereby constituting a more limited, onetime, or one-issue relationship. In the context of complex planning and public policy questions, collaboration implies a long-term, ongoing relationship.

Collaboration involves *stakeholders*, because individuals and organizations with a high stake in the outcomes must spend time understanding the problems before they can agree. The stakeholders create the depth of a collaborative approach. The process is also *deliberative*, allowing everyone to fully explore and debate the issues. This deliberation should also include a role for the public, which has a stake in the outcomes too, even if its interest is not as clearly defined. This helps ensure that agreements among the stakeholders are mirrored in the broader community, providing the breadth that supports the agreement.

In addition, collaboration requires *consensus* among the stakeholders and the public. Consensus may be defined by decision rules ranging from complete agreement to a simple majority, but in most cases it means an agreement that everyone can live with. This consensus defines the common goals and objectives, and the stronger the consensus, the more likely the stakeholders will support implementation.

Finally, collaboration requires *networks,* because reaching consensus is the easy part. The hard part is translating the consensus into results. This requires ongoing entities to guide implementation, rather than merely written plans or agreements. It also necessitates appropriate networks to support implementation and adapt management responses. This does not mean that all consensus-based processes require networks, but this book focuses on settings where the conditions demand an ongoing adaptive approach.

How Is Collaboration Different?

Collaboration has become a ubiquitous term in planning and management circles. It seems like what we used to call two people talking in a room has suddenly become collaboration. While some of this reflects the increasing popularity of collaboration, it also illustrates the tendency for management terms to wash through the literature and professions. The result is that the word has become somewhat diluted, and is now used to describe a wide range of processes and approaches.

To help explain collaboration, I like to compare and contrast several terms, which I call the "seven Cs." As defined above, *collaboration* captures a specific ongoing approach to planning and management. Each of the other Cs may be encompassed in a collaboration effort.

Communication involves the sharing of information. It can be one-way (a lecture or brochure) or two-way (an email exchange or a conversation). One-way communication can be done in effective or ineffective ways, but informing people is a relatively easy process. Two-way communication is inherently more difficult because it requires both parties to share information and listen. It is the core of any interactive process, and effective two-way communication is essential for collaboration.

Consultation is a formal process of communication with a community of people that may be conducted by governmental or nongovernmental organizations. Like communication, consultation can offer significant or little exchange of information. Furthermore, consultation can be carried out with significant or no effect on decision making. Presenting information to a room full of people is thus relatively easy, but it is much more difficult to design a process that allows those people to have meaningful and substantial input on an organization's decision. In collaboration, consultation can be important for stakeholder groups that need to obtain feedback from the broader public.

Conflict resolution describes a range of formal and informal processes for resolving the differences between two or more parties. Effective conflict resolution starts with effective communication, because the parties have to communicate and understand their differences before they can resolve them. Conflict resolution may simply be a negotiation, or it may involve more formal procedures like facilitation, mediation, and even arbitration. It is an integral part of collaboration, but it generally depicts a narrower process because it begins with a defined problem or conflict. This may constrain the type of approaches from the outset. In contrast, collaborative processes advance a shared vision, which begins with the stakeholders defining common goals and then resolves differences related to achieving those goals.

Consensus building refers to the series of steps through which individuals come together, share information, and reach a mutual agreement about problems, goals, and actions. Some people use consensus building interchangeably with collaboration, but I like to think of it as the planning phase of collaboration. Building consensus requires effective communication and conflict resolution, but it typically implies agreement through substantial or complete accord rather than simple majority rule. Consensus building produces agreements, although implementation often necessitates ongoing entities and networks to produce results.

Cooperation is defined as a process whereby participants work independently toward a common goal. The key term is independently. Cooperation can be an important implementation approach for a collaborative when the issues are well-known, the goals are clear, the setting is stable, and the implementation actions are not interdependent. Hence, cooperative approaches are frequently described as implementation through a plan or contract.

Coordination is defined as a process whereby participants work jointly toward a common end. A coordinated approach relies not only on a common goal but also on a process of functioning together that allows mutual adaptation and adjustment. Coordination is a crucial implementation approach for a collaborative group when there is less clarity regarding issues and goals, more dynamic settings, and interdependent implementation actions. This ongoing, interactive role also means that coordinated approaches require people, entities, or networks to support their work.

In short, collaboration has become a ubiquitous term because it is an umbrella concept incorporating many of the Cs listed above. Communication, consultation, and conflict resolution are an ongoing part of a collaboration effort. Consensus building is a core concept in the process of developing collaborative agreements, and implementation of those agreements may be carried out through cooperative or coordinated approaches.

When Do Collaboratives Need to Be Ongoing?

As this summary suggests, there are many deliberative planning and management efforts, and not all collaborative processes need to be ongoing. In some cases documented in this book, participants convened, built consensus, and then developed a cooperative plan that detailed implementation tasks to be carried out independently by different organizations. Many collaborative efforts, however, face complex problems with unclear data, changing conditions, and unclear intervention strategies. This often means there is a need for ongoing arrangements during implementation to respond to new information, make adjustments, and manage adaptively.

Adaptive management refers to a process of learning by doing in which the decision makers combine management activities with monitoring and feedback loops to allow for adjustment as well as improve future management (Holling and United Nations Environment Programme 1978; Layzer 2008; Webster 2009). When these monitoring approaches and management responses cut across jurisdictions, an ongoing structure that allows participants to coordinate their responses is needed. Most of this book focuses on issues and problems requiring these kinds of ongoing adaptive approaches.

While adaptive management has been described as a rational and scientific process, it has also been criticized as a trial-and-error process in which politics and science are intertwined. Several researchers have also questioned whether ongoing adaptive management approaches are able to respond effectively. In D. G. Webster's study (2009, 19) of adaptive management for international fisheries, she notes, "States try a cheap option, find that it doesn't work, and are left even more dissatisfied than before; escalation continues until a true solution is found or the fishery collapses, whichever comes first." Similarly, Judith Layzer (2008) contends that collaborative and adaptive approaches often lead to a lowest common denominator approach, because participants cannot achieve consensus on the most challenging issues. She also links adaptive management with flexible or voluntary management, and argues that learning and adjustment usually does not occur because of personnel turnover, resistance to changing established practices, and an unwillingness to address issues related to core value differences.

In her final assessment of adaptive approaches, Webster (2009, 32) is less pessimistic, asserting that national decision makers "have proven to be highly innovative, even within the constraints of international bargaining." She suggests that the institutional systems may continue to evolve and develop more nuanced frameworks that may help them to address a range of ongoing issues. Likewise, in John Scholz and Bruce Stiftel's assessment of complex water resources problems, they contend that the uncertainties of both the human and natural systems require fundamental changes in our approaches to governing. "Adaptive management, then, involves the evolution of new governance institutions capable of generating long-term, sustainable policy solutions to wicked problems through coordinated efforts involving previously independent systems of users, knowledge, authorities and organized interests" (Scholz and Stiftel 2005, 5).

In this book, I don't attempt to define the biophysical or socioeconomic conditions that may lead to the need for an ongoing and adaptive approach. When there is stability, clear objectives, and clear strategies to achieve those objectives, an adaptive approach may not be required. When there is uncertainty, changing conditions, newly emerging information, and even changing expectations, there will be a need to monitor and adjust activities based on feedback. By definition this requires an ongoing approach that can make these adjustments.

Why Has Collaboration Emerged?

There is a rapidly growing interest in collaboration across a range of fields. This interest stems from the shift from more single-issue, single-organization approaches to more holistic and cross-jurisdictional responses. In their article about integrated and collaborative efforts, Stephen Born and William Sonzogni (1995, 168) state that it is a "response to much of traditional natural resource management, which has been largely reactive, disjointed, and for narrow or limited purposes." This does not always mean giving up government roles or powers. Instead, it means sharing power to address the range of human, societal, and ecological needs, and the result can be more or less government roles.

This book draws much of its findings from research in the environmental and land use sector, but collaboration has emerged in many different fields. In the area of social services, for example, there is increasing interest and even mandates for collaboration among the governmental and nongovernmental sectors. Gray (1989) notes that reduced government spending for social problems coupled with increased private and nonprofit roles has led to increased collaboration to solve the more intractable social problems.

There are several reasons why collaboration has emerged and taken root in planning and management. First, some of the problems being addressed through collaboration are diffuse problems that have not been adequately addressed through traditional approaches. Water quality management, for example, has traditionally focused on the control of point source pollution. Yet today, the dominant source of pollution in many watersheds is runoff from urban and rural areas (nonpoint source pollution). This requires action and management—some of it voluntary—from a wide range of individuals and institutions, such as farmers, urban landowners, and cities.

Second, we have come to understand more about natural and human systems along with how they function, which means that we are more aware of interconnections. For example, we understand that water quality is linked to the management of land, wetlands, and floodplains. As water pollution control has shifted to nonpoint sources, water quality has increasingly involved the coordination of policies, economic incentives, and voluntary conservation programs to protect and enhance these natural amenities.

Third, the distrust of government in urban and particularly rural areas has generated conflict around planning and management efforts. Community interaction often comes late in decision processes, which limits the opportunity for influence and increases public frustration. Lack of communication also leads to misinformation among both community members and government staff, leading to greater community mistrust. Collaborative processes provide opportunities for people to have more decision-making involvement and in some cases a direct role in management activities.

Fourth, many problems are not short-lived issues resolved through a single conflict resolution process but instead ongoing ones requiring adaptation and adjustment. Issues confronting water quality do not go away; they demand continual attention, adjustment, and problem solving. As a result, problem solving is not just a change in policy but rather an adaptive management approach in which key decision makers receive monitoring feedback and make adjustments.

Fifth, there is an increasing demand for integrated solutions. Many traditional approaches to planning and management are single-issue oriented. When community-based watershed councils get started, they often find that there are many efforts to address individual topics, but few to integrate them. One agency deals with water quality, another with water quantity, and another with wetlands; local governments address land use, and a myriad of state, regional, and local entities deal with transportation. None of these participants consider how these issues interrelate on a watershed basis.

Finally, there is greater competition for land, resources, and the use of them. National forests in the United States, for instance, were historically viewed as areas of resource extraction. Yet the increasing use of these lands for recreation and the increased recognition of their ecological value has made the management of these lands much more complex. The problem is compounded by the relationship with neighboring public and private landowners, which in many areas is becoming increasingly difficult with more rural residents.

While the term collaboration may change over time, the underlying forces leading to collaboration will continue. In fact, with increasing population pressures, more difficult global environmental challenges, and more understanding of social, economic, and ecological interconnections, the need for some type of holistic and interconnected approach will only increase.

Where Is Collaboration Being Applied?

Collaboration is being advocated in many countries throughout the world, and much of it has emerged from applied learning that has preceded detailed scholarship. In the United States, state agencies and regional bodies began undertaking collaborative efforts in the 1990s to manage watersheds and forest systems as well as plan for regional growth (Clark et al. 1991; Innes et al. 1994; River Federation 1994; U.S. Environmental Protection Agency 1993). In particular, there has been a rapid increase in locally based collaborative groups in the United States, many of which are focused on watershed efforts. A study of watershed management organizations identified 600 nationwide (Clark, Burkardt, and King 2005). A study by Douglas Kenney and his colleagues (2000) identified 346 watershed partnerships west of the Mississippi, and William Leach, Neil Pelkey, and Paul Sabatier (2002) identified 150 watershed partnerships in California alone.

In public administration and public policy, the idea of collaborative and networked governance has emerged in response to complex cross-boundary issues and problems (Ansell and Gash 2007; Dukes 1996; May et al. 1996; Agranoff 1990; Mandell 1999, 2001). For example, David Chrislip and Carl Larson (1994) conducted detailed research on collaborative efforts involving local governments in six settings, and then tested some of the hypotheses from this work on another forty-six cases.

Collaborative approaches are also becoming increasingly common in the field of land use planning, particularly for regional and metropolitan scale issues (Helling 1998; McCann 2001; Lund et al. 2007; Margerum 2002b, 2005). A quick online search revealed over fifty "visioning" processes to address land use, transportation, and economic development at a regional scale. At the metropolitan scale, there are also many collaborative efforts around issues like social services, drug and alcohol treatment, and criminal justice (Darlington, Feeney, and Rixon 2005; Gray 1985; Colby and Murrell 1998; Marans and Schaefer 1998).

Australia has also been a hotbed of collaborative activity at several scales and levels. Many collaborative efforts were first spawned by the Community Landcare Program, which is a government-sponsored effort to encourage groups of landowners to come together and work with government to address soil and water conservation issues. A study in 1996 of these groups estimated that there were over 4,000 groups and 120,000 volunteer members (Curtis and Lockwood 2000). These efforts led states such as New South Wales, Victoria, Queensland, and Western Australia to develop policies or legislation for collaborative watershed (or catchment) groups (AACM and Centre for Water Policy Research 1995; Burton 1992; Mitchell and Hollick 1993). More recently, there was a significant new infusion of federal funding and program guidelines, resulting in the amalgamation of these groups into larger natural resources management organizations (Robins and Dovers 2007a; National Audit Office 2008).

Many other countries have also applied collaborative approaches. In Canada, provincial governments have initiated integrated watershed and basin management efforts (Dodge and Biette 1992; Shrubsole 1990). The United Kingdom, Japan, and other countries have seen new collaborative initiatives too—many focused around watersheds (Barrett 1995; Shrubsole 1990). Jeroen Warner's (2007) edited volume profiles collaboration efforts from countries such as Peru, Mexico, Bolivia, South Africa, the Mekong region, and Uzbekistan and highlights their potential for change as well as their likelihood of failure when confronting fundamental social, economic, and political barriers. Finally, in Europe there has been increasing attention focused on collaborative approaches to solving environmental problems, especially around water resources issues. Some of the early attempts concentrated on large-scale systems such as the Danube River basin and the Mediterranean Action Plan, but more recently this has been bolstered by efforts undertaken by the EU Water Initiative (Lindemann 2008; Mostert et al. 2007; Haas 1989). While European approaches have traditionally been more top-down, the increasing role of the European Union, the inclusion of new eastern European countries into the union, and the increased attention on diffuse pollution has all led to a greater emphasis on collaborative responses (Mostert et al. 2007; Pahl-Wostl 2002, 2006; Warner 2007).

In summary, collaboration is being widely applied throughout the world—often ahead of the theories that fully explain it. Practitioners frequently learn by doing, and thus one of the missions of applied fields like planning and public policy is to study practice, critique it, and develop theories that guide future practice.

What Are Results?

This book explores the translation of agreement into results, but what do I mean by results? There is a variety of approaches to measuring results, and chapter 10 explains the range of indicators and measures that can be used in evaluating collaboratives. Some of these factors have been used in the cases that I describe, such as input measures that assess the quality of information applied to decision making. Some of these indicators are also incorporated in the assessment factors listed throughout this book. For example, several of the factors discussed in chapters 3 and 4 are measures of process quality. When most people think of results, however, they think of concrete changes that address problems and issues. These can be described as outputs, performance indicators (or intermediate outcomes), and final outcomes (or impact measures).

Outputs are the direct products of the planning process, such as plans, policies, and regulations. In metropolitan Denver, for example, producing a regional vision plan for a seven-hundred-square-mile region supported by thirty-seven of thirty-nine signatory local governments was a significant result. A similar regional plan for South East Queensland was one of the first plans for an area that had been growing rapidly for ten years.

Performance indicators are the intermediate results of a collaborative process. These results might be changes in knowledge, attitudes, and awareness. For instance, planners and elected officials noted that the SEQ 2001 plan encouraged people to think about the region for the first time and provided concepts that began appearing in local government plans. These may also mean more concrete intermediate results. The South East Queensland region began recording the number of new infill or redevelopment proposals as an intermediate indicator of population and density targets. Finally, voluntary intervention programs may document the number of participants or changes in program participation, such as the number of people attending rural land management workshops.

Outcome measures (or impact measures) are the actual changes in social, economic, and environmental trends. They are often the results that generate the most interest, and their contrast with interim outcomes highlights the difference of each. Thus, the intermediate result of infill development proposals is an interim measure of the final outcome of increasing overall density, increasing utilization of public transit, or reducing urban expansion into outlying areas (or a combination of all three). Participation in a workshop is also an interim measure of ecosystem restoration, but the outcome measure is the effect on habitat and biodiversity.

When many people think of results, they think of final outcome measures. Are there more fish in the stream? Are we controlling urban sprawl? Is the population getting healthier? The problem is that these results are notoriously hard to measure. It often requires lots of data over a long period of time and with a sufficient intensity of intervention for a definitive result to be observed. For example, it could take years of intensive streambank restoration efforts to improve the ecological condition of a watershed, and years of data collection to flatten out the effects of seasonal and climatic variation. Even then, these restoration attempts may be eclipsed by changes in water use, upstream urbanization, agricultural practices, or the introduction of exotic species.

For these reasons, it is important to think of a range of approaches to evaluating collaboration. Chapter 10 reviews some of the indicators for measuring outputs, intermediate outputs, and final outputs. I also review indicators for assessing collaborative process and program logic. Some of these indicators are identified throughout this book as well, and the goal of all this discussion is to provide approaches to assessing collaboratives at varying points to improve their ability to achieve results.

When Do Collaboratives Fail?

This book starts with the assumption that collaboratives can and sometimes will fail. For example, in Eugene and Springfield, Oregon, a planning effort called Region 2050 collapsed because city leaders and competing factions could not agree on regional objectives and strategies. In both Australia and Oregon, some watershed-based groups have disappeared. Some lost key leaders, some lacked a strong vision, and others could not gain enough momentum to generate long-range commitments from participants.

More important, collaboratives may survive but fall short of expectations, achieve few results, or constrain other responses from being undertaken. In Australia's Murray Darling River Basin, a federal-state collaborative management effort operated for over fifteen years to address water allocation, water quality, and land management. Yet its failure to resolve competing demands for water between the states ultimately led to the demise of the collaborative, which was replaced by a new federal authority with substantial powers.

Did the collaborative efforts lay the groundwork for the new authority or delay its introduction by over a decade? No one can answer this question, or even be sure that the new basin authority will be any more effective. We may also have a hard time defining failure. We can identify the measures for assessing collaboratives at all stages of the process, though, to allow them to self-correct and be evaluated. Therefore, this book is based on the assumption that there is a range of ways we can assess collaboratives to improve their performance or hasten their demise.

Overview of This Book

Beyond Consensus is divided into four sections: an introduction to collaboration, the consensus-building process, approaches to moving beyond consensus, and the implications for practice. Part I includes this chapter, followed by typologies in chapter 2 that delineate collaborative efforts and networks to support implementation. These typologies are used throughout the book to explain how collaboration—and particularly implementation—differs among groups. The typology of networks is discussed below. The typology of collaboratives places them along a spectrum, which is demarcated by three archetypes: action collaboratives, organizational collaboratives, and policy collaboratives.

Action collaboratives are community-based groups that focus their collaboration efforts on direct action (for example, watershed restoration, ecosystem enhancement, and on-the-ground activities). Organizational collaboratives are groups that concentrate on the programs, priorities, and rules of management organizations (government, private, and nonprofit), including collaborative efforts sponsored by government agencies (for instance, U.S. Forest Service management plans). In turn, these organizations carry out activities and jointly produce action on the ground. Policy collaboratives are groups that focus their efforts on building consensus on policies (legislation, programs, and administrative rules). These policies ultimately affect organizations and the activities that they deliver on the ground through a range of approaches.

While these are portrayed as distinct categories of collaboratives, they are really only archetypes. In practice, it is not unusual for collaboratives to span levels, and in chapter 2 I discuss several of these examples. I also describe examples in which lower-level collaboratives may be nested within higher-level ones. This does not make the typology any less relevant; it does mean that some approaches are complex.

Part II examines the process of building consensus (see figure 1.1), because the process of implementation cannot be separated from that of consensus building. Many of these early steps have long-term effects on a group's ability to produce results. Chapter 3 reviews the process of convening collaboratives, chapter 4 looks at stakeholder deliberations during consensus building and their relationship to public involvement, and chapter 5 explores the products from consensus-building efforts.

Part III focuses on the implementation of collaboration, which often means translating agreements, plans, or strategies into action. Chapter 6 centers on the collaborative itself as an ongoing entity and the factors that determine whether they are sustained over time. Chapters 7, 8, and 9 build on the typology of implementation approaches introduced in chapter 2. Specifically, these chapters describe different networks used by collaboratives to translate products into results. This includes the social networks that provide important interpersonal pathways for information exchange and influence, interorganizational networks that allow governmental and nongovernmental organizations to coordinate their activities, and political networks that allow political actors to develop an integrated approach to

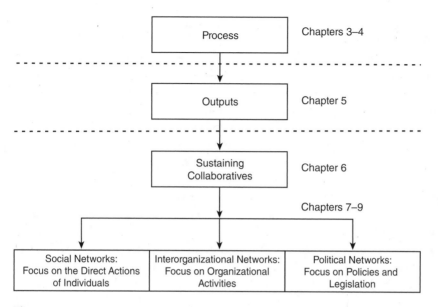

Figure 1.1
Overview of the book

policy implementation. Any given collaborative—regardless of where it is on the action-organizational-policy spectrum—may utilize one or more of these networks. Nevertheless, some collaboratives are better positioned than others to utilize certain networks.

Part IV examines how these different elements are translated into practice and prospects for the future. In particular, chapter 10 highlights the different forms and pathways that collaborative efforts might take, and the future opportunities and challenges for the array of people who influence collaborative practice. Chapter 11 reviews some of the trends facing collaboratives along with the communities, governments, and practitioners that support them.

Goals of This Book

My aim here is to improve collaborative efforts and make them more effective in translating their work into success on the ground. To do this, my book aspires to contribute two things. First, it strives to provide a better theoretical basis for assessing and explaining collaboratives as well as their ability to achieve results. Effective collaboration, as mentioned earlier, is not just about producing consensus but also about producing results from consensus. I believe that the typologies in chapter 2 underscore crucial differences between collaborative efforts, thereby helping direct researchers and practitioners to the theories and conceptual models that will be most useful for advancing their endeavors.

The typologies are not predictive models. Yet they better explain the variety of efforts and some of the reasons for their differences. Are these typologies perfect? Of course not; collaboration is a complex and dynamic phenomenon. But hopefully my contributions will improve the research and evaluation of collaboration, and spark alternations, amendments, or new typologies.

Second, my goal is to provide a set of concrete indicators for researchers and practitioners to assess collaboratives. Thus, rather than just talking generally about how collaborative efforts are convened, I have attempted to identify the specific factors that appear to define when they are effective. These factors are listed in chapters 3–9 and summarized in chapter 10. Where possible, these factors have been linked to specific methodologies and measures that can be used by researchers and practitioners. These indicators of effectiveness are also a work in progress. They draw on a diverse range of approaches and disciplines. I have applied some of these, but some are derived from other theories and researchers. Some are specific, others are vague, and still others may require entirely new methodologies. I don't view this as being the end of the discussion but instead hopefully the start of new deliberations about translating consensus into results.

2

Typologies for Collaboration

The Long Tom Watershed Council is a collaborative stakeholder group working to improve the water quality and restore habitat across 410 square miles in western Oregon. The group is led by a twelve-member steering committee, which is composed of a cross section of people with interests in the watershed. Operating by consensus, the group has worked over a number of years to build trust among diverse interests, agree on watershed conditions and restoration priorities, and ultimately help improve ecological conditions. On the first Thursday of every month, the steering committee meets in a small red building owned by the Bureau of Land Management affectionately know as the "red house." Looking out over wetlands and a used car lot, the committee works through its issues during three-hour meetings, which often creep past their 9:00 p.m. end time.[1]

The San Francisco Estuary Project was also a collaborative process for addressing water quality and quantity issues in a vast sixteen-hundred-square-mile system. It was led by a 49-member management committee composed of a wide range of stakeholders, several subcommittees, and a public advisory committee designed to incorporate some of the perspectives from the 7.5 million people living in the region (Innes et al. 1994). The group met in the downtown Oakland offices of the Bay Area Association of Governments, with many long and intense meetings led by a trained facilitator.[2]

The view from the red house is quite different from the one from the Bay Area Association of Governments offices, and the attire at the Long Tom meetings was usually more casual than at the San Francisco meetings. But if you overlook these differences, the process of these groups is remarkably similar. Many successful collaboratives start with a period of tension or mistrust, go through a phase of information sharing, reach a turning point when participants identify common goals, and move into a phase of implementation. Many less successful efforts have struggled through these phases or missed important steps, hampering their effectiveness.

On paper, the Long Tom and San Francisco cases meet the criteria of collaboration. They involved a cross section of stakeholders and the public. They worked to build consensus through intensive deliberation and creative problem solving. Additionally, they developed plans and structures for implementing their objectives. Having observed or participated in these forums in rural Wisconsin, urban Sydney, coastal Oregon, and the northern tropics of Australia, I have often been struck by the similarity of the lessons about group process and consensus building.

Yet a closer examination of the details of these two efforts reveals many differences in how collaboration has been translated into practice. While the Long Tom involves local landowners and managers, the San Francisco Estuary Project involved policymakers and major interest groups. The Long Tom focuses on direct action to restore local ecosystems, while the San Francisco Estuary Project concentrated on policies related to water quality and quantity. The Long Tom encompasses approximately twelve thousand people in its 780-square-mile watershed, while the 1,600-square-mile estuary contains over seven million people and the drainage basin encompasses 40 percent of California. These differences tell only part of the story, however.

To really understand how these collaboratives operate and how they worked to achieve results, it is necessary to understand more fundamental differences. First, the focus of collaboration in the Long Tom watershed is different from the San Francisco estuary. They operate at different levels, and therefore the nature of their interaction is different. Importantly, this difference is not just defined in terms of government participation, because government representatives were involved in both efforts. Instead, it is collaboration about on-the-ground actions versus collaboration about policy.

Second, these collaborative efforts utilized different networks for implementation. This does not refer to the network of trust, respect, and familiarity built up among the participants or stakeholders but rather the broader network that allows the consensus of the collaborative to produce results. The Long Tom relies heavily on social networks and, to a lesser extent, interorganizational networks. The San Francisco efforts depended on political and interorganizational networks. These networks allow the collaboratives to link with a broader set of decision makers, which is key to translating consensus into results.

This chapter introduces two typologies to explain these differences. To begin with, I use an institutional analysis framework to help identify a continuum of collaboratives based on their level of operation. Individual groups may fit anywhere along this continuum, and understanding where they lie assists in identifying the factors that will make them effective. Next, I introduce the concepts of social, interorganizational, and political networks to describe how the implementation attempts of collaboratives connect with a broader set of decision makers. While there is a natural affinity between the levels and types of networks (say, the link between action collaboratives and social networks), any given collaborative may utilize one or more network strategies, and many of the cases I present use multiple networks. Still, some choices about network strategies may create tensions or implementation difficulties.

Typologies from the Literature

Elizabeth Moore and Tomas Koontz (2003) note that typologies are helpful building blocks for theory. They also aid practitioners by providing a conceptual guide for analyzing and critiquing their work. In her groundbreaking book on collaboration, Gray (1989) starts with a broad definition of collaboration, and offers a typology based on the motivating factor and expected outcome. The result is a four-part classification of collaboration: dialogues like public meetings and policy discussions; information forums such as search conferences and community gatherings; negotiated settlements like regulatory negotiations and issue-specific disputes; and finally, collective strategies like partnerships, joint ventures, and cooperatives (see figure 2.1). This casts a much wider net over the term collaboration, resulting in many activities that I would place in the category of communication and conflict resolution.

Most collaborative efforts in the literature fall into the category of collective strategies, which are defined by groups advancing a shared vision through joint agreements. Groups are doing more than just sharing information; they are attempting to reach agreement on strategies and actions that can be undertaken. They are also doing more than simply resolving conflict; they are attempting to advance a

Author	Typology factors	Categories		
Gray (1989)	• Outcome: Information exchange or joint agreement • Motivation: Conflict resolution or shared vision	Dialogues		Negotiated settlements
		Information forums		Collective strategies
Moore and Koontz (2003)	• Government roles • Citizen roles	Government directed	Citizen directed	Hybrid
Cheng and Daniels (2005)	• Scale	Small: Community oriented		Large: Interest group oriented

Figure 2.1
Collaboration typologies

shared vision of what they want the future of their watershed, community, or region to look like. This shared vision is spelled out in a plan or agreement, and supported by an ongoing management entity.

Moore and Koontz (2003) use an approach developed by the Center for Watershed Protection (1998) to contribute one of the more refined typologies of collaborative watershed groups. They distinguish between groups that are government directed, citizen directed, and hybrid. A government-directed collaborative is one that is initiated, established, and sometimes supported by a government entity. A citizen-directed collaborative is one that is initiated, established, and managed directly by citizens. And hybrid models demonstrate some characteristics of both.

This typology is helpful because it begins to highlight some differences between groups based on their membership and leadership. Ryan Bidwell and Clare Ryan (2006) take a similar approach. They classify a group of twenty-nine watershed councils in Oregon according to the number and type of organizations participating in the collaborative. In doing so, they find several differences between agency-affiliated and independent partnerships relating to both membership composition and the nature of their activities. Independent partnerships, for example, are more likely to conduct scientific assessments or plans, while agency-affiliated partnerships more often rely on the priorities developed through a preexisting agency plan or program.

Anthony Cheng and Steven Daniels (2005) present another typology, which highlights the effect that scale has on group dynamics and the framing of watershed issues. They examine two nested watershed councils in Oregon: the McKenzie Watershed Council, the officially recognized body; and the Mohawk Watershed Partnership, a subregional group that includes many people who also serve on the McKenzie Council. Cheng and Daniels argue that the difference in geographic scale between the McKenzie (803 square miles) and the Mohawk (109 square miles) influences how watershed issues are framed.

In the small-scale watershed, issues are framed as a "direct relationship between watershed health and community well being." In contrast, in the large-scale watershed the issues are framed in terms of "regional conservation efforts, with no direct link between watershed health and community well being." The result is that in the larger-scale group, participants tend to view each other more as interest groups rather than individuals and tend to produce more contention than the smaller-scale group (ibid., 30).

As I have explored different collaboration cases, I have found that scale and membership do not fully explain differences among collaboratives. Scale is not the only way in which societal complexity may be expressed. There are watershed councils covering large rural areas in eastern Oregon and inland Australia that sound much more like the Mohawk (community driven). There are small urban watersheds in places like Portland, Oregon, and Sydney that sound more like the McKenzie (organizationally driven). Furthermore, organizational participation is not always a good predictor of group differences. I have discovered that what the group was working on (policy versus restoration) and who was involved from the organization (administration versus technical staff) were more influential than whether the organization was at the table. Similarly, Bidwell and Ryan (2006) noted that many agency representatives were participating as individual technical experts as opposed to representatives of their agency and its policies.

A Typology of Collaborative Groups

The collaboration typology I use in this book is based on the institutional analysis and design framework developed by Elinor Ostrom (1986a), and applied in a range of ways to study public policy settings (Gregg et al. 1991; Imperial 1999). One of the important principles of institutional theory is that management institutions emerge at different levels of decision making. This framework of levels can be used to describe institutional levels in different settings, including collaboration (Gregg et al. 1991; Imperial 2005; Margerum 2007, 2008). Frank Gregg and his colleagues (1991) use these three levels to locate collaborative groups along a spectrum based on where they focus their activities. Mark Imperial (2005) uses the same theoretical basis to highlight the different levels of collaborative watershed management.[3] Importantly, all collaboratives strive for actions that will support their goals, but all collaborative groups are not deliberating on the specifics of these actions. Collaborative groups are instead focusing their deliberations at a higher level, and actions are delivered through different means.

Typology Overview

At the action (operational) level, collaboratives stress direct action or on-the-ground activities, such as monitoring, education, service delivery, and community action (Margerum 2007, 2008; Imperial 2005). For example, Landcare groups in Australia engage local landowners to come together to address various land and water issues, such as invasive species, landscape restoration, and even the computerization of farm management. The key distinguishing feature of an action collaborative is that the subject of most stakeholder deliberation is on-the-ground actions and activities (see table 2.1).

At the organizational level, collaboratives focus on the roles and programs of organizations. As Imperial (2005, 293) observes, "These activities perform a steering function by improving communication among actors, coordinating actions, and integrating policies in ways that advance collective goals." State and federal agencies frequently are the targets of these efforts, but nongovernmental organizations and

Table 2.1
Typology and distinguishing characteristics

Typology	Institutional analysis and design framework	Characteristics
Policy	Constitutional	• Deliberation focuses on policy and higher-level administrative rules • Strong orientation to interest groups, policymakers, and significant stakeholders • Groups are created or sanctioned by government agencies or elected officials • Organizations represented by top administrators play a significant role • Often supported by quasi-governmental organizations with substantial resources
Organizational	Collective choice	• Usually focuses on information, priorities, and programs of organizations involved • Stronger agency/organization orientation • Groups often created or sanctioned by government agencies • Organizations represented by administrators or managers • Often supported by participating organizations
Action	Operational	• Focuses mostly on direct actions like watershed restoration and habitat enhancement • Stronger community orientation • Groups are often independent organizations or nonprofit corporations • Groups often created by citizens or community leaders • Often involves technical staff from organizations assisting with on-the-ground actions of the group

local government may also be included. For example, a collaborative effort to manage the Lake Winnebago system was primarily aimed at the policies and programs of the Wisconsin DNR and the local governments bordering the lake system. The key distinction with this group is that the deliberation focused less on the on-the-ground actions, and more on the set of agency programs and local government rules that would help improve water quality. In turn, organizations implement activities as a result of the collaborative, but these activities are not the main concern of the deliberations by the collaborative.

Finally, at the policy level, collaboratives work on government legislation and policies (Imperial 2005; Margerum 2007, 2008; Gregg et al. 1991).[4] The San Francisco Estuary Project, for example, involved a wide range of interest groups, local government entities, and federal and state agencies to develop a management plan. Among other things, the effort worked to develop new water quality standards for the estuary. The critical distinction with a policy collaborative is that the focus of its deliberative effort is on government policies at the highest levels, which in turn affect organizations and ultimately on-the-ground results.

The three types described above are better portrayed as archetypes across a spectrum of collaborative approaches. Some collaboratives will fit neatly under one of these archetypes, while others may be placed anywhere across this spectrum. Imperial (2005) points out that collaboratives can cut across categories, and I found ones that nest lower-level collaborative activities within a higher-level collaborative. As Graham Marshall (2008) remarks, this nesting may create complementary systems of governance if the roles are allocated appropriately. Some of these variations are discussed in the examples below and in chapters throughout this book.

More important, all groups are working to deliver results—whether the results are steps for prevention, restoration, operation, or education. Some groups deliberate about the specifics of the activities and play a direct role in making them happen, others deliberate about how organizations can better deliver management, and still others deliberate about the policies and standards that guide organizations and their activities.

Applying the Typology: Illustrative Examples
In several parts of the world where I conducted research, I ran across case studies that capture the differences highlighted by this collaboration typology. I will start this tour in the rugged terrain of southern Oregon before moving on to urban and rural instances from Australia.

Two different collaborative groups in southern Oregon reveal some significant differences in the approaches to collaboration at different levels. Each month, a diverse group of people living throughout the Lower Rogue watershed meet to

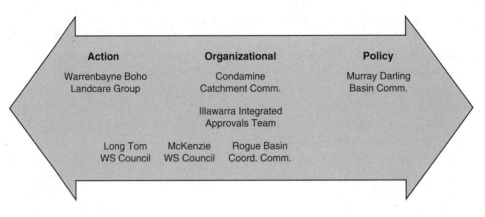

Figure 2.2
Spectrum of collaboratives

address issues of water quality and fish habitat in their creek. Sitting around a table in Gold Beach, Oregon, the Lower Rogue Watershed Council members conduct their business in an open and relaxed style—making decisions by consensus. The members are landowners, farmers, residents, fishing and environmental interests, and others concerned about the creek and its future.[5]

At a different time each month, a somewhat larger group called the Rouge Basin Coordinating Council meets in a range of locations: the Cave Junction Ranger Station, local community centers, and state agency offices. It is structured around the eight watershed councils in the basin, with participation from local, state, and federal government representatives (see figure 2.2).

If you sat through the meetings of these two councils, you would describe them both as collaborative natural resources groups. They are both involved in an ongoing effort to jointly manage natural resources. The participants are there voluntarily and don't have power over others at the table. Their process is open, with extensive discussion and consensus-based decision making. Even their topics are aimed toward at least one common end point: improving the region's ecological health.

Yet as you begin to explore the topics and approaches of these two groups, you recognize that they are fundamentally different: they operate at different scales, involve different types of participants, and crucially, function at different levels.

The Lower Rogue Watershed Council primarily deliberates on the direct actions it is trying to accomplish, such as removing fish barriers, removing invasive species like blackberries, and planting trees in the riparian area (action collaborative). After setting restoration goals around these issues, its focus is how to interact with individuals and organizations to deliver these restoration actions.

The Rogue Basin Coordinating Council is addressing similar kinds of issues, but its deliberations are targeted at a higher level. This council serves as a coordinating entity, and facilitates deliberation on a regional assessment, regional restoration priorities, and restoration initiatives (organizational collaborative). Its deliberations center less on the specific projects, and more on securing commitments, funding, and management efforts to support the on-the-ground actions of the participating organizations (Margerum and Whitall 2004).

Another Oregon-based collaborative that has been the subject of research is the McKenzie Watershed Council (see, for example, Cheng and Daniels 2005; Cheng, Kruger, and Daniels 2003). In contrast to the Long Tom watershed, which is 98 percent private land, the McKenzie watershed is approximately 80 percent public land. For many years, its funding, activities, and tenor have been guided by three major agencies: the Eugene Water and Electric Board, the U.S. Forest Service, and the U.S. Bureau of Land Management. Many of its activities have focused on public management issues and restoration efforts along with the organizational programs that will make this happen.

Both agency members and residents noted that the McKenzie group "never got down to the ground level," but while agency staff supported this, community members didn't like this "analytical" approach, and felt they should be "getting out and getting your hands dirty and digging to plant trees" (Cheng and Daniels 2005, 39). In contrast, agency participants said that they "lean towards the larger issues" and did not feel that they could "start getting into specific land use issues" (ibid., 39). These views reflect a difference between collaboration more toward the organizational end of the spectrum compared to a group more toward the action end.

Moving from Oregon to Australia, the Illawarra region south of Sydney is the location for two collaborative efforts that covered the same region and involved many of the same participants.[6] The Illawarra Catchment Management Committee was a stakeholder-based group working on improving water quality by reducing the impacts from land management activities in an area undergoing urbanization pressures. Its efforts were geared toward restoration projects as well as the education of developers and landowners to reduce water resource impacts (action collaborative).

The Illawarra Integrated Approvals Team (I Team) involved most of the Catchment Management Committee's agency personnel, who recognized that inconsistent environmental regulations among agencies and local governments in the region produced confusing decisions vulnerable to challenge. The I Team used a collaborative process to refine standards and develop a better scientific basis for applying them (organizational collaborative). It was not amending the state or local legislation and explicitly decided not to get involved in individual permit decisions. Thus, both Illawarra groups were concerned about water quality, but one sought to achieve this by deliberating about on-the-ground efforts (action collaborative), while the other focused on the scientific standards of regulations (organizational level).

Finally, Australia's Murray Darling River basin provides an example of a region where three types of collaboratives were nested.[7] The Murray Darling River is the largest in Australia, crossing five states and territories on its journey from Queensland to South Australia. Australia has limited environmental management powers. As a result, the basin was managed through a state-federal partnership called the Murray Darling River Basin Initiative that decided on funding priorities and negotiated policies on issues such as water allocation (policy collaborative).

At a organizational level, catchment committees operated in the states of Queensland, New South Wales, and Victoria. The Condamine Catchment Committee (Queensland), for example, worked at a subregional level to bring together the programs and initiatives of state agencies, local governments, agricultural groups, and groups of local landowners (organizational collaboratives).

At the action level, hundreds of small Landcare groups have been involved in efforts to restore streams, address erosion problems, eradicate exotic species, and reduce salinity. The Warrenbayne Boho Land Protection Group (Victoria), for one, planted thousands of trees, fenced off creeks, restored habitat, and conducted monitoring (Campbell 1994). These self-organized groups are composed entirely of local landowners working together to address problems and influence their neighbors to participate in conservation actions (action collaboratives).

The collaboratives described above operate at a range of levels with a range of participants. As the discussion underscores, this is a spectrum, and different collaboratives will fit in different positions along that spectrum. Nevertheless, understanding where they fit is important for both improving practice and focusing research.

Problem Characteristics of Different Collaboratives

There is clearly a range of other variables that make collaboratives different from each other, such as history, technical complexity, power dynamics, membership size, and resources (Gray 1989; Clark, Burkardt, and King 2005; Moore and Koontz 2003; Wondolleck and Yaffee 2000), but there are no consistent tendencies between these factors and where they sit on the action-organizational-policy typology spectrum. For example, there is a wide array of histories leading to the formation of collaboratives, yet there appear to be no characteristics in those histories that one can associate with a collaborative based on its position in the typology.[8] Based on my analysis of cases using the action-organizational-policy typology as well as work of E. Franklin Dukes and Karen Firehock (2001), I review five characteristics that tend to vary in relation to the collaborative typology: scale, population affected by

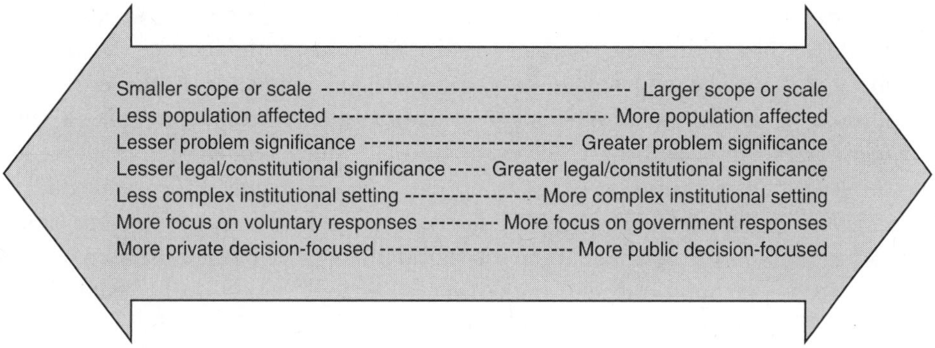

Smaller scope or scale -------------------------------------- Larger scope or scale
Less population affected ---------------------------------- More population affected
Lesser problem significance --------------------------- Greater problem significance
Lesser legal/constitutional significance ----- Greater legal/constitutional significance
Less complex institutional setting ---------------- More complex institutional setting
More focus on voluntary responses ---------- More focus on government responses
More private decision-focused ------------------------- More public decision-focused

Figure 2.3
The context continuum. *Source*: Based on Dukes and Firehock 2001.

the change, problem significance, institutional arrangements, and decision-making realm (see figure 2.3).

Collaboratives toward the policy end of the spectrum, first of all, are more likely to be addressing issues that cover a large scale. At a practical level, large areas limit the ability of stakeholders to interact, and the larger the scale, the more difficult it is to deliver results through direct action. At a conceptual level, the larger the scale, the less likely that people will identify with the area and the issues being addressed. Cheng and Daniels (2005) highlighted the different views about a sense of place when they compared the larger McKenzie Watershed Council to a nested collaborative working in the Mohawk subwatershed.

Second, collaboratives toward the policy end of the spectrum are more likely to encompass a larger population. Just as a target population's size and diversity affect the tractability of a policy problem (Mazmanian and Sabatier 1983), the number of people affected by its activities influences the approach of a collaborative effort. Collaboratives addressing highly populated regions like the San Francisco estuary or metropolitan Denver tend to fall toward the policy end of the spectrum. A collaborative effort encompassing a small population trends more toward an action collaborative, such as the Pringle Creek Watershed Council (Oregon) and the Black Earth Creek Watershed Association (Wisconsin).

The complicating factor with these first two variables is that scale and population may have opposing tendencies. Thus, collaboratives covering large rural areas with a small population may work at the action level. Those covering small areas in highly populated urban areas may work at an organizational level. It is not clear which of these may have a stronger influence on the type of collaborative that is formed, but where a collaborative group positions itself will have an effect on how they go about translating consensus into results.

A third tendency is that collaboratives toward the policy end of the spectrum are more likely to be addressing issues of regional or national significance (Dukes and Firehock 2001). The significance may relate to concerns such as the ecological importance of species and ecosystems (for instance, an ecosystem containing a critical species), the uniqueness or iconic value of a place (such as a national monument), or the legal or constitutional issues that are raised (say, state water quality standards). For example, the Trinity Inlet in north Queensland, Australia, is a small estuary along a vast coastline, but the ecological importance of the fishery combined with the economic importance of the Great Barrier Reef tourist traffic resulted in a process with high-level agency involvement. A similar high level of attention has been devoted to the management of Lake Tahoe despite its relatively small area and population.

Fourth, collaboratives toward the policy end of the spectrum are likely to involve more complex institutional settings. These institutional settings refer to the number of jurisdictions, organizations, and organized interest groups addressing environmental management issues. The collaborative growth management effort in metropolitan Denver, for example, involved fifty different local governments, across a large urbanized region. Most action collaboratives operate across a more limited number of jurisdictions, such as the four local governments covered by the Long Tom Watershed Council.

Finally, collaboratives toward the organizational and policy end of the spectrum tend to focus more on issues involving public decision making (Dukes and Firehock 2001). Oregon watershed councils with significant amounts of federal land, for instance, tend to concentrate more on the programs and management policies of those agencies (say, the Umpqua Watershed Council). In contrast, councils dominated by private land lean more toward direct action, such as education and restoration efforts with private landowners (for example, Mary's River Watershed Council).

Operational Differences among Collaboratives

The five characteristics listed above highlight differences in the problem domain and context of different collaboratives. Yet it is also essential to introduce two operational differences: stakeholder involvement and ongoing arrangements for sustaining collaboratives (see table 2.2). These issues are discussed in more detail later, but it is worth noting several key differences here.

Stakeholder Involvement

Stakeholder involvement is a crucial principle of collaboration, and the way in which stakeholders are defined illuminates an important functional difference across the spectrum of collaboratives. With collaboratives at the action end of

Table 2.2
Operational differences among collaboratives

Operational difference questions	Action collaborative	Organizational collaborative	Policy collaborative
Who are stakeholders more likely to represent?	Themselves; a sector of the community	An organization	A constituency; an interest group
Typical position of organizational representatives	Technical	Managerial	Administrative
What are the roles of citizen input?	Provide community contacts; support projects	Provide community perspective on agency programs and priorities	Provide community perspective on proposed policies
What are the groups discussing?	Projects; education efforts; direct action	Joint programs; management responsibilities; funding priorities	Policies; administrative rules; program oversight

the spectrum, there are usually more stakeholders representing themselves rather than organizations, which is a characteristic confirmed by other researchers (Cheng and Daniels 2005; Moore and Koontz 2003; Curtis, Shindler, and Wright 2002). Thus, an action collaborative may involve a representative from a state agency, but the person is involved because of their technical and professional knowledge rather than a role in coordinating the programs or policies of their organization.

Collaboratives in the organizational range of the spectrum tend to be heavily populated by individuals representing governmental and nongovernmental organizations (Cheng and Daniels 2005; Imperial 2005). Many of these organizational representatives are regional administrators, or midlevel managers of local, state, and federal agencies. The level of this person within the organization is particularly important, because the collaborative may be asking the organization to coordinate program implementation, commit staff and resources, and provide clarification on programs or policies. These groups may also involve citizens, but their role is more to provide public perspectives and input. In fact, one of the potential weaknesses of organizational-level collaboratives is to substitute this narrower stakeholder involvement for broader public participation.

At the policy end of the spectrum, collaboratives are composed mostly of stakeholders who represent organizations, interest groups, and others involved in the policymaking process, including elected officials. They are chosen to gain broad representation, and try to include all stakeholders with the potential to veto or block the policy outcome (Innes et al. 1994; Susskind and Cruikshank 1987). As such, they are often representing significant constituencies, and usually participate in a range of these kinds of policy negotiations and forums.

A consequence of these differences is that negotiations at the organizational and policy levels tend to be more difficult, because stakeholders are playing a bridging role between the collaborative and their organization or their constituencies. Furthermore, implementation may be more difficult because it requires an ongoing commitment from the organization and its constituencies. These differences are explored in more detail in chapters 7, 8, and 9.

Sustaining Collaboratives

The second functional difference relates to the type of ongoing arrangements that collaboratives develop for implementation. Ongoing collaboratives go through an information-sharing and consensus-building phase aimed at producing goals, agreements, and strategies for implementation, but different types of collaboratives require different approaches to sustain their collaborative role.

For an action collaborative, the differences between management arrangements for consensus building and implementation are often negligible. Most participants are the same in both phases, and even staff or working groups may not change the focus of their work. Stakeholders may come and go over time, but the core group is frequently composed of people who are the conveners and consensus builders, and who serve an ongoing role in guiding implementation efforts. Thus, the stakeholders generally make up a board that oversees staff members, who in turn carry out the day-to-day functions.

For an organizational collaborative, the organizations associated with the group usually do not change after the group shifts from consensus building to implementation. The individual participants are more likely to change, however, because people working for governmental and nongovernmental organizations change jobs, get promoted, leave organizations, and shift responsibilities. Sometimes ensuring ongoing commitment to collaborative management from an organization is therefore not just about personal dedication but also about the dedication of the organization as a whole (Imperial 2005). The on-the-ground actions are delivered through the organizations themselves—guided by the stakeholder group and inter-organizational networks.

In contrast, the management arrangement for the implementation phase of a policy collaborative may look different from that of the consensus-building phase. With the broad direction and policies established through a consensus-building process, the participants may disband or operate in more of a maintenance role because high-level representatives can't continue to participate in such an intensive process. Instead, the stakeholders set policies and establish programs that allow other people to carry out actions. This is especially true when collaboratives are populated with elected officials, who often delegate the day-to-day oversight to managerial-level staff, or a management organization with significant resources and staff. Hence, a collaborative process at this level frequently produces an ongoing collaborative organization, such as the International Joint Commission (Great Lakes) or the Murray Darling Basin Commission (Australia). The on-the-ground actions are delivered through these organizations with oversight by an ongoing stakeholder group.

In summary, some basic process principles of collaboration are common across all kinds of groups and levels. However, there are some key contextual and operational differences between collaborations and how they operate that are discussed in more detail in chapters 3–6.

A Typology of Networks

The typology of collaboratives describes the core stakeholder group, but to effect change collaboratives often have to influence a broader set of decision makers. To understand this process of influence I turn to the concept of networks, which actually encompasses several different bodies of theory. I define networks generically as sets of individuals bound by communication, relationships, positions, and/or interest area.

This is a generic definition because I suggest there are three types of networks used by collaboratives. Social networks are defined by interpersonal relationships of people through their work, family, friends, and community action (Putnam 2000). Interorganizational networks are defined by structures and processes by which organizations and people can interact with each other (Alexander 1993). Political networks are defined by power positions and configurations in the political system (Knoke 1990).

Social Networks

One approach to change is for collaboratives to utilize the personal social networks of stakeholders to spread information and influence. In many cases, the stakeholders themselves become agents of change through their political, social, and economic networks (Bender 1978; Moseley 1999). This model implies that collaborative stakeholders are linked into society, or as Cassandra Moseley (1999, 61) puts it, these groups are "imbedded in a community of place—a set of political, social and economic networks related to a particular landscape."

For example, the Pringle Creek Watershed Council helps restore its watershed by working through a number of community connections, including a network of master gardeners in the region.[9] The theoretical underpinnings of action collaboratives are found in the literature on social capital, civil society, and the diffusion of innovations (Putnam 2000; Hutchinson et al. 2004; Rogers 2003). This literature asserts that communities not only have physical capital (roads and buildings) and economic capital (businesses and employment) but also social capital (social networks and community organizations). Through community discourse, this social capital can be tapped to enable cooperative collective action toward a common goal (Putnam 2000).

Many social networks exist independent of the collaborative, but collaboratives can plug into these networks through the set of stakeholders around the table. As people gain a greater understanding of local problems, these stakeholders connect to community and other leaders to help bring about change. In the Pringle Creek area, the network of gardeners has adopted new gardening techniques that will reduce the impacts on water quality and riparian areas, and they have helped influence others to take similar actions. Whether government is a partner in this process or not, personal and political networks can become a powerful force in bringing about change. The role of social networks is discussed in more detail in chapter 7.

Interorganizational Networks

Another way that collaboratives can bring about change is through the programs, budgets, and priorities of organizations such as local governments, agencies, private firms, and interest groups. The theory of change is that more strategic and coordinated management among an array of organizations and stakeholders can improve their ability to solve problems (Bryson 1988; Lang 1986a; Imperial 2005). An array of organizations is networked through formal and informal linkages that are constantly evolving (Agranoff and McGuire 2003; Knoke 1990; Alexander 1995). As Robert Agranoff and Michael McGuire (2003, 122) note, the linkages between participants in these networks do not form by accident; they are "built for strategic jurisdictional purposes." Like social networks, these interorganizational networks exist independent of collaboration efforts. The collaborative group itself is a new node in this network, however, and it may be able to build a number of new networks to support its set of implementation activities.

For example, the Milwaukee River watersheds project was an effort to improve watershed health by integrating the management activities of state environmental and agricultural agencies with county conservation departments and extension education programs. Researchers examining these kinds of collaboratives are aided by theory relating to interorganizational coordination, networking theory, and organizations (Wondolleck and Yaffee 2000; Alexander 1995; Agranoff and McGuire 2003; Bardach 1998; Cortner and Moote 1999). This theory base sheds light on interorganizational network issues such as management, organizational behavior, and the structure of bureaucracy, which is discussed further in chapter 8.

Political Networks

The final avenue of change that can be pursued by collaboratives is through the network of political actors, which includes elected officials, interest groups, and other policy entrepreneurs. Political networks help negotiate rules and policies, and provide the ongoing support necessary for implementation (Roberts and Bradley 1991; Mandell 1999; Altman and Petkus 1994; Schlager 1995). They are defined by relationships and interactions among people holding positions in the political system, which David Knoke (1990) observes often does not change substantially even with changes in people in those positions.

Denver's Metro Vision process, for instance, involved fifty local governments negotiating to develop regional policies about land use and growth management. The strategy was to use federal transportation funding to create a significant incentive for local governments to adopt urban growth boundaries, and the Denver Regional Council of Governments (DRCOG) oversaw the implementation of that policy. In these settings, collaboration is negotiation about policies, programs, and budgets to solve large-scale, complex problems. The assumption is that the problems can be addressed through new policies or policy changes, and therefore implementation requires policymakers and interest groups with power in the policy process (Molnar and Rogers 1982; Innes et al. 1994; O'Toole and Montjoy 1984; Roberts and Bradley 1991).

Unlike advocacy coalitions or iron triangles that are organized around sets of like interests (Sabatier and Jenkins-Smith 1993), political networks in this context include a diversity of interests held together by trust, common goals, and/or agreement on problems. But political networks are dynamic, and may compete for stakeholder time, support, and positions. Furthermore, a political network for implementing collaborative problem solving will compete with other political networks for time and attention. The role of political networks in supporting the implementation of collaboration efforts is explored in chapter 9.

Network Typology and Its Application to Practice

All three of these network types have an extensive theoretical history, and in chapters 7, 8, and 9, I draw on some of this research to explain its application to collaboration. Importantly, social, interorganizational, and political networks encompass a wide array of human and organizational relationships, most of which have no relationship to collaboration. For example, people belong to religious organizations, social clubs, neighborhoods, poker groups, and interest groups without ever interacting with a collaborative or its activities. By developing new networks or tapping into existing ones, though, collaboratives can significantly improve their ability to translate consensus into results. Three additional qualities about networks make them complex (and often confusing) when these theories are applied to practice.

Collaboratives as Networks

First, an ongoing group of stakeholders (a collaborative) bound by trust, commitment, and rules is itself a network. This is most easily explained through examples. Australia's Landcare program is founded on groups of local landowners coming together to address land and water management problems. Thus, Landcare groups themselves have become a social network. This was obvious with some of the Landcare groups that I met. The members knew each other, worked together, and frequently shared social as much as work events.

At the same time, not all collaboratives—even at the action level—are part of a social network. Oregon's watershed councils bring together a diversity of participants who build trust and respect, but in many cases this does not create a new social network among them. When I was on the board of the Long Tom Watershed Council, we gathered for meetings, picnics, project tours, and potluck dinners hosted at board members' houses. We had a good working relationship among a group of people with varied professions, political persuasions, and interests who would rarely interact in social settings. Indeed, after stepping down from the board, most past members have not interacted except through council activities. Nonetheless, the council has always utilized the existing social networks of board members to connect with the broader community, and developed strategies for extending this network further.

In contrast, organizational collaboratives are generally a forum for exchanging information and coordinating activities, which makes them part of an interorganizational network. It in fact may be hard to clearly delineate the collaborative from the network. The Rogue Basin Coordinating Committee (Oregon), for example, has been both a collaborative group and an ongoing interorganizational network among watershed councils, state agencies, and federal agencies. The committee also set up a number of subcommittees, which have worked on an adaptive management model, fish access barriers, and technical assistance for restoration projects. Are these subcommittees part of the ongoing collaborative or are they an interorganizational network? In some respects it doesn't matter, because we would evaluate them the same way. Any ongoing collaborative involving organizations will need to respond to the factors that make interorganizational networks successful if it is going to manage adaptively.

Finally, policy collaboratives that maintain an ongoing role in decision making become a political network. What is unique about this network is that it is a group bound by problem solving, trust, and commitment, rather than serving as a coalition of like-minded interests. This potential to create an ongoing political network that includes a diverse array of perspectives and interests is what makes policy collaboratives such an interesting governance model. It is also what makes policy collaboratives so vulnerable to failure.

Networks and Interorganizational Levels

A second complex aspect about networks is that they may operate at multiple levels and venues. This is most relevant to collaboratives utilizing interorganizational networks to support implementation efforts. For example, the Long Tom Watershed Council has utilized a technical team of agency and university experts as an adviser on restoration projects. The team's role is to review projects and ensure that they are designed successfully. These people participate because of their technical knowledge and because their organization (university or federal agency) allows them to contribute their time. They are not committing resources or adjusting priorities, and they are not approving any permits that the council is required to obtain once the design work is complete. Thus, they are truly operating at an action level, but it is part of an interorganizational network bound by their positions rather than social interaction.

This issue of interorganizational networks operating at multiple levels was apparent in a study of social services collaboration in Multnomah County, Oregon. In our research with stakeholders from local governments, nonprofits, schools, and other organizations, we found two levels of need related to interorganizational networks (Community Planning Workshop 2006).

First, much of the previous collaboration had been around specific projects or in response to federal funding mandates. Once the project or grant was completed, the collaboration would cease. Yet there was a need for the organizations to build consensus around their relative missions, common needs, and priority areas. In other words, with limited resources and overlapping missions, they needed to develop a strategic view of who was doing what, and they needed to sustain this interaction over time to respond to new challenges, emerging issues, and funding opportunities. Hence, they needed to develop an organizational collaborative to build consensus and design an interorganizational network to support their ongoing roles. This network could then respond to individual grant opportunities along with new issues and challenges that emerged.

The needs of the frontline staff members were different from this organizational focus. The frontline staff members needed to develop systems for information sharing, client referral, and service coordination. This is action-level work, but it would not be created by an action collaborative, nor implemented by a social network. It would most likely be the product of an organizational collaborative that could generate the organizational commitment, protocols, and procedures for sharing potentially sensitive information. It would become part of an interorganizational network that would not only coordinate the strategic direction but also support the creation of these action-level systems and procedures.

Examples from three locations further illustrate how interorganizational networks may focus at the organizational or action level. First, as noted above the I Team in the Illawarra region of Sydney made a conscious decision to deal with the standards and data related to existing policy. The I Team was composed of regional managers working through an interorganizational network (organizational-level activities). They chose not to amend the existing policy nor did they want to become involved in individual decisions.

Second, the Trinity Inlet Technical Team *did* become involved in individual permit decisions. This process was limited to organizations with formal decision-making power, but on a regular basis they reviewed permit applications for developments and uses in the inlet, and each representative offered an assessment of the application. Many people referred to a "TIMP approval process," yet in fact all decision-making authority was retained by each organization and no new policy was created. For several years, however, this interorganizational network provided highly coordinated actions related to permit decisions (action-level activities).

Third, collaborative efforts in the Rogue basin demonstrate how an organizational collaborative may utilize interorganizational networks at both the organizational and action level. The committee's goal has been to coordinate the activities of member organizations in restoring land and water health in the basin. To that end, it has developed common aims, adjusted organizational priorities, and identified a range of efforts to support this. The group also recognized that there was considerable need for technical assistance to aid both public and private landowners in on-the-ground restoration activities (Southwest Oregon Provincial Interagency Executive Committee and South West Interagency Group 1999). This led to the creation of the Rogue Basin Restoration Technical Pool, which was a broad group of approximately eighty-five specialists providing technical assistance to private and public land restoration projects. Individuals requested assistance through an online form, and the interagency technical coordinator used the database to match specialists with assistance requests (Margerum and Whitall 2004). Once again, this was an interorganizational network functioning at an action level. The network of people and contacts was built not on social networks but rather on a database of experts and organizational commitments to support this work.

Political Networks and Multiple Venues

A final complication in describing networks relates to the multiple venues in which political systems operate, which includes city, state, and national venues. To reduce confusion, I avoid the term levels here, because whether they are local, state, or national political actors they are deliberating about policy.

I focus on a narrow view of these networks—namely, how a collaborative might develop political networks or utilize existing ones to support its implementation efforts. The complication is that political networks may involve local, state, or national political actors that come together to address an issue like water quality in the San Francisco estuary. These political actors operate in venues such as city councils, state legislatures, and the United States Congress. Yet when congressional representatives tackle an issue such as water quality in the San Francisco estuary, they may be developing policy, administrative rules, or precedent that extend to a national level. These multiple venues make a place-based approach inherently more complicated and make political networks incredibly complex and difficult to maintain.

Discussion of the Typologies

The two typologies presented here highlight some key differences between collaboratives and their approaches to producing results. Given that a collaborative may locate anywhere along the action-organizational-policy spectrum, and any collaborative may utilize one or more network implementation strategies, there is a wider array of combinations than what can be easily explained. Nevertheless, I believe these typologies shed light on several aspects of practice, including the criticisms of some collaborative approaches (see table 2.3).

Natural Collaborative: Network Affinities

As noted above, certain collaboratives have an affinity for certain types of networks: action collaboratives use social networks, organizational collaboratives use interorganizational networks, and policy collaboratives use political networks. Collaboration has drawn criticism from those who contend it is an effort to devolve power and decision making to more local levels of government (McCloskey 1996; Lane 2003). But different collaborative-network combinations assume different decision-making roles for government. Action collaboratives that deliver results through social networks have generally emerged to address problems that government has not effectively addressed because of limited resources, the ineffectiveness of government programs, an inability to regulate, or a lack of authority. In the environmental context, collaborative groups have formed to address diffuse problems such as nonpoint source pollution caused by private landowners, which requires thousands of people to change their land management practices. Government is often playing a supportive role through its funding and information efforts. There is little or no decentralization or delegation of authority, because there is usually no power being delegated; rather, there is only the delegation of limited resources.[10]

Table 2.3
Collaborative-network relationships

Network collaborative	Social networks	Interorganizational networks	Political networks
Action collaborative	• Natural affinity • Collaborative plays role in building social network • Little devolution of government power • Example: Landcare groups	• Potential tension with efforts to utilize social networks • Potential for collaborative to utilize action-level activities of networks • Some potential devolution of government power • Example: Long Tom Watershed Council Technical Team	• Potential tension with efforts to utilize social networks • Difficult for collaborative to access network • High potential for devolution of power or increased local influence • Example: Quincy Library Group lobbying efforts
Organizational collaborative	• Potential difficulty creating networks given organizational level membership • Little devolution of government power • Example: Mary River Catchment Committee riparian restoration program	• Natural affinity • Collaborative a component of interorganizational network • Potential devolution of government power • Example: Milwaukee River watersheds nonpoint source programs	• Potential tensions with efforts to utilize interorganizational networks • Difficult for collaborative to access network • High potential for devolution of power to organizations • Example: No cases found
Policy collaborative	• Significant difficulty creating networks given policy level membership • Little devolution of government power • Example: Murray Darling basin (catchment and Landcare implementation strategy)	• Common step to delegate new specified powers to interorganizational network • May create new power or devolve power to organizations • Example: Lower Wisconsin Riverway Board and coordinator	• Natural affinity • No devolution of power; retained in network • Hard to sustain • Example: San Francisco Estuary Project

For organizational collaboratives utilizing interorganizational networks, discussions about the role of government are focused on coordinating programs and problem solving. Coordination refers to the alignment of programs, policies, and activities across government sectors. This does not usually mean new roles, but the adjustment of existing ones. Wisconsin DNR staff used phrases such as, "making sure the right hand knows what the left hand is doing." The issue of flexibility arises because government organizations collaborate with stakeholders on how programs and policies are applied in light of local and regional context.

Importantly, organizational collaboratives that utilize interorganizational networks may involve a significant democratic decentralization of power, because power is often being delegated within the organizations to lower levels (Lane 2003; Layzer 2008). For large government agencies, this frequently means delegation to local and regional offices, which may raise the most concern about access and influence. When these collaboratives and networks include nongovernmental stakeholders, local interests may have more influence than nonlocal interests (Kenney 2000; McCloskey 2001). This delegation also may come without the kind of public scrutiny generated by groups operating at the policy end of the spectrum.

For policy collaboratives utilizing political networks, the role of government is that of a problem-solving partner. There is much less discussion about the decentralization of government, because policy itself is the focus of discussion. Issues arise in policy forums because existing policies have not been effective, and a crisis, lawsuit, or policy entrepreneur has brought the issue forward. The existing policies' lack of effectiveness may arise from increasing problem complexity, the failure of existing policies to consider cross-cutting issues, or increased conflict surrounding the policy problem. The role of government usually has little to do with delegation or decentralization; it is often exploring adjustments, shifts, and integration issues. In the case of collaborative growth management initiatives in places like Denver, collaboration may actually mean an expanded role for government.

Collaboratives Utilizing Other Networks

As noted above, collaboratives may utilize multiple networks to support implementation efforts. These combinations come with certain risks, mismatches, and difficulties.

Action Collaboratives and Networks

A number of action collaboratives routinely utilized interorganizational networks, particularly when network activities centered on action level activities. The most common example is watershed groups using a group of agency staff as technical advisers. These groups often focused on implementing private action through social network strategies, but because agency staff members were there as technical advisers, this created few tensions.

Tensions were more likely to arise when action collaboratives became engaged in interorganizational networks that operated at the organizational level. The Lockyer Valley Catchment Committee in Australia, for example, was focused primarily on efforts like streambank restoration by private landowners. Over time, the organization became more involved in regional land use decision making, and tensions arose about its role; some landowners began to mistrust the council and its increasing relationship with government.[11]

I believe that one of the most controversial collaboration cases in the literature is explained by a potential mismatch between the collaborative and its network. The Quincy Library Group formed as a coalition of local stakeholders concerned with the policies and plans of the region's national forests. This is an approach more consistent with an organizational collaborative, but the local group did not include the three national forest managers in the region. The group looked more like an action or organizational collaborative, but it ultimately decided to utilize its political networks. The participants sought out their congressional delegation to impose the plan on the agencies.[12] The mismatch between the type of collaborative and the collaborative's activities may explain why the Quincy Library Group has generated so much criticism (McCloskey 1996; Kenney 2000).

The Long Tom Watershed Council faced a similar decision point when I was on its board. A development proposed in the headwaters of one of its tributaries generated strong objections from people throughout Eugene. The development was within the urban growth boundary on land zoned for residential use, but the steep terrain and habitat value created a potential threat to the tributary and watershed. Some residents wanted the watershed council to help them advocate for the city council to stop the development and purchase the land for open space. We provided information from our stream assessment reports, although we unanimously agreed that we would not take a policy position. Our diversity of participants and political networks would have carried significant weight if we could have agreed about a position, but it would have shifted the organization into a different role. Most important, it could have undermined our role as a community-based group that people from across the political spectrum viewed as a trusted and unbiased resource. Becoming involved in the headwaters debate was a slippery slope because from there it would be natural to engage in decisions about urban growth boundary extensions, septic tank regulation, and other local government policies.

I believe that this distinction between network strategies is often what distinguishes community-based collaboratives from community-based advocacy groups. Each group may have a diverse membership working on similar problems, but advocacy groups utilizing political networks are pursuing a very different strategy from groups utilizing highly diverse social or interorganizational networks to deliver on-the-ground results.

Organizational Collaboratives and Networks

Many organizational collaboratives addressed conservation efforts among private landowners using interorganizational networks. For example, in the Milwaukee River watersheds case, the Wisconsin DNR worked with the University of Wisconsin–Extension office and county conservation efforts to promote agricultural land conservation that would improve the water quality. On the other hand, some organizational collaboratives have worked to utilize social networks to implement their efforts. The Mary River Catchment Committee (Australia) created a streambank restoration program and hired a local, respected landowner to be the outreach person. In turn, the landowner relied on word of mouth among participating landowners to encourage new participants.

Organizational collaboratives also experience constraints when trying to use a social networking strategy. The Wisconsin DNR faced this difficulty when it convened some collaboration efforts because of the agency's broad powers over environmental regulation, resource management, and state lands. The perception that the collaborative attempt was a "DNR project" often made it challenging to work with local communities and particularly hard to conduct outreach efforts with private landowners.

The McKenzie Watershed Council that was described above has pursued both action- and organizational-level approaches. Its strong organizational focus has made it difficult for the council to relate to private landowners, except in the Mohawk subwatershed, where an action-oriented group has emerged (Cheng and Daniels 2005).

The Johnstone Catchment Committee in northern Australia also pursued multiple network strategies but faced fewer tensions. The committee worked through interorganizational networks to reach farmers in the coastal areas who were involved in highly structured growers' cooperatives. In contrast, the graziers (ranchers) who farmed in the highlands did not have any strong organizations, and the catchment committee reached this audience through its social networks, such as well-connected graziers from the region.

Many of Australia's catchment committees would have had considerable difficulty reaching private landowners were it not for the Landcare groups that already existed across their region. Organizational collaboratives such as the Mackay Whitsunday Natural Resource Management Group and Port Phillip Westernport Catchment Management Authority developed resources and programs to support as well as foster these kinds of local groups. This allowed the organizational collaborative to concentrate on interorganizational network activities, and created action collaboratives that could more easily connect with local people through social networks.

As noted in table 2.3, I could not find any evidence from my cases of organizational collaboratives that utilized political networks. There may be several explanations for this. One, it may be rare because of the difficulties of bureaucratic interaction with political networks. Second, it may exist in other settings, but not in any of the cases that I examined. Third, organizational collaboratives may utilize political networks, but they may do so in quite subtle ways, or they may be reluctant to describe this role because government employees are not permitted to lobby.

Policy Collaboratives and Networks

Almost universally, policy collaboratives utilized both interorganizational and political networks in their implementation approach. The use of interorganizational networks is common because many of the details of implementation and ongoing decision making need to be delegated. Furthermore, policy collaboratives are most likely to emerge in complex and cross-cutting problems where there are overlapping implementation responsibilities.

Thus, in every one of the policy collaboratives that I researched, at least one entity was created or delegated authority to coordinate implementation. Paul Sabatier, Will Focht, and their colleagues (2005) refer to this as a collaborative superagency, and Imperial (2005) labels it a collaborative of organizations. In some cases, the policy collaborative continued to operate. The Murray Darling basin's ministerial committee and the Trinity Inlet's steering committee both met periodically to assess policies, review information, and make any needed adjustments. Yet much of the day-to-day coordination was delegated to the Murray Darling Basin Commission and the Trinity Inlet Management Program.

In other cases, the policy collaborative ceased to function altogether and was replaced by an organizational collaborative delegated with an implementation charge. The Lower Wisconsin River involved intense policy collaboration, but once the administrating framework was developed, the ongoing implementation of policy was delegated to an organizational collaborative called the Lower Wisconsin Riverway Board.

Policy collaboratives face even more difficulties than organizational ones utilizing a social networking strategy. The adoption of this approach appears to require an infrastructure of nested collaboratives that create more locally connected network opportunities. For example, the conservation efforts in the Murray Darling basin were delivered though the nested set of catchment management committees and Landcare groups described above. Most policy collaboratives, however, focus on policies delivered through organizations rather than the voluntary efforts typical of most social network strategies.

Conclusion

The typologies presented here are relatively simple in their basic approach. This simplicity is helpful for practitioners who can use them to better analyze, evaluate, and interpret collaborative efforts. It is also a weakness, because in practice many collaborative efforts and their settings are complex. Significantly, these typologies are not predictive, and do not suggest that any *one* collaborative is the most appropriate form. I believe the typologies are ultimately a starting point for understanding, critiquing, and evaluating collaboratives. I also view these typologies as works in progress, and hope that other researchers will refine, amend, or even replace them through their own studies and analysis.

II
Consensus Building

3

Convening Collaboratives

Every collaborative has a story. Sometimes it is a story about conflict and controversy. At other times it is a story about a new vision for an old problem. And sometimes it is a story about a leader going around to meet with others and seek out their participation in a new way to address old problems. Some stories involve all of these elements. The key is that there are conditions, processes, and reasons behind the convening of a collaborative. The way in which this convening process transpires can have a positive or negative effect on the ability of a collaborative to achieve results.

In Oregon today there are over ninety watershed councils, and the process leading to their formation provides an interesting cross section of examples. Controversies over the protection of spotted owl habitat in the early 1990s led a range of people to recognize that the potential endangered species listing of salmon and trout could produce even more contention due to the breadth of the impact. To encourage a more collaborative response, Oregon governor John Kitzhaber initiated the Oregon Plan for Salmon and Watersheds. Crucial to the Oregon plan was the idea of administratively and financially supporting the formation of community-based watershed councils that could work collaboratively to restore and enhance water quality and fish habitat. Rather than creating councils, the plan allowed groups to be self-formed. As long as these groups followed certain procedures, such as providing broad representation and getting county approval, they were eligible for grants to support operations and restoration projects (Curtis, Shindler, and Wright 2002). The stories of two councils highlight the different conditions and issues affecting the formation of collaboratives.

The Long Tom River runs from the city of Eugene through several smaller communities and agricultural areas before flowing into the Willamette River. The watershed is approximately 98 percent private land, with most of the public land held in the form of parks and recreation areas. A small group of citizens in the lower portion of the watershed met in 1996 to discuss watershed issues and consider forming a council. To become eligible for state watershed grants, the council needed approval from the County Board of Commissioners.

The Lane County commissioners agreed to approve the formation of a council as long as it covered the entire Long Tom watershed, which included not only agricultural landowners in the lower part but also a major portion of Eugene. In late 1997, two members utilized the momentum from the earlier efforts to write a grant proposal and hire a coordinator. The coordinator helped with outreach efforts, and soon after, meeting attendance swelled to as many as seventy people from many backgrounds (Long Tom Watershed Council 2008). A group of volunteers then set out to write a charter that reflected the grassroots nature of the organization. This charter created a steering committee, but most major council decisions were made at monthly meetings. Anyone who lived in the watershed was eligible to vote at a council meeting. The council's structure has changed over the years, including more powers granted to the steering committee so that the organization can operate as a nonprofit corporation. Yet, the council and its decision-making process still retain a community-based orientation.

The McKenzie River drains a thirteen-hundred-square-mile watershed, which begins in the Oregon Cascade Range and flows down ten thousand feet to the confluence of the Willamette River in the Eugene-Springfield area. Approximately 80 percent of the watershed is composed of public land, and it is the drinking water source for approximately two hundred thousand residents.[1] Lane County and the public water utility (Eugene Water and Electric Board) played a key role in convening the McKenzie Watershed Management Program. The council, formed to address watershed management issues, provides a framework for coordination among key interests, a forum for information exchange, and a mechanism to help resolve issues among the diverse interests in the watershed. The council also plays an important role in advising the public land management agencies in the region, as council documents reveal:

The agencies, organizations and interests represented on the Council are not obligated to adopt or carry out the recommendations of the Council, but are encouraged to give due consideration to the recommendations and take actions they consider appropriate. These agencies, organizations and interests report back to the Council on any actions taken in response to Council recommendations. (McKenzie Watershed Council 2008)

To this day, the different origins and context for the Long Tom and McKenzie councils affect the way they operate along with how they implement actions. For many years, both councils have successfully accomplished their primary activities: reaching private landowners in the Long Tom and coordinating public land management efforts in the McKenzie, respectively. But as new issues and opportunities have emerged, these groups face challenges. The Long Tom Watershed Council has been developing more partnerships with cities and federal agencies, for example, but it must determine how to do so efficiently without upsetting its grassroots reputation. Conversely, the McKenzie council has been initiating more conservation efforts on private land, yet it must address some community perceptions that it is an agency-led group.

Theory Related to Convening

There is a long and extensive history of research on groups, group decision making, and team-based work, but much of this explores deliberation processes once a group is formed. Furthermore, many of the studies look at member-assigned groups, such as when a manager appoints staff members to a team. The focus of this chapter is the context and process by which people voluntarily come together—often from different perspectives and organizations—to solve problems or achieve a common vision.

One of the fields that addresses convening is conflict resolution, which examines contextual factors such as issue maturity, stalemates, venue shopping, and problem conditions that stakeholders might weigh to consider whether to participate in a consensus-based effort (Schwarz 2002; Susskind and Cruikshank 1987). The chief difference with these kinds of forums is that they frequently concentrate on developing an agreement, as opposed to forming a group that plays an ongoing governance and management role. The growing literature around collaboration is beginning to look more specifically at ongoing collaboratives and their formation (Mattessich, Murray-Close, and Monsey 2004; Born and Genskow 1999; Koontz et al. 2004). There also appears to be growing interest in questions about the social, economic, and ecological conditions that make collaboratives more likely to form.

Literature in public administration, public policy, and management has also examined convening in relation to collaborative governance (Mandell 1999, 2001; Schneider et al. 2003; Ansell and Gash 2007). This work hones in on the role that government entities play in convening collaborative efforts at a range of levels.

Some of the categories of findings across these bodies of literature include the context for collaboration, the roles in convening, the steps in convening, the convener characteristics, and the process of stakeholder selection.

Context for Collaboration

Researchers studying the emergence of collaboratives raise the issue of context—namely, what are the types of problems, settings, and situations conducive to collaboration? In their review of the theoretical frameworks explaining watershed partnerships, Paul Sabatier, William Leach, and their colleagues (2005) provide one of the more comprehensive reviews of the theories and literature relating to partnership formation.

The institutional rational choice literature hypothesizes several categories of factors affecting collaborative formation (Sabatier, Leach, Lubell, and Pelkey 2005).

First, there are resource attributes, such as whether problems are homogeneous or heterogeneous, whether the problems are severe, and whether knowledge about the problem is good (Sabatier, Leach, Lubell, and Pelkey 2005; Leach and Sabatier 2005). Second, there are institutional attributes, such as the initial transaction costs, whether existing institutions are effectively addressing the problem, and whether higher-level institutions grant local autonomy. Finally, there are community attributes, such as the extent of the social capital, heterogeneity of beliefs, distribution of costs and benefits, types of industries in the region (e.g., extractive versus service), and willingness of stakeholders to trade short-term costs for long-term benefits (Sabatier, Leach, Lubell, and Pelkey 2005).

To these sets of conditions, the literature on advocacy coalition frameworks would add whether there is an intense policy core conflict among potential stakeholders. Are there different normative assumptions about human nature or the role of government that make it hard to bridge differences, for example? The advocacy coalition frameworks and dispute resolution literature also highlight the importance of a "hurting stalemate." This makes the status quo unacceptable to stakeholders and the avenue of a collaborative forum more attractive (Sabatier, Leach et al. 2005). Finally, the social capital framework underscores the critical role of existing ties within communities to build new partnerships and collaborative relationships (Putnam 2000).

Roles in Convening

Another theme in the literature is the multiple roles involved in moving an issue, problem, or conflict into a collaborative setting. Chris Carlson (1999) identifies the roles of sponsors, conveners, neutrals, and participants. Sponsors are individuals or organizations that support the initiation of a group. In some cases, this may simply be through providing a forum or information about the potential for collaboration, but frequently sponsors give resources or staffing to support the convening process. When the sponsoring organization is one of the stakeholders, this can make convening more challenging because the stakeholders may perceive it as biased.

Conveners help with the process of identifying stakeholders, bringing them to the table, and often finding resources to support the process (Winer and Ray 1994; Carlson 1999). The literature around collaborative and integrative leadership describes this in terms of a catalyst role (Morse 2010). In particular, researchers examining the role of interagency and boundary-spanning efforts cite the communication networks and external relationships of these individuals as important to building bridges across organizations (Chrislip and Larson 1994; Morse 2010; Crosby and Bryson 2005). Conveners may be individuals or organizations, and Sonia Ospina and Erica Foldy (2010) emphasize the collective capacity of organizations to exhibit the leadership qualities to build bridges with others. In some cases, in order to avoid perceptions of bias, sponsoring organizations may hire or solicit a third or neutral party to help convene a collaborative (Gray 1989).

Then there are the participants themselves, who are usually referred to as stakeholders. These may be people representing themselves, interest groups, or organizations. One of the issues with convening stakeholders is that organized interests are likely to have more resources and capacity to participate than those who are not organized (Innes et al. 1994; Carlson 1999). Gray (1989) also points out that representation and its legitimacy can be an issue for some stakeholder groups if there is dissension or the lack of a clear spokesperson. In addition to raising questions about access, stakeholder capacity can also bring up issues about the equitability of the deliberation process (Kenney 2000; McCloskey 2001).

Steps in Convening

Another theme relates to the steps involved in convening a deliberative or collaborative effort. There has been less research on this topic, but many guidebooks and publications describe this process (Mattessich, Murray-Close, and Monsey 2004; Justice, Jamieson, and NetLibrary Inc. 1999; Thomas and Kilmann 1974). For example, the Wilder Foundation produced a series of publications about collaboration best practices and the role of nonprofit organizations (Winer and Ray 1994; Mattessich, Murray-Close, and Monsey 2004).

Carlson (1999) and Michael Winer and Karen Ray (1994) identify some similar steps in the convening process. First, there is the initial assessment where a convener needs to identify the issues, determine what the collaborative wants to accomplish, identify potential stakeholders, settle on the convening steps and potential obstacles, and determine potential resource needs. Second, there is the step of identifying and engaging participants. Third, the necessary resources to convene the effort need to be secured, including resources for training, hiring support, and reaching out to constituencies and the public. Finally, there is the planning and organization of the consensus-building process.

Convener Characteristics

Another area of discussion in the literature is the convener's characteristics. Researchers cite a wide range of characteristics, but the overarching theme is the importance of conveners being viewed as unbiased or trusted. Gray (1989, 72) notes that if a convener is suspected of bias, "other stakeholders may refuse to participate or even try to subvert the collaborative attempt." Government agencies often face this challenge due to fear and mistrust. Carlson (1999) argues that government representatives can reduce this by clarifying their objectives, stating their commitment to implementation, giving it their time and attention, and being clear about the form the agreement needs to take, including statutory limitations and responsibilities.

Another characteristic that can be significant for convening some groups is the convener's power, such as the power of holding formal office or the courts' power to require that parties come together. The tasks of these kinds of conveners are frequently distinct from those of a third-party mediator or facilitator (Gray 1989).

Several researchers allude to some more nuanced skills, such as a sense of timing and the ability to identify stakeholders (Gray 1989; Carlson 1999). Gray (1989, 72) suggests that they also need to have appreciative skills—meaning that "they need to appreciate the potential value of collaborating." Carlson (1999) maintains that the process also requires an external assessment to determine how other stakeholders view the issue and whether joint negotiations are feasible.

Stakeholder Selection

The final theme that many authors in conflict resolution highlight is the importance of a stakeholder selection process that includes adequate representation of all interests so the full range of perspectives is considered (Carlson 1999; Susskind and Cruikshank 1987). Some convening efforts face the situation of too many stakeholders and too few places at the table. This leads to issues about the criteria for choosing potential members, which can be difficult. In their handbook on collaboration, Winer and Ray (1994) identify a range of potential criteria, ranging from the ability to work collaboratively to stakeholders' capacity, familiarity with the topic, power, and impact. Similarly, several researchers mention the power to block a decision as a criterion (Innes 1991). Yet these kinds of filters have also raised concerns among those who fear that stakeholder selection will be based on existing power structures rather than the range of actual voices and interests—including those who are highly critical of existing policy or management (Lane 2003).

Assessing Convening

In this section, I draw on the literature as well as findings from my own research to present factors for assessing the convening process and its likelihood of achieving results. As with all of the factors presented in this book, it is difficult to trace a cause-effect relationship between these variables and the results of the group. This is particularly true for the convening steps, because it is hard to follow success or failure all the way back to the formation stage. Still, I believe there are some common assessment factors.

In explaining these factors, I attempt to identify specific measures or indicators of these factors to help researchers and practitioners with evaluations. Each factor can be assessed through self-evaluation or qualitative methods, such as interviewing participants, but I try to describe more objective measures that can be collected to corroborate self-evaluation or observational data. As shown in table 3.1, these factors are broken down into four categories: supportive context, legitimate broker, selection and structuring, and attractive forums.

Context Conducive to Collaboration

Since 1909, the International Joint Commission has worked collaboratively to manage the waters of the Great Lakes. The commission is composed of six members: three appointed by the president of the United States, and three appointed by the prime minister of Canada. Through treaties, quasi-judicial authority, and joint

Table 3.1
Assessing convening of collaboratives

Factors	Measures of factors	Related references
Supportive context: Setting that allows room for collaboration to emerge and develop solutions	**Problem context** • Problem characteristics with opportunities for win-win options • Relative power symmetry among stakeholders • Less heterogeneity of environmental problems **Community context** • Communities with strong social capital • Potential participants with established social networks • Low cultural or belief heterogeneity • Economic interlinkages don't limit potential for collaboration • Media, political, and interest group attention • Institutional complexity does not create significant barriers	Ostrom 2005; Putnam 2000; Sabatier, Leach, Lubell, and Pelkey 2005; Kenney 2000
Legitimate broker: An individual or organization with legitimacy that helps initiate a collaborative	• Broker has the respect or perception of neutrality that allows them to bring parties together • Broker connections or networks contain the individuals necessary to convene the effort • Adequate resources (time or funding) to initiate collaboration	Leach and Sabatier 2005; Bidwell and Ryan 2006; Koontz et al. 2004

Table 3.1
(continued)

Factors	Measures of factors	Related references
Selection and structuring: Legitimate process for stakeholders	• Process is somewhat insulated from the politics of selection • Range of individuals or organizational representatives at the table • Communication between lay and technical participants	Susskind and Cruikshank 1987; Depoe 2004
Attractive forum: Forum is more attractive in terms of problem solving, time, and costs compared to other venues	• Hurting stalemate that major stakeholders find unacceptable • Benefits from participation are commensurate with contributions • Stakeholders perceive that benefits exceed transaction costs • There are financial incentives to convening • There is a mandate that convenes a collaborative	Weber 2000, 2003; Innes et al. 1994; Moore and Koontz 2003

funding arrangements, the commission has tackled a range of issues in the Great Lakes, developing policies and programs implemented across the two governments, eight states, and two provinces. For example, the commission is sometimes called on to approve applications for dams or canals in the waters of the Great Lakes system. If it approves a project, the commission can set conditions limiting water levels and flows, protect shore properties and wetlands, or address the interests of farmers and shippers. In some cases, the International Joint Commission (2008) may continue to play a role in how the dams or canals are operated.

A cross-jurisdictional regional structure was also developed for the Sacramento and San Joaquin river and estuary systems of northern California. In response to significant drought and conflicts between water users, federal agencies worked collaboratively with the state of California to develop a new approach. In June 1994, these state and federal partners signed an agreement to coordinate activities in the Delta, particularly for water quality standards, which was the beginning of a California-federal partnership called the California Federal Bay-Delta (CALFED). The partners worked six months to develop a science-based proposal for water quality standards, which then led to an agreement known as the Bay-Delta Accord. The accord along with the accompanying agreements and memorandums of understanding resulted in a total of twenty-five state and federal implementing agencies that agreed to work collaboratively toward achieving balanced improvements in the Delta (California Bay-Delta Program 2008). But CALFED's road has been rocky, with state and federal partners failing to fully fund the efforts, calls for restructuring, and critical reviews of the agreements and management structure (Heikkila and Gerlak 2005; Innes, Connick, and Booher 2007; Little Hoover Commission 2005; Owen 2007). Many suggest that CALFED has failed.

The question confronting these cases is, What has allowed a group like the International Joint Commission to maintain its role and activities for almost a hundred years, while CALFED has faltered after fourteen years of activity? One set of factors that may help explain this relates to context.

Assessing Context

Identifying clearly defined and measurable factors for assessing context is challenging, because there are so many factors and a cause-effect relationship is difficult to establish. In the course of my research I have noted contextual differences as part of case study analysis, but my work has not focused on contextual variables. In this section, I draw from the literature to help explain some context factors, but this topic certainly requires more attention and research.

Problem Characteristics

There are many researchers who assert that the characteristics of a problem have an important impact on the likelihood that participants can reach agreements or address problems collectively (Lord 1979; Sabatier, Leach et al. 2005). One of the principles of collaboration is to develop win-win solutions by "expanding the pie" rather than focusing on how the pie is divided. Yet some problems lend themselves to those kinds of solutions more than others. For example, many collaborative efforts in Oregon focus on restoration and enhancement, which typically uses financial incentives to encourage people to undertake these efforts on their property. The win-win scenario here is that the public gets conservation benefits, and the landowner receives funding or compensation for their efforts or land.

If the conflict is over water quality flows—as in the case of CALFED—the reduction in flows to one sector may be at the cost of another sector. There may not be a readily available win-win scenario. Thus, reducing irrigation flows for rice production benefits the river and estuary ecology, but it also affects rice production, migratory birds that use the rice fields, and the secondary industries supporting rice production. In other words, there are sometimes settings that involve the reallocation of costs and benefits, or that confront value differences that cannot be easily overcome (Sabatier, Leach et al. 2005; Lord 1979). While stakeholders may not be able to determine this during the convening stage, collaboration is more likely to fail when potential solutions do not offer win-win outcomes.

Another factor impinging on stakeholder power and dynamics around collaboration is whether there is symmetry in the setting (Kenney 2000). The classic theoretical example compares dischargers emitting waste into a river versus a lake. A river system creates an asymmetrical power relationship between upstream and downstream dischargers, because the upstream actor's actions affect the downstream actor, but not vice versa. In contrast, dischargers emitting waste into a lake must also bear the impacts on that lake system, and they both have equal impacts on each other. So there is a built-in incentive to collaborate because they are sharing a resource and their power is symmetrical. In his critique of collaboration efforts, Kenney (2000, 34) notes:

Issues such as water supply are probably not so readily amenable to resolution through western watershed initiatives in most situations since any group action that increases supply is likely to produce benefits accruing exclusively to the next appropriator in line. In contrast, group efforts to improve ecosystem health promise benefits for all, given the greater symmetry of the situation, and are presumably well suited to collaborative problem-solving strategies.

A third factor identified in the institutional rational choice literature is the extent to which the environmental problems being addressed are heterogeneous (Ostrom 1999). The more multifaceted and multidimensional the problem is, the more difficult and complex the solutions. In contrast, more homogeneous problems tend to create less complexity. A collaborative addressing water quantity, say, can focus on the allocation of demand, but a group dealing with wetlands may require deliberations about land use planning, water quality, water quantity, and habitat.

Community Characteristics

Another category of context factors relates to community characteristics, which are particularly important for collaboratives relying on community support and implementation through social networks (see chapter 7).

Human and Social Capital

One variable that may be significant in assessing community context is the local social capital. Researchers from the institutional rational choice (Ostrom 1986a, 1999) and the political contracting framework (Sabatier, Leach et al. 2005) assert that communities with high existing social capital are more likely to be places where collaborative efforts emerge. The theory is that the community already has networks in place that allow stakeholders to be selected who can be connected into these networks and the community. These communities are also more likely to trust public institutions. These linkages are key for building a consensus that reflects community concerns, developing trust for the collaborative within the community, and helping to support implementation efforts. For example, farmers who participated on a groundwater management committee in the lower Willamette Valley were already involved in farming organizations, social clubs, and other community groups. When they brought their perspective to the table, they could provide a sense of what other people in the region were thinking about the issues. The committee also relied on them to take information back to their own groups for feedback.

When collaboratives address issues at the organizational and policy levels, however, the concerns encompass larger regions with larger populations. In these circumstances, the stakeholders' social networks in relation to the community are less critical. Instead, the personal networks that stakeholders have among organizations and policymakers become the more significant factor. One of the representatives on the CALFED Bay-Delta Program governing board, for instance, was the chair of a bank in Yuba City, which is in the heart of the Sacramento River region's rice industry. He also had a history of involvement with the rice industry, having served on the board of directors for the California Rice Industry Association and as the California delegate to the USA Rice Federation. Stakeholders in policy collaboratives thus have important networks, but their participation is valued most for their networks with organizations, interest groups, and elected officials, rather than their personal networks in the community.

Measuring the social capital to assess community context is difficult, because data tend to be time-consuming and expensive to collect. Many trends of social capital are based on national surveys, market information, and organizational participation data, and are often not available at a regional or local level (Putnam 2000). Some locally available data may nonetheless provide indications of trends or comparisons to other localities. These data include voting participation, club and organization membership, religious organization membership, or even the density of community and social organizations.

Another method that can be used in conjunction with existing collaborative efforts is social network analysis. Utilizing a range of qualitative methods, researchers identify the network of people who are communicating and interacting with each other. An analysis of these networks can reveal the density of the overall network and centrality of any one individual to it (Burt 1992; Granovetter 1983; Prell, Hubacek, and Reed 2009).

Low Cultural or Belief Heterogeneity
Another factor that researchers suggest has an effect on a collaborative's ability to achieve results is the degree to which community culture and beliefs are heterogeneous (Ostrom 1999, 2007; Libecap 1989). In other words, the more variation there is in a community about what it values or believes about the environment, the more difficult it may be for collaboration to work.

Conceptually this idea makes sense, because collaboration is built on finding common ground. The more distance there is between people at the beginning, the more difficult it will be to reach this mutual interest. Yet there are many examples of collaboratives that have emerged out of just this kind of divisive setting. Several stakeholders in the Johnstone Catchment Committee (Australia) previously had been combatants in a bitter dispute about rain forest protection along the escarpment in tropical north Queensland. An environmentalist involved in the group even described being verbally abused by people in the community when she went into town to shop. At the same time, this history of conflict was what brought people to the table to find a more constructive way to address the issue.

I believe it is also important to recognize the differences between action, organizational, and policy collaboratives in relation to cultural and belief heterogeneity. One of the common messages I have heard from action collaboratives is that they are able to overcome deep differences about values and policies because they can agree on the need to undertake restoration or education actions. All the participants on the Johnstone Catchment Committee were excited about the restoration efforts that the group was sponsoring and the success it was having in promoting best practices among agricultural landowners. They could agree that these actions had benefits. When it came to issues of organizational programs and government policy, though, it was more difficult to find common ground. Hence, the sugarcane farmer and the environmentalist developed considerable respect for each other and their positions, and they could agree on restoration actions. They could not agree on agency policy regarding alterations to a local weir (dam) that would reduce the size of a coastal wetland, despite two years of deliberations.

As with social capital, measuring belief heterogeneity is difficult. Interviews or surveys targeted to key community members may provide some insights into these issues. These differences may also be revealed through an analysis of data, such as voting patterns (as an indicator of political homogeneity or heterogeneity), newspaper coverage of controversies, or an assessment of letters to the editor (as an indicator of community controversy and conflict, and opinion polling about beliefs and attitudes.

Economic Interlinkages

A final community characteristic that may affect a collaborative's success is the economic interlinkages associated with the problem that the collaborative is addressing. For instance, the institutional rational choice theorists suggest that watershed partnerships are less likely to form in areas dominated by extractive industries as compared to those dominated by service industries (Sabatier, Leach et al. 2005). The classic example of this in the western United States has been timber-dependent communities significantly affected by timber policies on federal lands.

The research is unclear, however, as to whether interlinkages have an effect on convening collaboration efforts. For example, several collaboratives that I researched in Australia and the United States existed in areas where there were significant extractive industries, such as gravel mining and timber harvesting. A key motivator in these cases was a perceived external threat, such as government intervention, which is discussed further in the next section.

In her study of the adoption of collaborative efforts among Bureau of Land Management field offices, Tamara Laninga (2005) reinforced this finding. She expected to discover a contrast between the offices located in the "old West" (extractive-based economies) and the new one (amenity-based areas). Instead, the uptake of collaborative approaches was better explained by areas experiencing human or environmental change, and where there was community capacity and a supportive field manager. Perceived threats to agriculture and the environment from oil and gas exploration were also a factor.

In contrast, many collaboratives have experienced difficulty in engaging individuals who are *not* dependent on the land for their livelihood. Rural residential landowners in both Queensland and Oregon, for example, were often more well educated and had higher incomes than the general population. But these people were generally unaware of land and water management issues. This issue was highlighted in a small study I conducted in the Bundamba Catchment in the rural areas outside of Brisbane. My students and I found that many agricultural landowners were aware of the exotic species and erosion, while many rural residential landowners had no idea that these problems were present and thought one of the most prolific weeds was "kind of pretty."[2]

It *is* important to recognize that economic interlinkages may help get people to the table, but may make it more difficult to achieve successful outcomes. For example, agricultural landowners may be motivated to join a collaborative watershed effort, yet they may be constrained on what they can do because they depend on the land as an income source. Rural residential landowners, by comparison, are hard to bring to the table, but many have the potential to undertake conservation efforts because their income does not depend on the land.

Economic interlinkages can be assessed through an analysis of local economic and job activity by industry type. For instance, employment by job category could indicate the extent of dependence on resource- versus tourism-related activities. This could provide rough measures of economic dependence or interlinkages with the issues being addressed.

Problem Attention

Another contextual category relates to the attention given to a problem, including the iconic value of a place, perception of a crisis, or fear of outside intervention.

Lake Tahoe is a relatively small area, for instance, yet the region's management has been the focus of high-level state and federal attention for more than a hundred years, because the lake and its surroundings are a national icon.

In several cases I have researched, the perception of a crisis has played an important role. For example, Australia's Murray Darling River sustained a thousand-kilometer-long blue-green alga bloom that led to a state of emergency, with the army transporting drinking water to the riverside communities (Sinclair 2001). This focused significant media and political attention on the river system, leading to new policy negotiations and joint funding to help restore the river basin.

Another common source of attention is a fear of government regulation or intervention (Weber 2003; Koontz et al. 2004). In fact, concerns about the Endangered Species Act may be one of the best explanatory variables for the emergence of collaborative watershed efforts in the West—particularly where there is a strong interlinkage with the resource in question. Similarly, the emergence of watershed efforts in other parts of the United States is explained as much by fears of water quality regulations as concerns about the actual quality of water.

Finally, elected officials, interest groups, and the media may raise concerns about a particular problem or place. The Steens Mountain area of southeast Oregon, say, received relatively little media and public attention, outside the few landowners, agency people, and environmentalists who were debating about how the highly unique ecological landscape could be maintained. Yet when U.S. Department of the Interior secretary Bruce Babbitt arrived in the region and asked locals and agencies to craft a plan together "or he would develop one in Washington," there was an immediate impetus to begin discussions.[3]

In many of the cases I examined, I found examples where problems, perceptions, or actions raised an issue's profile. It is more difficult to determine the conditions under which this helps a collaborative convene an effort and those under which it inhibits convening. Raising the profile of a problem can lead to pressure to solve it; this pressure can also make the process of resolving it more difficult.

Assessing problem attention may depend on looking at both the attention given to a problem or region and the response that this attention generates. Some indicators may be the media coverage of problems, elected official involvement (particularly at high levels), and the attention raised by interest groups. Participants themselves often provide the most insight into the factors and fears that motivated them to join a collaborative effort.

Institutional Characteristics

A final contextual factor affecting collaboratives is the institutional characteristics. By institutions, I refer to the array of organizations and government entities as well as the formal and informal structures among them. This issue is especially relevant to organizational and policy collaboratives that are attempting to bring players from across this institutional landscape into a collaborative setting.

Two growth management case studies that I explored highlighted some of the challenges confronted by complex institutional settings. In South East Queensland, a collaborative growth management process involved eighteen local governments and a half dozen state agencies.[4] In metropolitan Denver, a similar process involved fifty local governments and little state agency participation. The more limited number of local governments in South East Queensland allowed for considerably more direct interaction among the local elected officials, compared to the metropolitan Denver process, which relied on a governing board and numerous subcommittees. As a result, in Denver it was harder for participants to have a big picture view or even keep up with what was happening across the region.

The research literature and cases I have investigated lead me to highlight three measures of institutional context (Gray 1989; Alexander 1995). First, there is the complexity of these arrangements in terms of the number of organizations as well as formal and informal structures. The greater the complexity, the more difficult it is for a collaborative to link together with key stakeholders and initiatives. Thus, in the Denver region, elected officials were critical of the committee structures used to develop the regional growth management approach, but the number of local governments made a committee structure difficult to design.

Second, the extent of jurisdictional overlap among management organizations increases the institutional complexity. Estuaries, for example, often create more complex institutional settings than terrestrial systems. Many estuarine systems involve overlapping local, state, and federal jurisdictions that relate to navigation, commerce, fishing, and the environment.

Third, the extent of interaction between levels also increases the complexity and may make the work of some groups more difficult. For instance, watershed councils in Oregon's Columbia basin must consider two levels. They work at the action level to implement restoration activities and encourage improved management practices. They also interact at the organizational level, because decisions about restoration, water flows, and other issues affect the ecological and hydrologic functioning of the entire Columbia River basin. Yet this basin-level activity provides the councils with access to conservation funding from the Northwest Power and Conservation Council as well.

In summary, the context in which a collaborative effort is convened involves numerous factors with a wide range of measures—many of which are hard to quantify. The direction of influence is also not always clear. For example, does attention to the problem motivate or constrain action? Does a threat of government intervention motivate collaboration but reduce the potential to achieve results? While I am skeptical that context can be examined as an isolated factor in determining the effectiveness of collaborative efforts, it obviously has an influence. It is also apparent that there is a need for more research in this area.

Legitimate Broker

A second factor important in convening collaboratives is the presence of a broker who helps bring the parties together. The literature spotlights a number of different roles, including convener, champion, and neutral (Carlson 1999; Crosby and Bryson 2010). In practice, I have found that these roles may overlap and be subsumed by one person, or they may involve several people in distinct roles. I will refer to these roles collectively as a broker role, but discuss the different aspects. A broker may be a federal or state agency, a local government, a university representative, or simply an individual who is able to spur people into action.

In the natural resources collaboration field, the brokerage role is best exemplified by the well-told story of how Oregon's Applegate partnership emerged. After years of conflict between timber and environmental interests, an environmentalist named Jack Shipley and a logger named Jack Neal got together to explore whether they could use a more collaborative approach to land management issues. They quietly began going around to the major stakeholders in the region, asking if they would be willing to work together. This led to a series of weekly roundtables involving a wide cross section of people. A group representing a diverse cross section of stakeholders voluntarily formed out of this process to work through the issues of natural resources management and economy in the region (Red Lodge Clearinghouse 2009; Moseley 1999). Clearly, the spotted owl controversy and the stalemate emerging between the interests were significant factors as well, but the role of the two leaders as brokers of a collaborative process was a critical precondition.

In the history of Australia's Landcare program, there are similar stories of brokers who helped initiate discussions that evolved into collaboratives to address local problems. In the Tragowel Plains of Western Australia, for example, several young farmers became concerned about the amount of salinity appearing on area farms. Marg and Rob Agnew hosted a meeting of eleven farmers, who agreed to jointly address the problem: "First, we got all the members together at the top end of the catchment and followed the drainage lines through each farm. . . . Now we have 23 farmers, covering the whole catchment" (quoted in Campbell 1994, 65).

In Wisconsin, staff members and administrators within the DNR were key to initiating a collaborative approach on the upper Wisconsin River. Staff members in one of the regional offices recognized that over a ten-year period, a large number of federal dam licenses would be expiring in the same river basin. Rather than creating a separate process for each individual dam, they established a basinwide collaborative planning process. The district information officer described the process that they used to kick off the effort:

We spent weeks traveling up and down the river all the way from the headwaters down to the confluence of the Mississippi getting input from people, going community to community giving out information, and gathering comments from people about their concerns. A lot of them we already knew, but they helped validate the areas we were concerned about. It also helped us to create an extensive mailing list of people who were interested that we could correspond with through newsletters and so on. During the first phase, we identified who the key people were along the whole stem of people we felt were key to involve. So during the issue identification process, we appointed a citizens' advisory committee that helped us identify and prioritize issues that the technical committee folks could use to get at the meat of the project. That whole process took about one and a half years.[5]

Assessing Brokers

While the story of brokers has been told in the literature, there has been less research focused on the characteristics, approaches, or lessons surrounding this role. One factor noted in the literature, which I have also identified in my cases, has been the perception of a broker (or brokers) as being neutral or unbiased (Carlson 1999). It thus can be challenging for a broker to convene a group when they are considered a stakeholder, because participants may be suspicious about their motives. Alternatively, the broker may be able to convene the group, but may not be able to easily lead it because they are a significant stakeholder. For this reason, some efforts have used a third-party facilitator or chair who was not a key stakeholder to help convene the effort. Perceptions of bias also may be overcome by having multiple participants involved in initiating the collaborative. It was important that not only Shipley (again, a local environmentalist) but also Neal (a local logger) convened the Applegate project. The fact that the brokers represented two ends of the spectrum in previous debates provided a sense among participants that the process was going to be open to a range of voices.

When a broker is not neutral, another factor identified in the literature is that the individual must not be wedded to specific problem definitions, and they also must be able to set a course that will engage a diverse set of stakeholders (Crosby and Bryson 2010; Huxham and Vangen 2005). In several of the cases I researched that were initiated by the Wisconsin DNR, this open course was critical to convening. Even in the case of the Lower Wisconsin River, where previous controversy had scuttled management efforts, the open approach of the new process convinced many stakeholders to come to the table.

A third factor for assessing a broker—and one frequently cited factor in the collaborative leadership literature—is their connectedness and communication linkages. These connections and linkages have been described in terms of "boundary spanning leaders" (Crosby and Bryson 2005) and "relationship capital" (Morse 2010). These studies and others assert that brokers do not start from scratch but instead often build on a network of cross-cutting relationships (Weber 2003). For

Table 3.2
Assessing broker legitimacy

Collaborative type	Factors influencing broker legitimacy
Action	• Broker connections to the community often an important factor • Government-based brokers can make convening more difficult
Organizational	• Broker validity includes both personal connections and organizational affiliation • Resources to initiate consensus building important aspect of legitimacy
Policy	• Broker validity includes both policy-level reputation and connections • Resources to initiate consensus building essential aspect of legitimacy

example, conveners from the Wisconsin DNR were usually seasoned veterans of the agency who had established sets of relationships and interaction.

Although these three factors appear in the literature and many of my cases, I have found that the factors impacting the effectiveness of the broker vary depending on the type of collaborative (see table 3.2). At the action level, the goal is to convene a broad group of people who are well networked into the social structures and organizations of the community. The broker must often be someone who is known to these people and well connected in the community. For this reason, it can be more difficult for a person affiliated with government to act as a broker of action collaboratives (Bidwell and Ryan 2006; Leach and Sabatier 2005; Koontz et al. 2004).

For organizational collaboratives, the goal is to convene all of the organizations with a stake in the management activities. Government affiliation can be an asset rather than a liability, because it connotes a sanctioned and supported process. As such, the broker's relationship capital is important, but the concept of "shared leadership" can also play a role. Shared leadership is the distributed set of leadership activities practiced by a group or organization (Pearce and Sims 2000). "Organizational legitimacy" may therefore be just as important for convening these efforts, and it may be hard for a citizen to act as a broker for an organizational collaborative. Stakeholders also know that collaboration requires resources, and an organization that commits resources to convene a group is more likely to gain legitimacy.

At the policy end of the spectrum, convening stakeholders involves assembling policy-level actors such as elected officials, agency administrators, and interest group leaders. This means that the broker must often have relationship capital among the actors at this level. The broker may be one of these stakeholders or a leader of a key organization (such as a university president, foundation director, or corporate

CEO). Prior to any meeting in which stakeholders gather, the broker may have to engage in an extensive process of quiet consultation and "shuttle diplomacy" to identify the participants as well as scout out their interest in participating. The individual who makes these contacts generally must have the political legitimacy just to get appointments for meetings or have phone calls returned. Furthermore, a simple kick-off meeting of a policy collaborative can involve a substantial effort to convene participants, schedule the event, prepare background material, and handle potential media coverage. Significant resources are thus frequently critical even before the stakeholders are convened.

Stakeholder Selection and Structuring

A third key factor in convening a consensus-building effort is a process of stakeholder selection that is perceived as fair. This is critical, because it sets the tone for the group and its legitimacy. When selection processes are understood as fair and transparent, few people pay attention to them. It is only when they are not deemed legitimate that their significance becomes obvious. Gray (1989, 64) notes, "The question of who should participate in a collaborative negotiation is a very important one with serious implications for the outcome of collaboration." Similarly, a study of over one hundred mediated environmental disputes found that participation by those in authority to implement the decision greatly influenced the likelihood of the agreement being implemented (Bingham 1986).

The process used in the Australian state of New South Wales highlighted the difficulties of a controversial selection process. The New South Wales government established catchment management committees in the late 1980s to address land and water conservation on a regional basis through citizen-government collaboration. The majority of the committee members had to be local residents, and the committees were meant to represent a cross section of interests. Membership in a committee required ministerial approval, however, and over the years elected ministers of both conservative and liberal parties politicized the process.

A conservative state minister removed one landowner from the selection panel of a north coast committee because she had been active with a local environmental group. Several years later, she was appointed to the selection committee under a more liberal government and remarked, "We came up with a really good committee. It had a wide variety of people on it from real estate agents to farmers to environmentalists. The list went down to Sydney and they made it into a totally 'green' [environmental] committee."[6]

Several other members of the same committee observed that the selection process had created ill feelings and made it difficult for the committee to operate. One committee member said that the committee was inhibited by:

political "rorting" [Australian slang for "con job"] of the public representation by our local member [elected representative]. . . . [There is] widespread public perception of the above mentioned "rorting" resulting in a tainted image and general apathy among the community at large.[7]

Similarly, another member commented:

The committee was initially stacked; i.e., it was interfered with by the local members of the National Party [rural conservative political party] and seven members did not apply in the formal sense. As a result a group of people from the old families in the area now represent the whole community.[8]

This type of political interference is contrary to the purpose of a collaborative approach, which is to build a broad base of understanding and achieve consensus, despite interests and political affiliations (Gray 1989; Wondolleck 1985). What New South Wales elected officials failed to understand is that the power of the catchment committees was not in how they were "stacked" but rather in the breadth of their consensus and support. Broadly supported consensus will help produce a strategy that is more cognizant of the range of issues and perspectives supported by diverse individuals and organizations (Mitchell 1991), and will also increase the likelihood of implementation.

The difficulty of stakeholder selection comes when participation has to be limited, and the competition for stakeholder seats tends to increase as one moves across the spectrum from action- to organizational- to policy-level collaboratives. This correlates with the tendency for higher-level collaboratives to cover larger areas, encompass a larger population, and involve more substantial policy issues. For example, there are a large number of potential stakeholders and community members who could be involved in policy collaboratives addressing issues like the San Francisco estuary, Chesapeake Bay, and Great Barrier Reef. Action collaboratives in sparsely populated communities often face the opposite problem. Their challenge is to find people willing to participate who are not already overcommitted to work, family, and other community volunteer efforts.

Assessing Selection and Structuring

Based on the literature and my research, there are at least three key variables in assessing stakeholder selection and structuring: an insulated selection process, an underlying principle of inclusiveness, and an appropriate structure.

Insulated Process

Several New South Wales cases demonstrated that a process appearing politicized might create a lasting reputation for the collaborative. It is important, then, that the process insulate itself from some of the politics and community biases. In some cases, the convener may have already laid the groundwork for committee membership. The initiators of the Applegate Partnership and Long Tom Watershed Council sought out a diverse spectrum of stakeholders, invited them to participate, and solicited other suggestions from participants. This kind of snowball process can be a quick way of generating a cross section of participants, especially when the potential stakeholders are known and the conveners have legitimacy.

The state of Queensland developed more structured selection processes to help insulate it from some of the politics. Local initiators of a collaborative group had to convene a selection committee, which identified appropriate government representatives and created a slate of citizen positions that would result in a citizen majority. These citizen representatives were often designated by subwatershed and/ or type (farming, urban, and environmental). The committee advertised for these positions, selected a slate to fill the management committee, and then the selection committee disbanded.

Ultimately, the steps and rules in a selection process should be judged against transparency and opportunity. Transparency refers to a clear process for selection. Opportunity relates to a clear mechanism by which someone can become a stakeholder—but without a guarantee that every potential stakeholder will be selected.

Inclusiveness

Another measure is the degree of inclusiveness in the stakeholder selection process. Lawrence Susskind and Jeffrey Cruikshank (1987, 103) suggest that it is better to start with too many people or groups, rather than too few: "The parties to a public dispute must agree that it is necessary to involve all legitimate 'stakeholding' interests in whatever negotiations are planned. If they leave out a key group, even unintentionally, the credibility of ad hoc consensus building may be irretrievably damaged." The goal of a collaborative approach is to achieve consensus through information sharing and conflict resolution, which cannot happen if the full range of interests is not included. Hence, collaborative groups are generally much larger than the optimum number cited in the conflict resolution literature.

A planning process in the Lower Wisconsin River valley initiated by the Wisconsin DNR used a group with thirty-four members that included as many views and opinions as possible. As one DNR staff person noted, "Without [this involvement] it would not have survived . . . largely because that part of the state is very conservative and very Republican. With a Republican governor, it was understood that it would not be passed unless the citizens were satisfied with the project."[9]

Even this large a committee still required additional efforts to involve stakeholders. One participant commented that there was a "perception that the initial committee was adjusted too far away from locals." To rectify this situation, a DNR administrator set up a local officials advisory committee to further expand participation.[10]

Similarly, the stakeholder committee created to address issues in the San Francisco estuary had forty-nine members. Although this made for a cumbersome consensus-building process, participants emphasized that it was important to have the full range of interests represented at the table. A developer representative said that it was critical that all of the different people involved got to know each other. Another participant noted that having everyone involved was essential: "Everyone participated; everyone had a sense of stakeholding. Everyone was lining up behind the effort; everyone was working together and it was really quite exciting."[11]

Inclusiveness also means the ability to expand or contract as the process unfolds. Clearly, having all stakeholders involved from the start has advantages, but as Susskind and Cruikshank (1987) observe, it is not always obvious which individual or interest should represent a particular stance. As details of a collaborative effort begin to be fleshed out, it will be more apparent whose interests are at stake, and thus stakeholder membership may change. In a collaborative case study in Wisconsin, the project manager explained that they tried to anticipate all potential interests, but also allowed the committee to expand as needed: "We sort of crystal balled it. As we got going in the committee process, we would find people to get involved that we needed."[12]

What is the optimum group size? The answer tends to vary by the setting's conditions, but it also tends to vary by the type of collaborative. Policy collaboratives usually involve high-level deliberation on prominent policy decisions, resulting in new policies or programs that government entities will implement or coordinate. Because the policy outcome has the potential for wide-ranging effects across a large area or population, the consensus decision can require a large stakeholder group to produce effective agreements (see table 3.3). As one moves across the spectrum from organizational to action collaboratives, the population affected decreases and the decision-making focus shifts from public issues (e.g., public land management) to private ones (e.g., restoration of private property). For action collaboratives, the stakeholder selection process is often guided by the need to find people with community connections, and in turn, this sometimes requires active recruitment.

Appropriate Structure

Structuring refers to the ways in which stakeholder input is organized during the consensus-building process. It is common for collaboratives to use subcommittees or working groups to do the "groundwork" on issues that they then bring back to the full stakeholder group. This can speed up the consensus-building phase by allowing several concerns to be explored in parallel. Subcommittees also create participation opportunities for stakeholders who are not part of the lead group. For example,

Table 3.3
Collaborative types and stakeholder selection

Type	Examples	Factors affecting group size and structure
Action	• Oregon watershed councils: 10–20 • Australian Landcare groups: 4–40	• Represent the range of perspectives in the community • Include people connected into community social networks • Some use other forums for broad-based input
Organizational	• Australian catchment committees: 12–20 • Rogue Basin Coordinating Committee: 8	• Represent the range of organizations involved in management • Stakeholders have key roles in management activities • Subcommittees provide a broader range of input
Policy	San Francisco Estuary Project: 49 Lower Wisconsin River: 26 Denver Metro Vision: 50	• Represent the range of policy interests surrounding an issue • Include stakeholders with the power to block or veto proposals • Executive groups and broader forums are often both used • Supporting agency is a significant factor in maintaining group

in the San Francisco Estuary Project, a technical advisory committee, a public advisory committee, and six subcommittees supplemented the work of the interest-based stakeholder committee (Innes et al. 1994). The subcommittee addressing water quality issues brought together scientists to develop a model for examining habitat and water quality issues, which was important for establishing some of the key water quality standards related to the estuary.

From my research of collaboratives, structuring becomes more of an issue as one moves across the spectrum from action to policy collaboratives for several reasons. Policy collaboratives tend to encompass larger areas, more population, and issues of greater significance, which results in more potential stakeholders. Furthermore, the complexity of science and policy standards at this scale frequently requires more detailed technical input—leading to technical advisory committees. And effective subcommittees often necessitate staffing to support the work, so some collaboratives are limited by capacity.

Although subcommittees offer more opportunity for input and technical assistance, they can also create difficulties, because some participants may not have the chance to hear each other or deliberate over key issues. A citizen representative involved in the Winnebago case noted:

It was less effective when you were in with the subdivided groups. You couldn't work with another group when we broke into smaller groups. . . . There was some confusion about who was involved where. It wasn't really clear how the other internal DNR committees were going to mesh with our committee. It seemed at times that they were operating separately from the [citizens' advisory committee]. There were a lot of people with a lot of differences.[13]

A similar problem was cited in the Denver Metro Vision planning process, which involved numerous subcommittees. This allowed the process to pull in a wider range of stakeholders besides local government elected officials, but as a county planner remarked, it also had important limitations:

The problem is that the [DRCOG] board sets out tasks and then gives them to committees. But these issues get broken down into more and more fine parts and details, and we don't have a good vision or idea of where we are supposed to be heading.[14]

When policy issues are interlinked with technical ones, it may be important to combine technical and lay committees. For example, Stephen Depoe (2004) documents the deliberations surrounding the rehabilitation of the Fernald nuclear weapons site. At the core of the rehabilitation debate was the question of standards and risks for exposure to radiation release. As is often the case, scientific and public perceptions of risk were different, so delegating this task to a scientific panel would have been unlikely to resolve the problem. The deliberation process instead involved both scientists and laypeople. This greatly increased the time required to build consensus, but Depoe (2004) contrasts the group's success with a similar advisory group that used a separate technical committee and encountered significant difficulties.

These findings and research suggest two factors in assessing the structure of a collaborative. First, the more that technical issues are intertwined with policy concerns, the greater the need to bring together both perspectives in a single forum. This will increase the time required for deliberation, but is more likely to produce a result supported by understanding and commitment. Second, subcommittees should have a clearly defined role, clear communication lines, and a clear process for decision making.

Attractive Forum

The final factor in convening collaboratives is the forum's attraction. In 2002, I participated in a study tour of the Klamath irrigation area a few years after it had been embroiled in a series of high-profile conflicts. In brief, low flows were affecting salmon survival in the lower Klamath basin, leading to a cutoff of water into the Klamath irrigation areas.

The actual events were dramatic. Bureau of Reclamation engineers wearing bulletproof vests and flanked by Federal Bureau of Investigation agents had to walk through a cauldron of protesters to shut off the irrigation water, which had been sabotaged by irrigators. While environmental groups were going to federal court to require the bureau to take action, irrigators were on the phone to the vice president's office seeking administrative relief. The conflicts and conditions offered little opportunity for consensus or collaboration. The local watershed council had determined much earlier that the water flow issues were well beyond its scope, and it chose to focus on restoration projects in the basin. There was little incentive for stakeholders to give up their existing avenues of influence (courts and the administration) and sit down to work collaboratively. Furthermore, there was no forum that provided an attractive alternative to addressing the issues, because neither the courts nor the administration was pushing the stakeholders in this direction.

The Applegate and Johnstone regions faced similar kinds of historic tensions as well as conflicts between environmental and resource-dependent interests (logging and sugarcane farming). Yet when forums emerged to provide a venue for discussion and deliberation, these participants were able to find some common ground. Why did forums work in these areas but not in the Klamath? One reason included a stalemate in the conflict that meant existing venues appeared less attractive than a collaborative one. Another factor was that the conflicts had an extended history, and the idea of moving away from confrontation had become more attractive. Finally, in both cases a forum was created—one by local stakeholders, and the other by government—that provided a venue for stakeholders to begin sitting down at the table together.

Assessing Forums

Although conveners and stakeholders have only limited control over the conditions that lead participants to join a collaborative forum, it is important to recognize that the reasons stakeholders meet together can affect implementation. Any parent or teacher understands that there is a fundamental difference in the behavior of kids when they *want* to do something versus when they *must* do something. It is reflected in their enthusiasm, dedication, and ultimately the quality of work. Adults are no different. They are much more likely to enthusiastically work with a group when they join because they want to as opposed to when they are told to do so. The chief difficulty with assessing the attractiveness of forums is the lack of objective data.

Forum as an Opportunity for Influence

One way of assessing a forum's attractiveness relates to whether potential stakeholders view it as a means for input into decision making. In some cases, this may be a desire to influence outcomes because the stakeholder is concerned about the issue. Often the motivation is a concern that someone else, such as a government agency, will make decisions. In fact, I have found this concern about what decisions a group *might* be making a surprisingly common motivation for those who have joined collaboratives.

In interview with stakeholders in the Oregon watershed councils, I found open acknowledgment that they became involved primarily because they were concerned of what would happen if they didn't have a say in decision making. Stakeholders in Australia stated that they got involved in a collaborative catchment committee because they wanted to prevent action such as new regulations, rather than wanting to take action. Even advocates of localism admit that collaboration is frequently supported because the alternatives are much worse. As Edward Weber (2000, 256) notes, "If the top-down superstructure of law and bureaucracy disappears, it is not clear that industry will maintain its participation in grassroots environmental management." It is a surprising theme, because it does not fit the feel-good, community well-being image that collaboration generally presents, but it plainly is a strong reason why stakeholders are willing to become involved.

Common Vision

A second way of assessing forums is to determine whether stakeholders share a common vision of the things that they could achieve collectively. For example, watershed councils came together with state and federal agencies in southern Oregon to form the Rogue Basin Coordinating Committee. They could see a mutual benefit in pooling resources, sharing information, and coordinating efforts at a basin scale.

Sometimes this common vision has to develop, but at other times it already exists. From the convening stories I have heard, strong social and interorganizational networks can help this common vision emerge more readily. Action collaboratives are often built on and facilitated by social networks, and communities that have strong social networks may offer richer seedbeds for collaborative efforts. Organizational and policy collaboratives also depend on networks among the array of actors and decision makers who are potential participants. Thus, a history of past interaction may be an important prelude for recognizing a common vision.

Costs and Benefits of Participating

Innes and her colleagues (1994, 21) maintain that participation in consensus building often depends on "stakeholders making an implicit cost-benefit calculation," or an assessment of their best alternative to a negotiated agreement (see also Susskind and Cruikshank 1987; Fisher and Ury 1981). A watershed stakeholder representing environmental interests in a rural region of southern Queensland explained her calculations about participating in a catchment committee: "I'm supportive of the catchment committee as long as my views are being taken seriously and the group is productive, but if not, I have got better ways to spend my time and energy. I'm always willing to find other forums."[15]

All potential stakeholders may assess collaboratives against a range of other forums, such as agencies, courts, legislatures, city councils, or even the "court" of public opinion. As a result, the parties may not be willing to collaborate until these forums are exhausted or some kind of stalemate is reached. The difficulty for stakeholders is that the initial stages of collaboration do not always present a clearly defined issue or conflict about which they can calculate the costs and benefits of participation.

The attractiveness of a collaboration forum is important because it also involves transaction costs and power sharing. The transaction costs include the participants' time, the resources needed to support the effort, and the time delays associated with the process. It also involves power sharing, because participants need to commit to sharing information, providing their perspectives on goals, and working on an agreed set of actions. These are inherent barriers to collaboration that inhibit participation.

Because of the transaction costs, incentives can help make collaboration a more attractive option. One of the most successful examples of using incentives to spawn collaborative efforts has been the Australian Landcare program. The National Landcare Program supplied funding and technical assistance to people who wanted to form Landcare groups and address natural resources problems in their area. Some groups might have formed regardless of this program's existence, because landowners recognized that they were confronting problems that extended beyond the scale of the individual property. Yet the opportunity to tap into funding and expertise through the National Landcare Program was an impetus for the creation of over four thousand Landcare groups across Australia (Curtis and Lockwood 2000).

Oregon is also noted for the large number of collaborative-based watershed councils. There are certain conditions that have helped lead to the emergence of these groups, but the proliferation of these councils has not been spontaneous. An essential motivator has been the incentives provided by the state of Oregon through the Oregon Watershed Enhancement Board (OWEB). Between July 2007 and September 2008, OWEB (2008) gave almost six million dollars in funding to over fifty different watershed councils for their operations and over forty-six million dollars in funding for watershed restoration efforts.

Finally, mandating collaboration can change stakeholder assessment by making the collaborative an essential forum. The Australian state governments of Victoria and New South Wales mandated the creation of catchment committees that covered the entire state. The state required the groups to have a majority of community members, but many also involve local governments or state agencies. As such, some of these groups became valuable forums where stakeholders could interact with decision makers.

Discussion

The four factors listed above are those that have commonly appeared in my research and the literature. These critical components are described in simple and succinct terms, but the convening phase frequently involves fits and starts, dead-ends, regroupings, and iterations. The convening process also raises several issues that require further discussion. Most prominent among these concerns are the relationships between stakeholders and the public, the constraints on convening collaborative efforts, and the factors that stakeholders may use to assess whether they should be involved.

Stakeholder versus Public Involvement

One of the common criticisms of stakeholder-based efforts is that they can mirror existing power structures in society and may exclude potential stakeholders who are not part of this structure. For example, an analysis of collaborative forums in Australia by Marcus Lane (2003) demonstrated that Indigenous people were usually left out of important decision-making processes. Some observers suggest that stakeholder selection should hinge on identifying those with the potential power to block or veto a decision (Innes et al. 1994). While these stakeholders are crucial, it is also necessary to consider those who are affected by a decision—whether they have veto power or not.

The risk of any stakeholder-led process is that the participants don't represent the range of perspectives in the community. Choosing participants with extensive networks and linkages is more likely to exclude minorities isolated by community prejudice. Furthermore, time commitments and involvement expectations will create barriers for certain people, including single parents, shift workers, the working poor, individuals with young children, and the less well educated. It is not uncommon to look around the table of a stakeholder group and see it dominated by older, higher-income, white males in amounts disproportionate to the local population.

For these reasons, some collaboratives work to build a broader constituency among the public. This group of people may attend only a few events, just provide input or feedback, or only read the group's newsletter. The broader public, however, can be a sounding board for the stakeholder group, a critical source of information, and a pool of future potential stakeholder participants. The role of the broader public during deliberation is discussed further in chapter 4.

Constraints on Convening

Just as certain conditions may support the development of a collaborative approach, certain preconditions may limit its potential. Three of the most common constraints cited by participants were reluctance due to time and transaction costs, restrictions related to policy or legislation, and limitations related to agency turnover.

When I asked participants in the United States and Australia about the factors influencing their reluctance to participate, the most oft-cited reasons were efficiency and time. Similarly, Donna Wood and Barbara Gray (1991) found that organizational barriers to participation in collaborative efforts included efficiency and access to resources. It can take a collaborative group months or even years to develop an agreement or plan. Agencies and elected officials generally prefer faster processes in which they make a decision with narrower involvement and then move forward. This decide-announce-defend approach is efficient, but it can also produce poor decisions, limited support, and more important for agencies and elected officials, lead to public backlash. The result may be court battles, adverse public reactions, or even protests that can produce significant delays.

In Eugene, Oregon, there has been a twenty-five-year-long battle over the construction of the West Eugene Parkway to ease congestion. It has been approved and rejected by various city council votes, and narrowly approved twice in public referenda. In 2004, Mayor Kitty Piercy was elected on a no-parkway platform, and the road has been the litmus test for many voters in council elections. In 2006, Piercy proposed a collaborative process for addressing the parkway issue, and hired outside consultants to interview a cross section of potential stakeholders and determine whether there was the potential for common ground. The consultants recommended exploring a collaborative process. According to reporter Edward Russo (2006, B3), Oregon Department of Transportation director Matthew Garrett

urged leaders not to embark on the uncertainty of the collaborative effort. . . . He also said he's concerned that the search for an alternative would last longer than Eugene's proposed 18 months. "I'll cut to the point," Garrett said. "I just think it's time to call the question, make a decision and move on."

In an opinion piece I wrote for the same Eugene newspaper, I commented that the previous processes had certainly been more efficient—for twenty-five years they had been producing answers. Unfortunately, these answers did not move the city or state any closer to a solution for traffic and land use in west Eugene.

A second common constraint on collaboration is the limitation or narrow focus of legislation and policies. In fact, this was the other unspoken constraint in the West Eugene Parkway debate. The Oregon Department of Transportation had to decide whether to allocate funding for a new parkway, not whether to solve a transportation and land use problem. This framed the issue from the outset as a parkway versus no-parkway debate rather than a broader problem-solving process. This kind of narrow, silo approach to funding and management is a typical constraint when bureaucracies are asked to engage in a collaborative effort.

In another example, prior to the passage of the U.S. Electric Consumers Protection Act, legislation prevented managers on the Upper Wisconsin River from addressing environmental and recreation issues during dam relicensing. The new act required regulators to consider a much wider array of issues than just hydropower. This allowed considerably more flexibility in the deliberation process, opening new options and concerns.

In Australia, state agency staff members involved in a catchment collaborative met resistance when they incorporated environmental restoration provisions and funding into a proposed sugarcane irrigation project. The administering federal agency required them to delete those components, because they did not meet the policy objectives of improving sugarcane productivity. Thus, one set of federal funds promoted an integrated approach even as another explicitly prohibited it.[16]

A final common constraint is the turnover of people within organizations that are potential partners. This is particularly true for government agencies, which may change managerial and administrative staff on a regular basis. For instance, for many years the U.S. Forest Service policies have expected managerial and administrative staff members to move locations in order to be promoted (Doppelt, Shinn, and DeWitt 2002). The philosophy is to build consistent approaches across the organization while also making staff members more loyal to the organization and its mission. But each time a person working for an organization changes, this breaks the networks and connections that may help a collaborative.

Evaluation by Nongovernmental Stakeholders

A final convening issue for nongovernmental stakeholders is the factors they use in assessing whether to participate. Some of their reasoning may relate to organizational factors, such as limited resources or a collaborative effort that is not central to short-term needs. Another set of factors affecting participation, though, relates to the context, structure, or process established for the collaborative.

In an effort to provide more guidance for environmental groups considering potential roles in collaborative processes, Dukes and Firehock (2001) identify different characteristics to consider about a collaborative process (see figure 3.1). They argue that this creates a continuum of caution, where collaboration at one end requires greater caution and collaboration at the other end allows for more freedom. Although this continuum is targeted at environmental collaboratives, many issues are relevant to a range of collaboratives and potential stakeholders. This continuum

More Freedom and Flexibility	**Greater Caution, Consultation, and Process Discipline**
Limited scope ⟵————⟶	Large scope
Limited constituency represented	Larger constituency represented
Private lands and resources ⟵————⟶	Public lands and resources
Briefer impact	Long-term impact
Direct action/Implementation ⟵————⟶	Policy/Regulatory
Unique to a particular setting	Precedent for other settings
Less authority ⟵————⟶	Greater authority
Voluntary formation ⟵————⟶	Mandated
Power balance	Power disparities
Lesser significance ⟵————⟶	Fundamental values at stake
Minor conflict	Extensive conflict
Dialogue and information exchange ⟵————⟶	Bargaining and agreement-seeking

Figure 3.1
Continuum of caution in a collaboration process. *Source*: Based on Dukes and Firehock 2001.

is helpful to review, because it examines the collaborative from the perspective of a potential participant rather than the collaborative. The factors that may make stakeholders unwilling to become involved in collaboration efforts can be divided into concerns about substance, process, and participants.

Substance
First, potential stakeholders could be concerned about the substance of the deliberation. Dukes and Firehock's framework (2001) includes a number of substantive issues that could limit participation, such as policy implications and potential value conflicts. Stakeholder groups assessing a collaboration effort may recognize from the outset that there are fundamental value differences that cannot be negotiated. For example, the Lower Wisconsin River case revealed a dilemma in stakeholder nonparticipation. A property rights group chose to drop out of the process because it was steadfastly opposed to any government land use regulation and did not want to participate in a process that was considering this option. Thus, situations involving fundamental value differences at the core of the process may restrict participation.

Although the conveners of a collaborative effort cannot change the substance of the problem, they can affect how a problem is framed. A collaborative process about a parkway proposal leaves little room for options. The negotiation starts with a highway option at one end and no highway at the other end. In between are different versions of the highway. If the process is framed as a deliberation about transportation, congestion, and land use, however, there is ample room to consider a host of alternatives that may include a highway or other options that could address the problems without a highway. One of the more famous Oregon examples of this comes from the 1970s, when transportation planners presented Portland residents with two route options for a circumferential highway. A group of concerned interests (including residents along both routes) formed a group that rejected the highway option in favor of increased investment in Portland's MAX light-rail system.

Process

A second category of concern relates to the perceived fairness of the consensus process. Several of these issues are noted in figure 3.1, including power disparities and the type of bargaining or dialogue. The elements of an effective process are described later in this book, but it is important to note here that these perceptions of process fairness may prevent a collaborative effort from ever getting started.

Participants

For stakeholders, the third concern in deciding whether to participate in a collaborative effort relates to the other participants. A history of conflict may create a climate of distrust. Unilateral decision making by powerful interests or government entities may create a sense that these participants are not willing to share their decision-making powers.

One of the critical dynamics to recognize about stakeholder willingness to participate is that it can change at any time. Stakeholders are not always able to evaluate their participation in a collaborative process from the outset. The scope of deliberations and even the definition of the problem may change during the deliberation process, and stakeholders may find themselves uncomfortable with the direction or their role in the process. The collaboration and environmental mediation literature also raises some concerns about the ability of inexperienced volunteers from community organizations and nonprofit groups to fairly participate in a stakeholder forum that also includes paid professionals from agencies and private companies (McCloskey 2001; Amy 1987).

It is also crucial to point out that many of the issues cited by Dukes and Firehock in their continuum of caution are parallel to differences across the action-organizational-policy collaborative spectrum. These parallels stem from the difficulties of smaller and more localized interest groups participating in collaboratives that are addressing issues at a broader scale, those that affect a wider range of people, or that have more far-reaching administrative, legal, or policy implications.

The implication for convening collaboratives is twofold. First, some potential stakeholders may be unable or unwilling to participate at the organizational and policy ends of the spectrum. In simple terms, the stakeholders may not believe they can adequately participate in a collaborative at the level at which it is working.

Second, in some regions it may be difficult to convene groups that represent the full range of interests. This is particularly relevant for organizational collaboratives in regions that don't have organized interest groups, because the collaborative conveners are asking individuals to personally represent a constituency for which there is no means for communication other than personal networks. This issue is discussed more in the chapter 4, but it is relevant for the convening process because this may be a barrier to launching a collaborative.

Conclusions

This entire chapter has been about convening—or getting people to the table. These people haven't even started deliberating yet! Some groups may fly through this phase with few difficulties or complications. As illustrated by several examples in this chapter, though, the ways in which the group is convened can have a lasting impact on its ability to reach consensus and produce results from its agreements.

This chapter also highlights many gaps in our knowledge about convening collaborative efforts in relation to the social, economic, and ecological contexts in which they take place. The issue of problem solving and management responses has been addressed in other contexts, but there is a need for additional research into the contextual factors that support and constrain the convening of collaborative efforts. As a watershed coordinator once put to me, "Why do watershed councils form in some places but not in others?"[17]

My research and the literature have nonetheless identified some common themes about what aspects of convening lead to results. The positive and negative effects of the convening process also spill over into the next phase—deliberation.

4

Stakeholder Deliberation and Public Participation

On a warm, sunny morning in April 2006, the Southern Willamette Groundwater Management Advisory Committee—affectionately known as the "gwa-ma"—was hurriedly trying to wrap up its business. The committee included a cross section of elected officials, community members, businesspeople, and other stakeholders who were called together to develop a plan for addressing nitrate contamination in groundwater. It was 10:05 a.m., five minutes past the meeting's appointed ending time, and the facilitator was attempting to push through a final agenda item about measuring progress and approaches to implementation. The committee members expressed many different views on the implementation issues, including questions about lead agency roles that led to additional questions about agency funding. Several members were packing up to head to other meetings, while others were discussing these concerns. At this point, the facilitator pulled back and recommended delaying the conversation until the next meeting to give the group more time and information to make their decisions.[1]

It was an obvious move for an experienced facilitator, but this is not always how group processes work. Sometimes an impatient chair will try to push things forward or frustrated staff members will craft something on their own without stakeholder buy in. The result could be a lack of understanding, agreement, or commitment among stakeholders to the products of consensus building.

The consensus-building process involves a series of steps that start with convening, and then moves through deliberation to a consensual agreement or plan. Many participants in collaboration point out that it is not just important *whether* stakeholders reach agreement on a plan or policy but instead *how* they do so. Consensus-based processes are not the same as those used by city councils or legislatures, because group decisions rarely carry the force of law or administrative power. The participating stakeholders are independent, so if they are not satisfied with the process, they may reduce their commitment or withdraw. This means that a simple majority may not be a successful result.

Stakeholders often need a stronger level of agreement, which may not mean complete satisfaction with the result but rather a willingness to "go along with it." These decisions all take place under the umbrella of a highly deliberative process that allows people to learn about the issues, hear different perspectives, explore alternatives, identify goals, and deliberate about actions. In addition to stakeholder input, public participation can also be a key part of collaboration, because stakeholders represent only a small cross section of views, and the stakeholder process of information exchange and learning may not be mirrored in the broader community. Thus, the agreements they reach may not be understood or supported by their neighbors or colleagues.

In summary, a good collaborative process can lead to better plans or products, and also help garner support. This means that the participants will be more likely to act as champions and advocates in other forums as well as support implementation efforts. It also means that the broader public will have opportunities to express their concerns, learn about the issues, and have input into the decisions.

Theory Related to Deliberation and Participation

A collaborative approach to planning and management involves a shared process of decision making in which a range of participants is engaged in an extended, face-to-face process of communication and deliberation (Gray 1989; Innes 1996, 1999; Innes and Booher 1999a). For over fifty years, researchers in the fields of social psychology, communication, and sociology have been conducting studies related to groups. Many social psychologists have explored these decision-making issues through extensive experimental research on groups in laboratory settings (see, for example, Gigone and Hastie 1993, 1997; Stasser, Taylor, and Hanna 1989; Stasser, Vaughan, and Stewart 2000).

Using field research, scholars from a range of disciplines have also looked at decision making in groups. Because of the limited number of settings available to examine these phenomena, much of this research is based on case study data (see, for example, Wondolleck 1985; Depoe 2004; Derry, DuRussel, and O'Donnell 1998; Hamilton 2004; Wondolleck and Yaffee 2000; Talbot 1983; Innes 1994; Yaffee et al. 1996; Weber 2003; Susskind and Cruikshank 1987; Susskind, McKearnon, and Carpenter 1999; Gray 1989). Some researchers have scrutinized more substantial data sets by studying cases from mediation of environmental and legal disputes, but these explorations have generally focused on outcomes rather than the process (see, for example, Bingham 1986; Buckle and Thomas-Buckle 1986; Sipe 1998).

Across this range of literature, there are at least four broad categories of findings relevant to effective deliberation and participation: group communication, shared interpretations, managing conflict, and public involvement.

Group Communication

Research from a range of disciplines has found that information sharing is critical for effective collaborative decision making, but there are different findings about the ability of groups to share knowledge effectively (Susskind and Cruikshank 1987; Wondolleck 1985; Bingham 1986; Susskind and Weinstein 1980; Stasser, Stewart, and Wittenbaum 1995; Stasser and Titus 1985; Gigone and Hastie 1993, 1997). Experimental research has raised questions about the ability of groups to achieve common understanding through group process, because discussion is often dominated by the information that members hold in common beforehand. Participants determine that certain pieces of information are more important when shared by the group, while information that they hold by themselves they judge to be less significant (Gigone and Hastie 1993). Daniel Gigone and Reid Hastie (1993) conclude that groups tend to use an implicit or explicit averaging combination rule to join their members' judgments, which may make group judgments no more accurate than the average of individual judgments.

The limitation with these experimental data is that they do not take into account the changes that occur within groups that repeatedly interact over time. Empirical field research has found that stakeholder groups are often able to effectively pool information even in the face of highly technical topics. For example, Depoe (2004) and Jennifer Duffield Hamilton (2004) analyzed two citizen advisory committees involved in decisions about nuclear weapons plants, and concluded that the variation in effectiveness between the two groups could be attributed in part to differences in the way that the groups received information and technical advice. Similarly, an evaluation of twelve case studies by Innes and her colleagues (1994, 43) found that through long-term deliberation, stakeholders developed a shared base of knowledge or "intellectual capital." This is supported by survey and case study research, but the cases also highlight that developing a shared base of knowledge takes considerable time, creating barriers to collaboration in terms of resources, timelines, and stakeholder participation. This may result in the systematic exclusion of lower-income and less well-educated stakeholders, or stakeholders whose time is at a premium (Amy 1987; Helling 1998; Margerum 1999d, 2002a; Wondolleck and Yaffee 2000; Selin, Schuett, and Carr 2000; Weber 2003).

Shared Interpretations

Even when participants are able to effectively pool information, collaboration will be ineffective unless participants can also share their interpretations of the information. Each participant in a collaborative process interprets and translates information in different ways, depending on their expertise, experiences, and concerns (Innes 1998). When groups are able to share the interpretations and meaning that they draw from shared data, they can supplement scientific data with observation and insights—and more important, they can offer insights that will inform policy choices (Ehrmann and Stinson 1999; Innes 1998; Innes and Booher 1999a; Margerum 1995a). Innes (1998, 57) notes that in collaborative processes involving both experts and laypeople, "the experts sometimes changed their views, not about the findings, but about their implications."

Shared interpretations develop when participants are able to freely communicate in effective and creative ways (Innes and Booher 1999a). This requires an open dialogue that allows the messages of both the sender and receiver to be interpreted in the same way, which results in greater depth of processing (Johnson 2000; Harrington and Miller 1993). Field research on collaborative groups has shown that an effective consensus-building process is influential on the ability of groups to share knowledge and interpretations. Nevertheless, the ability of stakeholders to individually comprehend information and attach meaning to it also depends on how information is presented (Forester 1999; Innes 1998; Selin, Schuett, and Carr 2000; Wondolleck and Yaffee 2000).

Managing Conflict

Another theme common across a range of disciplines is the need for collaborative approaches to manage conflict (McKearnon and Fairman 1999; Innes and Booher 1999b; Priem, Harrison, and Muir 1995). Clear communication prevents misunderstanding and promotes exploration, but it can also reveal differences, which means that stakeholder groups need to be able to manage conflict effectively. The concept of managing conflict is important because it encompasses a range of potential actions (Buntz and Radin 1983; Leach and Pelkey 2001). Groups may resolve the conflict within the group, defer it to a later time, refer it to another forum or group, or work around it by addressing other issues. When the conflict is central to a group's efforts and mission, the literature highlights a wide range of strategies and techniques that can help produce consensus, including using a third-party facilitator or mediator. A key concept relates to the idea of integrative bargaining, in which participants seek outcomes that satisfy the entire group's needs. This notion of "win-win" outcomes is often contrasted with typical "win-lose" or distributive bargaining, where participants seek to maximize their own outcomes. Integrative bargaining encourages participants to seek solutions that expand rather than divide the pie (Carpenter and Kennedy 1988; Fisher and Ury 1981; Susskind and Cruikshank 1987). These concepts have been popularized in books like *Getting to Yes* by Roger Fisher and William Ury (1981), who stress several critical principles for resolving conflict: separate the people from the problem, focus on interests rather than positions, invent options for mutual gain, agree on objective criteria for assessing outcomes, and make sure everyone understands what has been agreed to.

Public Involvement in Collaboration

Collaboration involves a broad set of stakeholders that includes individuals from agencies, local governments, interest groups, affected parties, and representatives of certain sectors of society. It is therefore a form of public involvement. Sherry Arnstein (1969) refers to these types of approaches as partnerships in which power is distributed through negotiations and decision making is shared with the public through stakeholder groups that make collective decisions. James J. Glass (1979, 182) calls this "representative input" because it is an effort to identify the entire community's views on particular issues "in order to create the possibility that subsequent plans will reflect community desires."

Like any representative form of input, however, some individual perspectives are not represented. Jean Pasquero (1991) notes that one shortcoming of a collaboration is that it underplays the significance of societal-level factors. Critics also contend that it delegates too much power to stakeholders who have a direct interest in the issues—at the expense of the broader public. In particular, authors such as Michael McCloskey (2001) and Kenney (2000) argue that natural-resource-based stakeholder processes tend to favor those local residents who are the most closely tied to resource extraction industries. Because these processes are discussions about the management of public lands with habitat and recreation values, other people with an interest in the management of these lands have limited access to crucial decisions. These people may include environmentalists concerned about habitat, or urban recreationists concerned about recreation trails.

In their review of the roles of various forms of interest representation in resource management, L. Graham Smith, Carla Nell, and Mark Prystupa (1997, 145) contend that each of the current models of stakeholder, public, and interest group involvement has limitations, and advocate for convergence between the various approaches. They suggest that strategies need to be based on empowerment, accountability, and a balance between equity and efficiency. "These elements may be achieved through an interplay of interest representation forms that build upon EDR [environmental dispute resolution] strategies, modified lobbying approaches, and/or advanced public involvement methods" (ibid.).

Assessing Deliberation and Participation

The literature on stakeholder deliberation and public involvement provides some important principles for collaboratives. Based on the literature and my research, I have identified four actors for assessing the effectiveness of consensus building: facilitated process, open communication, conflict management, and public involvement. Each of these variables may be evaluated through self-assessment interviews or surveys, but in table 4.1 I have also identified some additional approaches.

Table 4.1
Assessing deliberation and participation

Factors	Measures of factors	Related references
Facilitated process: Process of consensus building is facilitated to maximize participation	• Presence of a facilitator or person with facilitation skills • Full participation by stakeholders • Clear agreements on scope and role • Organizational policies that support collaborative processes • Adequate resources to support a facilitated process	Schwarz 2002; Kaner 1996; Justice, Jamieson, and NetLibrary Inc. 1999
Open communication: There is a rich and effective exchange of communication	• Information-sharing procedures • Two-way flow of information • Communication with participating organizations	Justice, Jamieson, and NetLibrary Inc. 1999; Schulz, Israel, and Lantz 2003; Beierle and Konisky 2000
Conflict management: Conflicts are managed to support progress on results	• There are clear rules in place for decision making • Conflicts arising in the group are managed	McKearnon and Fairman 1999; Lord 1979
Public involvement: Broader public is involved	• The approach to public input is tailored to the collaborative • Public input techniques are appropriate for the collaborative	Smith, Nell, and Prystupa 1997

Facilitated Process

Because the consensus-building process brings together a wide range of people to address complex, often-controversial issues, facilitation is an important factor in achieving results. A facilitated process does not necessarily require a trained facilitator but it does need to be guided by someone who can ensure effective deliberation.

For example, a staff person from the Wisconsin DNR who led a planning effort for the Lake Winnebago system was a fisheries biologist. He did not feel well equipped to manage a complex process that was going to involve local elected officials, recreational users, lakeshore homeowners, and other DNR technical staff, so he took several training classes to prepare. Many of the participants complimented him and the effectiveness of the consensus-building process.

In contrast, some Australian catchment groups that I studied were experiencing difficulties with the way their processes were being facilitated. About 8 percent of the respondents did not feel that their coordinator had the necessary skills (n = 191), and a survey of catchment coordinators identified group process skills as the second-highest type of training needs.[2]

Before discussing the characteristics of effective facilitation, it is useful to look at the roles of chairs, staff members, and facilitators in collaboratives. A committee chair or board president is usually the administrative and symbolic head of the group. This person often presides over meetings, and is involved in setting the agenda and planning for those meetings. Frequently, this person is a stakeholder, which can complicate their participation in discussions because they are attempting to manage the process while also engaging in it. For some small collaboratives at the action end of the spectrum, the chair may also play the role of facilitator and coordinator, which can further complicate their role.

Some collaboratives have staff members to support their work from the early stages of formation. These individuals serve various roles according to how the group operates, but they often provide logistical support, prepare information for the group, and liaise with stakeholders, organizations, and the community. It is also not unusual for collaboratives to ask their staff members to undertake substantive tasks (such as education or outreach) even before they have reached consensus on their full set of priorities.

Some collaboratives have facilitators to guide them through the consensus-building process. In particular, collaboratives operating at the organizational and policy end of the spectrum generally have professional facilitators or trained staff. These collaboratives frequently have more resources, but the greater complexity and higher profile of the issues they face increase the need for a professional facilitator. In the San Francisco Estuary Project, the U.S. Environmental Protection Agency brought in a trained facilitator to help guide the large stakeholder group through a complicated process. A stakeholder representing development interests noted that the process had "lots of problems—in fact it was terrible; but then the EPA got a facilitator, and it really began operating."[3]

In summary, a facilitated process is important for reaching an agreement that ensures buy in, whether there is a formal facilitator or not. A facilitated process means that some combination of a chair, staff person, and facilitator ensures that the *process* is facilitated.

Assessing a Facilitated Process

As with all the factors in this book, one way of assessing a facilitated process is to query participants. Table 4.2 lists a range of questions that can be posed to participants involved in a consensus-building process. This approach is limited, however, because it depends on participant evaluation. Participants may not have similar

Table 4.2
Facilitated process measures

Category	Sample measures	Related references
Communication	• Open and clear lines of communication • Deliberation between participants focuses on consensus • How much do people in the group feel comfortable expressing their point of view? • How much do you feel comfortable about expressing your opinion at group meetings? • How much is your opinion listened to? • How much are you willing to listen to others' points of view?	Selin, Schuett, and Carr 2000; Beierle and Konisky 2000; Schulz, Israel, and Lantz 2003
Debate and discussion	• Use dispute resolution to try to handle impasses • Clear ground rules about how the group operates • Process facilitated by a neutral third party • How satisfied are you with the way the group deals with problems that come up? • Do you feel pressured to go along with decisions even though you might not agree?	McKearnon and Fairman 1999; Frame, Gunton, and Day 2004; Selin, Schuett, and Carr 2000; Schulz, Israel, and Lantz 2003
Exploration	• Create joint gains • Explore interests and the positions of others • Brainstorm options • Create packages to try to reach agreement • The process produced creative ideas	McKearnon and Fairman 1999; Frame, Gunton, and Day 2004

Table 4.2
(continued)

Category	Sample measures	Related references
Decision making	• Groups seek consensus but don't require it for closure • Deliberation between participants focuses on consensus • Deliberation between participants is fair • Mutually agreed on decision-making process • How committed do you feel to decisions that are made by the group? • How satisfied are you with the way the decision-making process is working?	McKearnon and Fairman 1999; Beierle and Konisky 2000; Dedekorkut 2000; Schulz, Israel, and Lantz 2003

senses of high- and low-quality practices; they may not share their true feelings about a group out of concern about how the responses will be used; and those who respond may be people who are more motivated to respond because they are positive or negative about the process. This kind of outcome self-evaluation also may not help a group during its early stages to improve its practices.

The following sections highlight other criteria for assessing a facilitated process, including assessment of the person acting in the facilitation role, the extent to which the group follows facilitation procedures, and whether the group has adequate resources relative to its facilitation needs.

Effective Facilitator
An effective facilitator is a person (or people) with the time and skills to support the consensus-building process in a way that allows participants to work through a process smoothly, efficiently, and deliberatively. As noted above, the facilitator may be a volunteer, government employee, or professional facilitator. For groups with more resources, even having a facilitator does not ensure that the process will be well facilitated. I often describe the difference between bad and good facilitation as that between bad and good wait service in a restaurant. In chain restaurants, overtrained staff will interrupt a group every ten minutes, asking, "Is everything OK?" They hope that the more they interrupt, the more you will tip, and the faster they can get the next group into your table. In contrast, good waitstaff will politely interrupt when it's important, refill glasses without asking, and be watching carefully

for a customer who needs something. Like good service, it's my view that good facilitation should be unobtrusive, and sometimes it's most effective when you hardly notice the role of facilitator.

In both the United States and Australia, I found that those facilitating the process were usually coordinators and chairs, and their approach had fundamental influences on how well the group operated. Two comments from Australian survey respondents illustrate these subtle and not-so-subtle influences of these leaders:

[Our committee is inhibited by:] The chairman is also a real estate agent who has allowed his personal bias to influence his actions, like speaking on behalf of the committee without prior consultation.[4]

[Our committee is inhibited by:] The chairman does not support community consultation; protects interests of his industry (cane and dairy); pushes funding for farmers only; lack of knowledge of environmental impacts; strong dislike for environmentalists and Landcare groups; instigator of disharmony and disruption of discussion.[5]

One of the key characteristics of an effective facilitator is that they must be someone who can operate in a way that participants feel is unbiased. In his book on facilitation, Roger Schwarz (2000) stresses that facilitators are never "neutral," because pretending they don't have their own opinions is unrealistic. Instead, he argues that facilitators should be *substantively neutral*, which means that they facilitate the discussion without sharing their opinions so that group members cannot tell what the facilitator thinks about the group's issues. This can be difficult when the facilitator is also a participant, convener, or chair, because the person may need to give up some of their substantive role.

The case studies revealed several important qualities of a well-facilitated process regardless of the facilitator's position within the collaborative. When a facilitator was effective, participants often recognized the person's significance, and praised their skills and approach. When asked about the staff person facilitating a group in Wisconsin, one person commented: "The role was key; I don't know how he did it. Someone without the team interrelation skills he had would have failed."[6]

Table 4.3 lists these qualities, but you will notice that the list focuses more on the qualities of the process than those of the facilitator. Even books that concentrate entirely on the facilitator discuss more about the characteristics of the process than those of the person doing the facilitation. This is because different people can achieve the same results in different ways. To come back to my restaurant service analogy, high-quality service can be delivered in a casual or formal manner. Facilitators, in other words, have their own personal styles and approaches. It is important to consider the style and approach that is most appropriate for a stakeholder group, but there is no general style that is always effective.

Table 4.3
Commonly cited facilitator roles

Listening	Able to paraphrase, observe, clarify, and elaborate
Interpreting	Able to observe and assess verbal and nonverbal behavior
Guiding	Able to design structured activities and processes
Balancing	Able to confront others, entice participation, and create opportunities for participation
Collaboration	Able to provide tools and approaches to managing and resolving differences
Managing	Able to manage meetings, processes, and logistics

Sources: Based on Schwarz 2002; Kaner 1996; Justice, Jamieson, and NetLibrary Inc. 1999.

Support of Facilitation Principles

Besides examining the facilitator and their role, another way to assess a facilitated process is to look at the operating principles of a group during its consensus-building process. Sam Kaner (1996) offers four core values of participatory decision making that are useful in thinking about what a facilitated process should *feel* like, including full participation, mutual understanding, inclusive solutions, and shared responsibilities. The extent to which a group achieves these principles may be reflected in the operating principles or ground rules that it develops, but for each of the four there may be other indicators.

Facilitated processes require full participation, which means being at meetings and forums as well as being engaged in them. Yogi Berra has been quoted as saying, "Eighty percent of winning is showing up." In facilitated processes involving difficult issues, 90 percent of the people should to be engaged 90 percent of the time. In several cases I examined, an analysis of the meeting minutes revealed attendance patterns that often reflect a lack of participation by one or several stakeholders. It can be even more frustrating when participants attend meetings but are not engaged. One stakeholder group I observed began keeping track of participant contributions to try to get participants more engaged, with one member providing a "tally" of people who did not speak at each meeting.

Facilitated processes also require mutual understanding and inclusive solutions. These issues will be addressed in the communication section below, but it is important for participants to feel that they understand the issues and problems, and that they have bought into the solutions developed by the group. Indicators of the acceptability of solutions include the outcomes of recorded votes on recommendations, minority reports or opinions, or the number of times issues are brought up for reconsideration.

Another way of assessing support of facilitation principles is to examine whether there is agreement on the scope, role, and mission of the collaborative. This may appear in memorandums of understanding, agreements, and other documents that specify the roles, expectations, and scope of an organization's involvement in a collaborative. These provide crucial indications from participating organizations that they support this scope, even if the documents are more symbolic than legally binding.

In a survey of local government advisory committees in Oregon, I found that one of the key weaknesses of these groups was an unclear mission or role in relation to the city and city council. A collaborative group needs to clarify with its participants whether they are providing advice or committing to group decisions, for instance. This is particularly relevant for government agencies that may not be able to delegate power to a collaborative forum.

Finally, assessing organizational support of facilitated processes could involve a review of the internal policies and reward structures for staff and programs. Internal policies can include job descriptions, work plans, and job performance criteria that may reward or discourage staff participation in a collaborative. In several cases I examined, government participants noted that their participation is limited by the time and importance that their organization places on the collaborative effort.

Supporting Staff and Resources

The facilitator is not the only support person needed during the consensus-building process. Often there is a need for people to take minutes, organize meetings, assemble data, prepare documents, meet with stakeholders and other organizations between meetings, and help prepare the group's outputs, agreements, and reports. When I visited with catchment committees created in New South Wales in 1995, there were marked differences in the progress that they had made. Some groups had racked up a list of accomplishments, completed a strategy, and compiled data, while others were still in the consensus-building and planning phases. While the age of the council, history of the issues, and problem context all affected their progress, one common difference between the groups was whether they had a full-time coordinator. Several groups had spent more than three years working on a catchment plan because they had only a half-time coordinator. This placed more pressure on participants to prepare information, and led to greater frustration and burnout with the consensus-building process.

Different types of collaboratives also have different resource needs, particularly for the administration of the group. Some action collaboratives are coordinated solely by volunteers and have no paid staff. In the United States, many of the collaboratives that have emerged over the past ten years are nonprofit organizations

Table 4.4
Watershed council staffing

Watershed council	Staff (full-time equivalent)	Contractor (full-time equivalent)	Total (full-time equivalent)
Bear Creek	0.0	0.5	0.5
Calapooia	0.0	1.0	1.0
Coast Fork Willamette	0.0	0.3	0.3
Elk Creek	0.0	0.5	0.5
Luckiamute	0.3	0.0	0.3
Johnson Creek	3.0	0.0	3.0
Long Tom	1.0	2.0	3.0
Yamhill Basin	1.3	0.0	1.3

Source: Data collected by Bodane in 2006.

that obtain grant funding to support one or two staff members. For organizational collaboratives, the focus on organizational activities makes it difficult to use an independent or volunteer coordinator. Many of these efforts instead are funded directly by one agency or through a multiagency arrangement. Many of the policy collaboratives require a coordinating organization to support the array of activities necessary at such a large and complex setting. These organizations are responsible for supporting the collaborative effort and usually have substantial paid staff through government funding.

Different types of collaboratives, in short, will require different levels of resources. Yet comparing similar types of collaboratives along with their levels of resources and staffing provides an indication of their support. For example, in our survey of forty-one watershed council coordinators in Oregon, staffing levels ranged from 9.0 to 0.3 full-time equivalent positions (Parker et al. 2010). Table 4.4 summarizes the staffing capacities of several councils with a similar action-level focus.

Effective Communication

A second factor in building consensus is that participants must communicate effectively. This sounds like an obvious statement, but when people come to the table with a history of distrust, misinformation, antagonism, and frustration, it can be difficult to communicate effectively. Good communication doesn't always come naturally; we are much better at shouting, not listening, and simply voting. One way of assessing communication is to ask participants to evaluate their activities.

When I surveyed Australian stakeholders about communication, over 84 percent of the respondents said their groups were engaged in constructive communication

Table 4.5
Self-assessment group communication measures

- People on the committee communicate openly
- I have the opportunity to contribute to committee discussions
- I am comfortable expressing my ideas and views
- People on the committee listen to each other
- People are respectful of each other at the meetings
- When people on the committee raise an issue, we discuss it
- We are able to discuss difficult issues effectively

Sources: Based on Beierle and Konisky 2000; Frame, Gunton, and Day 2004; McKearnon and Fairman 1999; Schulz, Israel, and Lantz 2003; Selin, Schuett, and Carr 2000.

(n = 195). Self-reported satisfaction did not always equate to effective communication, however, as I found out from some of my field observations. I attended a two-day retreat of an Australian catchment committee, whose members had provided a positive assessment of their communication in a mail survey. The communication I observed in practice revealed problems and confusion about roles. For example, both the coordinator and committee chair felt unsure of their roles in managing the group, and there was considerable debate about what kind of information government participants should (or could) share. Several members did not participate in discussions at all, even when asked by a facilitator to share their perspectives. An important outcome of the discussion was that the committee clarified what things they wanted to handle, what role they wanted the chair to play, what boundaries they wanted to place around the coordinator's activities, and the expectations among themselves for communication. This was not a brand-new group; it had already been operating for two nearly years.

Assessing Communication

As with a facilitated process, one of the ways in which communication can be assessed is through self-evaluations and self-assessments by the group. In several studies, I have used this kind of approach to examine communication practices (see table 4.5). The advantage of self-assessments is that the assessor gets feedback on the overall communication experience of a group from the participants' perspective. These kinds of assessments can also allow information collection across a large number of groups in a relatively short time.

This kind of assessment has the same disadvantages as other self-assessments, though, including different experiences and expectations about what is "effective," a bias due to the higher motivation of those who are dissatisfied to respond, a bias based on fear of how the results will be used, and responses based on what respondents think the evaluator wants to hear. This is not to suggest that self-

Table 4.6
Personal role on stakeholder committee

Two-way roles (37 percent)

• "Provide knowledge about [my agency's] operation in the catchment, receiving feedback and altering—when appropriate—[my agency's] direction to fit the committee's direction."
• "To represent department policy and listen to the community."
• "To communicate the views of my department, to advise in my area of expertise, and to inform my department on the views and expectations of the committee."
• "To represent and report back to the council."
• "Liaison and coordinating [my council's] activities with the committee."

One-way roles (63 percent)

• "To encourage members to believe that the government is serious about integrated catchment management."
• "To provide technical advice."
• "To represent [my department's] perspective on catchment management issues."
• "To provide expert advice in relation to the management of forested land within the catchment."
• "To ensure that local government perspectives are considered in the resource management process."

Notes: Based on a survey of 550 catchment committee participants with 197 responses (36 percent). Responses above include all respondents affiliated with an organization (n = 67).

assessments are not useful but rather that it is important to consider other assessment approaches.

One way of assessing communication is to determine whether a consensus process involves a two-way flow of information. This means that participants must share and receive information, which can be assessed through group observation or questions about stakeholder roles. For example, when I surveyed participants on Australian collaboratives I included an open-ended question that asked stakeholders to describe their role on the committee. Content analysis and classification of these responses revealed that over two-thirds of government representatives (including agencies and local government) view their role as one-way (providing information and expertise to the committee) rather than interactive (supplying information to the committee *and* taking it back to their organization) (see table 4.6).[7]

Information-Sharing Procedures
Another way of assessing communication is to evaluate a group's ground rules or operating procedures. Table 4.7 summarizes some of the more common ground rules that groups use either formally or informally. In assessing information-sharing

Table 4.7
Examples of ground rules

- Everyone is encouraged to participate
- One person talks at a time
- Every idea and comment is valid
- Say what you mean and mean what you say
- Every effort will be made to reach consensus
- People need not agree
- Require mutual respect
- Keep an open mind
- Seek common ground
- Maintain a put-down-free, safe environment

Source: Justice, Jamieson, and NetLibrary Inc. 1999; Schwarz 2002.

procedures, it may help to examine whether group members have developed the ground rules together, and whether they review and assess their processes to ensure that they are following the ground rules (Justice, Jamieson, and NetLibrary Inc. 1999; Schwarz 2002).

Adopting a list of "packaged" ground rules may not translate into effective information sharing, because the group needs to understand and support them. With some groups it may be important to develop such rules from scratch so that they can state them in their own terms and develop more ownership. The members of the Lake Winnebago Comprehensive Plan team, for instance, spent their entire first two meetings discussing operating and communication procedures. The coordinator of the project explained the approach they took:

We used an "if I had my druthers" sheet in which each person individually filled out a sheet of who they wanted the team leader to be, how they thought we should operate, etc. Through nominal group [effort] we boiled it down to how we were going to operate and it was smooth sailing from there because everybody had agreed to: be honest, listen to other people, [and] understand there were differing viewpoints.[8]

Other participants found the early focus on these process issues tedious and were concerned that they were "wasting time," but by the end of the process they recognized it had been effective and efficient because of the early efforts they put into discussing their operation.

In addition to adopting written rules, it is critical for groups to periodically review and assess their information-sharing procedures. Facilitators will often ask participants to undertake a quick evaluation of a meeting after it is completed, and groups may also benefit from a "two-minute drill" in which they are asked to provide two minutes of feedback on what aspects of the meeting went well and two minutes on those aspects that could be improved. It may also help if groups undertake more thorough and formal evaluations, including feedback through an anonymous process that allows communication concerns to be discussed.

Communication with Organizations

Equally significant for effective consensus building is communication between individuals and the organizations they represent. Thomas Colosi (1983) refers to this as the two-table issue—meaning the relationship between the consensus-building effort and the decision-making processes within the represented organization. This can be an issue for interest groups, which may have to convene their own collaborative process to determine their position on a particular issue. Yet it can also be of concern for a government agency, which may have unclear or vague policies and rules. A participant in one of the collaborative efforts examined by Innes and her colleagues (1994, 17) portrayed their agency in this way:

An agency is a consensus group. Internally the managers do not agree, but we try to iron out these differences and present a common face. Agencies do have policies but these are very general and could be given in one seven-word sentence. Different staff interpret it differently. For example, Joe has a different view from Paul. One is "fish sensitive" and the other is "politics sensitive." Both tried to represent their organization the way they saw it.

Communication with organizations becomes more of an issue with organizational and policy collaboratives, which not only involve more organizations but also involve more issues that may require clarification and discussion within those organizations. In other words, if the issue is technical or relates to specific regulations, programs, or policies, a person working for the organization may be able to provide an immediate response based on established policies and technical expertise. If the issue involves broader interpretations of organizational priorities, program goals, administrative rules, or legislative intent, the process for clarifying this can take considerable time and effort.

One indicator of effective communication with an organization in a collaborative is whether the people representing the organization have clear guidance. For example, one-quarter of the Australian stakeholders I surveyed believed they had insufficient guidance from their organization (16 percent were not sure, and 59 percent believed they had sufficient guidance). The type of guidance needed varied by person, organization, and project, but many staff members found that their agency and the collaborative had different expectations about their communication.

Another indicator of effective communication with organizations is the presence of procedures or mechanisms for information exchange between stakeholders and the organizations they are representing. In small organizations this may be relatively informal, but within larger government organizations these communication procedures and channels can be critical. For example, the lead staff person working on the Lower Wisconsin River project held regular briefings with the head of the state natural resources agency and several division heads to ensure that he was representing the consensus of the agency. Some Australian catchment committees complained that their state agency representatives did not communicate regularly with their organizations, which created conflicts later in the process.

A third indicator of effective communication with organizations is when groups develop clear procedures and expectations for information sharing. In a study of regional transportation collaboratives we found that some groups were lacking input from metropolitan planning organizations, because elected officials were representing their own local governments rather than the metropolitan planning organization (on which they also served). A role or procedure for such representation had not been clearly specified (Brody and Margerum 2008).

Conflict Management

A third factor for effective deliberation is conflict management. In 1996, I was observing an Australian catchment committee meeting in southern Queensland. About twenty committee members sat in a square around tables, while I sat in the back of the room. It was difficult to silently observe, because the group was mired in conflict. It was difficult not because there was a conflict but instead because the conflict was being buried and avoided.

Several speakers stated points and positions, and each successive person spoke as if they were making an independent statement unrelated to what the others were saying. At no point during the process did anyone note where there was agreement or disagreement, or even acknowledge that there were differences of opinion. As a result, the speeches went on for quite awhile until the chair stepped in, saying: "Well, I think we need to move on here. We should take this issue up again at a future meeting." It was clear to me that they had little chance to resolve the conflict, because they hadn't even acknowledged that a conflict existed.

In every U.S. case that I examined, there were stakeholder conflicts capable of undermining the consensus process. In Australia, 18 percent of stakeholders surveyed believed that their committee did not handle conflicts effectively (n = 191). Their self-evaluation of their group's conflict management effectiveness, committee accomplishments, and functioning were all strongly correlated (see table 4.8). Many researchers of collaboratives consistently emphasize that consensus processes require constructive conflict management (Susskind and Ozawa 1984; Innes et al. 1994), but stakeholders that I interviewed and surveyed often remarked that it could be difficult to achieve in practice.

Why is consensus hard? One reason is because it is different from the typical government decision processes with which many participants are familiar. When a

Table 4.8
Correlations between accomplishments, conflict resolution, and functioning

Variables	Correlation	Significance	n
Committee accomplishments and conflict resolution	.473	< .0001	189
Committee accomplishments and effective functioning	.635	< .0001	189
Conflict resolution and effective functioning	.577	< .0001	189

city council votes and decides by a five-to-four majority, the decision carries the weight of city policy, and staff members have the authority to implement it. Elected officials may openly criticize the decision, but by and large they live with it, and raise their concerns during elections. City councils and legislatures make hundreds of these decisions each year through this kind of process, and periodically voters have the option to vote for the representatives that they want.

The stakeholders involved in a consensus process have not been elected to that position (although some may be elected officials). Most stakeholder groups also do not have direct authority. They may have some personnel and a budget, but they have few powers to enact and enforce decisions. They rely on grant funding, the participating stakeholders, and their organizations to help get decisions implemented. If a stakeholder group makes a decision by voting and arrives at a five-to-four outcome, this means that nearly half the participants don't support the issue and thus may help prevent its implementation.

As this section's heading states, consensus building requires a process to *manage* conflict. This means that sometimes a group must work to bring differences to the surface, so that participants can have constructive discussions about the issues. In some cases there may not be a conflict—just miscommunication. In other cases there are conflicts, and the group is able to resolve them effectively. It is also not unusual for groups to set aside or bypass conflicts, or refer them to other forums. Therefore, managing conflicts involves a range of practices and responses, but the management of differences and the ways in which they are resolved are important.

Assessing Conflict Management

One way of assessing the effectiveness of conflict management is to ask participants to evaluate the group's processes and approaches. Table 4.9 summarizes some of the measures that can be used to conduct this kind of assessment. This kind of approach provides a quick assessment of a group's effectiveness, and it can be applied across a range of groups to assess their approach relative to their accomplishments.

As noted in other sections of this chapter, there are also limitations with a self-assessment, including bias among those who are motivated to respond, a range of

Table 4.9
Conflict management measures

Category	Sample measures	Related references
Dispute resolution	• Use dispute resolution to try to handle impasses • How well do you feel that the group handled these conflicts? • Do you feel pressured to go along with decisions of the group even if you don't agree? • Do certain individuals have more influence over the decision-making process than others?	McKearnon and Fairman 1999; Schulz, Israel, and Lantz 2003
Consensus building	• Create joint gains • Explore interests and the positions of others • How well do you think the group has been able to work together to solve problems? • Groups seek consensus but don't require it for closure • Deliberation between participants focuses on consensus • Deliberation between participants is fair	McKearnon and Fairman 1999; Schulz, Israel, and Lantz 2003; Beierle and Konisky 2000

respondent experiences with conflict management processes, and respondent "editing" of feedback based on how they think the information will be used. Furthermore, this kind of assessment may not allow a group to review its approach in the midst of its deliberations. Two alternative approaches that can be used for assessing conflict management include the presence of clear rules for managing conflict and making decisions, and the history of conflict management by the group.

Rules in Place for Decision Making

Stakeholder groups involve people associated with a wide range of organizations that use many different decision processes. It is generally argued that consensus is the best decision-making rule for collaboration (Gray 1989; Innes et al. 1994; Pasquero 1991). Susan Hill MacKenzie (1993) found that consensus is important not only for reaching an acceptable decision but also for building long-term trust and support.

The exact definition of consensus varies among stakeholder committees, but it generally means an agreement of opinion. It may produce decisions that don't meet everyone's full expectations, but it should not produce decisions through a narrow majority. Other methods such as voting or appeals to other parties result in an outcome, but often do not resolve differences. Consensus can greatly increase the time required to make decisions, yet it helps build mutual support and trust in the decision-making process.

The professional facilitators working with the forty-nine-member San Francisco Estuary stakeholder group devised a particularly creative consensus process— probably out of necessity because of the group's size. The members used a six-finger voting system to check in on issues as they were proceeding. A state agency staffer described the scale: "One meant that you loved it, two meant you supported it, three was somewhere in the middle, four meant that you didn't like it, but could live with it, five meant that you couldn't live with it, and six meant that you didn't like it, but thought you could work with it." The voting system allowed the group to quickly identify areas of agreement and disagreement, so they could then work more efficiently. The state agency representative noted, "When it got time to do a straw poll, everyone would start by scanning the room looking for fives and sixes."[9] At this point the process continued with clear ground rules. The members had to explicitly state their opinions; they had to explain their concern with the issue, and had to try and articulate "what they *could* live with."

As shown in table 4.10, when we examined the decision procedures of watershed councils in Oregon, we found a range of approaches.[10] Most groups worked to reach agreement through consensus, but had developed a fallback option such as two-thirds majorities, supermajorities (70 to 80 percent), and complete consensus minus one. Complete consensus creates the risk that one stakeholder may "hijack" the process. Alternatively, complete consensus may assure everyone that they will have an equal decision-making say and hence cannot be railroaded into an agreement.

History of Managing Conflict

Another approach to assessing the effectiveness of a group is to evaluate how well it has managed conflicts over time. While this is a post process assessment, it does provide an indication of how well the group is working. When I examined collaboratives in Wisconsin, I asked participants to describe the two most significant conflicts that they confronted during the process.

To help with this analysis, I used a typology based on Bill Lord's work. Lord (1979, 1227) defines *cognitive conflict* as "rooted in different understandings of the

Table 4.10
Sample consensus rules of Oregon watershed councils

Group	Primary decision rule	Deadlock procedures
Mid Coast Watershed Council	Consensus (no dissenting votes)	None specified
Lower Columbia River Watershed Council	Open discussion with Robert's Rules of Order	Majority vote
Tillamook Bay Watershed Council	Consensus	Two-thirds majority
Umpqua Basin Watershed Council	Consensus with option to block	Blocked decision tabled for seven to sixty days; approval requires consensus minus one, and dissenting statement can be submitted
Seven Basins Watershed Council	Consensus	Simple majority
Clackamas River Basin Council	Consensus	Two-thirds majority
Long Tom Watershed Council	Consensus with option to block	Table decision for subcommittee to resolve; after two fails, vote by supermajority (70 percent)

Note: Compiled by Samuel Fox in August 2005.

conflict situation." It is usually ascribed to differences in factual information or technical judgments. For example, in the Upper Wisconsin River case, management agencies differed with dam operators on fish mortality rates from hydroelectric turbines. Resolving these differences can often occur through additional data or analysis. Another type of conflict is *interest conflict*. It takes place when parties perceive impacts on their own well-being, such as when the beneficiaries and cost bearers of a proposed project are different. There is not disagreement on facts but rather a concern over who wins and who loses. In the Winnebago case, conflict arose over a proposed breakwater and the benefits to water quality versus a reduction in the boating area. Resolving these issues frequently happens by negotiating the distribution of costs and benefits, or offsetting the costs to some people through other means. Lord (1979) notes that *value conflicts* arise from different assessments of the desirability of outcomes. For example, in the Lower Wisconsin River case, the Wisconsin DNR personnel disagreed about land management for recreation and aesthetics versus historical hunting and trapping uses. These are the most difficult to resolve, because they can often be addressed only through some reassessment of values or adjustment in the implications of those values for management.

When I analyzed forty-four of these different conflicts in detail, I found that the conflicts during the consensus-building phase were more difficult to resolve than those that arose during the implementation one (Margerum 1995a). Over one-quarter of the conflicts had to be bypassed or resolved by third parties. The rest were resolved through additional research, extensive discussion, and/or careful deliberation. The open-ended, direction-setting approach of the consensus phase reveals more fundamental differences in value and interest. In contrast, cognitive conflicts usually dominated the implementation phases. This appears to reflect this phase's focus on the details of implementing actions and policies identified during the planning phase. Cognitive conflicts were generally resolved through research, new data, or communication, while interest conflicts usually required communication and bargaining. Value conflicts were sometimes resolved through communication, but often involved appeals to authority or collective decision (Margerum 1995a). Importantly, the conflicts were managed successfully in all the cases, in contrast to some of the Australian catchment committees where conflict undermined group legitimacy.

Effective Public Involvement

The final element that I have found to be significant for consensus building is effective public involvement, which is often not cited as critical in the collaboration literature. In both the literature and in practice, collaboration frequently is directed at stakeholder processes, and the assumption is that stakeholder involvement is equivalent to public involvement.

Many Australian stakeholders interviewed about their efforts responded with statements such as, "We need to do a better job of consulting the public."[11] Only 27 percent of catchment committee participants believed that they were doing a "sufficient job" of consulting the public (n = 192). In several of the Wisconsin case studies, participants noted that public involvement was an essential complement to stakeholder processes and key for gaining implementation support. Before discussing the ways in which the public is effectively involved, it is worthwhile to consider why both forums are important.

Stakeholder processes allow diverse groups of people to share information face-to-face, learn about issues from each other, gain an appreciation of different perspectives, and when successful, agree to work toward common goals. This is viewed as a progressive form of public involvement, because participants have substantial influence over decision making. Yet the limited participation and ongoing role of these groups also makes them distinct from efforts to involve a wider cross section of the public (hereafter referred to as the "general public").

The general public also has a stake in the decision making, but it is not involved because it has not been invited, is not interested, or doesn't have the time or inclination to become involved. Stakeholder groups are learning from each other, gaining respect for the positions of others, and developing new thinking and ideas about how to solve the problems. The general public, however, is often not exposed to these deliberations, and stakeholder solutions may be inconsistent with public views.

The potential gap between stakeholders and the public becomes more acute as one moves across the spectrum from action to organizational to policy collaboratives. For action collaboratives that cover small regions and/or small populations, the stakeholders themselves ideally have an array of social and community connections. These connections allow the stakeholders to consult with community groups, interest groups, social organizations, and business or agricultural organizations that can be just as widespread as traditional public involvement efforts. In the words of a farmer participating on an action collaborative, "I check in with them [agricultural groups,] and they keep me honest."[12]

As one moves to organizational- and policy-level collaboratives, the size and geographic distribution usually become significantly greater. It is impossible to expect a stakeholder group working in the Columbia basin or San Francisco estuary system to have personal connections that can reach the millions of residents encompassed by their collaborative. Therefore, public involvement must often be a separate process, requiring more resources, more expertise, and more careful planning.

The typical weaknesses of limited public involvement were demonstrated in two regional growth management cases that I examined. The planning process for Denver Metro Vision 2020 relied heavily on stakeholder input, which tended to be dominated by elected officials and staff from cities and counties. Rick O'Donnell, policy director for Governor Bill Owens, stated, "If you took a poll in metro Denver, and you asked, 'Do you know what the . . . Metro Vision 2020 plan is?' less than 4 percent would have a clue" (quoted in Shaping the Future 2000). Similarly, a city councillor commented that "most people don't know about it."[13] A local government planner described the direct effect that this lack of awareness had for planning officials:

The only time [the public] find[s] out is when something gets rejected. If we say we can't do something because of the [Urban Growth Boundary], they will ask, "What is that?" And then we will tell them about DRCOG [Denver Regional Council of Governments], and they will say "Who?"[14]

Besides the direct impact that these policies might have on landowners, the lack of public involvement can also undermine the long-term viability of the growth management efforts. Elected officials in both regions expressed concern that the lack of awareness meant there was little support for the policies. When decisions had to be made to reject development proposals, it was the local governments that had to bear the pressure of that decision. Without the public or a constituency to lend support for the plan, many felt the regional plan would not succeed.

Assessing Public Involvement

Public involvement effectiveness can be difficult to assess. One way to assess public involvement is for the stakeholders themselves to evaluate the extent to which they have involved and consulted the public, although this kind of assessment may be biased because it is using those already involved to ask about the adequacy of involvement. Another option is for groups to conduct opinion polling, but this is expensive and can be difficult to design. Other approaches to public involvement rely more on inputs, such as its function in relation to the type of collaborative and the design of the process (see table 4.11).

Tailoring Public Involvement to the Type of Collaborative

As noted above, public involvement often varies by the type of collaborative. In the following section, I consider this issue at the two ends of the spectrum (action and policy collaboratives) and then for groups in the middle (organizational collaboratives).

ACTION COLLABORATIVES

For action collaboratives, the purpose of public involvement is to maintain the group's legitimacy in the community and increase its ability to reach out to the public. Action collaboratives therefore tend to rely heavily on the stakeholders as the primary avenue for sharing knowledge, crafting solutions, and gaining support for implementation. In fact, it could be argued that the spectrum of interests obtained through a stakeholder process will be far more diverse than the best-planned and best-executed public participation forum.

For collaboratives like the Siuslaw Watershed Council, stakeholders belong to local religious organizations, farm cooperatives, interest groups, and social service organizations, and they are local residents with friends, family, and neighbors. On numerous occasions, participants express this role with statements like, "What are they saying about this down at the grange/feed store/café?" One of the key assessment questions to ask is whether the stakeholders at the table have well-connected networks, and whether they share information through those networks.

Even with good stakeholder participation, many action collaboratives still find more general forums for public input important for maintaining their community contacts, increasing their exposure, and identifying new volunteers and participants. Many action groups hold forums while they are developing a plan, link their meetings with demonstration projects and tours, or use public events to celebrate the

Table 4.11
Assessing public input

Types of collaboratives	Purpose of public involvement	Assessing stakeholder input	Assessing public input
Action	• Maintain legitimacy of collaborative in the community • Increase outreach and education potential	• Representativeness of stakeholder group • Community connections of stakeholder group	• Number of participants involved in public events • Forum and events linked to outreach and education efforts
Organizational	• Solicit public input on government policies and plans • Ensure stakeholder group is aligned with public views	• Representativeness of stakeholder group • Links to organizations involved in decision making	• Forums and events designed to solicit public input • Participation in forums and events
Policy	• Solicit public input on government policies and plans • Build broader coalitions and support for policy agreements	• Representativeness of stakeholder group • Links to interest groups that may take positions	• Breadth and depth of public involvement efforts • Opportunities for broad based public input

council's accomplishments. Thus, these groups can also be assessed by tracking the public attendance at these kinds of events.

POLICY COLLABORATIVES

For policy collaboratives, the public often plays a significant part in supporting policies along with the coalitions that can help or hinder their implementation. Because of policy collaboratives' prominent role and link to agencies, rule-making, and legislative processes, there are usually more resources for public participation. Yet the scope and scale of the efforts of these collaboratives frequently make public engagement both daunting and expensive.

To overcome the challenge of involving the public in large-scale issues, some planning efforts have looked to more intensive public processes that fall under the banner of deliberative democracy. These attempts tend to de-emphasize the role of stakeholder groups in favor of more intensive and extensive public involvement projects. For example, Ed Weeks describes several initiatives that he led to help local governments provide substantial public input for major budget and planning decisions. These efforts utilize workshops, newspaper inserts, and media outlets to supply the public with succinct but informed choices. In a budget process for the city of Eugene, for instance, voters were given a breakdown of the city budget in a two-page newspaper insert. Citizens could review both revenue and expenditures, but were asked to either vote for the budget option they liked the best or create their own budget (as long as it balanced). These attempts require substantial funding and expertise, but they have also helped resolve significant funding dilemmas, and informed the public on budget revenues and expenditures (Weeks 2000).

Assessing these kinds of efforts can be difficult, yet an accounting of the activities can provide some indication of their intensity. For example, a regional planning project called Envision Utah documented its own extensive array of involvement strategies, which included 135 public meetings with more than 4,500 people in attendance. It distributed 930,000 questionnaires that generated approximately 23,500 resident responses, and helped produce a documentary that aired on local commercial and public television stations.[15]

ORGANIZATIONAL COLLABORATIVES

For several reasons, organizational collaboratives face some of the most difficult challenges with public involvement, because their actions have a broader impact than those of action collaboratives without the high profile of policy collaboratives. They tend to deal with organizational policies, priorities, and programs that are often overlooked by both the public and interest groups. Furthermore, this lower profile can make it difficult to find resources for broad-based public input and design a process that garners much public response. There is a tendency for organizational collaboratives to rely solely on stakeholder input, and then use traditional comment and review processes for public input.

Despite these limitations, organizational collaboratives can incorporate broad-based public input. Some of the organizational collaboratives that have made the most concerted effort to reach out to a broader public are in fact those focused primarily around a single agency. For example, Julia Wondolleck and Steven Yaffee (2000) describe a collaborative effort centered on a recreation plan for the Tongass National Forest in Alaska. A team of U.S. Forest Service staff members used a wide range of innovative and publicly visible participation opportunities, including brightly colored mailings, media stories, and public meetings that allowed one-to-one contact.

Similarly, several projects led by the Wisconsin DNR included not only diverse stakeholder input but also broad-based public participation opportunities. The extensive outreach efforts in the Upper Wisconsin River valley is probably the best illustration, since the DNR staff members estimated that they held over four hundred hours of public meetings. As a result, when stakeholders gathered to discuss the issues surrounding hydropower dam relicensing, they not only had a good cross section of interested parties, they also had important observations about water and fishing conditions, and a broad set of concerns about the future of the river basin. These public input assessments are examples of measures of inputs (resources, staff time, and events) or outputs (the number of people participating and response rates).

Discussion

In terms of the critical factors for stakeholder deliberation and public participation, there are several issues and themes that need to be considered. This includes the need for training, the limitations of conflict management, the risks of poor public involvement, and the issue of power.

Skills and Training

One implication is that a good, deliberative process does not just happen; it requires people with skills to support it and often resources. Thus, one of the needs for those leading and facilitating collaboratives is access to training and mentoring to support their work. Studies of staff working with action collaboratives have found that many coordinators tend to be young and inexperienced, and many groups are dependent on a few key individuals (Byron and Curtis 2002; Parker et al. 2010). Even agencies and interest groups that are engaged in collaborative efforts recognize that their staff members need training and support to work in collaborative settings (Doppelt, Shinn, and DeWitt 2002).

In Oregon, this need to train and mentor watershed council coordinators and boards was one of the factors that led to the formation of the Network of Oregon Watershed Councils. The network hosts annual meetings and mentoring opportunities to improve the facilitative and managerial capacity of these groups.

Skills and training may also extend to the stakeholder group itself. Some groups need assistance because they frequently have limited experience in consensus-building processes or are dealing with issues that have raised significant differences. For a number of groups I studied, this has meant bringing in a trained facilitator to help them work through a particular issue or improve their process skills generally. For example, one of the aims of the two-day retreat organized by the Clarence River catchment group was to help improve its process by improving the participants' skills. The goal of bringing in outside facilitators for its meeting was not just to help the group work through a particular problem but also to build understanding about how to do so in a constructive way.

This is known as developmental facilitation. Schwarz (2002, 50) notes that in developmental facilitation, "the group uses a facilitator to learn how to improve its process and applies newly developed skills to solving a problem." In contrast, under basic facilitation, "the group uses a facilitator to temporarily improve its process to solve the problem" (ibid.).

While developmental facilitation leads to the long-term improvement of group functioning, it does have some limitations. It can take groups longer to work through a developmental facilitation process, because the facilitator is working with the group to understand where it is performing well and poorly. If the group faces time pressures or limited time for participants, spending time on group process may not be feasible.

Limitations of Conflict Management

Another issue that has been raised in the literature as well as cases I examined is the limitations of conflict management. In both the U.S. and Australian instances, I found that conflict was common and difficult to resolve, but important to address for stakeholder success. Some conflicts involve legal precedent, intractable problems, or fundamental value differences, or extend beyond the scope of the stakeholder group.

In these situations, the stakeholder forum may not be the place where conflict can be resolved. A conflict over lowering a weir in Australia's Johnstone Catchment Committee exemplifies one of the common dilemmas facing collaborative decision making. On the one hand, it can be viewed as a successful management of conflict. The group deliberated and gathered information, but it ultimately decided that it could not reach consensus and agreed to let the issue be resolved through other forums. On the other hand, it could be argued that this is the core weakness of collaboration. It only resolves problems that are relatively easy to figure out—the so-called low-hanging fruit—while the more difficult and complex ones are left unaddressed.

Based on my research of collaboratives, I believe that those at the action end of the spectrum are the most likely to become frustrated by the limitations of their group. They are addressing problems "on the ground," which allows them to focus on the details of direct involvement in restoration, protection, and enhancement efforts.

They also see the on-the-ground effects and conflicts in government policy, interest group positions, and expert advice, however. Thus, the Mary River Catchment Committee in Queensland has spent years working to restore the river system and reestablish the native Murray cod, only to be faced with a state government proposal for a massive new water storage dam on the river's main stem.

These kinds of issues have often led these groups to shift their focus upward to agencies, agency policies, and elected officials. For example, almost three-quarters of the catchment committees observed in Australia spent time developing or drafting letters to an elected official because of concerns about legislation or policies.[16]

Risks of Poor Stakeholder Public Involvement

Public involvement, as noted above, is frequently overlooked or downplayed in stakeholder-led efforts. Whether the collaborative effort takes place at an action or policy level, it is important to have some interaction with the public. In some cases, this may mean simply stakeholder communication with the community. In others, this may mean extensive involvement efforts run by consultants or experts. When there is inadequate public involvement, stakeholder processes pose several risks.

Stakeholders, for one, offer only a sample of views and perspectives compared to those that may exist in the broader community. They are chosen because they have a particular interest or "stake" in the outcomes of management efforts. Yet the community also has a stake in the outcomes, albeit a less well-defined one (Margerum and Born 1995). If stakeholders develop strategies without efforts to consult with the public, they may find that their views are quite different from those of the public

Second, the public often possesses significant information based on its observations and knowledge, some of which may provide historical insights extending beyond the range of scientific data. In a number of U.S. cases, agency staff members were surprised to learn how much information the public could offer them. There is an assumption that technical people are the experts, when in fact local residents who have carefully observed changes in the environment around them can supply a critical temporal perspective not covered by data. If there is no opportunity for community input, this information may never enter into the strategy development process, which could lead to incorrect assumptions and inappropriate actions.

Third, the consensus reached by stakeholders may not be mirrored in the larger community. Stakeholders are not representatives (in the sense of being elected) but are instead people who participate because they represent an organization or are indicative of a certain *type* of person (farmer, landowner, or concerned citizen). As they sit around the table, sharing information, learning about their region, and understanding different perspectives, they are usually developing a new, more holistic, and integrated view of the issues and problems. As stakeholders identify common goals, however, "their mutual learning and consensus . . . [are] not always being mirrored in the community" (Margerum 1999d, 159). Many stakeholder groups need to think of their consensus process as part of a broader objective to reach consensus in the community.

Fourth, a lack of public support may limit political support. Community involvement can be central to building public and political support for activities and programs. Participants in a Wisconsin regional management strategy recognized at the outset that they would be addressing difficult and controversial issues. Therefore, they designed a stakeholder-led effort supported with an extensive process of community participation. One participant in the project commented:

At least 50 percent of the process was public input. . . . Without citizen involvement it would not have survived and [we] would not have gotten the support we did in the end. . . . Early on we had legislators show up and tell us there was no way the project would get passed. These same people were later sponsors of the bill.

Fifth, when the public is not involved, stakeholders and organizations miss an important opportunity to tap into the public. Many managers now recognize that the public is valuable not only as a participant in the strategic planning process but also as a monitor and watchdog of activities on the ground. One manager noted that the public helps "call attention to problems. Many [people] are very knowledgeable about the river and the impacts on the river. They are our eyes and ears." Even the increased familiarity that stakeholders and managers bring can help improve communication and trust with the community.

Stakeholders and Power

Power is an essential issue in consensus building, including the power of managing the process, knowledge and information, not collaborating, and autonomous decision making.[17]

One category of power relates to the capacity to influence process through the control of agendas, information, and persuasiveness (Amy 1987; Gray 1989). For example, stakeholders involved in several of the Wisconsin cases were concerned about the overinfluence of the DNR because of its wide range of powers, expertise, and resources. Similarly, a community representative on a New South Wales committee expressed concern about the power of government departments and industry organizations to influence the process:

At first glance, it would appear that citizen members have better than equal representation on the committee. In practice this is often not the case because their attendance is not always certain and they are not paid, but mainly because representatives of government departments have much greater access to office assistance, photocopying, printing, and research. Hence, they can drive agendas with superior presentation, leapfrogging, and squeezing out some citizen-initiated items.[18]

The second category of power is the ability to mobilize, influence, and organize action or resistance through stakeholder constituencies (Amy 1987; Bingham 1986; Susskind and Cruikshank 1987). This form of power is substantially more complex to address. Minority interests, such as environmental representatives, most commonly express concerns about this form of power. For example, an Australian community representative observed:

The committee has allowed a cross section of power brokers in the district to meet with the few environmentally concerned groups and provide some reasonable working conditions, but it is my clear impression that the cane growers and executive are there to make sure their plans are not significantly compromised.[19]

The literature offers a range of views about how to respond to these power differentials during consensus building. Steven Selin and Deborah Chavez (1995) suggest that consensus building is inhibited when significant power differences exist among the parties. While Gray (1989) agrees that major inequities will deter collaboration, she contends that parties involved in consensus building will *not* be equal in power.

A number of authors argue that consensus building requires a kind of power sharing that will produce a stalemate. Gray (1989, 119) maintains that stakeholder groups are successful when they have "mutually authorized each other to reach a decision." Likewise, Jane E. McCarthy and Alice Shorett (1984, 13) suggest that "power parity is reached when each interest group is unable to impose its proposed solution on the other affected parties." The parties must in some way become dependent on each other. In Douglas Amy's review (1987) of environmental mediation, he asserts that participants may have to be forced into power stalemates to resolve their differences. The critical issue for the practice of collaborative planning is how interdependence and power stalemates are created.

Using complete consensus is one way of promoting power sharing. In fact, Julian Edelenbos and Erik-Hans Klijn (2005) suggest that if the expectations of deliberative process are met, then participants should expect to have veto power. Others claim that consensus is important for effective process and to ensure that a substantial minority is not ignored, but complete consensus is not required (Innes et al. 1994; Susskind and Ozawa 1984).

About 48 percent of Australian participants said they operated by general consensus, 50 percent said they operated by complete consensus, and 2 percent by voting (n = 189). Similarly, an analysis of forty-four different conflicts in the U.S. cases revealed that participants used a range of voting and consensus processes. Yet the few case study committees that did adhere to complete consensus appeared to foster a greater balance of power. For example, participants in the Upper Wisconsin River project operated by complete consensus to decide on dam relicensing issues, and unresolved issues were left to be decided by the Federal Energy Regulatory Commission. Both government and nongovernment participants commented that complete consensus lent considerable strength to individual viewpoints, but the collective power of consensus in front of federal regulators encouraged participants to work together.

The Johnstone River committee also operated by consensus from the beginning and developed several projects that were used as models across Queensland, but it also reached a stalemate on a wetland alteration proposal. Although a majority of the committee was composed of farming interests that supported the proposal, the committee respected the opposition of environmental representatives, and did not produce a position on the proposal. As noted in the discussions about process, however, consensus-based decision making is difficult for many committees, and even the wetland dispute was debated on and off for almost one year before the group agreed to disagree.[20]

The case studies also suggest that power sharing may require a deliberate effort on the part of powerful organizations. Government agencies in particular may need to be encouraged to give up some of their autonomy in exchange for increased respect and consensus. In three Wisconsin case studies, for example, participants were especially impressed with the way the DNR used stakeholder and public input to shape the plan. A participant in the Lake Winnebago plan noted,

When I first moved here people just hated the DNR. . . . People felt they were power hungry. [In the Lake Winnebago Plan] it felt like the DNR was part of it, but they did not dominate. I have not heard near the anti-DNR sentiment as when I first got here. It seems to be a more cooperative atmosphere.[21]

Concluding Remarks

The discussion here implies a linear process of consensus building leading to implementation. As many researchers and participants emphasize, consensus building is an ongoing process. This means that many of the processes described here must become ingrained in the structure and operations of the collaborative. For this reason, sustaining collaboratives (explored in chapter 6) is often an important dimension to achieving results.

Another reason why consensus building is a cyclic process is because of the changing conditions and participants. Collaboratives frequently deal with dynamic and complex problems—and as such, problems are prone to change. These changes usually bring new challenges, new information, and new problems. For instance, watersheds in Australia plagued by drought can find themselves suddenly confronted with flooding and its impacts. Recent increases in commodity prices have had significant impact on agriculture and the places in which farmers operate. Global price changes may affect conservation programs, leading to crop changes that generate different kinds of problems. These kinds of changes—which are generally outside the collaborative's control—can require a group to go back and evaluate a plan, an agreement, or the strategies it is using to achieve its outcomes.

Even without changes in external factors, consensus building must also be a cyclic process because the participants in the collaborative change. People leave the group, organizations shift priorities, or individual liaisons between a collaborative and an organization may move on to a different job. Nevertheless, the underlying principle is that the group has to constantly build trust and respect for as well as commitment to the collaborative's goals. In summary, even when a collaborative moves from consensus building to implementation, stakeholder deliberation and public participation will continue to play a significant role.

5

High-Quality Collaboration Products

In 1994, the state of Queensland finalized the Regional Framework for Growth Management—a regional plan developed collaboratively by state agencies and eighteen local governments. The initiative grew out of concerns about the impacts of rapid growth, including the loss of open space due to development. Yet the process also created significant controversy, which led to a plan with vague goals and objectives, and few means for carrying it out. For example, one of the objectives called on councils to develop and adopt local planning policies that include "*advice on options* available for the protection on vegetation of freehold [private] land" (Queensland Department of Infrastructure and Planning 2008, 30; emphasis added). Given that there were no criteria for measuring progress or specifying outcomes, however, it was essentially a meaningless objective. In 1999, I led an evaluation of the effect of this regional plan on local environmental planning. We found that the concept of open-space networks and their protection had filtered into the language of many local governments and their plans, but many local governments had not developed information, tools, and resources for implementation (Margerum 2001b; Margerum and Holland 2000).

In my research in both Australia and the United States, I found groups that produced low-quality plans or plans with sections that were inadequate to guide implementation. For instance, in 1992 the North-West Catchment Management Committee (Australia) prepared a management plan for the 94,510 square kilometer (36,490 square mile) watershed. Although some of the actions contained in the plan were well defined, others were vague and unclear. Strategy 1 in the water quality section, for example, was to "ensure a coordinated water quality program." Under this strategy the Department of Water Resources and "agencies" were assigned to "investigate problem areas" with a time frame of "when required" (North-West Catchment Management Committee 1992, 26). In another case, the Wisconsin DNR led a collaborative management effort for the Milwaukee River. Five years after the initial plan had been developed, DNR staff members reviewed the progress and found that few of the actions had been implemented. As one staff person commented, "We listed what we *wished* could be accomplished rather than what we were *willing* to accomplish."[1]

Does Collaboration Produce High-Quality Products?

Some researchers have found that a process of consensus building that meets good practice criteria will lead to high-quality products. A survey of 239 published cases of stakeholder involvement revealed that more intensive participatory processes allowed more exchange of information and analysis along with higher-quality decisions (Beierle 2002). Other research has indicated that effective consensus-building processes lead to plans that reflect local conditions as well as incorporate a wider range of information and perspectives (Innes and Booher 1999a; Innes 1996; Burby 2003; Wondolleck and Yaffee 2000; Cortner and Moote 1999).

Based on my research, I conclude that there is a correlation between good process and good plans, but I don't believe we can assume that good process will always generate good products. In fact, I believe that collaborative efforts are sometimes at greater risk of producing weak products for several reasons. First, in an effort to reach consensus, participants may adopt vague language that becomes difficult to interpret or specify. The importance of clear criteria for evaluating agreements is highlighted in the consensus and conflict resolution literature, but in practice the desire to reach agreement in a timely manner sometimes undermines this principle. Second, collaboration often involves many players and participants approaching an issue from different perspectives. This makes the complexity and interpretations of goals and objectives more difficult. Third, there are frequently multiple users of the products besides those who are directly involved. People change jobs, new participants come on board, actions are delegated within organizations, and suddenly people are attempting to interpret vague documents.

These weaknesses were exemplified by a state agency staff person whom I interviewed about her role in coordinating the implementation of a collaborative plan prepared by her predecessor. As she explained, the plan "does not distinguish actions that are part of agencies' core business versus those it would like to do versus those that are a priority for regional planning." She read out one of the objectives listed in the plan that was assigned to her agency and with an exasperated look exclaimed, "I have no idea what the hell that means, and there are dozens of pages listing things like that."[2]

Types of Products

Collaboratives may produce a range of plans or products, and several examples demonstrate the variation of these outputs. For one, a collaborative effort to address water quality in the Milwaukee River basin was led by the DNR, and involved the university extension service, the metropolitan sewer district, local governments, other state agencies, and citizens. The product of this process was two sets of plans for each subwatershed. The nonpoint source pollution control plans documented watershed conditions and identified restoration priorities that allowed county staff to work on them with agricultural landowners. The integrated management plans identified the array of potential programs and projects for the DNR and other agencies. These were typical agency plans that defined the problem, specified goals and objectives, and listed actions for the implementing agencies.

Second, several collaborative groups in Australia treated their plans as working documents and produced them as a three-ring binder. The first draft of their plan provided the basic framework of data, goals, and major objectives. As they refined each objective and developed an action plan for each one, they would publish a new set of pages to be inserted into the binder. Alternatively, as new data and information became available, the groups could amend or replace sections of the plan.

Third, watershed councils in Oregon are required by the OWEB to develop a watershed assessment. The purpose of this document is to determine watershed conditions, identify restoration needs, and help councils prioritize the restoration projects they undertake in their watershed. These documents are essentially technical ones that set the restoration priorities for the group and then become the basis for work plans to translate these priorities into projects.

Finally, some smaller community-based Landcare groups in Australia did not produce plans at all. These groups reviewed issues, identified problems, and developed goals and objectives. This material was often summarized in other documents like grant applications, research reports, information programs, and demonstration projects, but the groups did not develop a formal written plan. For example, Andrew Campbell (1995, 116) documented a group in Western Australia experiencing water quality problems. Until the collaborative group emerged, "many studies had been completed on the catchment, but nothing substantial had been done on the ground to prevent further degradation of the estuary. . . . [The collaborative] signaled a change in emphasis from measuring the problem to initiating activities to reduce its major component-nutrient levels."

Products and Outcomes

Throughout this chapter I will refer to the "products" of a collaborative, because there is a range of direct and indirect outputs that are important. The direct products include things such as the plans, assessments, and agreements described above. The indirect outputs (process evaluation) include things like a shared fact base as well as trust and commitment, which are critical to sustaining implementation efforts.

Ultimately, the success of any effort is determined by its ability to achieve outcomes, but results are difficult to evaluate because of the time lag associated with implementation. The success of a flood mitigation plan, for example, might be evaluated by performance measures, such as the acres of wetlands or floodplain that are reconnected to a river system to increase flood storage capacity. The long-term outcomes would be the reduction of flood severity and frequency, even though it would take many years of data to assess this success. Therefore, evaluating products can be a crucial indicator of future effectiveness in achieving outcomes.

This chapter reviews theory related to collaboration products, presents criteria for assessing outputs, and discusses some of the implications of this evaluation. As noted in this chapter's conclusions, some of these issues dovetail into the implementation approaches explored in chapters 7, 8, and 9.

Theory Related to Products

There is an array of disciplines that address the issue of products, outputs, and agreements along with their quality. The field of urban planning has for many years examined the issue of plan quality, and the factors supporting and limiting implementation. For example, William Baer (1997) developed a set of plan evaluation criteria, and Larz Anderson (1995) identified the components of effective plans. Similarly, the fields of public policy and public administration have looked at the implementation issue, focusing on the factors that allow policies to be implemented or that undermine their success. Traditionally this literature tended to focus on single policies and view implementation from a top-down perspective (Bardach 1977; Bunker 1972; O'Toole 1986; Sabatier and Mazmanian 1979). Over the years, though, there has been increasing attention paid to implementation from a bottom-up view (Elmore 1982; Fraser et al. 2006; Sabatier 1986). More recently, the increased interest in collaborative and ecosystem-based approaches to environmental policy have led people to identify the types of plans and agreements that allow integrated sets of actions to be implemented (Layzer 2008; Steelman 2010).

Two other fields have focused more specifically on agreements and their quality. Conflict resolution often emphasizes the importance of both "high-quality agreements" and stakeholders developing evaluation criteria for those agreements (Carpenter and Kennedy 1988). Similarly, the literature on group process has examined the quality of agreements from the standpoint of participant support and the quality of substantive outcomes. Unlike other fields that have concentrated on these issues in real-life settings, this research has explored these topics by constructing experimental scenarios that allow for "better" or "worse" outcomes (Schwenk and Cosier 1993; Stasser, Vaughan, and Stewart 2000; Sunwolf and Seibold 1999; Wittenbaum 2000). Yet these experiments are often limited to student subjects in one-off scenarios, rather than settings where stakeholders interact over time. Several categories of themes have emerged from the literature: high-quality products (plans or agreements), high-quality information, and trust and commitment.

High-Quality Products

The quality of plans or agreements has been evaluated in a number of ways, including research on whether consensus-based efforts reduce conflict or legal challenges over time (Sipe 1998; Bingham 1986). Significantly, this kind of evaluation frequently assesses the agreement not just from the perspective of those who were a party to it but also from the vantage point of those who were not involved or who have been affected. While this provides insights into the relative success of products, it doesn't help identify the factors that make them high quality. The elements that address the issue of quality can be grouped into three categories.

First, the literature indicates that clear goals and objectives are key for group processes, whether they are identified at the outset or developed by the group. Goals and objectives help motivate groups to resolve conflicts (Mattessich, Murray-Close, and Monsey 2004; Susskind and Cruikshank 1987), and translate agreements into clear strategies (Harbin et al. 1991). When groups identify common goals, they usually realize that they have more in common than they thought and more potential to work together than initially perceived (Gray and Wood 1991; Innes and Booher 1999b).

Second, research in group communication and conflict resolution emphasizes the extent of support or even enthusiasm for the agreement. These evaluations underscore that resolution means participants must be willing to "live with the agreement," but the fewer the reservations, the greater the likelihood of success (Innes 1999; McKearnon and Fairman 1999; Susskind and Cruikshank 1987).

A third aspect of a high-quality agreement is the extent to which the participants believe it is sound, well developed, and has the desired influence on implementation. For example, Amy Schulz, Barbara Israel, and Paula Lantz (2003) identify a number of criteria for judging agreements, such as whether the group is having a positive effect on the community, whether it has chosen to focus on important problems, whether agencies and groups in the area know about the efforts, and whether the group has been effective in informing decision makers. Similarly, some researchers have applied normative criteria to judge whether a plan or agreement is high quality.

Philip Berke and his colleagues (Berke and Conroy 2000; Berke et al. 1996) led several evaluations of plan quality in which they assessed plans against sustainability and hazard mitigation goals.

High-Quality Information

In chapter 4, the role of sharing information during consensus building was described in terms of the process of building trust and effective solutions. High-quality information is also an output of the consensus-building process, and the quality of this information can be assessed. One measure is the quality of the data and science developed by the collaborative. The importance of good science has been stressed in several collaborative efforts involving large-scale systems (e.g., Chesapeake Bay) or highly technical issues (e.g., Fernald nuclear weapons plant) (Schneider et al. 2003; Failing, Gregory, and Harstone 2007; Depoe 2004; Ozawa 2005).

Another measure of information quality is whether it incorporates a broad range of sources and perspectives. Research indicates that when the collaborative process is effective, it leads to agreements reflecting the local conditions while incorporating a wider range of information and perspectives as well (Innes and Booher 1999a; Innes 1996; Burby 2003; Wondolleck and Yaffee 2000; Cortner and Moote 1999). For example, Raymond Burby's analysis (2003, 44) of sixty comprehensive plans found that "broad stakeholder involvement contributes to both stronger plans and the implementation of proposals in plans."

Another element of high-quality information is whether there are shared interpretations of it. This factor can be particularly significant in cases where public, stakeholder, and scientific views of data and its interpretation lead to different conclusions (Derby and Keeney 1981; Keeney and von Winterfeldt 1986). When scientific processes are separated from lay stakeholder processes, there may be different interpretations of the same data. Furthermore, focusing only on the physical science perspectives may ignore or devalue social and economic scientific perspectives. The expectation for shared interpretations, however, can significantly increase the time requirements and timelines for collaborative processes to produce high-quality products (Depoe 2004).

Trust and Commitment

Trust and commitment are the indirect products of collaborative efforts, but a wide range of research emphasizes the importance of this for implementation (Gray 1985, 1989; Wondolleck and Yaffee 2000; Margerum 2001a, 2002b; Bingham 1986; Johnson and Johnson 2000; Innes 1996). For example, my survey of over two hundred stakeholders in Australia highlighted links between weaknesses in interactive communication and a perceived lack of commitment among government participants (Margerum 1999b). In contrast, when stakeholder groups built strong communication norms and supporting institutional structures, local government officials became champions of regional planning efforts, even though they initially objected to such a regional approach (Margerum 2002b).

Trust and commitment create a sense of belonging and support that allows stakeholders from different perspectives to work together (Selin, Schuett, and Carr 2000; Schulz, Israel, and Lantz 2003). They also make the members feel committed to the group's goals, and more willing to put in time and effort to meet them (Alper, Tjosvold, and Law 1998). This is critical for participants representing organizations, because supporters are more likely to act as champions for implementation within their organization (Frame, Gunton, and Day 2004; Innes 1999).

Assessing Products

As noted in earlier chapters, the process of consensus building leads to an agreement, strategy, or plan, which is usually a written document providing the foundation for implementation. For simplicity, these documents will be referred to as plans throughout this chapter. Plans will often describe the context and setting, document the consensus process, and specify the goals and actions that the participants have agreed on. They are also essential communication tools as the participants change, new people take over implementation activities, and other people are asked to interpret and carry out actions. Therefore, it is important to look at the quality of the plan itself in terms of both its substance and its ability to communicate information.

In addition to the plans, it is also crucial to examine the increased understanding and mutual support developed through consensus building. Many of the participants I interviewed commented that plans represent the understanding and agreement among stakeholders at a particular point in time. More bluntly, one Australian coordinator remarked, "Most plans are obsolete the day they are published."[3] Assessing high-quality products thus should include an evaluation of group outcomes and their secondary effect.

Table 5.1 lists a series of factors from the literature and my research that can be used to determine whether the products of consensus are high quality. These assessment factors start with the assumption that collaborative processes can produce good or bad plans, but they must be evaluated critically.

Clear Goals and Objectives

An important principle of consensus building is that groups need to identify clear goals and measurable objectives. These goals and objectives are often what bring

Table 5.1
Assessing high-quality products

Factors	Measures of factors	Related references
Clear goals and objectives: Goals of plan are clear and supporting objectives are specific	• Clear goals agreed to and supported by stakeholders • Objectives that clearly specify measurable outcomes • Goals and objectives that are integrated	Levy 1997; Hoch 1992; Hoch, Dalton, and So 2000; Anderson 1995
Plan communication: Plan should document and explain the collaborative's process and approach so they can be communicated with a broader audience	• Adequate explanation of context and scope • Clear explanation of plan purpose and role • Explanation of plan-making process • Effective communication and format	Anderson 1995; Baer 1997; Talen 1996
Shared high-quality fact base: There is an adequate base of shared factual information to support the plan, or a system for research and information gathering	• Scientific information and expertise is built into the process • There are procedures for external or scientific review • There are procedures for disseminating, sharing, and clarifying information among experts and laypeople	Ozawa 1991, 2005; Beierle and Konisky 2000; McKearnon and Fairman 1999
Sound intervention strategy: Intervention approach assigns and funds actions that will leverage change to achieve goals	• Responsibilities for implementation are clearly assigned and resources are allocated • Implementation activities will induce the desired change and lead to accomplishing objectives • Actions are aligned with the type of collaborative	Mazmanian and Sabatier 1983; Elmore 1982; Pressman and Wildavsky 1973

disparate parties to work together. For example, on watershed councils across Oregon, traditional farmers, organic farmers, pesticide companies, lumber companies, environmentalists, and recreational boating and fishing interests have joined to restore and enhance local rivers. I have sat in numerous Oregon watershed council meetings where people who could never agree on politics or policies can agree that there is a need to restore salmon or trout in a local watershed. Conservative landowners who rail against government wistfully tell stories of fishing in local streams during their childhood and proudly show off pictures of restoration projects on their land carried out with government funding. A watershed council coordinator noting the diverse cross-section of people attending its annual meeting remarked to the audience, "I think we all cancel each other out at the voting booth."[4]

The key to goals and objectives is not just a general agreement that fish or clean water is good. There must be a clear aim that all participants can rally around, and measurable targets specifying how they will assess progress. Clear goals and measurable objectives are emphasized by public policy and conflict resolution scholars, because this is usually the area of agreement that participants can rely on when they face conflict. In fact, compared to a top-down model, a collaborative approach needs to be even clearer on these criteria because of the large number of decision makers who may be interpreting a plan or agreement (Margerum 2002b).

The potential risk is that in the process of trying to reach consensus on goals and objectives, a group may produce terminology and wording that is written ambiguously. In a study of Atlanta's collaborative visioning process, for instance, Amy Helling (1998) concluded that the effort yielded few significant and immediate results because it did not define clear outcome aims. Similarly, my evaluation of the collaborative growth management process in South East Queensland revealed that the regional plan highlighted some crucial ideas, but also produced vague objections and action items—particularly on the topic of open-space protection.[5]

Assessing Goals and Objectives

One approach to assessing goals and objectives is to determine whether the participants believe they are clear and whether they agreed with them. There are examples of survey instruments, including the Wilder inventory, which stress several elements of a good plan or agreement, such as a shared vision, the development of clear goals and policy guidelines, and concrete, attainable goals and objectives (Mattessich, Murray-Close, and Monsey 2004).

I used this kind of self-evaluation approach to examine over eighty local government advisory committees through a survey of almost seven hundred committee members. In the survey, I asked participants to self-assess their group's process, products, and accomplishments. I looked at several different models of accomplishment, including direct questions, process variables, product variables, and outcome variables. The one variable that was significant in almost all these models was whether the group had clear goals and objectives.

When my survey respondents answered open-ended questions about committee strengths, weaknesses, and recommended changes, committee goals was one of the most common themes. Respondents underscored the need for the committee itself to review its goals, so that the members had a clearer sense of its focus and agenda. For example, one committee member noted that the "goals and responsibilities of the committee are not clearly defined." A respondent on another committee observed that their committee needs to "clearly stay to the mission that it was set up for, rather than diversions into policy areas that the group should really not be taking." Conversely, respondents noted that the strengths of their committees were "a common vision" as well as a "shared vision and goals."[6]

The weaknesses of participant assessments such as this include variable definitions of quality, bias among respondents, and self-censorship by respondents who are concerned about how an assessment will be used. Two alternative approaches to assessing goals and objectives are based on normative criteria.

Well-Crafted Goals and Objectives

Goals are difficult to evaluate because they are "feel good" statements that articulate in broad terms what participants want to achieve. Anderson (1995) explains that goals should describe a desired future condition and create a sense of common mission. In some cases, groups may need to identify superordinate goals that are above the current conflict. Disagreements over a specific action may appear less problematic if these higher-level, overarching goals can be established. In other cases, there may be a common mission that brings about an obvious reason to work together. In situations where participants don't start with a common vision, there may be common goals with different benefits, different goals with compatible ways to achieve them, or a way of incorporating other issues to find common ground (Wondolleck and Yaffee 2000).

The vague nature of goals means that it is important to have clear objectives for defining and evaluating progress toward achieving goals. Objectives should describe specific future conditions to be attained within a stated period of time (Anderson 1995; Levy 1997; Hoch, Dalton, and So 2000). Anderson identifies several key criteria for evaluating the quality of objectives:

• They are similar to the goals but more specific
• They should be consistent with the goals

- They should be clearly attainable
- They should be measurable
- Their time period should be specified
- They involve an expenditure of effort

Integrated Goals and Objectives

Another criterion is the extent to which goals and objectives are integrated with other ones. A common advantage of collaborative efforts is that they bridge areas of expertise, jurisdictions, and responsibilities. Their approaches are often contrasted with traditional decision making that focuses on single issues or narrow "silos" (Baer 1997; Margerum 2002b; Mazmanian and Sabatier 1983).

For example, groups like the Coos Watershed Association have worked to tie watershed restoration efforts to economic strategies. Because of employment declines in the fishing and timber industries, the association has utilized federally funded job programs to help train local residents and contractors in landscape restoration skills. This allows the association to restore watershed conditions while tapping into a pool of local, skilled professionals and providing local employment opportunities.[7]

Because goals and objectives are context specific, it is difficult to develop a general assessment framework, but there are several questions that participants or evaluators might ask, including:

- Are the objectives in their plans and strategies interlinked?
- Do the objectives link with the plans and approaches of other entities?
- Do the objectives consider the range of social, economic, and environmental factors?

Plan Communication

A second factor important for assessing the quality of collaboration products is the plan's effectiveness in communicating information. By the end of an intensive collaboration process, the participants are usually highly knowledgeable about the final plan. Yet there are many more people who will use or be affected by it. An Australian watershed coordinator stated, "We wanted to write our plan so that if I leave or if the entire steering committee changes, the new people would understand our goals and agreements, and why we were doing what we proposed to do. We want them to be able to pick up the plan and keep the momentum going, rather than having to start all over again."[8]

Assessing Plan Communication

In general, a plan as a written document is more important for organizational and policy collaboratives. For many action-level collaboratives, the "plan" is frequently just an agreement of how to proceed and where to focus their attention. It may not even be formally written as a separate document. This approach, however, relies on both the stakeholder group as the lead implementer and the continued involvement of stakeholders who are familiar with the agreed-on approach.

In contrast, organizational and policy collaboratives produce plans that must be interpreted by a range of individuals within the implementing organizations. Some of these people may have been involved in the consensus-building process, but many of them may have had no involvement, or may have found particular objectives and actions delegated to them from within the organization. In these cases, the kinds of plan communication criteria listed below are crucial for relaying this information.

Assessing plan communication can be conducted by stakeholder evaluations, but evaluations can also use normative criteria. Table 5.2 lists a range of criteria for effective plan communication for urban planners. In 2004, I used a modified version of these criteria to evaluate natural hazard mitigation plans in Oregon. The plans had been prepared over several years in response to impacts from floods throughout Oregon in 1996. We were interested in whether the plans were being implemented, whether they were influencing decision making, and whether the quality of the plan influenced effectiveness. In our preliminary evaluation, we found that the plan itself was a significant factor in laying out a specific course of action—especially when the people who were involved in implementation were not the ones who developed the plan.[9]

Our pilot natural hazards plan study examined only a handful of cases, but some of the stories offered insights. In one jurisdiction, the entire plan had been prepared by a consultant with a "fixed template" and numerous pages of general hazard information. The staff person in charge of coordinating hazard mitigation efforts found the plans frustrating to use and hard to interpret. When asked about the plan, he noted that it "sat on the shelf" and "nobody knew we had it."[10] Furthermore, plan actions were not interlinked with other important county plans, such as those used for planning roads and infrastructure investment.

A similar plan was prepared in Clackamas County, but it was based on Federal Emergency Management Agency guidelines and a best practice approach developed by the Oregon Natural Hazards Workgroup. The planner who inherited the document commented that the plan was well structured, easy to use in terms of finding information, and clearly articulated its role and the proposed actions. She summarized it by saying that the plan was "very active" in terms of being an implementation guide.[11]

Table 5.2
Plan communication evaluation criteria

Criteria	Specific assessment measures
Adequacy of context	• Are the political, legal, and administrative contexts of the plan explained? • Are the purposes of and reasons for the plan explained? • Is it clear whom the plan is for?
Underlying theory of the plan	• Is the plan clear about the criteria that will be used to judge its success? • Are the problems clearly identified? • Are the goals and objectives clear? • Is the tone appropriate to the type of plan? • Are alternatives listed and explained?
Procedural validity	• Is the process for developing the plan clearly explained? • Does the plan explain how stakeholders and decision makers were involved? • Does the plan explain how the public was involved? • Does the plan explain how data was used? • Collaborative plans: Does the plan have adequate stakeholder commitment? • Collaborative plans: Is there public support and commitment?
Quality of communication	• Is the plan convincingly presented (are the recommendations consistent with the objectives)? • Are the rationales behind the decisions effectively presented? • Are the criteria by which the plan is to be judged clearly explained?
Plan format	• Is the plan attractively presented and appropriate for the subject? • Are graphics used effectively? • Is basic information provided (publication date, page numbers, and table of contents)? • Are the rationales behind the decisions effectively presented?

Source: Based on Baer 1997; Hoch 1992; ONHW 2002.

Shared High-Quality Fact Base

A third essential factor for high-quality plans is the quality of the fact base. Many group processes are dealing with complex problems that cross multiple jurisdictions, physical boundaries, and disciplines. This often means that groups have to assemble information that has not been brought together before. Because collaboration involves participants from a wide range of perspectives, backgrounds, and organizations, one of the significant challenges of collaborative processes is producing a shared, high-quality fact base (Layzer 2008). For some, high-quality information means rational-scientific data that measure outcomes: Is the water quality improving? Is housing becoming more affordable? Is the ecosystem getting better? This kind of fact base has several limitations: it takes many years of data collection to assess these trends accurately, the degree of change necessary to influence outcomes is substantial, many complex outcome questions are difficult and expensive to assess, and it is difficult to eliminate the effect of external influences (e.g., economic trends or climate change).

The difficulties of assembling and interpreting data were highlighted in Oregon's Rogue River basin, where watershed councils, federal agencies, and other stakeholders came together to share information and identify restoration priorities. The goal of this effort was to create a decision support model that would allow all these organizations to assess ecosystem quality and target their restoration projects. But the team quickly discovered that assembling and interpreting the myriad of data from the different organizations presented several problems. First, each agency had their own internal criteria and formats for collecting, storing, and reporting data. Jack Williams, a former U.S. Forest Service supervisor, noted that from the Bureau of Land Management's perspective,

it may be more appropriate to organize their data in Medford, Oregon, the same way they do in southern Arizona. Of course, from an ecological perspective, it would probably be more important to organize their information the same way as Oregon [Department of] Fish and Wildlife.[12]

Second, differences in agency funding and mandates limited the availability of some critical data. As a regulatory agency, the National Marine Fisheries Service is required to collect data on endangered species, while the Forest Service manages large tracts of federal land and must respond to a broader array of land management objectives. The team working on the project thus had to reject a number of indicators because the data were not available across the entire region. They also had to use data as proxies for other kinds of measures and trends. For example, the team had to use road density data (correlated with geology) as an indicator of potential erosion rates.

Table 5.3
Data quality and interpretation measures

Criteria	Specific assessment measures	Related references
High-quality information	• Team members are concerned about the quality of the work • Decisions are based on reliable data • Process lacked adequate high-quality information for effective decision making • The technical aspects of the problem are well understood	Alper, Tjosvold, and Law 1998; Selin, Schuett, and Carr 2000; Frame, Gunton, and Day 2004; Beierle and Konisky 2000
Shared interpretations and learning	• We engage in joint fact finding to understand the problem • I have increased my knowledge about important topics through this group • How much do you have a sense of ownership over what the group does? • As a result of the process, I have a good understanding of the issues	McKearnon and Fairman 1999; Schulz, Israel, and Lantz 2003; Frame, Gunton, and Day 2004

Third, different organizations use different criteria. Even something seemingly straightforward, such as combining map layers of hydrologic systems, raised significant difficulties in the Rogue River basin. The Bureau of Land Management hydrologic layer included all stream courses, including low-order, ephemeral streams, while the Forest Service layers mapped only higher-order, fish-bearing intermittent and perennial streams. Moreover, the Bureau of Land Management data were based on remote-sensing analysis of the terrain, while the Forest Service maps were usually "ground truthed." Thus, when the different basin maps were combined, the density of streams was significantly different, and some streams on the bureau maps did not match up with streams on neighboring Forest Service ones.

Despite these limitations and difficulties in the Rogue River basin and other cases, stakeholders have been able to compile high-quality data. A range of research illustrates the importance of high-quality data and shared interpretation of those data among stakeholders. Assessing data quality and interpretation can be conducted through procedures such as self-assessment surveys (see table 5.3), but in addition to the aforementioned limitations of self-assessment, these surveys would not be good measures of what stakeholders don't know. In other words, stakeholders may not know that they have poor-quality data. It is therefore helpful to consider other approaches to assessing a shared high-quality fact base.

Assessing the Fact Base

The quality of the fact base for a collaborative effort is highly dependent on the issues, problems, and context being faced by the collaborative. As such, a generic assessment must often focus on the structures and processes for establishing as well as reviewing the fact base. This includes the information inputs and shared understanding.

Information Inputs

One measure of a fact base is the extent to which scientific information and expertise is built into the collaborative and its processes. For groups operating at the action level, this may mean ensuring that there are scientific perspectives among the stakeholder group or creating a technical advisory committee. Many of Oregon's watershed councils, for instance, use technical advisory committees to help review restoration project proposals and designs based on sound science. The stakeholders set the goals and objectives for the restoration program, but the technical input ensures that the projects are a sound investment and technically correct.

On a much larger scale, the effort in the Sacramento–San Joaquin rivers basin and estuary (known as CALFED) was underpinned by an attempt to integrate high-quality science into all decision making. There were three different science boards created to support the program, including the Independent Science Board to advise and make recommendations on science for all program elements; the Ecosystem Restoration Science Board to assist management with restoration efforts, and the Water Management Science Board focusing on water supply and quality in all CALFED program elements (Little Hoover Commission 2005). Innes and her colleagues (2006) suggest that the CALFED science efforts signaled a shift from internal agency science to independent science review. Nevertheless, they also noted that the science program has struggled from a lack of funding along with a tension between the positivist approach of the scientists and the more deliberative, negotiated ones of the stakeholders.

Another measure of data quality can be based on procedures for external reviews of collaborative efforts. For example, OWEB convenes a seven-member independent multidisciplinary science team to review watershed council projects. OWEB (2006) also monitors statewide progress in achieving goals through an interdisciplinary monitoring team involving twelve state and federal agencies. In the Columbia River basin, federal agencies and Indian tribes created two scientific groups to review forty-five plans covering the fifty-eight subbasins in the region. For each plan, the review teams evaluated "the likelihood that the plans would succeed in their attempts to recover fish and wildlife," and provided a "general view of the technical merits of the subbasin plans as a whole" (Independent Scientific Review Panel/Independent Scientific Advisory Board 2004).

Shared Understanding

A second key aspect of collaboration products is a shared understanding of the fact base among the stakeholders involved (Beierle and Konisky 2000; McKearnon and Fairman 1999). This is more difficult to assess, because it may be impossible to accurately evaluate whether laypeople understand technical information. There is also not complete agreement about the extent to which technical information *needs* to be understood by all stakeholders. Still, based on my research, I believe some level of understanding among stakeholders is important, and may be critical when technical analysis is central to management and policy decisions.

Connie Ozawa (2005) has examined the role of science in a range of dispute resolution and collaboration processes, and has highlighted criteria for effective processes, including disseminating information regularly, sharing technical expertise, pursuing joint fact finding, publicly clarifying science discrepancies, and monitoring progress. In some cases, stakeholders may identify particular technical questions that they want to refer to a technical team, but often it is essential for them to see both the data and analysis so they can understand these concerns.

For example, when members of the Southern Willamette Valley Groundwater Management Area Committee began reviewing data about nitrates in monitoring wells, the information appeared to be conflicting and confusing. In discussing the data with technical staff, however, committee members learned about geology, the effects of soil types, well depths, and the fate of nitrates over time. These conversations provided some clarity to the members about what was known (such as variations in susceptibility to contamination) and the need to invest in a better monitoring network so the group could track its implementation progress.[13]

In addition to helping stakeholder groups make better decisions, a shared understanding can also influence the individual decisions of stakeholders. To assess this impact, one can analyze the effect of data on organizations' policies, plans, and activities. Local planners in South East Queensland, for example, noted that the collaborative growth management efforts compiled information that had not been brought together before, and this affected the way that local governments looked at environmental planning. The new information raised the awareness of local governments, and, according to a staff member from Logan City Council, it helped them to "look beyond our boundaries." This staff member also stated, "The SEQ process has required local government since 1990 to think as a cohesive unit."[14]

Staff members from both Ipswich and Logan City observed that the data-gathering process also required them to improve communication and information sharing within their councils. One council employee said, "It forced us to respond across council, which made us integrate our information and analysis."[15] The improved quality of information was often apparent when we compared local plans prepared before and after the regional plan process (Margerum 2001b).

Sound Intervention Strategy

A final factor in a high-quality product is a sound intervention strategy; the lack thereof is one of the most common weaknesses I have seen in plans. Because of the difficulties of reaching consensus about goals and actions, stakeholders involved in a collaborative process often fail to adequately address how their plan or agreement will "leverage" change.

In some cases, this failure stems from a lack of planning and public policy insight. In 1995, when I interviewed coordinators and participants in Australian watershed councils, I was struck by their frustration with the plans they had produced. One coordinator pulled out a colorful, nicely written watershed plan, but looked at it with exasperation and said, "I can't understand why it has not been implemented."[16] There was almost an expectation that the plan was self-implementing. The council had done all of the hard work reviewing the information, resolving conflicts, and reaching an agreement, and now it was time for the plan to do its job. But the council had not fully considered an intervention strategy.

In Queensland, the Mackay Whitsunday Natural Resources Management Group has embarked on an ambitious plan to improve water quality that will reduce impacts to the Great Barrier Reef. To accomplish this, it developed a Water Quality Improvement Plan that identifies key targets for a range of pollutants, and allocates those targets back to each of the thirty-three subwatersheds in the region. These targets are then cross-checked with a range of land use practices for the activities in that subcatchment. Major categories of land use that produce pollutants include sugarcane lands, grazing (ranching), horticulture, and urban development. For each of these categories, the organization estimated current management practices and adoption rates, and then projected the changes in both the practices and adoption rates that would be necessary over time to meet the group's objectives. Importantly, it took each of these practices out to groups of landowners and managers within each category to assess the likelihood of adoption, the effort required to adopt new practices, and the private and public costs of adoption. For the horticulture industry, for instance, the group assessed the incentives required for moving from the current practice of applying fertilizer at one rate across the entire crop to more sophisticated techniques of using soil data to apply different rates to different fields, and even using global positioning systems to apply different rates within a field (Drewry,

Higham, and Mitchell 2008). In summary, it is not enough to identify the changes needed. Plans must also determine what actions are necessary to make the changes happen.

Assessing Intervention Approaches

Key issues in assessing intervention approaches are whether the intervention efforts have assigned responsibilities and resources, and whether the intervention approaches are based on a sound theory. I also suggest that intervention approaches should be aligned with the type of collaborative and its capabilities. These factors can be evaluated through an analysis of plans and documents, but often interviews or self-assessments are required to do so.

Assigned Responsibilities and Resources

As noted above, I led an evaluation of local government plans prepared before and after a collaborative regional growth management process. Our plan analysis revealed that many of the issues and ideas had been picked up in the plan, such as the recognition of regional open space. Yet the resources and commitment for implementing the effort varied significantly. For example, Ipswich City Council developed a wide range of programs, and allocated staff and funding to implement them. Beaudesert Shire Council, in contrast, allocated few resources, and its staff noted that the plan had not identified management programs to support these efforts (Margerum and Holland 2000; Margerum 2001b, 2002b).

The failure to allocate responsibilities and resources is a common weakness among the cases I examined. Also problematic is when unrealistic expectations are placed on the collaborative itself. On more than one occasion when I have reviewed action plans, a "coordinator" is listed as the responsible party under almost every action. A coordinator in a watershed south of Sydney noted that this was a significant problem when she took over the committee. The previous coordinator had taken on most of the duties, so that "when anything came up, it got delegated to me. . . . I had to delegate things back, because I was getting burned out."[17]

In order to delegate back to the stakeholder group, there must be people around the table willing to take on responsibilities. This can be difficult when many of the people are volunteers with limited time, or when people from agencies and organizations have competing demands for their time. Thus, assessing intervention strategies often means looking at a plan for the specific allocation of responsibilities, and assessing the commitment of resources and time by stakeholders.

Logical Leverage Points

Another key question to ask of an intervention approach is whether it has a clear set of logical implementation steps that support the plan goals. While this is self-evident for those who have expertise in strategic planning, it is usually not obvious to community volunteers, natural scientists, and groups involved in a complex institutional setting. For example, the Cooks River Catchment Committee's plan of 1993 identified thirty-nine policies that were grouped into high, medium, and low priorities. One of the high priorities assigned to the New South Wales Environmental Protection Authority was: "A strategy is needed to reduce unnecessary and nonbiodegradable packaging" (Cooks River Catchment Management Committee 1993, 35). Another medium-priority implementation item assigned to the eight local governments in the catchment stated: "Efforts must be made to control weed species" (ibid., 36). Both of these implementation activities are laudable and important, but they offer little guidance. They are broadly assigned without a clear explanation of the steps required to carry them out, or the role that the committee will play in helping to make the activities happen. It was also not apparent what steps had to be put in place to ensure organizational commitment.

There are many researchers in the implementation field that emphasize the need to identify the leverage points that will translate current practices into desired practices (Mazmanian and Sabatier 1983; Elmore 1982). This means that participants identify the specific behavior that is generating the need for a response along with the tools that will influence this behavior. These tools are leverage points or intervention strategies. They can range from information campaigns that create change by informing people about the effects of their behavior, to incentive programs that produce change through financial rewards, to formal regulations that help ensure change by enforcing compliance (Margerum and Hooper 2001).

For example, the Wisconsin DNR had a nonpoint watershed program that offered farmers cost sharing for adopting conservation practices. A significant source of pollution was runoff from dairy barnyards. Rainwater flowed through those areas around the barn where the dairy cattle concentrate, and the nutrient-rich runoff went into the local streams, thereby creating quality problems. Studies showed that the most significant reduction in runoff came from the most inexpensive intervention step: installing gutters on barns and redirecting runoff away from the barnyard. The "logical" policy choice would be to spread the limited funds across a wider area by focusing the program on barn gutter installation.

In talking with farmers, though, the DNR staff discovered that farmers weren't motivated to install barn gutters but instead were interested in improving their manure collection areas to make them easier to manage. The staff recognized that getting farmers to agree to the voluntary program meant that installing barn gutters needed to be "packaged" with installing concrete manure collection areas. Thus, there are important links between policy goals, intervention steps that support those goals, and the policies that will induce change.

There are three critical logic connections in developing leverage points (Margerum and Hooper 2001). First, the participants need to determine what behaviors are necessary or must be changed to reach management goals. In the area of air quality management, say, vehicle trips for noncommuting activities like errands, school drop-offs, and events are a growing source of the total number of vehicle trips. Therefore, policies directed at simply changing commuting behavior will address only part of the problem.

Second, the intervention itself must be able to induce the correct kind of behavior or change in behavior. Information campaigns, for example, have often been used by air quality agencies to induce different travel behavior. But when residents live in areas where it is difficult to walk, where public transport is poor, and stores and residential areas are separated by large distances, this information may have little effect on behavior, even among those who want to change.

Third, collaborators need to consider whether the changes in behavior would lead to accomplishing the desired goals. For instance, efforts to reduce emissions through changes in travel behavior need to have realistic assumptions about how much change is necessary to achieve the goal (Elmore 1982; Margerum and Hooper 2001; Mazmanian and Sabatier 1983; Pressman and Wildavsky 1973).

These logic connections can be difficult in a well-developed policy area such as air pollution, and they are frequently even more difficult for collaborative groups. These groups are generally dealing with problems that have not been solved by traditional information, regulations, or incentives. They are addressing concerns that have fallen between existing programs and jurisdictions. Furthermore, they are trying to approach the issues with limited staff or else responsibilities spread across several organizations.

Leverage Points Aligned with Implementation Networks

The other crucial factor in assessing leverage points is to ask whether they are aligned with the networks through which the activities will be implemented. This does not mean that the collaborative itself will be leading all the efforts but rather that the collection of people or organizations sitting around the table match the implementation strategy being developed. This connection between the type of collaborative and its approach are discussed in more detail in chapters 7, 8, and 9, yet it is helpful to preview these issues here.

Many collaboratives are working to implement their activities through their social networks in the community. These networks allow a collaborative to connect its action plans to volunteers and other people interested in implementing actions. It also can help appeal to people who aren't traditionally involved or are not interested in government-led efforts. For example, the Long Tom Watershed Council is composed of landowners, farmers, and other local community leaders. To build off its community networks, it initiated a subwatershed program in which it finds a local landowner to host a meeting, and then invites neighbors to meet with council staff members and volunteers. By tapping into new and existing social networks, the council reached unique audiences with a tailored message and a package of incentives to take action. In Rebecca Flintcroft and her colleagues' description (2009, 36) of the Long Tom, they note:

Project sites are identified using three criteria (in priority order): ecological priority of the location and site potential for restoration success, anticipated commitment of landowners, and social network connections in the neighborhood. Social network connections are important for long-term maintenance of project sites and also to facilitate future work in the subwatershed as neighbors speak positively to neighbors about action.

Other collaboratives are delivering their implementation efforts more through the network of governmental and nongovernmental organizations. The collaborative influences their priorities, programs, and implementation efforts. Australia's Liverpool Plains in northwest New South Wales, for one, was facing significant problems with salinity. The source was naturally saline groundwater that flowed onto the land along the bottoms of hill slopes, destroying the land's capacity. A collaborative group called the Liverpool Plains Land Management Committee helped bring together local landowners and state agencies to fund research, which revealed that removal of native vegetation was one important cause. Deep-rooted trees in upland areas that were tolerant of saline groundwater were replaced with shallow-rooted grasses that did not tap into the groundwater. The groundwater level increased to the point where it intersected with the land downslope, causing salinity damage.

The logical policy goal was to replant native trees, but this approach faced two barriers. First, the upland areas where the trees needed to be planted were not always owned by the same people where the salinity was appearing. Furthermore, planting adequate numbers of trees would require taking pastureland out of production, which many landowners could not afford. The Liverpool Plains Land Management Committee considered land buyouts, but there were no clear sources of funding and little landowner support. As a result, the committee recognized that it needed to find a new way to induce change. So it began exploring agroforestry options with state agencies in the region to determine the types and quantities of trees needed to reduce groundwater levels, the supply area needed to create an agroforestry market, and the government and industry steps needed to secure commitments. Addressing these issues required the group to develop networks for coordinating the programs and efforts of a range of governmental and nongovernmental organizations. The work of the Liverpool Plains committee continues to this day, but it demonstrates the effort and creativity required to translate a goal like "reduce salinity" as well as an intervention step like "plant native trees" into a clear policy that will produce the desired effect.

Collaboratives implementing through networks of political actors and stakeholders are often developing new policies and programs that can address problems with funding, incentives, or regulations. One of the innovative cases of this occurred in the Denver metropolitan region, where local governments all agreed to limit the expansion of urban areas by creating urban growth boundaries. They key issue was not creating the boundaries but rather enforcing them. So through the regional Metro Vision process, local governments decided to use federal transportation funding as an incentive to adopt and maintain this boundary. In other words, without an urban growth boundary, the local governments were unlikely to get federal transportation project funding. The incentives built into this policy were clearly adequate to change local government policies across the region, because all fifty cities and counties adopted an urban growth boundary. A critical element in this instance was that it built off the political network of elected officials to create a regional policy that was linked to federal funding. The ongoing challenge of the effort is to sustain commitment to this policy over time (Margerum 2005).

Discussion

The factors listed above coupled with the approaches to assessing them provide the basis for collaborative participants and external parties to evaluate the products of consensus building. Nevertheless, this discussion also raises some broader implications for those involved in collaboration, and larger questions about the effect of collaboration on governance.

Expectations and Standards

One implication related to high-quality collaboration products is the potential for funding and oversight organizations to improve these outputs by raising expectations, providing guidelines, or offering best practice examples. This is less relevant to unique or one-off collaboration processes, which may need to be judged on a case-by-case basis, but it is quite relevant for governments and foundations funding collaboration efforts on a state or national basis. For example, the Federal Emergency Management Agency developed a checklist of criteria that local hazard mitigation plans had to pass in order for the local government to receive agency approval. This approval is important, because without an approved mitigation plan the local governments have less access to hazard response funding. In our pilot evaluation of natural hazard plans prepared before the new Federal Emergency Management Agency criteria, we found that the plans would have been improved if they had been required to meet the new standards.

There are several challenges with this approach. First, different settings and contexts are unique, so the standards or expectations in one place may be unrealistic in another place. A common example of this is data-rich versus data-poor regions. Remote, rural areas, say, may have little information on which to base decision making, and therefore standards about baseline data and analysis may be unrealistic. The second challenge is that when funding organizations set expectations and standards, collaboratives may be less willing to be forthright with self-assessments and reports because they do not want to be penalized for being honest.

These challenges were highlighted during my work with federal researchers in Australia (Robinson, Taylor, and Margerum 2009). The research examined plans and evaluations prepared by regional natural resources management organizations in response to federal funding criteria. The federal agency developed a set of national environmental objectives, which these regional organizations had to address—whether they were located in remote desert communities, intensive agricultural areas, or heavily populated urban coastal cities.

The data from interviews and focus group meetings revealed that national performance objectives were vague and sometimes inconsistent with regional conditions. Moreover, the Australian government was expecting these newly developed, moderately funded, nongovernmental organizations to report on goals that neither the commonwealth nor the state governments had been able to fulfill previously. The staff members working for these regional organizations described the reporting process as "exhausting," "time-consuming," "requiring an endless effort," and an "overwhelming waste of time" (ibid., 207). And because the reporting process was tied to funding and the national performance reporting was designed to assimilate information across all regional organizations, there was little opportunity for feedback and learning. One staff member for a regional organization observed that if performance assessment was about reporting on success, "how can we learn . . . [including] what to do with failure?" (ibid., 209).

Approaches for Plan Commitment

Another issue that arose in several cases I researched is the issue of how to obtain and sustain commitments to plans produced by the consensus-building process. Chapter 6 discusses the issue of ongoing commitment to implementation in more detail, but I want to briefly mention the approaches to plan commitment here.

One approach is to view commitment as an interpersonal "contract" among participants. Stakeholders participate in a consensus-building process, and agree to attach their names or signatures to the outputs of this process. This may be formalized in a recorded vote or acclamation. As one moves toward the organizational and policy end of the spectrum, though, the role of organizations, interest groups, and formal bodies becomes increasingly important to convey support for an agreement.

For example, the U.S. Forest Service policy of moving administrative staff among offices means that a plan based on the personal commitment of a district ranger may mean little when that person moves to a new job.

More formal mechanisms are often necessary for committing organizations, interest groups, and even governments for two reasons. By requiring a formal cross-approval step, the participating organizations may have to take a much harder look at the products of the process and be more realistic about their commitment. These mechanisms also can have symbolic weight, encouraging organizations to support implementation over time—even when there are changes in the organization's leadership.

Plan commitment mechanisms may take two general forms. The most common is the symbolic commitment of a memorandum of understanding or organizational signature on the plans. In Oregon's Rogue River basin, for instance, one of the products of this process was a memorandum of understanding among the participating organizations. The memorandum had symbolic importance in communicating to agency administrators the support of their predecessors. But it did not prevent the two federal regulatory agencies—the National Marine Fisheries Services and the U.S. Fish and Wildlife Service—from pulling back on their commitment due to budget cuts. These organizations were supportive of the collaborative efforts, but they also had regulatory and legal mandates that took priority.

A second form of commitment relies on legal and regulatory enforcement. The Endangered Species Act requires habitat conservation plans to be scientifically sound, and the plans must have the financial and management commitments in place to ensure implementation. For example, in the Balcones Canyonlands of Texas, an ambitious effort involving federal agencies, state agencies, and local governments produced a habitat conservation plan for more than two dozen species. One of the keys to obtaining approval for this plan was securing the $134 million in land acquisition funding to ensure implementation (Beatley, Fries, and Braun 1995). If the parties to the habitat conservation plan fail to follow through on funding and intervention efforts, approvals for the plan can be revoked. Thus, habitat conservation plans and the resulting agreements bind the participants to the ongoing funding and financing of plan implementation.

Concluding Remarks

This chapter highlights the importance of high-quality products. They are crucial both to those involved in the process of consensus building and those who will work on implementation for years to come. The difficulty of developing products through a consensus-based process also means that these tangible and intangible products are essential to celebrate. I remember visiting a catchment group in Queensland that paused in the middle of its monthly meeting to share a traditional Australian dessert called Pavlova. The group was celebrating the recent completion of its catchment plan, and as the chair prepared to cut the dessert, he commented, "The problem with our work is that we don't produce things that ministers can screw brass plaques into, so we need to celebrate our accomplishments whenever we get the chance."[18]

Still, the products of consensus are only the end point of the first phase of collaboration. As I remarked to a stakeholder group that worked tirelessly for several years to develop its plan, "That was the easy part; now the real work begins." It was clear from their faces that this message was not what they wanted to hear. In the following chapter, I delve into the details of the efforts, approaches, and strategies that allow stakeholder groups to move beyond consensus, translating their plans, programs, and policies into results.

III

Beyond Consensus

6
Sustaining Collaboratives

This book focuses on collaborative efforts that involve ongoing implementation with adaptation based on feedback. The form of these ongoing collaboratives will vary. Some are community-based entities that depend entirely on volunteers. Some collaboratives are associations or nonprofit organizations with employees. Other collaboratives are "sponsored" by one or more organizations through funding or staff secondment. Finally, some are created as government-based collaborative organizations or "collaborative superagencies" (Sabatier, Focht et al. 2005). As ongoing entities, all collaboratives face a range of challenges in sustaining their efforts.

In discussing a collaborative's ongoing role, it is important to recognize that a group may change after the consensus-building phase. In particular, a group that operates at one level in the action-organization-policy spectrum during the consensus-building process may "downshift" to a different level during implementation. In the Lower Wisconsin River case, for example, an intensive, policy level deliberation led to new state legislation, but a regional coordinator and a riverway board direct an ongoing collaborative focused at the organizational level. In these kinds of situations, there is still an ongoing, adaptive management role, but it is focused on the coordination of organizations implementing new policies. Although activities have shifted to an organizational level, there still remains a need for an ongoing entity to support implementation.

One of the implicit assumptions with this discussion is that these collaboratives *should* continue. Clearly, this is not always the case. Some groups may be ineffective or inefficient. Collaboratives therefore must also be judged on their ability to achieve results, which is explored in more detail in chapter 10. The underlying assumption of this chapter is that the collaborative is worth sustaining.

What Do Ongoing Collaboratives Look Like?

Because collaboratives exist in a range of forms, it is helpful to describe some typical examples. This is not an exhaustive list, but looking at these cases helps illustrate the issues they face.

Volunteer Groups: Cloncurry Landcare Group

In his book on Landcare, Campbell describes community-based efforts that emerged in Australia to address land and water conservation. One of the groups he profiles is the Cloncurry Landcare group in Queensland (Campbell 1994). Its history, structure, and organizational issues are typical of many Landcare groups. Cloncurry is a remote and sparsely populated place in a region dominated by beef cattle on grazing (ranching) properties ranging from 15,000 to 200,000 hectares (approximately 37,000 to 494,000 acres). The group emerged from a meeting called by the Cloncurry Shire Council (the local municipality), but it was led by a group of people who agreed to participate on a steering committee.

The leader of the group was Daniel "Bood" Hickson, who is typical of some of the Landcare leaders I have met. He is involved in many other community organizations, tends to think outside the box, and was willing to personally confront bureaucrats to make his case. At one point the group had over 150 members who were addressing several different issues in the region. Over time, however, the group faced declining attendance and burnout issues.

The chronic shortage of people means that the same people are committed to several different organizations, for example the Country Women's Association, Cattlemen's Union, United Graziers Association, Show Society, Rotary, Isolated Children and Parents Association etc, and simply have neither time nor resources to give meaningful support to another organization. (ibid., 86)

The declining attendance and time constraints of the group led it to refocus on fewer issues. The group exists today under the umbrella of the Southern Gulf Natural Resources Management Organization.[1] These new regional natural resources management organizations were created by the Australian government to increase problem-solving capacity at the regional level.

Associations or Nonprofits: Long Tom Watershed Council

The Long Tom Watershed Council is a collaborative group focused on restoring watershed health in Oregon's Southern Willamette Valley. Through my role as a board member, I gained new insights into collaboratives not just as a movement or process but also as an organization with employees, budgets, work plans, and contracts.

Like many collaboratives, the Long Tom is more than just a forum for bringing together diverse stakeholders. It is an ongoing entity that must secure resources to employ its 2.5 employees, support an office, pay for travel and supplies, and maintain communication with stakeholders and the community. Its operating budget for 2007 totaled almost $97,000; $54,000 of that was funded by the OWEB (56 percent) and $43,0000 (44 percent) was funded by a cross section of agency, city, business, and community partners. Over the same year, the council's income for monitoring totaled $49,000, and its budget for projects and restoration efforts was more than $385,000.

One of the reasons that Oregon figures prominently in collaborative watershed efforts is the funding provided by state and federal agencies to support restoration projects along with the ongoing operations of councils. Yet the funding for operations is far more limited than that for projects. With many groups competing for a limited pool of funding, about one-third of the councils in Oregon struggle to perform.[2]

Organizational Partnerships: Rogue River Basin

The Rogue River drains a twenty-two-thousand-square-mile basin in southwest Oregon, which is characterized by rugged mountains, forestry, and farming.[3] The Rogue River is world renowned for its "wild and scenic" white water character, and the basin includes habitat for threatened and endangered species such as steelhead trout, coho salmon, and the northern spotted owl. Eight watershed councils are currently active in the Rogue basin. The mission of these locally organized groups is to improve watershed health through voluntary efforts (OWEB 2004).

The eight watershed councils in the Rogue recognized that their long-term objectives related to the health of the entire basin. Therefore, they came together to create the Rogue Basin Coordinating Council with regular participation from state and federal agencies. The council helps coordinate seven basin priorities, including fish passage, water quality, stream flow, basinwide coordination, interagency cooperation and collaboration, outreach and education, and monitoring.

When Debra Whitall and I analyzed the Rogue Basin Coordinating Council in 2002, its efforts were funded by state and federal grants, but one key to its ongoing operation was the position of a coordinator funded by the U.S. Forest Service and the secondment of staff from other agencies to support the council's work. Participants noted that the coordinator position was important for keeping the project moving and acting as the liaison between the team and the agencies. Craig Tuss of the U.S. Fish and Wildlife Service and Brian Barr of the World Wildlife Fund both commented that this role required someone who could be a liaison as well as someone who could build a team vision and be an advocate for the group.

Collaborating Organization: CALFED and CBDA

The final example comes from the deliberation over water management and restoration of the Sacramento and San Joaquin River basins, which became known as CALFED. The implementation programs were led by an agency called the California Bay-Delta Authority (CBDA), which was established by an act of the state of California in 2003. The CBDA had no direct authority, but it coordinated a cross-cutting budget that by some accounts totaled between $500 and $900 million annually (Little Hoover Commission 2005; Sabatier, Focht et al. 2005; CALFED 2007). It employed a substantial staff, supported an independent science board, and coordinated four CALFED program priorities: ecosystem restoration, water supply reliability, water quality, and levee system integrity.[4] One of the difficulties faced by CBDA has been the failure to obtain long-term funding commitments from either the state of California or the federal government.

Summary

These case snapshots illustrate the range of entities that support collaboration efforts, and the variation in their size and resources. Some of this variation is due to history, stakeholder preferences, context, and other variables. Where the collaborative is located in the action-organizational-policy spectrum, however, often correlates with organization size and capacity. Groups at the policy end of the spectrum are more likely to have significant funding through direct allocation of resources from legislative and executive branches of government (see table 6.1).

Table 6.1
Range of collaboratives

Collaborative type	Case	Entity	Staff*	Funding sources
Policy	Murray Darling	Federal-state commission	≈20	Federal
	CALFED (CBDA)	Federal-state agency	≈30	Federal and state
Organizational	Trinity Inlet	Agency partnership	2–3	State agencies
	Rogue basin	Interorganizational committee	2–3	State agencies
Action	Long Tom Watershed	Nonprofit organization	2	State and other grants
	Cloncurry Landcare	Volunteer group	0	Small federal grants

Note: *Estimates at the time that the research was conducted; actual staff levels for the Murray Darling and CDBA were not available.

Many of the organizational collaboratives rely on fewer staff, with resources contributed by state or federal agencies and other organizations. Finally, groups operating at the action end of the spectrum tend to have a small staff (or no staff), and they rely on grants and contributions from partners. These differences in funding sources are particularly relevant to the issue of sustaining groups through the implementation phase.

Theory Related to Sustaining Collaboratives

It may sound contradictory, but the literature relevant to sustaining collaboratives is incredibly vast while at the same time sparse. By this I mean that there is a significant literature on organizational theory, nonprofit organizations, management, and leadership, but only some of this literature addresses the unique roles and circumstances of collaboratives.

The large organizational theory and management literature covers several subareas that examine issues related to decision making and interorganizational relations. There is also a significant literature in the fields of management, business, and public policy about leadership relevant to collaboratives, such as the roles of boundary spanners, policy entrepreneurs, and facilitative leaders. Finally, the nonprofit literature is particularly relevant, not just because some collaboratives are nonprofits, but also because it addresses issues like board governance and board-staff relationships. Four themes from this literature that relate to collaboratives include the concept of collaborative leadership, the issue of governance, the issue of organizational change as it relates to complex management environments, and external pressure and its impact.

Collaborative Leadership

A theme emerging from the literatures on management, organizations, and public policy is the importance of collaborative leadership (Chrislip and Larson 1994; Huxham and Vangen 2005). Other leadership concepts focus on the characteristics of the individual, the style of the leader, or the relationships between the leader and "the followers" (Northouse 2007). Collaborative leadership—including theories like transformational leadership, facilitative leadership, integrative leadership, and team leadership—views leaders as enablers that allow groups of people to increase their performance through processes of communication and support (Pearce and Sims 2000; Northouse 2007; Morse 2010; Huxham and Vangen 2005; Chrislip and Larson 1994). The leader is seen less in a traditional CEO role, and more in the role of a person who helps convene people, communicate ideas, and allows them to work together effectively (Zaccaro and Klimoski 2001; Burns 1978; Northouse 2007). Crucially, several studies of the public sector highlight that organizational effectiveness requires contributions by leaders at multiple levels rather than just top executives (Fernandez, Cho, and Perry 2010; Dutton et al. 2001).

This does not mean that collaborative leaders are exempt from all traditional leadership actions but instead that the overall style reflects leadership through interaction. In David Chrislip and Carl Larson's book (1994) on collaborative leadership, they stress some key roles for leaders, such as: having commitment from high-level, visible leaders; obtaining the support or acquiescence of established authorities and powers (like city councils and chambers of commerce); and strong leadership of the process rather than strong advocacy for a particular point of view.

Other researchers point out the significance of collaborative leaders as boundary spanners, able to work across different organizations, interests, and people (Huxham and Vangen 2005; Linden 2008). Barbara Crosby and John Bryson (2010, 222) note: "The development of informal leadership is likely to be especially important, since participants often cannot rely on clear cut, easily enforced, centralized direction." Finally, Chris Silvia and Michael McGuire's empirical study (2010) of four hundred emergency managers confirmed some consistent themes about leadership in a network setting, particularly the importance of people-oriented tasks like treating everyone as equals, freely sharing information, and creating trust among participants.

Board Governance

Although not all collaboratives are nonprofit organizations, there are some relevant themes that Kate Bodane (2006) identified from the board governance literature.[5] Boards may take the form of a nonprofit governing board, a steering group for an interagency committee, or a committee of elected officials. While the board training literature emphasizes that boards should set policy and staff should implement it, many empirical researchers note that the distinction is seldom so clear in practice (Wood 1996; Edwards and Cornforth 2003; Rochester 2003; Renz 2004).

A study focused on small nonprofits conducted by the London School of Economics' Centre for Voluntary Organisation found the ambiguity of roles to be particularly prominent in smaller organizations (Rochester 2003). Colin Rochester (ibid., 128) explains that in small nonprofits, "the roles of staff and board are so entwined as to suggest that the functions of governance are carried out by the active elements in the agency rather than reserved to the board."

Rochester attributes this trend to three interrelated problems that confronted the small nonprofits he studied. First, these organizations struggle to recruit and keep board members. Second, board members who serve often lack the capacity to perform all the governance responsibilities. Third, staff directors are too overworked to provide the board with the necessary amount of support (ibid.; Bodane 2006).

The divergence between role prescription and practice is not unique to nonprofits, as shown by Shirley Otto's comparative research on public, private, and nonprofit boards and directors. In Otto's sample, however, role ambiguity was an especially acute issue for nonprofit boards and directors, with respective uncertainty about the "nature/extent of their authority" and "their responsibilities" (Otto 2003, 140). Otto argues that one reason for a nonprofit's comparative difficulty in obtaining role clarity is that nonprofits must negotiate roles between paid staff and volunteer boards. Unlike public and private boards where both boards and staff are paid to perform their duties, a nonprofit introduces different expectations related to being paid or volunteering that complicates the process of defining roles (Otto 2003; Bodane 2006).

Rochester (2003) also notes that small voluntary organizations usually rely on a few actors to do most of the work, but this approach frequently backfires because it creates the potential for turnover to leave a vacuum of institutional knowledge. Ian Byron and Allan Curtis (2002) found volunteer dependence and burnout was common throughout volunteer and community-based organizations in Australia. In addition, even if turnover can be avoided, individuals who try to do everything will likely not be able to keep up the pace indefinitely, and when they do attempt to reduce their contributions, they are plagued by feelings of guilt and failure (Bodane 2006; Byron and Curtis 2002).

Organizational Change
Another theme in the literature addresses the issue of change, and how organizations are able to cope or adapt to it. In several studies of agency involvement in collaborative efforts, researchers have found that organizations are challenged by the new communicative and interactive roles that collaboration requires (Wondolleck and Yaffee 2000; Clark 1993; Doppelt, Shinn, and DeWitt 2002; Cortner and Moote 1999). As a result of these new demands, organizational participation may range from full involvement and participation to little interest. In the former, individuals are fully intended to be organizational representatives, while in the latter the individual is effectively collaborating in their own capacity. "The only contribution from their organizations is the allowance to the individual of the time spent working with the collaboration" (Huxham and Vangen 2005, 130).

Concepts like watershed management and ecosystem management require organizations along with their leaders to work across jurisdictions, share resources and data, and develop joint management approaches. As Jeanne Nienaber Clarke and Daniel McCool (1996) document in their study of federal natural resources organizations, some adapt well to this new environment, and recognize the need for interactive and preventive work, while others recede into a focus on so called "core business." Similarly, the literature on organizational development and management emphasizes the importance of leadership in steering new directions and innovating in the face of change (Chrislip and Larson 1994; Bryson and Crosby 1992). This has led researchers to examine organizational innovation, and people's ability to adapt to new settings and changing conditions (Rogers 2003; Danter et al. 2000; Bonnell and Koontz 2007). This also increases the pressure on organizational representatives to lead their organization's role in collaborating, and Chris Huxham and Siv Vangen (2005, 210) observe that "the practicalities of making this happen are frequently not easily surmounted."

External Pressures for Collaboration

A final theme in the literature is the issue of external pressure and its impact—not just on convening, but also on sustaining participation in a collaborative over time. John Kingdon's contribution (2003) on policy windows and its elaboration by other researchers provide some principles for how external pressures may sustain ongoing activity. Kingdon (2003) asserts that there are three "streams" that flow through a policy system that couple at critical points in time. These streams include problems, policies, and politics. Problems attract policymakers' attention based on factors such as magnitude, feedback loops that bring them to the fore, and dramatic events or crises. Policies are the set of ideas generated by specialists in policy communities that float around and receive attention based on factors such as technical feasibility and value acceptability. Finally, politics consist of forces such as the national mood, pressure group campaigns, and administrative and legislative turnover (Zahariadis 1999).

An important feature of Kingdon's multiple streams (2003) is the coupling argument—where two or more of these streams come together at critical moments in time to produce change. For example, an airplane crash occurs at a time when new policies regarding airline safety are being floated. Kingdon refers to these moments as "policy windows," and states that policy entrepreneurs with the time, energy, reputation, and money can size up the opportunity to initiate action. He also asserts that the policy window is fleeting and the opportunity for action may be lost fairly quickly. Yet Elaine B. Sharp (1994) contends that some windows are continuously activated, because of particular characteristics about the issue. Nikolaos Zahariadis (1999) maintains that when windows are opened in the problem stream, coupling is likely to be consequential—that is, a solution to a given problem is found. When windows are opened in the politics stream, they are likely to be doctrinal—that is, a problem for a given solution is found.

Assessing the Sustainability of Collaboratives

Based on the literature and my research, there are five categories of factors that can be used to assess collaboratives' ability to sustain themselves (see table 6.2). It is important to note that this chapter relies heavily on findings from groups operating at the action and organizational end of the spectrum, though. In general, the issue of sustaining collaboratives has not received much attention in the literature, particularly in relation to policy collaboratives. There is thus clearly a need to further test these concepts and explore their applicability across all collaboratives.

Board Leadership and Capacity

The issues of board leadership and capacity are significant for all types of collaboratives, because they affect the ability of a collaborative to gain access to funding, plan strategically, manage its volunteers or employees, and work effectively. Leadership and capacity are especially acute for groups at the action end of the collaboration spectrum, because these groups often rely on a few volunteers.

My experience on the board of the Long Tom Watershed Council exemplifies some of the leadership and capacity tensions faced by collaboratives. The council is led by a steering committee composed of people from across the region who are representative of the subregions, residents, and organizations in the watershed. At the same time, selecting members with management and organizational skills has also been critical for sustaining the council. As the council transitioned into a nonprofit corporation, we had to revise bylaws, change operating procedures, develop employee manuals, and adjust financial oversight and management roles. This required people with the skills, expertise, and leadership ability to manage an organization, but it was still important to maintain our community connections. The group also faced leadership weaknesses due to illnesses, work changes, and family circumstances that reduced participation on the steering committee, requiring a concerted effort to recruit new board members.[6]

Assessing Leadership and Capacity

Action collaboratives often depend entirely on volunteer support. Organizational collaboratives frequently involve people with management experience, but their experience working in interorganizational settings may vary, and competing demands may limit their time. Finally, policy collaboratives generally have significant professional staff, but may have difficulty sustaining political-level leadership.

For most collaboratives, the ongoing role of facilitating the group does not fall on a professionally trained facilitator or mediator. Instead, the group is led by a

Table 6.2
Assessing the sustainability of collaboratives

Factors	Measures of factors	Related references
Board leadership and capacity: Effective leadership and capacity	• Leaders with collaborative leadership skills; ability to support vertical and horizontal linkages • Board members with management, technical, and other skills	Agranoff and McGuire 2003; Bonnell and Koontz 2007; Weber and Khademian 2008
Collaborative stability: Stable staffing and participation	• Staff experience and tenure • Staff turnover • Relationship between staff and board • Funding levels and diversity	Rosenberg and Margerum 2008; Parker, et al. 2010; Edwards 1991
Information capacity: Information, data, and scientific capacity	• Collaborative as a trusted source of information and data • Information management capacity	Connick and Innes 2003; Heikkila and Gerlak 2005
Commitment: Ongoing commitment by stakeholders and their organizations	• Interpersonal trust and social capital • Benefits exceeding transaction costs demonstrated by allocation of time, resources, or agreements	Huxham and Vangen 2005; Weiss 1987; Logsdon 1991
External pressures: Influences that encourage participants to maintain participation	• Legislation or policy legitimizing or supporting collaborative • Monitoring or reporting puts spotlight on issues • Legal and regulatory pressures • Pressures from elected officials	Thomas 2003; Zahariadis 1999; Kingdon 2003

person—often called the chair—who runs meetings, helps to set the agenda, and usually serves in some administrative capacity for the organization. In their national review of watershed efforts, Stephen Born and Kenneth Genskow (1999, 49) wrote: "All of our cases benefited from strong leadership of individuals who took the initiative, were committed to the concept of a watershed partnership, where influential, possessed networking and coalition-building skills, and stayed active over time."

A key staff person, who is often in the position called coordinator or executive director, typically supports the chair. While this staff person is theoretically supposed to carry out board direction, my research of coordinators and boards revealed that coordinators were taking on a substantial role, including representing the council, developing priorities, maintaining communication within the council, and even introducing new ideas and proposals. These kinds of roles exceed what is usually envisioned for lead staff, but this also confirmed two observations from my case study research. First, the efforts to sustain collaboratives on an ongoing basis require substantial time and energy. Second, stakeholder leadership groups are frequently composed of volunteers who do not have adequate time to provide continuous support. The leadership role, as a result, may be distributed between the chair and the coordinator.

Rochester (2003) points out that in small voluntary organizations, there is an emerging view that a clear boundary cannot be drawn between board and staff roles. Instead, governance is seen as a function or responsibility of the organization as a whole. Similarly, Charles Edwards and Chris Cornforth's study (2003) of boards found that they often focused on the agenda of the executive director and had little involvement in formulating a strategic direction.

Collaborative Leadership

Across the range of my cases and the literature, a common theme is that leadership is important to sustain collaboratives (Agranoff and McGuire 2003; Ansell and Gash 2007; Chrislip and Larson 1994; Silvia and McGuire 2010; Edwards and Cornforth 2003). The principles of a collaborative and facilitated process are addressed in chapter 4, but the nature of leadership usually changes as groups move into an implementation phase. There tends to be a shift in focus after the consensus-building process from deliberations about major directions and options to more detailed implementation issues. As noted in my study of collaborative efforts in Wisconsin, the conflicts that arose during implementation were more likely to involve technical issues than the more interest- and value-based conflicts that arose during the consensus-building phase (Margerum 1995a).

The shift to implementation also means that the leaders of a collaborative have to work to maintain and enhance the networks that support their implementation efforts. These may be the social networks connected through the stakeholders themselves (chapter 7), the interorganizational networks charged with delivering implementation efforts (chapter 8), or the political networks required to sustain a major policy initiative (chapter 9). These networks behave differently, but in all three cases the leaders must work to help build these networks to support the collaborative's implementation attempts.

One assessment factor relates to whether leaders maintain vertical linkages, which depend on communication and interaction with higher-level decision makers (Agranoff and McGuire 2003). For example, the most highly regarded leaders among the Australian catchment committees I studied were not just actively engaging participants in their region but were also interacting with higher-level administrators and elected officials. One farmer who participated on local, regional, and national boards commented, "I farm committees now."[7] In their study of leader behavior in collaborative processes, Edward Weber and Anne Khademian (2008) also highlighted their key role in promoting and advocating for the group and its process. Importantly, this is not vertical interaction to advocate for a personal or organizational perspective; it is an interaction on behalf of the collaborative.

A second factor for assessing leadership and capacity is whether leaders are able to sustain horizontal linkages across the different participants, including those who are not at the table (Agranoff and McGuire 2003; Bonnell and Koontz 2007; Edwards and Cornforth 2003). These linkages are the networks that collaboratives utilize to work across different perspectives and jurisdictions (described in chapters 7–9), and leadership requires some critical interpersonal strategies and skills, such as promoting broad participation, creating trust among participants, freely sharing information, and making credible and convincing decisions that are acceptable to all (Ansell and Gash 2007; Huxham and Vangen 2000; Lasker, Weiss, and Miller 2001; Silvia and McGuire 2010).

The significance of these skills is also illustrated by case study research on the roles of collaborative leaders (Weber and Khademian 2008; Weber 2003), and counterproductive approaches by some leaders underscored the problems it could create.

When analyzing survey responses and interviews of Australian stakeholders grouped by catchment committee, leaders on two committees were consistently criticized. A member of one committee described how the chair allowed his personal bias to dominate group discussions and present his view as the committee's perspective. Another member of the same committee got "fed up" with the group and resigned, shifting her efforts to groups that she thought were more effective.[8]

Several members of another committee noted that their chair did not like community consultation and tended to push only for farming interests. Four of the eight respondents to the survey cited disharmony, parochialism, and politics as one of the most significant inhibitors to the group. One person remarked that "there is a bit of friction between members," and another mentioned a "definite us/them feeling between some members."[9] All committee members were asked to rate the accomplishments of their group, and these two committees were ranked twenty-seventh and twenty-third out of twenty-seven committees.[10]

A third factor is whether the leaders have adequate time and resources to support the effort, which several researchers contend can be significant (Huxham and Vangen 2000; Weber and Khademian 2008; Roberts and King 1996). Nancy Roberts and Paula King (1996) document the personal attributes of entrepreneurial leaders in policy-change processes, and note the need to be tenacious, plus the ability to work long hours and sacrifice a lot of their personal life. The importance of time for leadership was highlighted throughout my case study research, particularly since collaborative groups seek leaders who are already networked into community, interorganizational, or political networks. Critically, as our Oregon watershed study revealed, this leadership role gets shared with coordinators. Although leaders are usually paid for their work, the salaries are often low and grant dependent, and the workload is high. Coordinators used terms like "never-ending," and several studies have documented high rates of burnout among coordinator staff (Parker et al. 2010; Byron and Curtis 2002; Byron, Curtis, and Lockwood 2001).

Board Capacity

Another assessment factor related to board leadership and capacity is the management skills of the board. This is especially an issue for collaboratives at the action end of the spectrum. Boards often must perform a number of formal functions, such as supervising staff, developing bylaws, and overseeing financial reporting. Less tangible but essential roles for boards are developing the vision and direction for the group, communicating with other people and organizations, and contributing to deliberations. Allan Curtis and Penny Cooke (2006) analyzed survey responses from over 340 Landcare participants in Victoria, Australia, and evaluated a range of factors against an index of activity (as a measure of on-the-ground work and capacity building). They found that several leadership and board capacity issues were significantly correlated with the index levels, including people being in leadership positions too long, resources being shared among members of the group, and someone willing to take on group leadership roles.

Figure 6.1 summarizes some of the common skills necessary for boards, which my colleagues and I used to examine the board capacity of watershed councils in Oregon (Parker et al. 2010). When forty-nine coordinators were asked whether leadership tasks were performed predominantly by their boards or the staff, coordinators cited a dominant staff role for most activities, including organizational priorities (59 percent of councils), communication with partners (68 percent of councils), introducing new ideas and content (65 percent of councils), and even

Tasks	Board predominantly does this ← → Staff predominantly does this					n
	1	2	3	4	5	
Managing Projects	2%	2%	6%	19%	71%	49
Managing Personnel	2%	0%	14%	18%	66%	44
Monitoring the Budget	2%	9%	13%	34%	42%	47
Initiating Staff Development	0%	0%	14%	19%	67%	43
Setting the Agenda for Board Meetings	6%	0%	22%	33%	39%	49
Facilitating the Discussion at Board Meetings	15%	23%	32%	15%	15%	47
Taking the Minutes at Board Meetings	17%	13%	4%	9%	57%	47
Recruiting New Board Members	11%	11%	38%	24%	16%	45
Initiating Board Development	2%	5%	30%	35%	28%	43
Fundraising (not grant writing)	3%	10%	17%	25%	45%	40
Representing the Council in a Technical Forum	6%	2%	19%	28%	45%	47
Representing the Council in a Community Forum	2%	2%	47%	25%	25%	49
Representing the Council in Media	2%	2%	24%	29%	43%	49
Maintaining Relationships w/ External Partners	2%	0%	30%	35%	33%	49
Maintaining Relationships w/ Landowners	2%	2%	22%	45%	29%	49
Maintaining Communication within the Council	0%	6%	21%	26%	47%	47
Developing Organizational Priorities	6.5%	6.5%	28%	37%	22%	46
Developing Restoration Project Priorities	6%	8%	37%	33%	16%	49
Contributing Content to Board Meetings	8%	13%	43%	34%	2%	47
Introducing New Ideas and Proposals	0%	4%	31%	47%	18%	49

Figure 6.1
Board versus coordinator distribution of tasks. *Note*: Shading correlates with percent in each category. *Source*: Parker et al. 2010.

contributing content to the discussion (36 percent of councils) (ibid.). This indicated a limited capacity among many watershed council boards.

In Edwards and Cornforth's study (2003, 95), they found a similar difficulty with the ability of boards to offer strategic contributions. One reason they cited was the lack of governance process skills in carrying out their roles, noting that "members had received little training in, or lacked experience of, discriminating between significant and routine information. . . . There was little evidence of board members prioritizing strategic issues for discussion" (ibid).

The study also demonstrated the challenge for collaboratives that have dual goals for board membership. To meet their mandate of being inclusive, collaboratives have to consider both skills (accountant, lawyer, and manager) as well as interests (farming, forestry, and environment). A former coordinator with one of the Oregon groups said that the outlook for finding a good mix of skilled and representative board members is "bleak" (Parker et al. 2010, 481). In more populated areas, watershed councils are better able to satisfy both conditions, but in many rural watersheds, simply recruiting and retaining representative volunteers is difficult. The emphasis on representation can even lead to the recruitment of board members who have limited commitment to the council's work. As one coordinator commented, "It's totally different than when people join a board because they are passionate about the issue versus when you are a farmer and someone says, we need a farmer, come join the council!" (Parker et al. 2010, 481).

Finally, while much of this discussion has focused on collaboratives toward the action end of the spectrum, board capacity can also be an issue for organizational and policy collaboratives. The issues have less to do with survival, and more to do with board capabilities and time. For example, DRCOG is a metropolitan planning organization that has led collaborative growth management efforts. But its leadership depends on participation and engagement from over fifty local governments in the region, all of which have their own busy local political agendas. When these competing forums are combined with elected official turnover and the steep learning curve about regional issues, maintaining the capacity of the board becomes an enormous challenge.

Collaborative Stability

A second factor important to sustaining organizations is the stability of the collaborative. In discussions and research on collaboration, considerable attention has been focused on the stakeholders. These individuals are crucial because reaching consensus and translating it into results ultimately depends on their efforts. Yet the role of the collaborative "entity" and its staff is often overlooked. This role becomes increasingly important after a group reaches consensus, because staff members follow through on the details of implementation, manage the finances and personnel, and maintain communication with the stakeholders and the myriad of interested parties.

As noted above, the collaborative entity can take a variety of forms: an informal group composed entirely of volunteers, a nonprofit organization, a government partnership, or a new government organization. Stability refers to the ability of a collaborative entity to maintain high-quality staff with good experience, limit staff turnover, and develop adequate levels and diversity of funding that allows the entity to support its efforts. Instability places greater pressure on the stakeholders to manage the entity along with its staff and finances. Transitions also consume time and energy, reducing the time that people have to work on producing results. Finally, staff turnover breaks down relationships and the trust that has been built around them (Parker et al. 2010; Rosenberg 2005).

One of the common reasons for turnover is burnout among staff members. Byron and Curtis have studied burnout among community-based Landcare conservation group members, and found that staff members were in their current position for a median of fifteen months, and 60 percent of them had no prior experience as a coordinator or facilitator. Based on scaled indicators of burnout, Byron and Curtis (2002) found that 53 percent were classified as having high levels of burnout, over two-thirds indicated their contract hours were not adequate for the services expected, and 74 percent felt they were being pulled in too many directions.

In our study of Oregon watershed coordinators, the forty-eight coordinators who responded to our survey indicated that they had served a mean of 3.7 years, with tenure ranging from 10 years to a few days. At the time of our study, we estimated that 38 percent of watershed councils in Oregon had experienced coordinator turnover within the previous four years. Our interviews with fifteen former coordinators highlighted several reasons for leaving, including compensation and job security, personal reasons, and career advancement opportunities. Burnout was a secondary issue for a few coordinators, but six of fifteen listed poor relationships with their board as a factor in their departure (Parker et al. 2010). Among the coordinators who were serving at the time, relationships and work responsibilities figured most prominently in the factors they cited as being important to job satisfaction (see figure 6.2).

Assessing Stability

Because collaboratives build relationships across people and jurisdictions, stability is critical. This issue is relevant for all types of organizations, but particularly for collaboratives at the action and organizational range of the spectrum. These groups often employ only one or two staff members, and their experience and rate of turnover are indicators of stability.

Experience is essential for the coordinator, because less experienced people will take more time learning on the job and are more likely to make mistakes. In my research on Australian catchment groups, participants described their coordinator with phrases such as "the glue that holds the committee together." They were not simply there to facilitate a process; they were like program managers. They comprised an integral part of the institutional history, and provided lead roles in consensus building and implementation (Margerum 2002a).

High rates of coordinator turnover in a collaborative can indicate instability. Turnover can also affect the momentum, capacity, and reputation of the collaborative. For example, Rosenberg's study of landowners in Oregon watersheds found that one of the key factors for landowner participation in conservation projects was the trust they developed with outreach staff from the watershed council. The landowners wanted professional staff members who were experienced and could

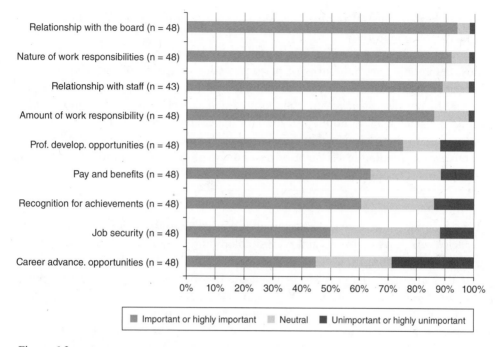

Figure 6.2
Factors important to coordinator job satisfaction. *Source:* Parker et al. 2010.

understand the need to accommodate the production needs of an agricultural property. When these staff members left a watershed council, it took time to rebuild these relationships (Rosenberg 2005).

Another indicator of sustainability is a good relationship between the staff members and the board of the collaborative. Research on job satisfaction suggests that people in coordinator type of roles may be more inclined to accept trade-offs in some areas of their job in exchange for qualities of greater significance (Edwards 1991; Maslach, Schaufeli, and Leter 2001). As shown in figure 6.2, Oregon coordinators rated their relationship with their board as highly important, and several interviewees indicated it was a counterbalance to less desirable aspects of the job:

My relationship with the board is excellent and I would not continue in this position if it were not. The challenges of funds and level of funding for the position would not warrant dealing with difficult board members! (Parker et al. 2010, 477)

Nobody is getting rich doing this, and the compensation is fairly moderate, so basically if I don't have some level of respect and professional latitude to do it, I would go somewhere else. (Parker et al. 2010, 477)

A final indicator of a stable collaborative across all action, organizational, and policy collaboratives is consistent and adequate funding. This funding is needed to support key administrative functions, such as coordinating programs and delivering implementation efforts.

When I surveyed Australian catchment committees in the mid-1990s, one of the most commonly cited inhibitors of progress was a lack of resources—not just for implementation activities, but also for supporting the group's operations (Margerum 1996). In my discussions with collaboratives that depend on grants and agency funding, participants in both Australia and the United States cited the importance of funding diversity. Groups that depend on one funding source are more vulnerable to changes in funding levels or priorities. Furthermore, organizations that support collaboratives financially often contribute other forms of support.

Information Capacity

A third factor for assessing the sustainability of collaboratives is their information capacity, which refers to the ability of a collaborative to serve an ongoing role in gathering, combining, collecting, and analyzing data. Collaboratives are unique in that they approach the problem through the lens of a diverse set of stakeholders and organizations, rather than through a single perspective. For example, a collaborative may assemble information from agricultural organizations, environmental interest groups, industry associations, environmental regulation agencies, local governments, and citizen monitors. This creates a shared set of information that is more comprehensive and integrated than the information held by any one organization or individual. Furthermore, shared analysis and interpretation of this information by a diverse set of participants will provide a better basis for management and decision making (Innes 1998; Cortner and Moote 1999).

High-quality data are noted as an important product of consensus building, but they are also relevant to sustaining collaboratives for two reasons. First, information gaps and problem complexity mean that a full understanding of the system frequently takes many years. Information gathering therefore must be an ongoing task of a collaborative rather than a one-off process. Second, the data collection role of the collaborative requires it to develop information capacity, including scientific expertise, systems for managing the data, and processes for updating it. If there is an adaptive approach to management, it also must be able to feed this information back to decision makers.

One crucial basis of decision making for the Long Tom Watershed Council, for instance, is an assessment that identifies problems and priorities in the watershed. The assessment was developed through a water quality monitoring program run by the council with funding from OWEB. At eighteen baseline sites, volunteers and the monitoring coordinator measured water temperature, dissolved oxygen, turbidity, conductivity, E. coli, nutrients, and suspended solids. The program has also collected data on macroinvertebrates (e.g., insects, crustaceans, worms, and mollusks), which provide important indicators of ecosystem health and biodiversity. These kinds of baseline data help the council target its work and ensure that restoration projects are selected for valid scientific reasons. Moreover, the water quality data and information is a critical part of outreach efforts; the council shares it with landowners to explain resource problems and potential restoration projects.[11]

A similar kind of data assembly process occurred in the Rogue River basin. Eight watershed councils and four federal agencies combined data from a broad cross section of sources to develop an adaptive management model for the basin. The model allows for the adaptive management of the ecosystem and provides guidance on management priorities for a wide range of decision makers, from federal land management agencies to private landowners (Margerum and Whitall 2004).

Similarly, CALFED led to the creation of a science program that assists state agencies, not by conducting science, but instead by integrating and managing science activities with a focus on the big picture (Heikkila and Gerlak 2005; Little Hoover Commission 2005). Sarah Connick and Judith Innes (2003) note that CALFED created several data assessment teams of technical experts from a diversity of stakeholder groups. This information was designed to feed into an "Operations Group" that could respond with specific management responses.

Assessing Information Capacity

A collaborative's capacity to gather, assemble, integrate, and analyze information will vary depending on the scale and complexity of the system it is managing. At the same time, all collaboratives can be assessed in terms of their information capacity.

One indication of information capacity is that the collaborative becomes a recognized and trusted source of information. This role often emerges because no one organization or entity is addressing the issues in a comprehensive or integrated fashion (Heikkila and Gerlak 2005; Connick and Innes 2003). This role also emerges because the collaborative produces information that is less likely to be partisan, and more likely to consider the range of implications and interpretations. In practical terms, this means that the collaborative is sought out for information and analysis; data collected by the collaborative is used by other organizations and agencies; and the collaborative produces reports and documents that are widely cited and used.

A second indication is that the collaborative develops an internal capacity to interpret and analyze information. The nature of this capacity will vary depending on the resources, level, and geographic scale of the collaborative. With a smaller-scale, action-level group like the Long Tom Watershed Council, its capacity may rest in a projects and monitoring officer along with a technical team composed of agency and academic specialists. The projects and monitoring officer brings data, reports, and monitoring plans to the technical team for review and input, which helps ensure that the group's analysis and data are sound. It also means that these agencies can use the data for their own purposes after they have been collected.

The policy-level group CALFED attempted to assume a key information capacity role through the creation of a science program. A lead scientist employed by the CBDA directed the program, and an eleven-member independent scientific review panel in turn supported the scientist. The panel's role was to provide an independent and objective view of the science issues underlying important policy decisions for the Bay-Delta (CALFED 2007). One of the concerns raised in the Little Hoover Commission review of CALFED, though, was the lack of data incorporated into CALFED programs. The Little Hoover Commission (2005) noted several difficulties faced by the program, including the complexity of the system, the lack of consensus on indicators, the inadequacy of monitoring infrastructure, and the difficulty of communicating data.

Commitment to Collaboratives

A fourth factor in assessing the sustainability of collaboratives is stakeholder commitment to the collaborative and its ongoing governance. The issue of commitment is also referenced in the chapters on consensus building and high-quality plans, so why is commitment an issue with sustaining collaboratives?

After consensus building there is often the relief, euphoria, and satisfaction related to producing a plan, strategy, or agreement, which can sometimes lead participants to view the process as being "over" and thus disengage. Yet ongoing consensus building is generally needed throughout implementation (Innes 1994; Margerum 1999b; Selin and Chavez 1995). New information comes to light, different challenges emerge, and perhaps most significantly, there are details encountered during implementation that raise new questions and debates. An ongoing role also relates to the tendency for participants to change over time, which requires new efforts to share perspectives and build trust. Finally, ongoing roles in sustaining collaboratives are more mundane, because they are frequently about management, overseeing budgets, providing leadership, and keeping the entity going. A group can lose momentum, which can result in a drop-off in participation and commitment (Linden 2008).

The issue of ongoing commitment has been one that I have explored in case studies for several years, and the one consistent theme was that ongoing commitment to the group could vary significantly. Some reasons for commitment are linked to organizational resources, costs, and benefits. For example, agency commitment in the Lake Winnebago system project was clearly linked to the costs and benefits of participation. For staff members from the Wisconsin Department of Agriculture, the issues being addressed were important, but their staff representative described his participation as moderate:

I felt I should be familiar with what was going on, but often I would skip meetings that I felt were not directly relevant. . . . There are five programs there and twenty-five others across the state, which is why I had to pick and choose. Our main problem is not having enough staff to work on all the projects.[12]

In contrast, a staff member for one of the county land and water conservation districts noted that they felt like a partner in the project, and "were very positive about the project" because it led to the designation of a priority watershed in their county.[13] This was a key source of state funding for county conservation efforts, so there were clearly recognized financial benefits.

Other reasons for commitment relate more to the personal dedication level of stakeholders. A catchment committee in the Sydney region had representatives from several local governments whose participation ranged from strong partners to almost nonparticipants. One city had an elected representative on the committee who was extremely involved and lobbied other councilors to support its work. Similarly, the city manager of another city was supportive, and encouraged the council to contribute funding and adopt policies. A planning department manager, in contrast, represented a neighboring city, and usually sent junior staff members on his behalf. The catchment coordinator commented, "The manager of planning is not really concerned about being involved with catchment management committees. I think there must be some turf concerns with him, but as a result we have had very little interaction with [the city]."[14]

Assessing Commitment

The factors and decision processes that determine commitment are not entirely clear. Jeanne M. Logsdon (1991) argues that the two essential preconditions to participation are perceived interdependence with other parties and high stakes for the potential participant. A lack of commitment may also be due to a tendency for some organizations to limit their concern to specific legislative functions, or the preference among some to "go it alone" regardless of the financial calculations of costs or benefits (Guruswamy 1989; Weiss 1987, 103).

Many researchers of collaborative forums emphasize that transaction costs are an important variable in determining commitment. These costs include the resources required for participation and the costs of delay. For example, Daniel Connell contends that one of the problems with the Murray Darling Basin Commission was the high transaction costs. For the Living Murray project, the six signing governments agreed to commit five hundred million dollars for implementation, but rather than consolidating this into a central fund, each government could nominate and implement projects that met defined criteria. They could also invest in each other's projects up to set limits. "Satisfying the State demand to maintain the maximum possible degree of autonomy took precedent over operational efficiency. . . . The required result is six compatible systems of registration" (Connell 2007, 168).

Stakeholder commitment to a collaborative effort can be quickly assessed through factors such as representation and the attendance of those representatives, but this often does not reflect the overall commitment of an individual or organization. Other indicators of commitment include interpersonal dynamics and benefits that exceed transaction costs.

Interpersonal Dynamics

One of the "secondary outcomes" of consensus building that researchers usually examine is the extent to which a collaborative creates interpersonal trust. Innes and her colleagues (1994, ix) refer to this mutually derived momentum as "shared capital," and emphasize that it is important not only for reaching consensus but also supporting implementation. For example, many Australian catchment management committees were effective in bringing together a variety of stakeholders, and fostering a shared understanding of problems, goals, and possible solutions. In catchments such as the Johnstone River in Queensland and Georges River in Sydney, the process engaged a range of parties with different and conflicting views, and identified joint goals that they could work toward.

Leach, Pelkey, and Sabatier (2002) studied the specific question of trust and social capital among watershed partnerships in seventy-six cases in the states of California and Washington. For groups older than three years, they found a positive and statistically significant relationship between trust and their evaluations of the partnership.[15]

Another finding from my U.S. and Australian research that related to interpersonal dynamics was the significance of people who were dedicated to the effort, and willing to act as an advocate within their organization. A Wisconsin DNR fisheries supervisor suggested that team attitude was the single most important factor to successful collaboration:

The only way [collaboration] can be put into practice is through the lowest level of the administrative tree. Unless a quality team is developed that can work together, it can't happen. No plan or paper can make it happen without a quality team at the lowest level.[16]

Similarly, a central administrator for the DNR stressed the commitment of the staff:

If you asked me what was most important, I would say the quality of the people chosen for the project and the fact that all groups were represented. . . . You have to pick carefully in terms of the quality of the people; the mistakes were overcome because of the quality of the people.[17]

Although personal dynamics are critical, they have limitations—particularly when the individuals represent organizations. People often move, change jobs, or shift responsibilities within organizations. When organizational commitment is entirely dependent on interpersonal trust, the loss of an individual can mean the withdrawal of the organization from the collaborative (Huxham and Vangen 2005). Therefore, it is essential to consider other factors that may commit organizations to collaborative efforts.

Benefits Exceed Transaction Costs

Community members who takes time out of their schedule and spends money to drive to a meeting is indicating a certain level of commitment to a collaborative as an ongoing forum. Likewise, organizations that maintain their involvement and/or provide resources demonstrate that they are willing to help sustain the group. This ongoing involvement shows that individuals or organizations view their allocation of time, resources, and funding to the collaborative group as worthwhile given the benefits of the forum. In turn, decreased attendance and participation over time is an indication that the perceived benefits are waning relative to the transaction costs.

Second, transaction costs may be overcome by allocating resources to the collaborative enterprise. The transaction problems pointed out by Connell about the Murray Darling basin were overcome in the Trinity Inlet by committing money up front. Rather than requiring it to solicit funding from participating agencies for each project or activity, the Trinity Inlet Program had an annual budget to spend across its set of implementation activities. This meant that the managers working TIMP activities had a sum of money to reallocate according to joint objectives. This helped ensure that projects and programs would not fall between organizational jurisdictions, or be dropped through changes in organizational priorities. This also creates a tangible incentive for these organizations to fully commit staff time and resources to the collaborative.

A third indicator of benefits exceeding costs is that the forum develops an ability to create win-win scenarios to alleviate impacts. Because stakeholders will "shop" among a range of venues, it is important that participants view the collaborative as a valuable forum for solving problems. Thus, I suggest that while transaction costs are critical, participants will often place far more weight on the substantive benefits they can gain from implementation. Collaboratives can be more attractive when they effectively allow participants to explore issues, concerns, and solutions. In a review of collaborative efforts in the San Francisco estuary, CALFED, and Sacramento Water Forum, Connick and Innes (2003, 187) assert:

Collaborative dialogues can produce high-quality agreements that genuinely alleviate, if not solve, problems; are widely acceptable among the parties whose support is needed, and among the public; and are practical and implementable. These agreements do so because they have the benefit of so many different perspectives and types of knowledge, which makes them more likely to be feasible and robust.

Conversely, critics of the CALFED process argue that it failed because it could not overcome the zero-sum game related to the ecosystem's goods and services

(Hanemann and Dyckman 2009). The win-win scenarios that were developed depended on enormous state subsidies that the collaborative process could not deliver (Kallis, Kiparsky, and Norgaard 2010). As a result, several observers contend that deliberations could not resolve fundamental conflicts and instead the efforts tinkered at the edges (ibid.; Hanemann and Dyckman 2009).

External Influences

A final factor in assessing the ability of collaboratives to sustain their efforts is the external pressures and influences that help keep people and organizations involved. Collaboratives often emerge in response to a perceived problem, crisis, stalemate, or directive from administrative, legal, or legislative sources. These pressures help to create a sense of urgency that gets stakeholders to the table and deliberating. Yet these pressures can change over time. The key question is what happens after stakeholders shift into implementation mode.

The public policy research tends to focus more on the factors leading to initial policy change or management reform (Kingdon 2003; Zahariadis 1999; Roberts and King 1996), and less on the need for ongoing involvement. The indications from my research are that the extent to which external influences continue to provide pressures and incentives is an important factor in motivating stakeholders to stay at the table.

The Rogue basin and Trinity Inlet cases both illustrate the role of external influences on sustaining a collaborative. In the Rogue basin, the Endangered Species Act loomed over all the participants, creating a strong incentive to develop demonstrable results. Also, OWEB allocated additional funding for basin and regional approaches to watershed restoration, citing the Rogue basin as a regional model.[18]

In the Trinity Inlet, strong public concern about development and impacts to the inlet were key motivators. In the 1990s, interestingly, several participants thought the program might become a victim of its own success as the public became more complacent about the threats to the inlet. In fact, a former coordinator with the program predicted that it would die a slow death "until the next crisis," when people would suddenly realize what they had lost.[19]

Assessing External Influences

Several external influences appear to help sustain individual and organizational commitment. Legislation or policy that legitimizes, supports, or funds collaboratives is one indicator of increasing commitment by governmental and nongovernmental organizations. When catchment management efforts were begun in Queensland, state policy was important for legitimizing the role of these groups and providing the funding to help them operate. The Oregon Plan for Salmon and Watersheds also established the framework and funding to support watershed councils in their restoration attempts. In both Queensland and Oregon, there were already collaborative groups emerging to address local problems, but having a statewide framework and funding helped catalyze as well as sustain many groups across the state. For some policy collaboratives, legislation may establish the powers, structure, and funding of a specific collaborative. Both the CBDA (the CALFED lead organization) and the Murray Darling Basin Commission, for instance, were created through legislative and administrative action. Conversely, reduced funding from the California legislature for CALFED has been a signal of waning commitment.

A second set of factors relate to monitoring, reporting, and oversight. This might include monitoring by the courts, media, legislative bodies, and other public entities. External monitors might be built into the system, or they might occur in response to scientific findings or an independent investigation. For example, in Oregon environmental groups have maintained pressure on the Oregon Plan through reports and evaluations about the progress of the collaborative efforts in restoring fish habitat and watershed health (Sommarstrom 1999). The collaborative itself may play a role in assessment and monitoring. For example, collaboratives working in the Milwaukee river basin of Wisconsin and the Mackay Whitsunday area of Australia produced annual report cards on watershed health.

A third set of factors relates to legal and regulatory pressures. In Craig Thomas's analysis (2003, 267) of the factors explaining agency cooperation in collaboration efforts, he remarks that it was not just important to have listed endangered species in the agency's region but that agency officials also had to believe it would be enforced against them: "Without the impending threat of a lawsuit that might constrain management autonomy, the presence of listed species did not prompt cooperation from line managers." This conclusion is supported by my interviews with both U.S. and Australian agency staff members, who often had to prioritize their involvement. They often described this using terms such as focusing on "the issues on the front burner." For example, in the Rogue basin, participation by the regulatory agencies was frequently variable due to resource and staffing constraints. In contrast, the federal land management agencies—the Bureau of Land Management and the U.S. Forest Service—were the most strongly committed to the efforts, because "the Northwest Forest Plan has required the BLM and the Forest Service to address fish habitat."[20]

A final set of factors relates to external pressures from elected officials, the public, and the media. The public policy literature notes that attention from elected officials, interest groups, and others raises the stakes by putting pressure on participants to accomplish tasks (Zahariadis 1999). For instance, ongoing media coverage may sustain attention to a problem and motivate participants.

In Australia's Murray Darling basin, public interest in crises has been key in applying external pressures for action. In December 1991, for example, a 1,000-kilometers-long (1,610 miles) blue-green algae bloom along the Darling River attracted widespread public and media attention. As John Pigram (2007, 97) observed, "This crisis and the state of emergency that followed raised public awareness of the vulnerability of Australia's inland river systems. Subsequently, a nutrient management strategy was developed and a National Water Quality Strategies adopted in 1992." Over time, the focus on the basin waned as new issues reached the top of the public and political agenda. Nevertheless, with the extended droughts that began around 2000, the system attracted new concern, leading to increased public and media criticism of the efforts by the Ministerial Council. The result was a restructuring of state and national powers in 2008, which effectively ended the collaborative approach in the basin.

In my research on the collaborative growth management efforts in the Denver metropolitan area, one of the pressures was the perception that population growth was leading to a loss of quality of life. There had been growing media attention, and interest groups raised these concerns in legislative and public forums. A survey of elected officials revealed that this external pressure was crucial for bringing a wide range of local governments together to develop the regional growth management plan, which was called Metro Vision 2020. When asked about support for the regional plan, one elected official mentioned the importance of these external pressures:

Yes, sufficient political support exists across the region to implement Metro Vision 2020, because: a) anti-sprawl sentiment is strong throughout the region; b) strong support for preservation of mountain views and open space all along the Front Range; c) traffic congestion irritates everyone and creates air pollution; d) realization of the need to effectively manage water resources as demand continues to increase.[21]

Discussion

The factors cited above are helpful for assessing collaboratives and their likelihood of being sustained. Yet the more important question is how to address weaknesses or shortcomings to improve management. These factors also raise larger issues about information management, the relationships between collaboratives and participating organizations, and collaborative success and failure.

Improving the Leadership of Collaboratives

Collaborative leadership was noted as a critical factor affecting success. The issue for collaboratives, evaluators, and funders is how leadership can be improved and enhanced. There are at least three areas where collaboratives can focus efforts to improve leadership: enhancing board leadership, clarifying coordinator responsibilities, and improving governance.

Enhancing Board Leadership

When a board is facing turnover or has limited capacity, collaboratives may need to take steps to enhance their board leadership. The literature on nonprofit boards indicates that it is the lead staff person's responsibility to support board members by ensuring that they have the skills and resources to do their jobs well (Parker et al. 2010; Herman 1989). More than half of the Oregon watershed coordinators we surveyed reported that they initiate board development. They also reported that time and interest by the board was a limiting factor. Relatively few coordinators had backgrounds in nonprofit management. Thus, training and professional development is a significant part of sustaining many collaboratives.

It is also important for collaboratives to prepare for transitions in their leadership group. One strategy is to foster leadership within groups through experience and mentoring. Several researchers have noted that collaboratives play a role in developing leadership capacity, particularly in smaller and rural communities (Wondolleck and Yaffee 2000). Leadership development may also include governmental and nongovernmental stakeholders. For example, several board members on one Oregon watershed council moved through a sequence of being a volunteer, subcommittee member, and then board member, and finally part of the board leadership group. The CEO of an agricultural company that supported a council commented that their employee had shown substantial leadership growth through their positions with the council.[22]

An implication for board members representing organizations is that they need to ensure their organization continues to support the collaborative. This was a concern among several Australian catchment management committees that I observed. When agency or local government representatives resigned from a committee due to a job change or move, it was important to ensure that they found a suitable replacement. One committee confronted poor representation from a state agency by sending a team of committee members to the administrator to request more support. Similarly, several watershed coordinators in Oregon have informally lobbied cities and agencies to make certain that their representatives were senior enough to bring crucial leadership skills and knowledge of the organization's strategic direction.

Clarifying Coordinator Responsibilities

Our study of Oregon watershed coordinators highlighted that the clarity of their responsibilities had an important effect on job satisfaction and turnover (Parker et al. 2010).[23] This issue is particularly acute among collaboratives at the action and organizational end of the spectrum, where the coordination staff may be comprised of one or two people. Written job descriptions, contracts, and work plans are frequently utilized as part of the hiring and training process, but the effectiveness of these documents can be hampered if they do not meet certain criteria (Lyons 1971; Edwards 1991; Otto 2003; Rochester 2003).

First, there needs to be a shared understanding among the board members about role expectations. Current and former coordinators indicated that problems arose when board members had not come to consensus regarding expectations, which resulted in inconsistent and unexpected demands.

Second, coordinators emphasized that written descriptions should be based on a practical assessment of the work that is required to accomplish the council's goals and objectives. A lack of knowledge about what is necessary to meet council objectives can result in overlooked and underbudgeted tasks.

Third, it may be important to have a written description of coordinator responsibilities developed through a process of consultation between the board and the coordinator, as opposed to development by one and acknowledgment by the other (Maslach, Schaufeli, and Leter 2001). A joint process not only helps to further the role clarity between boards and coordinators but it also provides a simultaneous opportunity for the negotiation of substantive issues (e.g., opportunities for professional development) that will lead to a better person-job fit. In other words, the process of going through such a document is just as essential as the document itself.

Finally, coordinators stressed that clarifying board responsibilities can be important for addressing workload. Several experienced coordinators mentioned the need to say "no" to some demands, being "brutal" or "ruthless" about prioritizing, and planning for only 80 percent of their time to allow for contingencies (Parker et al. 2010, 479). For some coordinators, having the latitude from the board to independently make strategic prioritizations is key to their workload management and job satisfaction. This is difficult, though, if coordinators do not have clear direction about their responsibilities. Some coordinators chose to share their prioritizing predicaments with their board, so that board members were aware of competing demands and trade-offs. This can produce more manageable workloads, more realistic board expectations, and reduced feelings of regret by the coordinator for tasks they cannot complete (Wolfred, Allison, and Masaoka 1999). But prioritizing did not always eliminate the problem. As one coordinator commented, "Sometimes they [board members] help me prioritize, but they don't get rid of anything on the list!" (quoted in Parker et al. 2010).

Improving the Governance of Collaboratives

Closely related to the issue of coordinator responsibilities is that of board and coordinator roles in governing the collaborative, including leadership, latitude, and oversight. In our Oregon study, some coordinators said their boards clearly outlined the actions that required board oversight and the actions they could take independently (Parker et al. 2010). Yet for the majority of interviewees this was not the case. Notably, several former coordinators suggested that having clearer role definition could have significantly improved their relationship with their former board. The more commonly described experience was an exploratory method of finding boundaries with the board that took time and often led to frustration. As one new coordinator still going through that process put it, "I don't know what I am allowed to make decisions on without their explicit approval" (Parker et al. 2010, 480). This issue also arose across a range of collaboratives. The executive director of the San Diego Association of Governments made a concerted effort to push elected officials toward driving the agenda and assuming an active role in decision making.[24]

Clarifying coordinator and board roles is particularly important during staff transitions. Carol Weisman and Richard Goldbaum (2004) highlight that overlap of staff members is critical for personnel and governance issues, because these issues are specific to the organization. These transitions tend to be more successful when time limits and goals for training are identified in advance. The hiring of a new coordinator is also an opportunity for a board to review the job requirements and ensure that there is internal consensus about the expectations for the new employee.

The decision to hire a new coordinator may be the result of a shift in the council's needs, and it can be an opportunity to recruit someone with a different set of skills, fresh ideas, and new energy (ibid.). When boards and coordinators do not initially discuss their respective expectations, the potential is great for not meeting them. When boards and staff cross roles, argue Weisman and Goldbaum (ibid.), it is a sign of weak trust and respect between them.

Multiple Oregon coordinators reported that they came to the position with the expectation that their board would provide more explicit direction, and this was frequently cited as a change they would like to see. Other coordinators discussed different expectations that were not met:

My struggles with it were more about the expectations of how watershed councils were supposed to work versus how it worked. The expectations on watershed councils are really huge; it's hard for the average board to live up to it. The work plan is so much more than what the staff can do, and there is the expectation that most will be done through volunteers and members. . . . Then coordinators get frustrated with their boards because they don't do everything you expect a watershed council to do. (Parker et al. 2010, 480)

Many coordinators used a gradual process of identifying expectations with their board. Participants in the Denver Metro visioning process also noted that collaborative efforts had improved significantly when the regional planning agency hired a new director with a more communicative and facilitative style. Similarly, the Little Hoover Commission review (2005) of the CALFED program emphasized the need for leadership with stronger negotiation and facilitation skills. For collaboratives with high turnover, however, coordinators may not be in a position long enough to improve their board relationship through trial and error. This suggests that discussions about governance should be held early during a coordinator's tenure and must be revisited when there is board member turnover. Clarifying governance responsibilities ultimately requires a collaborative to carefully consider its expectations and needs. As one former coordinator noted, "Often they [boards] have an idea of how they need a certain kind of person; but they really need this other kind of person" (Parker et al. 2010, 480).

Finally, improving governance may require ongoing efforts among the board and staff leaders to be strategic in their approach to sustaining the group. In addition to the traditional perspective of collaborative leadership that involves embracing, empowering, involving, and mobilizing, Huxham and Vangen (2005, 228) offer an alternative perspective that they call "collaborative thuggery." They contend that this more controversial view of collaborative leadership is often required to address participants not willing to work together or play the politics that inevitably become part of many processes. This kind of terminology is likely to raise suspicions about collaboration, especially among those less powerful interests who are more vulnerable to being pressured or squeezed out of a process. Still, Crosby and Bryson (2010) describe similar sets of strategies using more benign terminology, such as leaders who are skilled at process, promoters of change, and politically savvy. They depict leadership as being a champion of the process, and not being too wedded to a specific problem or solution, which requires some maneuvering to keep collaboratives operating.

As noted in the deliberation discussion (chapter 4), leaders in several of the cases I researched thought strategically (or politically) about who they invited to meetings, where and when they timed events, and who they asked to cut ribbons (i.e., dedicate projects or facilities). Many collaboratives put pressure on organizations to set up their participation and sought out leaders from organizations to reinvigorate commitment when it was not happening. Collaboratives spent time on the governance and leadership question as well, whether it was defining roles or increasing expectations for board member engagement. Cornforth (2003) asserts that the "how to do it" literature on board governance and leadership is flawed, because it assumes an overly idealized model. He suggests that the most important steps a board can take is to be more reflexive of its behavior, roles, and impact, and take time to address its own maintenance and development.

Funding Support for Collaboratives

Another implication relates to the critical role that funding and support play in sustaining the operations of a collaborative. The public, private, and nonprofit organizations that fund collaboratives need to be aware of the relationship between funding stability and effectiveness. In Oregon, the agency that administers funding for watershed restoration efforts has been under constant pressure from the legislature to "fund projects rather than people."[25] In other words, legislators want to see money spent directly on restoration efforts and are reluctant to have funds go for watershed council staff. For a number of councils this means that they can find funding for well-designed restoration projects, but have difficulty getting funding to keep the council itself going.

Likewise, Byron and Curtis found instability problems among Landcare facilitators and recommended that staff be provided with more long-term funding support. "Being forced to work and plan within 2–3 year time frame (at best) severely limits the capacity for strategic facilitation, without which efforts to manage complex long-term social and environmental problems are likely to have limited success" (Byron and Curtis 2002).

Some small collaboratives, moreover, rely entirely on volunteers to run the organization. These volunteers lead the group, write grants, and coordinate outreach efforts. The small groups that I researched in Wisconsin, Oregon, and Australia all noted the precariousness of these kinds of collaboratives, because the groups were often so highly dependent on only a few people. Collaboratives built around volunteer-only groups are unlikely to be sustained over the long term, but may play an important short-term role in addressing key issues or problems that generate a lot of motivation for stakeholders.

Although this discussion focuses on collaboratives at the action end of the spectrum, funding support has also been an ongoing issue for some organizational and policy collaboratives. As mentioned previously, federal agencies in the Rogue basin found it difficult to provide ongoing commitment to the collaborative, particularly when some of them were facing regular budget cuts. Similarly, the cost of CALFED efforts and its science program raised concerns among many elected officials in the region (Little Hoover Commission 2005).

Complexities of Information Management

Another implication for sustaining collaboratives relates to the expectations of their information management capacity. In theory, this is a clear role, but in practice it can raise many complexities—especially when it involves government agencies. From my research, I identified three common issues associated with information management, some of which were confronted by the Rogue Basin Coordinating Council.

First, the collaborative and the participating organizations must resolve issues about the internal criteria along with formats for collecting, storing, and reporting data. As other researchers have underscored, information technologies have made this process easier (Cortner and Moote 1999), but there are additional complexities that emerge when the goal is joint management.

As noted in chapter 5, the technical team in the Rogue case faced this problem when it wanted to combine hydrologic map layers from different agencies to create a single layer for the entire river basin. When the different basin maps were combined, the stream densities were significantly different, and some streams on the Bureau of Land Management maps did not match up with streams on neighboring Forest Service ones. To rectify the situation, the World Wildlife Fund provided funding for the Rogue Basin Restoration Technical Team to digitize existing maps, ensure the lines connected, and make the Forest Service layer denser to include nonfish-bearing intermittent streams (Margerum and Whitall 2004). This resolved the data issue in the Rogue basin, but created new issues for the agencies that had to decide whether they would allow more flexible systems for data management and risk complicating internal reporting consistencies. Alternatively, they considered working with parallel databases—internal ones and regional ones used for collaborative management efforts.

A second issue is the transaction costs to maintain, update, and manipulate the information systems. When participants share data to develop a more comprehensive understanding of a system, they rely on this knowledge to influence the understanding of participants and bring about change. For example, a hydrologist involved in a collaborative process may gain a much richer understanding of ecosystem functions, which then allows them to understand how certain water flow regimes relate to ecological health. In turn, they may be able to better apply their new knowledge to a project that affects the stream flow.

As the Rogue case demonstrated, though, the problem becomes quite different when the hydrologist is asked to integrate their data sets with information from other disciplines and other organizations to jointly manage the resource. There is not only the immediate time and resources required to understand the data; there are also ongoing transaction costs to maintain data sharing. Craig Tuss of the U.S. Fish and Wildlife Service summed up the hopes and concerns of data coordination in the Rogue basin:

The optimistic side of me says that after the initial investment, we will have systems in place and habits so they won't notice the additional work. Instead of being extra work, it will become normal work. . . . If we can get something in place where we can get the process rolling, it will become self-perpetuating. The pessimistic side of me says we are tired of rolling this rock to the top of this hill, and wishing that we were at the top so it starts rolling down and it is self-perpetuating. . . . I haven't gotten to the top of the hill yet. So, I'm not sure if it is a false peak . . . or if it's going to be a continual climb up for a long time yet.[26]

The final issue relates to the long-term management and security of information and analysis. Because some collaboratives will not be sustained, the participating stakeholders, partnering organizations, and agencies must consider how this information is documented, backed up, and managed. This issue will likely resonate with people who have had experience with small organizations or volunteer groups. For example, I was involved with a well-established professional organization that could not find its bylaws for over a year, because the paper copy had been lost and the original was on "someone's computer."[27] This could have been a substantial loss if it had been information such as monitoring data, summary reports, and other documents. Several watershed councils in Oregon have been careful to develop backup systems for data, and use academic and local libraries as depositories for information and data generated by the group. This is only anecdotal information; it is not known how many of Oregon's ninety councils have followed these kinds of procedures. In terms of collaboratives involving agencies or that have significant management organizations, more safeguards tend to be in place for information storage. Yet even in these cases, careful consideration must be given to the documentation and metadata that allow the information to be used and interpreted.

The Demise of Collaboratives

This chapter focuses on assessing collaboratives to determine whether they can be sustained, with the underlying assumption that this is a good thing. But sustaining collaboratives may not always be the best outcome. They end for a variety of reasons, and failure may not be bad because it allows some other entity, process, or organization to undertake a different approach. Why do collaboratives end? Besides the factors discussed in this chapter, there are in my view four underlying issues that may lead to a collaborative's demise.

While many collaboratives deal with significant and complex problems that require an ongoing role, some groups are short term or relatively narrow in scope. This means that participants may declare implementation successful at some point and end the collaborative. For example, a restoration initiative aimed at Australia's Berowra Creek involved a series of discreet actions by state and local authorities. With these efforts implemented, the parties wrapped up their collaborative effort. A similar history was evident in a restoration effort regarding Wisconsin's Starkweather Creek, and in a collaborative addressing state and local government riparian policies in the Illawarra region of New South Wales. In all these cases, there was no reason to maintain a sustained effort because the collaborative had achieved one or more of its primary goals.

Another reason relates to the interpersonal trust that develops among stakeholders. This trust leads to innovative, breakthrough ideas and ongoing commitment. As noted several times in this chapter, however, interpersonal trust is personal, and even when collaborative efforts are built around organizations, relationships play a big role. When these relationships break down, the collaborative itself may break down. The breakdown may occur because of a loss of trust, but it is also common for people to move, leave organizations, shift their attention to another issue, or become burned out working on a particular topic. If there is no process for transferring this trust to other stakeholders, or if participating organizations don't commit new participants, this could lead to the collaborative's demise. This issue is particularly germane to small, community-oriented collaboratives that rely on only a few leaders or groups that operate in sparsely populated areas where there is a small base from which to draw volunteers (Parker et al. 2010; Byron, Curtis, and Lockwood 2001).

A third reason why collaboratives sometimes end is because the nature of the problem (or the response to it) changes. These changes can be produced by a shift in scale, such as the change in some Oregon watershed councils from a localized approach to a larger-scale umbrella council that can attract more stable funding. These changes can also be produced by a shift in the nature of the problem. For example, many watershed efforts in the United States started with a focus on agricultural soil and water conservation. Changes in the Clean Water Act increased emphasis on water quality impacts from urbanization and storm water, leading to the initiation of many watershed efforts concerned with the cumulative impacts of urban and rural runoff. These total maximum daily load efforts include a regulatory component for cities, which has shifted the focus of collaborative watershed efforts in some states.

Finally, in some evaluations of collaborative efforts, there is dissatisfaction with achievements (Huntingon and Sommarstrom 2000; Koontz and Thomas 2006). This may be dissatisfaction with the rate or progress, or a feeling that a collaborative group is not achieving adequate results. A lack of achievement can have two effects. For one, if the group is not able to produce concrete products or outcomes, group members may begin to lose interest. Across many of my case studies, I heard participants refer to the importance of getting "runs on the board"— whether they were using a cricket metaphor (Australia) or a baseball one (United States). Joseph Bonnell and Tomas Koontz (2007) document the difficulties faced by the Little Miami River Partnership when the group was not achieving its objectives:

As building and sustaining the organization became the overriding goals, the roles of partners and other stakeholders became less clear and the board became increasingly isolated from the partner organizations. . . . Early on, the partnership was able to draw dozens of interested parties to establish the group, but participation dwindled later as the group failed to demonstrate results.

Second, a lack of accomplishment may also lead to questions from funding organizations. The issue of monitoring and evaluation is discussed in more detail in chapter 10, but the key concern here is that an outcome from an evaluation may lead to the loss of support for a collaborative or a change in its structure. For example, in Australia the outcomes from a review of the National Heritage Trust initiative (NHT-1) led to major changes in the approach to natural resources management efforts. One of the changes in NHT-2 was a shift from localized management efforts to more regional-scale natural resources organizations. Some of the reasons for this included concerns about the progress under NHT-1 and the transaction costs of numerous localized efforts. Interestingly, in current reviews of NHT-2, similar worries about the progress and effectiveness of regional natural resources management organizations are being raised (Robins and Dovers 2007a; National Audit Office 2008; Robinson, Taylor, and Margerum 2009).

Conclusions

This chapter emphasizes that many collaboratives are ongoing entities, which makes them distinctly different from groups formed to resolve conflicts, advise organizations, or make a recommendation on a particular issue. Collaboration thus is not just a movement or a process but also a collection of people formed into an ongoing entity or organization. Ultimately, the success of these efforts will be judged by what they accomplish. Yet they have little chance to achieve results if they are not sustained or are constantly struggling to survive. As noted in the introduction to this chapter, the diversity of collaborative entities makes it hard to generalize across all of them about the factors that will sustain them. Still, some issues and themes seem to appear consistently in case studies and the literature. I believe the factors identified here are only a starting point for researchers, evaluators, and groups looking to better assess their work and improve their approaches. In the following chapters, I explore the relationship between these sustained collaboratives and the social, interorganizational, and political networks that help collaboratives achieve results.

7

Producing Results through Social Networks

On numerous occasions when I have met with collaboratives working in a community, they have cited the importance of social networks for implementing their work. The first time I noticed the role of these networks was in 1995, when I was visiting a streambank restoration project with a catchment coordinator in Queensland. We drove out to the landowner's farm in a dusty flatbed pickup called a "ute." We arrived to find the landowner pulling weeds around an assortment of small saplings planted on a streambank. The landowner proudly showed off the project, describing how the erosion had been undercutting the banks and creating a hazard for cattle trying to access the river. With funding and technical support from the catchment committee, the landowner had graded the banks, removed exotic weeds, planted native trees, fenced off the river to prevent cattle from trampling into the streambed, and built an off-stream watering system. The landowner was farsighted and a typical "early adopter." He had heard about the streambank program from a friend on the committee and volunteered to participate. Thus, the interpersonal network of the committee participants had an influence on the landowner.

But the story does not end there. After the catchment coordinator had finished inspecting the saplings, the farmer commented that his neighbor had stopped by to talk to him about the project. The coordinator asked what the neighbor wanted, and the farmer replied that he had "all kinds of questions" about the project, how much it cost, and what kind of red tape was involved. The farmer recommended the program to his neighbor and gave him the coordinator's contact details.

"What did he say to that?" the coordinator asked.

"He said he'd think about it," replied the farmer.

As we drove away, the coordinator explained that this neighbor was typical of a lot of people in the area. The locals were fiercely independent, and reluctant to work with anything that might involve government funding or agencies, but they were facing some significant land management problems. The program was designed to offer technical advice and some financial incentives through the catchment committee to solve some of these problems. The coordinator's job was to make it as simple as possible for them. His approach was to let the work speak for itself. He never contacted landowners unless they contacted him, and he relied heavily on neighbors convincing neighbors that the program was worthwhile. This strategy meant that the program was slow to get going. But as word spread, there were more requests than funds, and the program was running at capacity.[1] I heard this type of anecdote repeated by coordinators and landowners in Australia, Oregon, Wisconsin, and Tennessee.

The literature on collaboration often describes the importance of social networks that can develop *among* the participants in a collaborative group, allowing them to communicate effectively, identify common goals, build trust, and seek consensus (Leach and Sabatier 2005). At the same time, social networks can serve as a means of translating the objectives of a collaborative into the broader community. These social networks are the friends, family, neighbors, and acquaintances that people have developed through informal interaction in their communities and participation in groups. Collaboratives pursuing this strategy need to be composed of stakeholders who not only bring a range of perspectives to the table but also bring their network of contacts and relationships. This allows the collaborative to influence (and be influenced by) the broader community through these networks.

What Are Social Networks?

The idea of social networks and "social capital" has been popularized in books like Robert Putnam's *Bowling Alone*. The argument that Putnam (2000) and others make is that communities not only possess physical capital (roads and infrastructure), economic capital (investment and assets), and human capital (people and skills) but also social capital (interpersonal networks). An interpersonal network is composed of friends, associates, colleagues, and acquaintances. It is built through work relations, participation in religious organizations, neighborhood networks, social clubs, and other places where people interact with each other.

Individuals can have extensive networks or limited ones. The network can be homogeneous, such as a farmer whose network consists only of other farmers. It can also be heterogeneous, such a farmer who has a diversity of acquaintances through participation in agricultural, social, religious, and political organizations. The implication for collaboration is that these are networks of trust and communication. These are also networks for the diffusion of ideas and innovations (Rogers 2003).

In discussing social networks, it is crucial to highlight several distinctions as I apply them to collaborative settings. First, the focus in this chapter is not on networks that develop within the collaborative among the participants but rather the broader networks in the community. These community networks may be linked to the collaborative through the stakeholders or other means of outreach. Second, social networks exist regardless of whether there is a collaborative. The implementation efforts of a collaborative may tap into existing networks or help form new ones, but networks are a social phenomenon. Third, there are social dimensions to interorganizational and political networks, although I suggest that they are not usually social networks. In other words, through interaction an interorganizational network may develop personal ties, trust, and familiarity, yet these are usually not networks built on social interaction.

These three distinctions are key for understanding how I describe social networks in this chapter. They are networks to solicit input as well as induce behavioral change or action among individuals. Since they are the means of diffusing ideas and innovations, as noted above, this also means that social networks can be utilized by action, organizational, or policy collaboratives. The means for doing this are more complicated for organizational- and policy-level groups.

In this chapter, I examine the concept of social networks and the opportunities that these networks offer to collaboratives. This is followed by a discussion of the factors for assessing a social network implementation approach, including the ways in which these elements might be measured. The final sections of this chapter look at some of the implications of this approach, including working in communities with weak networks, strategies for fostering networks, and connotations of this approach for action, organizational, and policy collaboratives.

Theory Related to Social Networks

Many researchers have addressed the role and influence that social networks have in behavior and attitudes. Whether it is referred to as social capital, diffusion networks, or institutional rules governing society (Putnam 2000; Rogers 2003; Ostrom 1990), several common themes emerge about these networks: their influence on social norms, ability to influence people's awareness of interlinked fates, and role in facilitating interpersonal communication and trust.

Social Norms
Social networks have several qualities that present opportunities for collaboratives and their implementation efforts. For one, social networks allow citizens to resolve collective problems more easily by helping them create social norms that promote certain desired behavior (see Putnam 2000). Many resource problems are what Ostrom (1986b) calls common pool resource problems. This means that there is a collective benefit in using the resource, but it is difficult to regulate or enforce individual behavior. Therefore, in times of drought when agencies call for reduced

water use or water restrictions, they rely heavily on social norms for compliance. They may undertake education efforts or selective enforcement, yet they cannot police an entire community. Neighbor "peer pressure" ends up being important for ensuring compliance. Similarly, landowners who undertake watershed restoration projects can create a norm or expectation of what landowners should do on their land.

A crop farmer in Wisconsin described the challenge he faced when he adopted no-tillage farming because other farmers perceived that he wasn't managing his land properly. They viewed it as "messy" in contrast to the "good" plowed fields that appeared each spring. Over time the practice became more accepted, and the social norms about what fields should look like changed. In some areas, no-till farming has become an indication of good farming practices.

This idea of a social norm is supported by a study of riparian landowners in Oregon. Stacy Rosenberg surveyed over nine hundred landowners and interviewed eighty individuals to explore their ideas about information, trust, and the factors that influenced their conservation activities. One of the common answers that emerged to the question of why they decided to undertake restoration efforts was a notion of "doing the right thing." The reasons why this was the right thing were varied, but the commonality of the message implied it was a community norm or expectation (Rosenberg 2005).

Interlinked Fates

A second quality of social networks is that they help widen the awareness of people's interlinked fates. "Joiners become more tolerant, less cynical, and more empathetic to the misfortunes of others. When people lack connections to others, they are unable to test the veracity of their own views, whether in the give-and-take of casual conversation or in more formal deliberation" (Putnam 2000, 288–289). This understanding of interlinkages makes people more aware of how their actions affect others and more likely to engage in civic activities (Sirianni 2007). For example, landowners are more amenable to messages about the impacts that land management has on their neighbors or water quality in general. When a collaborative comes along and presents information to landowners about what they can do, this message often resonates with people and appeals to their sense of community.

One of the qualities of collaboration is that it brings people together from different perspectives and backgrounds, and prods them to understand each other and recognize interlinkages. As noted in the discussion about consensus building in chapter 4, participants are frequently surprised by their ability to identify common goals with people they previously distrusted or with whom they openly argued (Wondolleck and Yaffee 2000; Weber 2003). The challenge for collaboratives in the implementation phase is to find ways that social networks can encourage understanding about interlinked fates not only within the group of participating stakeholders but also with the broader community.

Interpersonal Communication and Trust

A third quality of social networks relates to their role in promoting communication and trust among network members (Innes and Booher 2010). Even though mass media channels reach many people, they are not usually effective in persuading someone to accept a new idea. Rogers (2003, 18–19) notes that "most people depend mainly upon a subjective evaluation of an innovation that is conveyed to them from other individuals like themselves who have already adopted the innovation." Networks are the pathways for information and ideas to be distributed, and because they are based on personal relationships, the receiver is more likely to listen to the information. Bonnie Erickson (1982) refers to these networks as belief systems, and argues that these belief systems will constrain individuals and also facilitate important social processes. Thus, efforts by a collaborative to distribute information about its riparian restoration program may generate little community response. When a local farmer who is involved with the council speaks to neighbors or other farmers, however, this information is more likely to persuade these people to undertake a restoration project.

Once again, the study of riparian landowners in Oregon watersheds highlights the significance of interpersonal communication. Rosenberg asked agriculture landowners, small woodlot landowners, and rural residents where they obtained information and who they trusted. Across all demographics and types of landowners, friends, family, and neighbors were the most important decision-making influence (see figure 7.1). For nonagricultural landowners, this source of influence was even more important because many of them did not use the agricultural extension agency. Interviews with these landowners revealed some interesting phenomena about how information was exchanged. Most landowners had heard about watershed councils from friends, family, and neighbors, and many decided to do projects based on recommendations or advice from these people. Furthermore, many landowners who chose to do projects consulted with their neighbors beforehand. They commented that they had known their neighbors since childhood, and did not want to undertake a restoration project until they had their blessing (Rosenberg 2005). Thus, even if they believed in the council and its work, they did not want to do anything that would upset their neighbors' trust.

Detrimental Roles of Social Networks

While much of the literature on social networks emphasizes the role that they play in increasing personal opportunities and building a sense of community, these

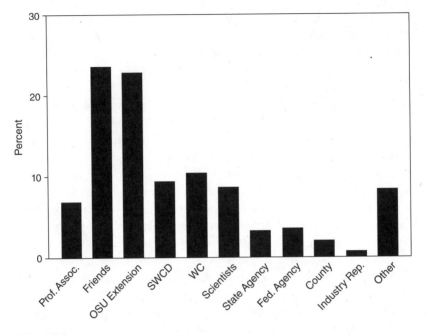

Figure 7.1
Trusted sources of information among riparian landowners. *Notes*: n = 393; Prof. Assoc. = professional association (cooperatives, forestry organizations, etc.); Friends = friends, family, and neighbors; OSU Extension = Oregon State University Extension Service; SWCD = Soil and Water Conservation District; WC = watershed council (includes five councils in study area). *Source*: Rosenberg 2005.

networks can also reinforce segregation, inhibit diverse participation, and serve as a means for negative influence (Erickson 1982; Putnam 2000; Schneider et al. 1997). Putnam (2000) notes that some researchers highlight the correlation between the decline of social capital in the 1960s and increased tolerance of society. But when he examined state-level data, there was a positive association between social capital and tolerance.[2]

Instead, Putnam (2000, 22) points to the differences between bonding and bridging social capital as a more critical component to potential detrimental effects (Granovetter 1982). Bonding social capital is inward looking, and tends to reinforce exclusive identities and homogeneous groups. In contrast, bridging social capital is outward looking and tends to cut across social cleavages. Ethnic-based fraternal organizations and church-based groups tend to be examples of bonding social capital, while civil rights and many youth service groups tend to demonstrate bridging social capital. This has been reinforced by other research, such as a study that found school choice programs designed to reduce segregation were not able to overcome the stratification effects of income and education (Schneider et al. 1997).

Mark Schneider and his colleagues (1997, 1220) found that blacks and Hispanics in choice districts had stronger networks than in nonchoice districts, but "higher status individuals are more likely to be exposed to more and better information about schools that they gather 'on the cheap' as part of their interactions with more highly informed and more highly educated discussants."

Concerns about the lack of bridging ties have also been raised in relation to collaboration efforts. For instance, Marcus Lane (1997, 2003) has highlighted the lack of Indigenous participation in collaborative decision-making processes in Australia. Several researchers emphasize the concerns among the environmental community that place-based collaborations reinforce existing power networks that are dominated by extractive industries (Hibbard and Madsen 2003; Kenney 2000; McCloskey 2001). Michael Hibbard and Jeremy Marsden (2003) note that a common theme among environmentalists opposed to the efforts of the Quincy Library Group related to concerns about industry domination. One activist commented, "I can unequivocally state that the Quincy Library Group represents a consensus of a certain people within our mountain community and does not represent a compromise reached by all affected parties" (quoted in ibid., 712).

Assessing Social Networks

For collaborative efforts in which social networks are central to implementation, there are several factors that can be used to assess their effectiveness. These factors determine the extent to which a collaborative is able to diffuse ideas, innovations, and behavioral change through a community. This diffusion model is more readily applied among action collaboratives that are operating at level where the links can be made more easily. As discussed in the implications section, though, policy and organizational collaboratives can also create structures that allow them to utilize a social network. In the following sections, I describe each of these factors, and list the ways in which they can be assessed through self-evaluations and interviews as well as more objective measures (see table 7.1).

Community Social Networks

The first factor relates to the strength and characteristics of existing community social networks, which researchers have shown to vary from place to place. This variation makes implementation through social networks easier in some places than in others. For example, many watershed councils have more difficulty reaching landowners in the rural residential areas compared to agricultural ones. In the agricultural areas, landowners tend to be long-term residents who are more likely connected to each other and the social fabric of the community. Many rural residents, in contrast, are newcomers with less history in the area and

Table 7.1
Assessing a social network strategy

Assessment factors	Measures of factors	Related references
Community networks: There are strong social networks in the community in which the collaborative is working	• Voter participation and turnout • Membership number and trends in clubs and organizations • Volunteer rates in community organizations • Participation in religious organizations	Putnam 2000; Australian Bureau of Statistics 2004
Linked stakeholders: Stakeholders are linked into social networks	• Representativeness of participating stakeholders • Membership networks of stakeholders • Amount of communication through networks	Rogers 2003; Prell, Hubacek, and Reed 2009
Connectivity: Collaborative is connected into the community through members and volunteers	• Membership numbers and meeting attendees • Volunteers numbers • Newsletter subscribers • Cross-sectional community interviews	Rogers 2003; Bandura 1986
Reputation: Collaborative has a good, established reputation in a community	• Longevity of collaborative • Staff experience and turnover • Change agent reputation • Community perception and awareness	Rogers 2003; Leach and Sabatier 2005
Implementation programs: Implementation programs capitalize on social networks of collaborative	• Implementation approach designed around existing linkages • Programs linked to reputation • Program targeted to leverage points • Evaluation of program outputs and outcomes	Elmore 1982; Margerum and Hooper 2001

limited community connections. Many of them work in nearby cities or towns, and may have more connections in urban areas than in the rural ones where they live.

The influence of interpersonal communication and networks is underscored by Rogers (2003), who reported on several studies examining the adoption of family planning strategies in communities in rural Korea. Although the national family planning program borrowed a "cafeteria" model of family planning options, the majority of people adopted different options in different villages. The result was "pill villages," "IUD villages," and "vasectomy villages," even though the same information program had been used in all the villages. Furthermore, overall acceptance of contraception was high in some villages (over 50 percent) and relatively low in other villages (10 to 15 percent). The differences could be traced to the nature of the intravillage communication networks. "An individual's network links were one important predictor of the individual's adoption of an innovation" (ibid., 333).

Some of the clearest examples of differences in social structures that I found were in the coastal watersheds in the northern part of Queensland. Several of these watersheds start in the high coastal plateau known as the tablelands, then flow through the tropical rain forests of the escarpment, and finally travel across the coastal plains. Both the tablelands and coastal areas have traditional social networks built on service organizations, religious communities, and other networks. In terms of agricultural communities, the tablelands are dominated by large grazing (ranching) properties and some dairying, while the coastal areas are dominated by smaller sugarcane, horticulture, and produce farming.

In 1996, I met with a catchment outreach officer who illustrated the strength and efficiency of this network. On several occasions he went out to meet with sugarcane farmers in a subcatchment about some proposed conservation projects. After meeting with the first farmer, he usually found that the other farmers in the area already knew the key messages he was going to deliver. "Fastest faxes in the West," joked the outreach officer.[3] A dense social network is created by the close proximity of landowners in the coastal areas along with strong sugarcane growers' cooperatives. Over time, the officer realized that it was occasionally more efficient and effective to work with the cooperatives.

In contrast, the farmers in the tableland areas were more independent, lived further apart, and did not have strong agricultural organizations. Some tableland farmers belonged to locally based conservation groups (Landcare groups), but many landowners were not members. As a result, outreach efforts in these areas often required one-to-one outreach to individual farmers. This not only meant that different strategies were necessary in different areas but also meant that outreach efforts in the tablelands were more time-consuming and expensive.

Assessing Community Networks

The interest in social capital has led to the rapid development and refinement of measurement frameworks. Wendy Stone (2001) points out that these measurement frameworks can be divided into those that measure the outcomes of social capital and those that measure social capital itself. In relation to collaboratives, we are interested in the latter—particularly the methods for studying informal and formal networks in a community.

Informal networks are those based around interaction among family, friends, and neighbors, while formal networks are based around social relations that emerge from work associations, participation in community groups, and civic participation (Putnam 2000). The strength of social networks can be measured by using secondary data, such as membership rates in organizations, participation in religious organizations, and voter turnout. Some of the types of measures identified for an Australian national framework of indicators include:

• network structure (size, intensity, density, openness, mobility, and power relations)
• network transactions (sharing support, sharing knowledge, negotiation, and sanctions)
• network types (bonding, bridging, linking, and isolation) (Australian Bureau of Statistics 2004).

The lack of precision in these measures and the emergence of other types of nontraditional networks (e.g., book clubs or Web-based communities) have led to the development of more sophisticated methodologies. Moreover, these methodologies are beginning to be incorporated into data collection frameworks. In many localities, however, data have not been collected specifically for measuring social capital. As a result, researchers and practitioners must collect their own data, rely on secondary measures, or assess the strength of social networks more informally. Some specific measures of local social capital include:

• rates of voter participation and turnout
• number of service and social organizations, and their membership numbers and trends
• volunteer rates and numbers among local schools, clubs, and organizations
• number and participation in religious organizations

Links into Community Social Networks

A second factor affecting the success of a social network implementation strategy is the extent to which the stakeholders participating in the collaborative are connected into community networks. In other words, the members themselves help act as change agents by spreading information and messages through their interpersonal networks. These networks may connect through groups like agricultural organizations as well as soil and water conservation districts, or they may be completely outside the sphere of the collaborative, such as a service club or religious community.

For instance, many of Oregon's watershed councils have utilized this strategy by building on the community connections of their members. Perhaps the effort that has capitalized on this the most is the Australian Landcare program. The program emerged out of interlocking concerns about the economic viability of farming and the effects of agricultural activity on both productivity and the environment. It was designed around the existing structures in society (Curtis 1998). In essence, Landcare is about "landholders working in their own local social group to solve their own local land conservation problems in their own way" (Poussard 1992, 233). While there is evidence that participation in Landcare reached a plateau, the program has still achieved remarkable success with over twenty-five hundred Landcare groups and sixty-five thousand volunteer members, accounting for 30 percent of the Australian farming community (Curtis 1998).[4]

To understand the relevance of linkages to a social network approach, it helps to also understand the role of "change agents" in the diffusion of innovation research. Change agents are individuals who influence decisions on behalf of a change agency. The two traditional challenges that change agents face are that the people they are attempting to influence are overloaded with communication inputs and they are socially marginalized because of their position with the change agency. In the classic centralized diffusion model of programs like the U.S. agricultural extension service, the change agents are technical experts and the information flows from the top down (Rogers 1974). Research on adoption behavior related to traditional extension models has shown that this approach is successful in reaching only a portion of the target population (Guerin 1999; Nowak 1983; Hooper 1995).

In contrast, decentralized diffusion models involve local experimentation, with the innovation bubbling up from nonexpert users (Rogers 1974). Change through this process often takes advantage of communication networks, but there is no guarantee concerning the quality of the information and strategies being dispersed. Hence, for an issue such as watershed restoration, the activities of uninformed innovators could actually be doing more harm than good.

This kind of interest in the role of communication and its influence on behavior has led to studies on networks along with their influence on attitudes and behavior (Granovetter 1982; Lin 1982). Each person possesses a personal network of individuals who are linked, and information and influence flows through these links. Rogers (2003) distinguishes interlocking networks from radiating ones. In interlocking networks, the networks consist of individuals who all interact with one another. In radiating networks, the network is linked to a focal individual, but the other members do not interact with each other. "Radiating personal networks are less dense and more open . . . and thus allow the focal individual to exchange information with a wider environment" (ibid., 338). These networks are important for decentralized diffusion models because they help explain the means by which information flows through a network and community.

Assessing Links

One indicator of a collaborative's ability to influence actions through social networks is the representativeness of the stakeholders involved in the effort. Representativeness is a relative measure, depending on the community attempting to be reached through the social network. A collaborative attempting to influence agricultural landowners may focus on enhancing its network of people that fit this category, and there may not be tremendous diversity within this group. Most collaboratives, though, have a range of people they are trying to reach. For example, the Yamhill Basin Council in Oregon seeks out a governing board composed of people who are representative of the significant types of people it is trying to serve (see table 7.2). This concept of representativeness has been a cornerstone of Oregon's watershed program.

A second approach is to ask stakeholders to map their social networks (Burt 1983; Wellman and Berkowitz 1988). Under these approaches, individuals map all the relations in their personal networks or communities (Wellman and Berkowitz 1988). This approach may reveal parts of the community that are missing and opportunities for untapped linkages. Several Oregon watershed councils, for instance, discovered that members belonged to several different religious faiths, several of which had active environmental stewardship groups. Like a survey sample, the more difficult question is whether the stakeholder group mirrors the range of people with a stake in the community.

A third approach to assessing stakeholder links is the degree to which participants on the collaborative are communicating with their social networks about the group's work. For example, a representative of a bushwalking (hiking) club that participated in a Sydney-based catchment committee expressed remorse over his role because he

Table 7.2
Examples of steering committee positions, Yamhill Basin Council

Agriculture	Forest industry
Soil and water conservation districts	Utilities
Environmental groups	Business
Confederated Tribes of Grand Ronde	Bureau of Land Management
Watershed resident	Counties

had been unable to attend the club meetings. This means that this community link was weak both in terms of the information he brought to the group and his role in helping to further the committee's work through the bushwalking club. On the other hand, some collaboratives I observed explicitly asked participants to check with their constituencies. This task is much easier when the constituency is organized, but stakeholders can also query their personal networks. Collaboratives and researchers can use discussions or simple surveys to assess the extent to which stakeholders communicate information both formally and informally with their networks.

Connectivity

The third issue for assessing social networks is connectivity, which is similar to the idea of stakeholder linkages, but refers to the connections of the collaborative entity itself. These connections occur through its membership, volunteer opportunities, meetings, workshops, or even just its newsletter. Connectivity is the result of the sum of these efforts to become known in the community.

As noted above, community networks and personal interaction play an important role in influencing behavior. Yet the influence of stakeholders is limited by their own personal connections and influence. Thus, even an active change agent will be able to interact with only a limited number of individuals. A collaborative as an organization can build more connections into a community through its network of programs and participants.

Another reason why collaborative connectivity into a community is key is because it can influence behavior in different ways. Some people are influenced by direct interaction with change agents or innovators who adopt a new practice and influence others (Rogers 2003). Another way in which people learn and behave is explained by social learning theory. In short, they learn by observing the behavior of others and modeling it (Bandura 1986; Rogers 2003). As Rogers (2003) notes, "The basic perspective of social learning theory is that the individual can learn from observation of other people's activities, so the individual does not necessarily have to experience verbal exchange of information in order for the individual's behavior to be influenced by the model."

In our study of riparian landowners in Oregon, we were interested to know whether watershed councils had become a source of information (Rosenberg and Margerum 2008). We found that a majority of the respondents were familiar with watershed councils (see figure 7.2). In fact, knowledge of the councils was at a similar level to an awareness about the university extension service as well as soil and water conservation districts—which is remarkable given that these organizations have been around fifty to eighty years longer.

Many of these councils have connected to their communities by designing programs that reach a broad audience. For example, many use volunteers to undertake

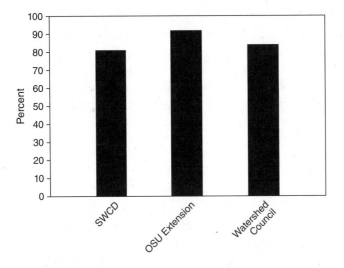

Figure 7.2
Landowner familiarity with organizations. *Notes*: *n* = 378; SWCD = Soil and Water Conservation District; OSU Extension = Oregon State University Extension Service; Watershed council includes five councils in study. *Source:* Rosenberg 2005.

monitoring and project work, which allows the work to get done and creates the potential for more people to become involved. Many groups sponsor tours of restoration projects, thereby allowing other landowners to see firsthand what a project looks like. Finally, many collaboratives sponsor workshops to address specific concerns in their area. Watershed groups in Oregon, for example, have held workshops for horse owners, some of whom have limited experience with managing properties and animals.

Assessing Connectivity

To assess the connectivity of a collaborative, it is instructive to look at the concrete ways in which it is linked to the community. Some of the simple measures are the number of meeting attendees, membership numbers, or newsletter subscribers. Although these numbers may have little effect on behavior, they can give an overall indication of community awareness of the collaborative. For example, whether membership requires a financial commitment or not, becoming a member of a collaborative indicates that the individual is willing to be formally associated with the group. As one Oregon farmer proudly said to me, "Yep, I'm a card-carrying member of the watershed council."[5]

A similar indication of organizational reach and connections is the number of people who attend workshops and volunteer for activities. Finally, surveys of landowners or community members can provide an assessment of connectivity. A general population survey can be time-consuming and expensive. In our Oregon landowner study, Rosenberg's interviews with landowners supplied some of the most informative insights into how watershed councils could connect with the community. A cross-sectional sample of community interviews therefore could offer the most insight into assessing connectivity.

Reputation

A fourth factor for assessing a social network implementation strategy is the reputation of a collaborative in the community. This reputation partly depends on stakeholder links and connectivity, but it also relies on the experiences that people in the community have while working with a collaborative.

When I took over as chair of the Long Tom Watershed Council, one of my concerns was the effect of my leadership role on the council's reputation. As an urban resident and academic, I was worried that rural and agricultural landowners might develop a negative perception. I brought this up with a fellow steering committee member who was a long-standing part of the farming community. He said that this might have been a worry in the early days of the group, but now that the council was well established he did not feel anyone would be concerned about the effect on its reputation. "Besides," he said good-naturedly, "we'll be watching you."[6]

The significance of reputation was also highlighted in Rosenberg's study (2005) of riparian landowners in Oregon. In one watershed, landowners interviewed by Rosenberg said they refused to work with one of the federal agencies because of their experiences with one of its staff members. The watershed council coordinator confirmed these problems and noted that the staff person had left many years ago. Furthermore, some landowners who refused to work with the agency had never interacted with this individual. It was clear that people in the area had long memories, and the damaged reputation of the agency lasted far longer than the staff person. Conversely, Rosenberg found that many riparian landowners who were working with watershed councils did not even know that they were community-based organizations with broad stakeholder representation. They based their decision on recommendations from friends, family, and neighbors, and the reputation of the staff. The staff members themselves had developed sufficient legitimacy and trust that the landowners were willing to allow them onto their land and undertake restoration projects even when they would not allow any government agency staff on their land.

Assessing Reputation

Based on the literature and my research, I believe there are several factors that may be useful in assessing a collaborative's reputation. First, the longevity of the collaborative is important, because it takes time for the group to gain name recognition and advance their reputation. The longer a collaborative operates, the more faith that people will have in it as an ongoing entity.

Second, the experience and turnover rates among the outreach staff can be indications of reputation. Staff members working for groups, as noted above, develop their own relationships and reputation over time that allow them to interact with community members. High rates of turnover not only slow organizational momentum but they also sever the interpersonal connections that staff members have with the community (Parker et al. 2010).

Third, the reputation of the change agents has a crucial effect on the reputation of the collaborative. Rogers identifies several factors that make these staff members or change agents successful. For one, the amount of energy they expend communicating and working on outreach efforts is positively related to success. So is the ability of the change agent to be oriented toward the people they are trying to reach, rather than the organization that employs them. Success is also correlated to the degree to which a change agent is able to diagnose people's needs and the extent to which the diffusion program is compatible with those needs. Then too, the more a change agent can be empathetic toward the people with whom they are working, the more likely it is that they will be successful (Rogers 1974).

A final factor for assessing reputation is community perceptions and awareness of the collaborative. Early in their formation, many Oregon watershed councils struggled to explain what they were. Some people thought they were environmental advocacy groups; others thought they were agricultural organizations; some thought they were a government agency. As noted in figure 7.2, our landowner survey revealed that watershed councils in Oregon have gained a familiarity almost equal to the much older soil and water conservation districts and extension agencies. Similar kinds of community surveys of familiarity and perceptions can be a direct way of assessing reputation.

Social Network Implementation Programs

The last implementation factor important for social networks is designing implementation programs to capitalize on the linkages, connectivity, and reputation described above. Implementation programs are necessary, because passive information exchange and networking alone are usually not sufficient for delivering results. Furthermore, for a collaborative that does not have a strong community orientation, it may need to develop a program that allows it to connect with these networks.

Studies in public health have found that knowledge of the need for change—by itself—is not enough to get individuals to decide to implement change. There also needs to be a process of persuasion, which is best delivered through interpersonal channels. As noted above, this diffusion of innovation model emphasizes that interaction on an interpersonal level is a crucial factor for persuading people that change is essential (Rogers 2003).

Several watershed councils in Oregon have developed outreach programs around existing community networks. In the Siuslaw, Coos, and Long Tom watersheds, a council staff member identifies a key landowner in a target subwatershed who will host a meeting and invite their neighbors. Gathering in the host's living room, the council staff member explains the issues in the subwatershed and the potential projects that the neighbors can do in conjunction with the council. The subwatershed program helps fund the restoration project, and the landowner pays a portion through cash or in-kind support (time and materials). The council provides all the technical assistance, including the project design as well as the federal and state permits. In return, the landowner gets a restored landscape, and often conservation easements or tax credits (Flitcroft et al. 2009).

These types of programs provide the vehicle for reaching these landowners through local networks, and the stories around these programs were remarkably similar—whether they were in the United States or Australia.[7] Not all the landowners agree to do restoration projects right away. Some are quick to sign up; others wait to see how the projects fare and talk to their neighbors before agreeing to do their own projects. In the end, many of the programs have been successful at creating a cluster of landowner projects, which increases the number of participants. A more concentrated group of restoration projects is also likely to lead to documentable environmental improvements as compared to projects scattered across the watershed.

In the Mary River in Queensland, the catchment committee was able to tap into community networks through its Voluntary Riverbank Restoration Grants Scheme (Kelly 1998). Like the Oregon efforts, this federally funded program provided money and technical assistance with cash or in-kind financing from the landowner. To help implement the program, the Mary River Catchment Committee hired a part-time outreach coordinator, who was a retired and long-term resident of the area. His agricultural background and particularly his history of personal connections provided the committee with an important avenue for tapping into the local community. Additionally, when landowners undertook projects it was common for neighboring landowners to also sign up or consider doing a project at a later date.[8] Within a short time, there was a waiting list of landowners to participate in the program, and in 2001 the program was recognized with a statewide river care award (Thompson and Pepperdine 2003).

Assessing Implementation Programs

There is a range of criteria that can be used to judge the likely success of an implementation program. Many of these criteria must be judged in relation to the specific context and program goals. However, there are also some subjective and qualitative criteria that can be used to assess a range of different programs.

First, a collaborative should design implementation programs around existing linkages. One way of assessing the role of a network in program delivery is to conduct a network analysis or analyze the path by which a landowner decided to undertake a conservation project. On numerous occasions when I have gone on field visits to restoration projects I have asked landowners what led them to undertake the project. Sometimes the path is serendipitous. Someone mentioned the council, or that they read about it in a paper or heard about the group from a friend. But in many cases I found that it was a result of a specific effort designed to tap into this network: a demonstration project tour, a meeting on a related topic of interest, or a subwatershed meeting organized by a watershed council. Thus, an assessment of implementation programs should consider whether there are logical connections between target audiences, outreach efforts, and implementation programs.

Second, the program needs to be designed with the collaborative's reputation in mind. It should be consistent with the mission of the organization, and capitalize on the organization's approach and philosophy. In evaluation terms, the question is whether the mission and philosophy of the program matches those of the organization. This arose with several collaboratives that I observed when they were approached with partnership opportunities. These partners included state agencies, local governments, nonprofit organizations, and businesses, and groups debated about the issue of reputation. For example, several Australian councils were concerned about appearing too closely aligned with state conservation programs because they feared they would lose their nongovernmental reputation. When I was on the Long Tom board, we were offered potential partnerships with private duck-hunting clubs and a regional council of governments, but in both cases the partnership raised concerns about whether these efforts were consistent with our core mission.

Third, the program should be designed with leverage points in mind (see chapter 5). It should, in other words, relate to the changes that the collaborative is seeking and the intervention efforts that will help induce this change. For instance, the Umpqua River Basin Council was successful in removing an irrigation diversion structure because it was able to identify the underlying needs and develop a solution that created leverage for change. The old, leaky irrigation canal in this case presented high maintenance demands and low water security for those at the end of the system. The council was able to find funding to replace the dam with an alternate system that delivered a more reliable supply of waters to all users. The change from the status quo was worthwhile for all the landowners, despite the difficulties of legal negotiations involving water rights.[9] The council and the river got one less barrier to fish passage.

A final approach is to assess outputs and outcomes against program goals. This kind of assessment can be undertaken through traditional program evaluation methods, as long as the program has clear and measurable objectives. By several measures, for instance, the Mary River Voluntary Riverbank Restoration Grants Scheme was a successful program. In terms of inputs, the program became so popular that all the available funding was being allocated. Some of the outputs from this program between 1995 and 1999 included: 300 kilometers (186 miles) of streambank fenced from stock access, 150 off-stream watering points, and the planting of more than 100,000 native seedlings. In terms of outcomes, it was estimated that the program helped reduce the amount of fecal contamination and nutrients from cattle by the equivalent of a sewage treatment plant servicing 50,000 people (Kelly 1998; Pickersgill, Burgess, and Wedlock 2007).

Discussion

The five factors of community networks, linked stakeholders, reputation, connectivity, and implementation programs are all important for successful implementation. Yet these factors also highlight implications for different types of collaboratives. In the following sections, I discuss how these are implemented across the spectrum of collaboratives, and explore the overall strengths and weaknesses of a social network implementation strategy.

Implications for Collaboratives

Collaboratives seeking to utilize a social network implementation strategy need to consider both the strength of existing networks and strategies for tapping into them. Depending on these two factors, collaboratives may need to employ a range of strategies.

Getting Results Where Networks Are Weak

If social networks are important for collaboratives to connect with their communities, places with weak networks present a significant challenge. This has implications for both the collaboratives and the organizations that fund them. For collaboratives, it is essential to recognize that existing networks may not revolve around natural resources, agricultural concerns, or other issues directly related to their work. Networks also exist in relation to neighborhoods, religious affiliations, and social memberships. Thus, collaboratives may be able to tap into these networks by exploring a wider range of networks.

In places where community networks are weak, collaboratives may need to take on the task of building networks and social capital. For example, many watershed councils in Oregon strive to make their meetings into forums where landowners can come to hear about current topics, meet other landowners, and socialize. This has a secondary benefit of fostering social capital among landowners where it is limited.

This was apparent during a watershed restoration tour sponsored by a watershed council that included two projects: one by a retired couple who purchased a rural residential property, and the other by agricultural landowners who had been farming in the valley for several generations. It was a classic social dichotomy: rural residential property versus working farm; newcomers versus established family. The project brought together both property owners, and they each remarked that a secondary benefit was a chance to get to know their neighbors. Still, this is clearly a tall order for collaborative groups—not only to ask them to improve watershed ecosystems, but also to improve the social fabric of rural communities.

This leads to another implication for collaboratives that are working in network-poor communities. Funders of these efforts may have to be more patient and provide more investment in capacity building. As noted above, outreach in these communities will take longer and cost more. This also means that short-term measures of success will look different because they will focus on more abstract indicators such as network development. Many governmental and nongovernmental funders are reticent to support these kinds of attempts, preferring to concentrate on "works on the ground."

A final implication in network-poor communities is that implementation through community networks may not always be a viable strategy. For example, natural resources collaboratives in northern Australia have struggled to implement actions, in part because of the sparse population and significant distances that limit social networks (Robinson, Taylor, and Margerum 2009). These are areas where travel is measured in days, the weather can cut off areas for weeks, and public schools teach classes over the radio and Internet. In these kinds of settings, implementation strategies based on expert-extension models, information dissemination approaches, incentive systems, or even regulatory strategies may be more appropriate.

Social Networking Strategies for Collaboratives

The factors listed above provide some output and outcome measures for assessing social networks. But the issue for many collaboratives is how to develop or enhance these networks to support their implementation efforts. Based on my research of collaboratives, I have noted several strategies used by these groups. While this is clearly not an exhaustive list, it highlights the types of efforts that groups can undertake.

First, collaboratives should consider diversifying stakeholder membership to ensure diverse social networks. Many Australian catchment committees, for example, emerged from agricultural communities, and several that I studied did not include rural residential landowners even though this was a significant proportion of the watershed community. Groups that reached out to this sector of the community found new participants with different networks and new skills.

Second, many groups keep records of volunteers and participants, and develop future leaders by involving them in these activities or subcommittees. One question I have asked many stakeholders involved in collaboratives is how they got involved. It was notable how often their response started with something like: "Well, I went to this meeting one day." Meetings and outreach events can attract new people, but there must also be personal invitations, follow-up, and other efforts to make people feel like they are part of something.

Third, collaboratives and the organizations that fund them are frequently reluctant to spend time and money on outreach programs, such as newsletters, workshops, and public meetings. Such outreach requires considerable time and effort, and it is difficult to connect these programs and events to measurable effects. Nevertheless, outreach events also increase the profile of the collaborative, bring in new volunteers, and create new potential connections in a community. For example, in our study of Oregon watersheds we found that 70 to 74 percent of landowners were familiar with their watershed councils, but in the Siuslaw the familiarity was 97 percent (Rosenberg and Margerum 2008). This was due in large part to the councils' free tree giveaway program, which not only raised the profile of the organizations and encouraged landowners to plant native trees but also increased interest in undertaking restoration projects. In fact, 62 percent of the landowners Rosenberg interviewed indicated that they had received trees through this program.[10]

Fourth, it is important for collaboratives to develop a clear mission and goals, and be able to articulate this clearly to the community. When collaborative groups emerged in places such as Queensland and Oregon, there was often confusion about their role, and many mistook them for environmental or advocacy organizations. Being able to describe and even market a collaborative's mission will help with its reputation and community linkages.

The stability of the collaborative and the experience of the staff (which were discussed in chapter 6) are also worth reiterating here in relation to social networks. As noted previously, Rosenberg's interviews with landowners emphasized the significance of outreach staff. Good experiences with these staff members led landowners to recommend them to other landowners, but when there is high turnover among staff members, these connections, experience, and reputation may all be diminished. In effect this means that staff members develop their own social networks, and the longer good staff members can be retained, the greater the extent of this network.

Social Network Approaches under Different Types of Collaboratives

In the discussions above, it is apparent that collaboratives at the action end of the spectrum are well positioned to utilize social networks to deliver implementation programs. Collaboratives along the organizational and policy parts of the spectrum

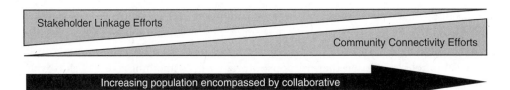

Figure 7.3
Connectivity and stakeholder relationships to population

can also use this approach, but they must consider how to develop the supporting structures and mechanisms.

The barriers to an organizational collaborative using a network strategy are exemplified by the case of the McKenzie watershed council in Oregon. As Cheng and Daniels (2005) note, since organizational participants (the U.S. Forest Service, the Bureau of Land Management, and the Eugene Water and Electric Board) dominate the McKenzie council, its initial focus was on restoration projects on properties managed by these organizations. As the council began shifting its focus to projects on private land, however, it encountered resistance because of its reputation as an agency-based group. It has had the most success in reaching private landowners in the Mohawk subwatershed, where a group of landowners have formed the Mohawk Watershed Planning Group. This action-level group is composed of landowners interested in promoting conservation efforts on private land, and their community connection is key in helping them do this work (ibid.).

One fundamental difficulty faced by organizational and policy collaboratives is that the larger the scale and population, the less the influence of stakeholder linkages (see figure 7.3). In simple mathematical terms, individuals are connected only to a limited number of other people. Thus, a stakeholder group can have significant connections in a region with a population of ten thousand, but relatively insignificant connections in a region with one million inhabitants. To translate implementation programs into action through a social networking strategy, organizational and policy collaboratives can utilize two types of community connectivity strategies: improve outreach and enhance institutional arrangements.

Increasing outreach requires an investment by the collaborative in education and information efforts in order to increase awareness of its objectives and programs. As mentioned in chapter 4, a regional planning effort called Envision Utah put a large amount of its energy into raising awareness about projected growth trends and the alternatives to existing land use patterns. The multimillion-dollar process involved 135 public meetings attended by over 4,500 people and 930,000 questionnaires that generated approximately 23,500 resident responses, and helped produce a documentary that aired on local commercial and public television stations.[11] The objective was to get the public to think differently about issues like urban development, density, infill development, and even travel behavior. Yet the specific planning decisions were left to each of the local governments in the region. Similarly, in places like the Fraser River basin (British Columbia), Milwaukee River watersheds (Wisconsin), and Brisbane River (Australia), collaboratives have used report cards to document conditions and trends.

One of the weaknesses of an implementation approach based solely on an outreach strategy is that there is a significant difference between knowing about the collaborative, learning about the issues, and undertaking actions to support the collaborative's mission. For example, research in the field of agricultural extension has shown that simply knowing about a conservation practice and even understanding its purpose does not necessarily translate into adoption (Napier, Thraen, and Camboni 1988; Napier et al. 1984). This is also supported by the diffusion and innovation literature, which observes that people are more likely to make changes when they are influenced by interpersonal interaction.

Therefore, a second strategy for organizational and policy collaboratives is to enhance institutional arrangements to utilize social networks. Institutional arrangements refer to the formal and informal structures that exist within a community, such as conservation groups, farming organizations, or neighborhood connections. Some of these groups may already be in a position to help with implementation programs, such as the Mohawk group in the McKenzie watershed. Other groups may be unsuitable or unwilling to take on this role, because it does not coincide with their mission and purpose. A farming cooperative may involve farmers interested in undertaking conservation efforts, for instance, but the cooperative itself may not be interested in delivering conservation programs.

Under these circumstances, organizational and policy collaboratives may have to help create new arrangements that will support implementation. These arrangements can be ongoing or have a limited tenure, but the key is that they are designed at a level where they are able to link into the community through social networks.

One illustration is Australia's creation of regional natural resources management organizations (commonly called regional bodies). Different states have approached the structure of these regional bodies differently, but one common trait is that many of them are larger in size and population than the catchment management groups that preceded them. The advantage of this structure is that the new regional bodies have greater capacity and are more sustainable as organizations (Robins and Dovers 2007a). The disadvantage is that they are less able to utilize a social networking strategy to implement programs. Still, several groups are developing or enhancing institutional structures to help deliver their programs. In particular, they are fostering action-level groups to support implementation.

The Port Phillip and Westernport Catchment Management Authority (Port Phillip CMA) encompasses a large region and population—taking in major parts of metropolitan Melbourne. The aim of the Port Phillip CMA (2004) is to "facilitate integrated catchment management and sustainability of the region's catchment." To deliver its implementation programs, the Port Phillip CMA has recognized that it is too far removed from local residents to link directly with landowners or even connect with the larger population to support its efforts. It has instead developed a set of policies, strategies, and programs to support and develop locally based groups.

In rural areas, the Port Phillip CMA has tapped into established Landcare groups. In suburban and rural areas, it has helped support groups working to restore and manage nature areas, parks, and public lands. And in other areas, the Port Phillip CMA has tried to foster the establishment of new groups through a series of programs, including offering funds for conservation and restoration projects, finding technical assistance, supplying self-assessment tools, and providing assistance with strategy and organizational development as well as volunteer recruitment. Thus, the Port Phillip CMA does not do on-the-ground projects but rather helps to coordinate and support the work of others. In 2008, it further emphasized this approach by moving from three catchment coordinators to employing nine coordinators. The impetus for this change was to provide more support for these groups and help foster new groups in high-priority areas.[12]

The role of social networks within collaboratives at the policy end of the spectrum may offer even greater challenges. In part this is due to an even larger scope and scale, but it is also because the parties involved in the collaborative effort must develop the organizational capacity to support and deliver the programs. The collaborative itself is composed of high-level stakeholders, such as elected officials, administrators, and interest group representatives, with limited time to devote to implementation activities. Therefore, these groups often create a new "collaborative superagency" to deliver implementation (Sabatier, Leach et al. 2005). This means that the collaborative and its supporting organization are charged with not only integrating policy but also creating the organizations and supporting institutional structures to implement it.

For this reason, it is not unusual for policy collaboratives to delegate this role to other organizations that are already positioned to undertake this. The former Murray Darling Basin Commission was a clear example of a policy collaborative that attempted to utilize social networks, and a clear instance of the challenges of this model. The Murray Darling basin is Australia's largest river system, draining one-seventh of the Australian mainland. The commission originated from the Murray-Darling Basin Agreement, which was initiated in 1985 and obtained full legal status in 1993. The agreement was a partnership between the federal government, Australian Capital Territory, and states of New South Wales, Victoria, South Australia, and Queensland. The commission was led by a Ministerial Council composed of the ministers from each of the states and the federal government (Pigram 2007).

In 2000, the council adopted a new approach for implementation based on integrated catchment management. The implementation strategy called for the strengthening of catchment management institutional arrangements and capacities, and delivering the integration of natural resources management through regional strategies and local action plans (Murray Darling Ministerial Council 2001; Pigram 2007). For a number of years, the council used the levers of funding, information, and technical assistance to support regional catchment management and local Landcare groups.

The commission would set priorities and provide funding to achieve those priorities using catchment and Landcare groups as key delivery mechanisms. At the same time, this model was criticized for its lack of progress in improving river basin health. Federal funding also began bypassing the commission, making it dependent on the states to fund several of its programs (Connell 2007). The problems with these arrangements and the failure of the Ministerial Council to address water reallocation in the basin led to new legislation in 2008 that created a more powerful regional agency (Murray Darling Basin Authority 2009). Many of the people I interviewed during the early stages of this transition noted that the commission's approach was producing positive benefits in terms of river restoration and land management, but it was unable to address some of the fundamental water quantity allocation problems in the basin.

In summary, social networks are relevant to all types of collaboratives, yet the larger the target population, the more infrastructure required to deliver implementation results through these networks.

Conclusions

The social networking approach applies to more than just the directly involved stakeholders. It can be a deliberate strategy for connecting the collaborative to the broader community, even when "the community" involves a large population. This approach has strengths and weaknesses that are important for translating collaborative efforts into results.

The strength of a social network strategy is that it is based on the idea that social and community pressures can help create the change necessary to achieve management goals. When successfully established, the community as a whole begins to adopt and reinforce certain behaviors in the way that community values have led to behavioral changes around littering and recycling. As social scientists have shown, these networks are important for the diffusion of ideas, because people often rely on their social networks to guide their actions.

In the context of natural resources management in places like Australia and the United States, another strength of the network strategy is that the messages and information come through nongovernmental sources. In many rural communities, landowners are highly distrustful of and even hostile toward governmental roles in their decision-making processes, even if they agree with the intended outcomes. Oregon watershed councils have found that one of the advantages they have is their nongovernmental status and community orientation. If friends, families, and neighbors reinforce their messages and advice, the councils can become a powerful force for change.

The weakness of a social network approach to implementation is that it depends on an adequate social network and the ability of a collaborative group to tap into it. As noted above, social networks may be weak in some communities or within certain sectors of a community. It is a tall order to ask a collaborative group to not only solve a problem but also build community social networks to help do so.

Another weakness—particularly for organizational and policy collaboratives—is that the presence of government agencies on the collaborative may create barriers for its work with the community. This was apparent in discussions with stakeholder and landowner assessments of catchment committees in the Australian states of New South Wales and Queensland. These groups had a majority of community members, but they all had significant participation by state agency and local government representatives. When I talked with community members and coordinators about community perceptions of these groups, many noted that this participation some-times cast suspicion on these groups.

A third weakness relates to the type of activities that are likely to be fostered through a social network. This approach is compatible with voluntary efforts, like watershed restoration and conservation. There also appears to be ample evidence that it is enhanced by a fear of government—meaning that a potential threat of government intervention or regulation helps to support action. Social networks are nevertheless unlikely to overcome fundamental economic or social forces. Thus, the multilayered network in the Murray Darling basin had moderate success around conservation efforts, but the structure was unable to effectively address water allo-cation or tree clearing.

Finally, as mentioned in the literature review earlier in this chapter, social net-works have the potential to be homogeneous in terms of race, income, education, and other characteristics. This was highlighted as an issue for the consensus-building process, but it is also a concern for implementation. There may be individuals who would be interested in participating in incentive programs or engaging in implemen-tation actions, but the collaborative does not reach them because they are not well connected to its social networks. The typical set of stakeholders I see around the table of many watershed councils therefore may not be well connected to rural resi-dential landowners, low-income residents, or minority landowners.

8

Producing Results through Interorganizational Networks

In the 1990s when I was working with the Wisconsin DNR, one of our administrator's goals was to improve support for the collaborative activities of the agency (Besadny 1991; Margerum 1995b).[1] The department was a large agency responsible for both resource management (e.g., forests, water resources, and parks) and environmental protection (e.g., water quality, air quality, and solid and hazardous waste). This dual responsibility created internal coordination issues, and the size and breadth of the organization often made this complicated. My first role with the agency was to research some of its exemplary collaboration efforts to help guide staff and the agency in future ones. Many of the cases I examined involved collaboration between other state and federal agencies, the university extension service, and local governments.

One of the common messages that I heard from participants in these cases was the importance of establishing connections for communicating information and resolving differences. For example, a DNR staff person working on agricultural and private land issues in the Wildlife Division noted that the issues he dealt with crossed many different agency jurisdictions, which made it difficult to build bridges. Yet "once you have built bridges, it is easier to travel them . . . [and] the product will be better because it represents a whole host of interests."[2] Another staff member commented that these bridges made the interorganizational work more proactive, because participants were dealing with issues early in the process rather than responding to problems once they had reached a crisis level.[3]

What Are Interorganizational Networks?

The bridges described by these interviewees are formal and informal networks created across organizations to sustain ongoing relationships. The activities associated with these relationships may include data sharing, joint analysis, joint projects, and management coordination. These networks are part of the institutional structure that affects decisions and actions, but these institutions are much broader than just the networks. Thus, a network may come and go, but there will still be an institution influencing decision making. Before discussing the role of interorganizational networks and where they occur, I want to clarify what I mean by them.

First, a network can be composed of the stakeholders participating in the consensus-building process, but often it extends beyond this core group. As pointed out by Chris Huxham and Siv Vangen (2005, 135), the structures that define a collaborative are parts of much more complex networks of collaboration. "Organizational members find themselves increasingly being part of multiple partnerships," which Snape and Stewart (2005) refer to as "pluralism in partnership." This is particularly true during the implementation phase, when there is a need for ongoing coordination among a wide range of actors.

In metropolitan Brisbane, for instance, a regional collaborative planning process led to the creation of subregional organizations composed of local governments. As some of these subregional councils began to take on new projects—such as habitat mapping, traffic issues, and power line corridors—they added more participants and working groups. These working groups interacted with other committees and groups as well. Thus, over time it was hard to define the boundaries of the interorganizational network working on the implementation of the collaborative planning effort.

Second, the network may operate at the same level as the collaborative or a different level. In the metropolitan Brisbane case, the regional framework developed at the policy level was translated down to a number of implementation objectives. Many of these objectives were delegated to formal and informal networks of organizations that were engaged in direct implementation activities. For example, an initiative called the Western Gateway project grew out of the regional planning process to address socioeconomic issues in a low-income region. Its goal was to bring together local government staff members, state agency personnel, and interest groups to address operational decisions, such as how to coordinate social services and bus routes in an area that was also bisected by a freeway.[4] These action-level efforts were being carried out through an interorganizational network.

Third, the interorganizational network may exist prior to the convening of a collaborative effort or it could be a direct product of it. In the Rogue River basin, the participants faced several difficult issues relating to federal agency priorities and the interpretation of federal law. The coordinating committee members were able to bring these issues to a group called the Provincial Interagency Executive Committee, which had been created to coordinate the implementation and monitoring efforts of the Northwest Forest Plan. The executive committee included regional administrators, who could collectively consider the issues that the coordinating committee was facing and help resolve them (Margerum and Whitall 2004).

Finally, interorganizational networks involve people, but the dynamics of linking organizations makes them different from social networks. Huxham and Vangan (2005, 125) also note this distinction, asserting that the collaboration literature often focuses too much on membership and "who is involved," in contrast to structure and "how they are involved." Interorganizational networks are influenced by organizational commitments, responsibilities, priorities, and even job descriptions. This is not to say that an interorganizational network may not overlap with a personal network, or that individuals don't have a significant personal influence in bringing participants together. For example, people who belong to the same religious or service organization may also participate in the same interorganizational network. The interorganizational network, though, is defined by their organization's links to the topic or issue under consideration, rather than just personal connections.

What Is the Role of These Networks?

An effective consensus-building process creates clear goals, commitment, and good quality products. Yet in my work as a researcher and state agency employee, I found that plans were not enough to deliver implementation results. Even when all the participating organizations were highly committed and the staff was competent, an ongoing network for interaction was important. Without regular interaction through the network, the attention given to the issues will frequently move to the back burner. If resource conditions and organizational factors are dynamic, and if implementation activities are interdependent, it is also essential for organizations to work together and adjust to each other as the details of the activities are finalized.

All this can be handled through informal or ad hoc arrangements of people from these organizations. In fact, this worked well in several cases I studied—until staff members left or new priorities came to the forefront, and these ad hoc arrangements disintegrated. In examining cases over time, I have become convinced that interorganizational networks need some definition and stability. Similarly, Huxham and Vangan (ibid.) assert that ambiguity about network membership often creates confusion. They suggest that it may be impossible to define all types of networks and alliances that may exist, but mapping these structures can help pinpoint where changes may be necessary. I likewise contend that these networks don't necessarily need to be formalized but rather that they need to be developed and documented by the participating organizations to ensure they operate effectively as well as survive changes in the participants.

Before discussing the literature on networks, it is helpful to look at two cases that illustrate some of the ways in which networks can operate. I conducted detailed sets of interviews with participants in both instances in order to research and assess how their networks functioned.[5]

Trinity Inlet

The Trinity Inlet is a natural marine and estuarine water body located in northern Queensland near the major tourist city of Cairns. The inlet is an important marine breeding and nursery area, a busy port for fishing and shipping, and the largest port for tourist vessels serving the Great Barrier Reef. Port expansions and development led to the filling of wetlands, reclamation of land for development, and clearing of mangroves. In response to public concerns about development and its impacts on the Trinity Inlet, the Queensland government and local governments bordering the inlet agreed to prepare a management plan. The four participating organizations were the Cairns Port Authority, the Cairns City Council, the Mulgrave Shire Council, and the Department of the Premier Economic and Trade Development.[6]

The ongoing management structure was led by a steering committee composed of high-level officials that met quarterly (TIMP Steering Committee 1992). The steering committee appointed three subcommittees: a technical committee, a consultative committee composed of community stakeholders, and an Aboriginal policy committee to solicit input from local Indigenous groups.

The activities associated with the technical committee demonstrated a well-developed interorganizational network created to support implementation. The technical committee's role was to coordinate day-to-day management activities, and in turn, it created working groups on water quality, sediment control, and visual quality. These groups involved a wide range of organizations and individuals engaged collecting data, analyzing data and trends, and making management recommendations. As other researchers have highlighted, this type of network involved a complex set of groups with overlapping memberships (Huxham and Vangen 2005).

The key to this network was a clear structure and role for the technical committee, which met monthly to share data, exchange information about organizational programs and policies, and manage research projects. Most significantly, the committee jointly reviewed all use and development permit applications. Each organization maintained its approval authority and power, but the consultation process allowed representatives from each organization to share their perspectives and identify potential problems (TIMP Steering Committee 1992). Each representative took the recommendations back to their organization, which made the final decision, but the consensus of the technical team carried considerable weight. As a result, applicants and staff members began referring to a "TIMP approval process" even though the committee had no direct authority. Between March 1992 and October 1997, the committee reviewed ninety-seven different permits and applications, including applications for development and port expansion, permits for guided boat tours, and permits for firework shows (Margerum 1999c).[7]

Rogue River Basin

The Rogue River drains a twenty-two-thousand-square-mile basin in southwest Oregon, characterized by rugged mountains, forestry, and farming.[8] Most of the mountains and foothills are under the jurisdiction of the U.S. Forest Service and the Bureau of Land Management, while the lowland areas tend to be mostly privately owned. As mentioned earlier, the Rogue River is world renowned for its wild and scenic white-water character, and the basin includes habitat for threatened and endangered species such as steelhead trout, coho salmon, and the northern spotted owl. There are eight watershed councils, which are supported by state and federal funding to restore watersheds, and they focus considerable attention on implementing conservation efforts on private lands.

In 1998, the watershed councils came together to create the Rogue Basin Coordinating Council (Rogue Basin Council). The eight voting members, one from each watershed council, govern the Rogue Basin Council, and invite participation from state and federal agencies. The U.S. Forest Service and the Bureau of Land Management have been significant participants because of their substantial land-holdings in the basin as well as responsibilities to protect threatened and endangered species there. The Rogue Basin Council helps coordinate seven basin priorities, including fish passage, water quality, stream flow, basinwide coordination, interagency cooperation and collaboration, outreach and education, and monitoring.

One of the council's goals has been to develop a coordinated, consistent, and streamlined approach to basin-scale restoration planning, implementation, and monitoring. To accomplish this, the agencies created the Rogue Basin Restoration Technical Team. The technical team's primary goal was to combine data from a range of sources into a model that would allow all the organizations working in the Rogue region to assess basin conditions and identify priorities for restoration efforts. The group started with almost twenty members operating under an interorganizational memorandum of understanding, but the technical nature of the work and time demands meant that the bulk of the effort was led by five core members. The result of their modeling work has been adjustments in priorities for management and restoration projects by each of the participating agencies and watershed councils.

In the following sections, I define interorganizational networks, examine the theories on which they are based, and discuss the criteria for evaluating their efficacy. I will relate these concepts to the cases I have researched, particularly the Trinity Inlet and Rogue River basin.

Theory Related to Interorganizational Networks

The concept of interorganizational networks is raised in several disciplines, but before reviewing this literature it is helpful to define the terms cooperation and coordination. Cooperation occurs when participants work together to achieve a common end or goal, while coordination refers to functioning together or bringing things into common relation (Merriam-Webster 1983). A cooperative approach is more of a contractual model in which participants identify an agreed goal or objective, and then independently work toward it. Participants attempt to anticipate future joint needs during the planning process by identifying compatible actions along preestablished schedules and summarizing them in a written strategy (Hage, Aiken, and Marrett 1972). Regardless of whether the strategy is binding, the assumptions are that the interaction necessary to integrate activities is largely completed, and that the participants can be guided by their agreement or plan. As Gray (1989) states, "Self-executed agreements are either implemented at the time of agreement or formulated so that adherence will be self-evident." The shortcoming of a cooperative approach is that changing conditions, new information, and new issues limit the ability of participants to anticipate actions (Lindblom 1959, 1979; Banfield [1959] 1973; Alexander 1984).

A coordinated approach is based on a comanagement model, which assumes that interaction is a continuous process of joint decision making. James March and Herbert Simon (1958) referred to this as an adaptive approach in which structures allow for real-time monitoring and feedback (see also Alexander 1993; Hage, Aiken, and Marrett 1972). Groups of organizations or individuals are interacting on a regular basis, sharing information, comparing analyses, and adjusting decisions and policies based on this interaction. The parties may still create a plan or agreement, but this often serves as a guide rather than a specific plan of action. Gray (1989, 88) notes that when implementation requires these kinds of new relationships, "stakeholders should remain closely involved during implementation."

In light of these definitions, interorganizational networks are formal and informal linkages between organizations that coordinate a set of activities. While social networks are built on social arrangements and interpersonal connections, interorganizational networks are a result of both interpersonal and interorganizational relationships (Huxham and Vangen 2005; Margerum 2008). The term network is relatively new, but the concept of interorganizational coordination has a long history spanning several fields.

Public policy and urban planning literature has been exploring these issues for many years, especially in relation to social services, metropolitan governance, and environmental management (Alexander 1993; Gray 1989; Colby and Murrell 1998; Stone 2000). As Laurence O'Toole Jr. and Kenneth Meier (2004) observe, however, much of the work on this issue is descriptive, and less commonly generalizable or empirically tested. The field of organizational theory also examines organizational behavior along with the factors that lead organizations to work together or independently, such as issues of embeddedness in networks, the role of organizational power, concerns with organizational culture and leadership, and the type of work performed by the organizations (Scott 1998). The institutional analysis literature focuses on the structures and patterns of decision making in society, extending far beyond the sets of rules that define organizational interaction (Hill and Lynn 2003; Ostrom 1990). On the other hand, this literature has been helpful when used to analyze interorganizational settings (Margerum 1999c; Margerum and Born 2000; Imperial 2005). There is also increasing attention being paid to interorganizational collaboration in the nonprofit and business management literature, with the concept being defined in terms of strategic partnerships and the "collaborative advantage" (Huxham and Vangen 2005; Mattessich, Murray-Close, and Monsey 2004; Winer and Ray 1994). Finally, transaction cost economics, game theory, and conflict resolution all provide insights into costs, benefits, and the factors affecting interaction (Hjern and Porter 1981). Four of the common themes and findings from this literature relevant to the discussion here are: the elements of coordination, components of coordination networks, factors affecting participation, and organizational dynamics in coordination.

Elements of Interorganizational Coordination

One long-standing theme from the literature is that coordination is composed of communication and the resolution of differences (Lang 1986a, 1986b; Parker, Peddicord, and Beyle 1975). Communication is necessary to share information, analyses, goals, and objectives (Mattessich, Murray-Close, and Monsey 2004). As Aubrey Sanford and her colleagues (1976) note, the transfer of information is what enables a system to operate. Stakeholders that use the same information and share analyses can develop a common basis of understanding (Parker, Peddicord, and Beyle 1975).

The process of communicating exposes conflicts in data, analysis, and goals (Mattessich, Murray-Close, and Monsey 2004). Therefore, conflict resolution is the second dimension of coordination (Parker, Peddicord, and Beyle 1975; Winer and Ray 1994). Mitchell (1986) suggests that even if participants communicate effectively and reach consensus on goals, conflict will inevitably appear between collaborating agencies during implementation. Francis Parker, Thomas Peddicord, and Thad Beyle (1975) found that a lack of coordination among organizations could be directly attributed to conflicts or inconsistencies in policies and objectives. "What is needed in such cases are mechanisms capable of mediating or authoritatively resolving these differences" (ibid., 97). This does not mean that conflict should be avoided. Gregory Buntz and Beryl Radin (1983) point out that there are positive aspects to conflicts if they are resolved effectively. Therefore, the key is to respond with effective resolution approaches (Winer and Ray 1994).

In practice, the functions of communication and conflict resolution are carried out via numerous mechanisms or tools. The literature identifies a range of communication tools, including data exchange, one-to-one consultation, group communication, joint review procedures, and information exchange steps. When communication reveals differences, participants can apply a range of techniques depending on the type of conflict, such as additional research, negotiation processes, facilitation and mediation procedures, and appeals to another party (Alexander 1993; Margerum and Born 2000; Winer and Ray 1994).

Coordination and Networks

There are several factors used to analyze coordination and networks, including the extent of hierarchy and degree of formality. Hierarchy refers to the degree of top-down, central control, which is often resisted, insufficient, or inappropriate for providing coordination (Bührs 1991). As Donald Chisholm (1989, 10) notes:

Central coordination does work well when the task environment is known and unchanging; where it can be treated as a closed system. . . . [Yet] the rigid character of standardized procedures inherent in formal centralized structures precludes adaptive responses to surprise, and the organizational system suffers accordingly.

A number of researchers focus on the degree of formality in a coordination configuration to assess its permanence. Other authors concentrate less on formality, and describe it as being regularized or nonregularized—meaning the degree of institutionalization among organizations (Guetzkow 1966; Imperial 2005; Alexander 1993). Huxham and Vangan (2005) highlight the complexity of these relationships, but suggest they can be depicted and even diagrammed to help articulate what exists as well as analyze what is needed. One key to understanding this portrayal is to view networks as "lasting patterns of relations among actors" or a social structure defined by an "organized set of rules."[9]

To better understand these rules, it is instructive to examine the institutional analysis and design literature. Ostrom (1986b, 5) defines institutions as sets of rules that are created by the individuals interacting to produce a degree of order and predictability within defined situations. These rules are "prescriptions commonly known and used by a set of participants to order repetitive, interdependent relationships" (ibid.). Sets of rules regularize human conduct through formal means such as statutes and regulations as well as less formal means such as unwritten agreements. Ostrom proposes a typology for classifying rules into several categories that define the scope, structure, and process of interaction. Ostrom's typology encompasses a much broader set of variables in a decision environment. At the same time, the framework can be applied to interorganizational settings to distinguish ad hoc networks from those with more permanence.[10]

When used to analyze coordination networks, the institutional analysis framework emphasizes two types of issues: the extent of shared power and coordination processes. The scope, position/boundary, and authority rules define the power of the coordination network to impose collective decisions. Importantly, authority does not refer to the power of individual actors but rather the power of the network. An arrangement in which the network itself has collective authority is different from a network that simply allows information exchange, for example. Thus, these rules define what the network will coordinate and what power it has over the autonomy of individual participants (Margerum and Born 2000; Imperial 2005).

Coordination processes refer to the procedures that participants have worked out for sharing information and reaching decisions (Alexander 1984). This parallels the components of coordination discussed above (information sharing and conflict resolution). For a network, crucially, these rules need to be clearly defined and commonly understood rather than ad hoc or serendipitous (Margerum and Born 2000). Hence, even when a committee undertakes a mundane task like "going around the table" at each meeting to provide updates on organizational activities, this informational sharing norm can be an important rule for coordinating activities in the network.

Factors Affecting Network Participation

Another theme relates to the reasons why organizations agree to participate in a network and maintain their involvement. Rational choice perspectives assert that organizations will be willing to participate if they determine that the benefits outweigh the transaction costs (Hill and Lynn 2003; Sabatier, Leach et al. 2005). The transaction costs include the time and staff resources to work jointly, share information, and reach decisions together. The literature on teams, conflict resolution, and group decision making defines these benefits more broadly, noting that the benefits may include access to information from others in the network, improved understanding of issues by the network, reduced conflict, and greater support for implementation (Moreland, Levine, and Cini 1993; Gigone and Hastie 1993; Cragan and Wright 1990; Hill and Lynn 2003; Susskind, McKearnon, and Carpenter 1999; Sabatier, Leach et al. 2005).

Another participation factor proposed by the game theory and group process literature is the role of historic, repeated interactions. As participants interact over time, they learn about each other, their operating procedures, and their reputations, which then can influence their future willingness to participate in a network (Cragan and Wright 1990; Innes 1998; Johnson and Johnson 2000; Justice, Jamieson, and

NetLibrary Inc. 1999; Moreland, Levine, and Cini 1993; Propp 1997; Schwenk and Cosier 1993).

Organizational and resource dependence theories both underscore several factors affecting organizational participation in networks. First, some organizations desire to maintain conceptual control over their implementation activities. Second, issues such as organizational turf and culture may support or constrain a willingness to engage in a network. The nature of the work also may affect participation. When outcomes are not easily observed or quantified, say, organizations are often less willing to grant the discretion necessary to support a coordination network (Hill and Lynn 2003).

Finally, the interorganizational coordination literature notes that organizations are more likely to participate in networks when they recognize their interdependence (Alexander 1998; O'Toole and Montjoy 1984). This interdependence may be "pooled" in the sense that different organizations are focused on the same goals or actions. Alternatively, the interdependence may be sequential—meaning that there is a set of linked or dependent actions involving several different organizations. These interdependencies will also tend to occur in situations where the implementation objectives are complex, ambiguous, or changing, so coordination is necessary to carry them out (Hill and Lynn 2003). For instance, Thomas (2003, 269) observes that the high fragmentation of the Bureau of Land Management lands made the agency recognize its interdependence more than the National Park Service's lands, which tended to be viewed as "biological islands."

Organizational Dynamics

A final theme revolves around the effect that this participation has on organizations and their internal workings. First, participating in a network requires the leaders of an organization to be open to its staff allocating time for this role. Organizational leaders can support coordination structures or undermine them (Thomas 2003; Huxham and Vangen 2005). For example, Agranoff and McGuire (1999) analyzed local government involvement in economic development initiatives, and found that it was important for a city's executive branch to have support and encouragement from the city council.

Second, shared values and culture within an organization can affect behavior and attitude of staff members in the organization, leading to stronger notions of autonomy or more willingness to work with others (Hill and Lynn 2003). Several authors have noted how the culture within various federal agencies has adapted to the demands of collaborative interaction or resisted them (Clarke and McCool 1996; Thomas 2003; Danter et al. 2000). Researchers point to the significance of field-level empowerment (Danter et al. 2000) or discretion in operating procedures (Thomas 2003).

A third issue is the impact that coordination has on internal assignments, training, and individual activities (Hill and Lynn 2003). Researchers have given this only limited attention, but coordination requires organizations to be open and flexible to making these adjustments (Agranoff and McGuire 1999; Rogers 1982). Coordination also requires organizational leaders to have new management skills consistent with facilitator roles rather than traditional directive roles (Mandell 2001; Gray 1989; Koontz et al. 2004; Huxham and Vangen 2005).

Assessing an Interorganizational Network Strategy

As noted in chapter 5, not all settings require an adaptive approach to implementation. Organizations can be assigned tasks, and carry them out individually with their own internal structures and resources. When there is a need for ongoing adaptation and adjustment that involves organizations, however, interorganizational networks may be necessary. The shift to implementation activities may also require linkages with new sets of people and participants—some of whom were not involved in the consensus-building phase.

Based on my research and the literature, I have identified three major factors that are important for assessing the efficacy of an interorganizational network strategy: support for the network, shared power in the network, and procedures that support ongoing coordination (see table 8.1).

Support for the Network

One factor that can be used to assess networks is their support. Organizations and particularly government entities tend to be funded to address issue-specific problems. Collaboration efforts often address problems that are diffuse, cut across organizational boundaries, cross jurisdictions, or lie in vague areas between jurisdictions. Therefore, no single organization views the problem as central to its management activities. This means that some organizations will see network activities as an "add-on" and not place a high priority on supporting it.

In my survey of Australian catchment committees, I asked participants to evaluate the commitment and support of agencies. The range of evaluations of one agency highlighted that the reasons for support were complex and varied. While 12 percent rated the support of the New South Wales Department of Agriculture as very low, 16 percent rated it as very high (see figure 8.1). This was confirmed in my interviews with committee members, who described strong support by the agency in one catchment and nonexistent support by the same agency in a neighboring catchment.

The Trinity Inlet and Rogue basin cases both provide examples of clear organizational support for coordination networks. The organizations involved in the Trinity Inlet Management Program all committed resources up front to support the

Table 8.1
Assessing an interorganizational network strategy

Factors	Measures of factors	Related references
Support for network: Participating organizations sustain network efforts	• Support through allocation of resources and staffing • Changes in goals, objectives, and priorities of participating organizations to support network goals	Bührs 1991; Alexander 1995; Huxham and Vangen 2005
Shared power: Willingness on the part of organizations to share decision-making power in the network	• Clearly defined scope for coordination activities • Clearly defined participants in the network, and clear rules for how organizations enter or leave the network • Clear authority about coordination authority of the network	Margerum and Born 2000; Ostrom 1986
Coordination procedures: Structures and processes for coordinating are clearly articulated and documented	• Clear rules about the information being exchanged among organizations, including form, timing, and procedures • Clear rules about how participating organizations will reach decisions	Margerum and Born 2000; Ostrom 1986; Huxham and Vangen 2005

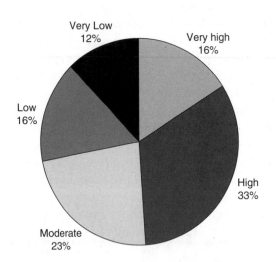

Figure 8.1
NSW agriculture support assessed by committee members. *Note*: *n* = 69.

management expenses and projects. The total funds allocated to the program and its projects ranged from $300,000 to almost $750,000 in Australian dollars per year (or $192,000 to $480,000 in 1996 U.S. dollars) for a coordinator and project implementation budget (TIMP 1996).[11] Similarly, in the Rogue basin, a key factor in the group's success was U.S. Forest Service funding for a coordinator and staff position for the technical team. Participants noted that agencies had to come up with more than $100,000 to support the effort, and the U.S. Forest Service agreed to fund the coordinator position.

Assessing Support

Several factors can be used to assess organizational support, including the commitment to power sharing and coordination processes, which are discussed in the next section. Support can also be assessed through qualitative interviews and questionnaires. In this section I summarize several empirical approaches to assessment, such as the allocation of resources and substantive changes in organizational programs.

Resources

One clear indicator of organizational commitment is a financial commitment by participating organizations to the coordination network. Assessing resource commitment is a simple principle in theory, but often difficult to apply in practice. Cash contributions can be easily documented. For example, I collected data from OWEB about financial support for council operations and found wide variation in its funding sources (see figure 8.2). In the 2003–2005 budget cycle, the South Coast Watershed Council obtained 100 percent of its council support funding from OWEB, while the McKenzie Watershed Council obtained 100 percent of its funding from non–OWEB sources, such as land management agencies and the U.S. Environmental Protection Agency.

In addition to financial resources, Koontz and his colleagues (2004) point out that human resources (personnel time) and technical resources (information, knowledge, and data) are also important. But assessing support in the form of staff, facilities, or other in-kind efforts is more difficult. For instance, many watershed councils in Oregon utilize networks of federal and state agencies to provide technical advice, project assistance, and information to carry out their functions. The support by these organizations is crucial, but not as easily quantified.

Substantive Changes

Another indicator that can be used to assess support is to examine whether the network has influenced the goals, objectives, and programs of the participating organizations. Along with Rachael Holland, I evaluated the effect of a collaborative regional growth management effort in Queensland based on a

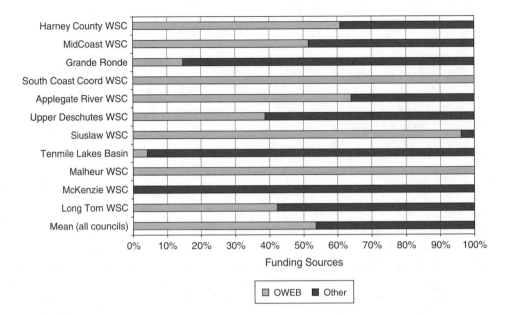

Figure 8.2
Sources of support for watershed council operations. *Notes*: From records of OWEB for the 2003–2005 funding cycle. Other sources of support include federal agencies, local governments, utilities, and Indian tribes.

review of local government plans prepared before and after the regional planning process. We found that the subregional networks of local governments played a significant role in supporting changes to local government policies and programs. In particular, local governments in the western part of the region began coordinating data collection and the analysis of environmental resources. This influenced the policies of several jurisdictions, and one council established a conservation easement program based on some of these efforts. In contrast, the more pro-environment councils in the northern part of the region were never able to maintain a coordination network, and their plans revealed less substantial changes in relation to regional conservation issues (Margerum and Holland 2000; Margerum 2002b).[12]

Shared Power

A second factor in assessing an interorganizational network is the extent of shared power among the participants. Huxham and Vangen (2005, 175) maintain that "power in the context of collaboration is not always thought about in terms of its use by one party over another party for that party's gain." Instead, power often is motivated by mutual gain or the "power to do" (ibid.; Agranoff and McGuire 2003;

Winer and Ray 1994). Power may also relate to "power for" or altruistic gain that creates a "shared transformative capacity" (Bryson and Einsweiler 1991, 3).

I have examined collaborative groups in which organizations participate in collaborative processes, share information, and develop a joint plan. Yet when it comes to implementing this plan, a critical question is whether they are willing to share power over ongoing decision making. Sharing power may occur in a range of forms, including joint decision making about priorities, program design, resource allocation, and policy interpretation. Data sharing, which is also a form of power sharing, is addressed in the next section.

Sharing power does not mean that the organization gives up its power but rather that it allows others to influence its decision making. In practical terms it means that there is an interorganizational network in which some decisions are made jointly. A participant involved in the Rogue Basin Coordinating Council noted that this process of sharing is not always easy. After identifying a common vision for the basin and sharing information about environmental conditions, the participants worked to develop regional restoration priorities that would have the greatest benefit for watershed health. This meant that the federal agencies, state agencies, and watershed councils working on the effort had to review their own goals as well as adjust their priorities. Alan Henning, an Environmental Protection Agency employee involved in the Rogue Basin Coordinating Council, commented:

It's a lot easier if you don't have to share your priorities with someone else and focus on your own priorities. It's harder to set your priorities, and then lay them out on the table and have other agencies come in and say, "Well, let's change that for you." . . . It changes your work plan; it changes your focus; it changes what people do on the ground. There is a lot that goes into giving up your autonomy.[13]

Assessing Power Sharing

To assess the extent of shared authority in an interorganizational coordination network it helps to utilize the literature on institutional analysis. As noted in the literature review, this framework does not offer a normative model of which *type* of coordination arrangements are more effective, but it does allow the analyst to deconstruct the arrangements and assess the extent of shared power (Margerum and Born 2000; Imperial 2005). A key concept in this framework is the idea of rules that define arrangements, which may be formal agreements, written committee procedures, or norms of operation that develop over time that are not written down. Thus, it is not so much whether the rules are formal or written down but instead whether they define the norms and practices of interaction. The risk with rules based entirely on unwritten norms is that organizations may not be committed to them or they may not be sustained when participants change.

Scope

One way of assessing the extent of power sharing is to examine the rules that define the set of concerns being addressed through the coordination arrangements (Margerum and Born 2000). This defines the purpose of the collaborative network and "the choice of issues that the members attend to" (Huxham and Vangen 2005, 179). If this scope is not clearly specified, there may be confusion among the participants about what they are coordinating (or not coordinating). When it is specified, the set of activities that the network is asked to address offers insights into power sharing. For example, the I Team was established to address policies and regulations related to urban waterways in the Illawarra region. Early in its process, the I Team identified a clear scope that it would focus on policy, but not participate in individual permit decisions or case disputes.

Position and Boundary

A second way of assessing power sharing is to look at the participants in the coordination network. This is defined by who holds a place in the network (referred to in the literature as position rules), such as whether an organization participates on a technical committee. As Huxham and Vangen (2005) observe, these members also influence the agenda and the other partners that may be involved in the effort.

Participation is also defined by the rules and procedures for people to enter as well as leave those positions (referred to as boundary rules), such as appointment through a steering committee (Margerum and Born 2000). When these rules are unclear, there may be confusion about who is participating in the network. A lack of clarity may also be a sign of reluctance on the part of an organization to share power. When the rules are clear, they provide insight into who is involved, who is missing, and who has been excluded.

When I studied the technical committee that was helping to coordinate regulatory and permit decisions for the Trinity Inlet Management Program, for example, I was surprised to see that it did not include other agencies such as the state planning department. The boundary rule for this group was appointment by the Trinity Inlet steering committee. The committee refused to seat the department on the technical team because it noted that the team was composed of individuals directly involved in regulatory decisions, and the state planning department did not serve in that capacity (Margerum 1999d). This offers insights into how this group viewed its role and where it limited power sharing.

Authority

A third way of assessing power sharing is to evaluate the extent of the interstakeholder authority imposed on the participants involved in the coordination network. Applying the institutional analysis framework to coordination settings, authority rules are defined by three components (Margerum and Born 2000). For one, the rules specifically establish the array of coordination activities in which the participants can or cannot participate (information exchange or conflict resolution). The authority rules also define how binding or permissive the coordination authority is on participants (i.e., the degree to which unilateral action is precluded). Finally, the rules specify the basis of authority (e.g., law, plan, administrative policy, or informal agreement) (ibid.). These rules parallel a set of questions that Huxham and Vangen (2005, 185) ask about the use of power in collaborative settings, such as "How can joint power 'to do' be executed?" and "How can power be shared between parties?"

The coordination authority may be assigned to a group (such as a committee) or an individual (such as a coordinator). In the Trinity Inlet case, the technical committee served a defined coordination role. The committee's authority was grounded in the management plan, which the principal officials of each participating entity signed (basis of authority). The participating organizations agreed to bring all pending permits to the committee, so that it could collectively review them and make a joint recommendation (array of coordination activities). The legal power of the jointly signed plan was unclear, but the participating organizations could apply peer pressure to attain compliance with these procedures (degree to which authority is binding). The Trinity Inlet Management Program did not influence legislation or even the formal policies of state and local organizations but were instead involved in the gray areas of interpreting and applying legislation and policies.

The authority delegated to the coordinator was less clear, though. In the early days of the Trinity Inlet Management Program, the coordinator assumed a significant substantive role. The coordinator in turn relied on the authority of the Trinity Inlet Plan to guide advice and actions. Participants indicated that this role was important in the early period of TIMP because it reduced the pressure on individual organizations. Thus, it appears that the collective authority of TIMP was exerting a stronger role in permit review than individual organizations had been accustomed or willing to assume. A number of participants noted that the organizations were "hiding behind the mantle of TIMP."[14] The disagreement about the roles and different expectations of the coordinator's role led to a high turnover in the position. With each coordinator change, the authority of the position and TIMP gradually shifted toward more of a process role. Throughout this time, the lack of clear coordination authority for this position created confusion and some controversy (Margerum 1999d).

Coordination Procedures
A final factor for assessing interorganizational networks relates to coordination procedures developed by participants to facilitate ongoing information sharing and joint decision making. A critical foundation of collaboration is information sharing

among participants, but implementation through a network of organizations requires procedures for this to happen on an ongoing basis. Wondolleck and Yaffee (2000, 27) explain that as information is exchanged, "it becomes part of the shared knowledge base necessary for problem solving that is 'owned' by all members of the collaborative group." Others have suggested that as people understand the different sets of data, they get a more comprehensive picture of the problem area (Innes 1996; Cortner and Moote 1999). Nevertheless, there is an important difference between data sharing that becomes a basis for understanding a problem and data sharing that is integrated into decision making. Layzer (2008, 280) analyzed collaborative cases, and found that implementation was impeded in part by the "unwillingness to create institutions that can coordinate collection and analysis of data across jurisdictions and agencies."

For a network to be effective, the participants need to establish the rules or procedures for coordination. Once again, the concept of institutional rules helps with the analysis of these arrangements. These rules define the arrangements for information exchange and those for decision making (Margerum and Born 2000). Rules, as noted above, may be formally adopted procedures or accepted norms, but the key issue is that they are regularized and ongoing. Although information sharing and decision rules are discussed here in terms of coordination procedures, they are also a form of power sharing, because they provide insights into the information, priorities, and analysis of the participants.

In Australia's Trinity Inlet case, the technical committee developed a well-defined process for reviewing applications. Proponents submitted applications to the relevant organization, which then brought it to the technical committee. The committee considered the proposal in light of the inlet management plan and policies of individual organizations, discussed these issues, and made a recommendation to the approval agencies. It made decisions by consensus, reflecting the view that the group's power was its ability to agree on analysis and evaluation of impacts. If the proposal was substantial or involved policy issues, it was usually referred to the steering committee for input, direction, or clarification. Importantly, these information exchange and decision rules preserved the powers of the individual agencies, although they encouraged them to use the process to produce more consistent and well-informed decisions.

The Rogue Basin Coordinating Council established a technical team that developed a joint database using twelve different physical habitat indicators along with a model for determining watershed condition and restoration priorities. This process presented significant technical challenges, because of the difficulties of combining data sets, working across different agency data procedures, and developing a model that would pass muster with a peer review process. The ultimate goal of the process, however, was to develop a model to allow watershed councils and land management agencies to adaptively manage the ecosystem as well as provide ongoing guidance on management priorities. Brian Barr, a staff scientist with the World Wildlife Fund who participated in the effort, described the purpose for a model:

The real benefit and beauty of [the model] is that it not only tells you which [watersheds] are healthy and less healthy but also has the ability to pinpoint within each watershed what are the weakest links. So it becomes less about assessment and more about diagnosis; so it helps you prioritize where you are going to do work and what kind of work you are going to do.[15]

Once again, the key here is that information sharing is not a one-off process conducted by stakeholders during a consensus-building process but rather an ongoing system to support management and implementation decisions.

Assessing Coordination Procedures

The institutional rules framework can be adapted to assess coordination structures in terms of their clarity and specificity, but does not prescribe a better or worse approach. The procedures for coordination are obviously interlinked with the sharing of power for decision making. In particular, *who* is involved in the coordination network needs be specified before participants can establish *what* they will be coordinating. Still, even in cases where the structure is clear and there are entities in positions to coordinate, coordination may not be occurring when the procedures are unclear or ad hoc (Margerum and Born 2000). An ad hoc approach means that participants have no set procedures for sharing information or making joint decisions, which often makes decisions time-consuming, complicated, and capricious.

In complex interorganizational networks, it is important to clarify procedures so they are fully understood and able to be utilized (ibid.; Huxham and Vangen 2005). Clarifying the procedures means defining the rules for information exchange and decision making. Information rules specify the content of the information that the participants must exchange, the form of the information, and the timing of the exchange (Margerum and Born 2000). The rules may specify general guidance, such as reports on activities at monthly meetings. They may relate to more specific procedures, such as the process for referring permits to other organizations used in the Trinity Inlet case. The rules may specify more detailed information-sharing procedures, such as the joint database and modeling efforts undertaken by watershed councils and federal agencies in the Rogue basin.

Decision rules lay out the processes by which the position holders in the network reach decisions. These rules may be general consensus or voting procedures, such as unanimity, super majority, simple majority, or plurality (ibid.). For example, the decisions of the Rogue technical team were based on consensus, which reflected the need to develop a model that all the parties could use. Researchers and evaluators looking for "evidence" of these rules may find them in: a plan or strategy signed by each organization; a memorandum of understanding that outlines roles and support; contracts or agreements that outline roles and support in more formal terms; and informal written agreements by participants.

Some procedures may emerge as norms, but participants should be able to describe these norms, and the norms should be evident in agendas and meeting minutes. Several Australian catchment committees, for instance, established an expectation that at each meeting, agency representatives would attend and provide a written update on activities and projects.

Discussion

The criteria described above focus on the factors for assessing interorganizational networks. Organizational collaboratives are well positioned to utilize interorganizational networks, because the collaborative itself is part of the network. Action and policy collaboratives can also utilize interorganizational networks, though. For example, one of the early innovations of the Australian Landcare Program was to hire regional Landcare facilitators, who then helped link action-level Landcare groups with the network of agency staff. Campbell (1994, 205) depicts the facilitators as the "meat in the sandwich" between Landcare groups and government agencies. He notes their importance in supporting the groups, acting as a "bureaucracy buster," and working within government agencies to provide landowner perspectives.

Action-level collaboratives also utilize interorganizational networks to support technical functions, monitoring, and other efforts. They are typically not coordinating organizational policies or programs but rather action-level advice and expertise from several different agencies. As noted previously, many watershed councils in Oregon use technical teams of agency staff to support their restoration projects.

Finally, it is quite common for policy collaboratives to utilize interorganizational networks for implementation. As mentioned in chapter 2, even with a strong policy collaborative in place, there will be a need to delegate many management functions. It is also likely that many of these management functions will cross organizational boundaries and jurisdictions, making an interorganizational network critical to success.

In this section I explore some of the implications and complications of developing as well as sustaining interorganizational networks, including the barriers to developing networks, the costs and benefits of coordination networks, and organizational dynamics.

Barriers to Developing Networks

As noted in the discussions about power sharing and coordination procedures, coordination networks are most effective when the rules defining these networks are written down in agreements, plans, or even meeting minutes. Yet this often fails to occur for several reasons. Participants are reluctant to develop and document networks because this takes time, they are anxious to "get on with the job," or the group appears amicable. The conflict resolution literature nonetheless emphasizes that spending time on operating rules at the beginning of a group frequently makes it operate more efficiently over the long run, because there are shared expectations about group process (Susskind and Cruikshank 1987; Susskind, McKearnon, and Carpenter 1999). Furthermore, it is much more difficult to step back and change those patterns when a group is in the middle of a difficult deliberation (Susskind and Cruikshank 1987; Susskind, McKearnon, and Carpenter 1999; Gray 1985). A participant involved in one of the Wisconsin cases, for example, highlighted their operating rule problems: "You thought that you would have settled an issue, and you would come back to the next meeting and people disagreed that it was resolved."[16]

Another barrier to developing and documenting networks can be the approvals required by the participating organizations. In the cases I observed where a coordination network existed, it developed through the initiative of a stakeholder forum where organizational representatives had some organizational authority. In other words, there were managers or administrators in the group who had the power or influence to commit the organization to the network. In both the Rogue basin and Trinity Inlet cases, there were high-level forums that provided a crucial venue for clarifying policy interpretations and agency commitments. Agency participants in the Rogue basin instance used the regional interagency committees established for the Northwest Forest Plan to address high-level agency issues. In the Trinity Inlet case, the steering committee itself was composed of mayors, ministers (elected officials), and high-level administrators who could address similar issues.

This is not to say that a network could not evolve from the bottom up, but if the organizations are hierarchical it may be difficult for staff-level representatives to gain their organization's commitment to a network. For example, regional natural resources management organizations in Australia have had difficulty obtaining state agency support, often because they are relying on lower-level staff as liaisons.[17] Similarly, Huxham and Vangen (2005, 130–131) underscore the ambiguity faced by representatives of organizations, and point out that the role of the individual can be seen as a continuum:

At one extreme the organization takes little interest in the collaboration. The individuals are effectively collaborating in their own capacity. . . . [T]he only contribution from their organization is the allowance to the individual of the time spent working with the collaboration. . . . At the other extreme, organizations are fully involved in the collaboration with full commitment to its aims and objectives and to ensuring that these are met.

The Costs and Benefits of Coordination Networks

A question that arises with interorganizational networks concerns the costs and benefits of participation. Mark Lubell and his colleagues (2005) stress several reasons why people coordinate, including the desire for information as well as to improve conditions, protect one's interests, and achieve the goals of one's organization. A difficulty with participating in a network, however, is that its costs are generally immediate and easier to quantify than the benefits. Benefits are often diffuse, indirect, and long term.

In concrete terms, individuals working for an organization know how much of their time is consumed with a coordination task relative to other tasks. As a result, they usually have to make choices about participating. Participants in several cases noted that there were more groups operating in their jurisdiction than they could cover. A regional manager for an Australian fisheries agency had seven catchment committees in his region. He had to pick and choose the committees and their meetings depending on the topics they were considering.[18] Likewise, Thomas (2003, 275) found that travel time to interagency meetings was important for explaining the duration of coordination activities, even in the presence of other motivating factors.

In contrast, the benefits of coordination are harder to assess and less immediate. The benefits might include preventive activities (which have less immediacy than responsive actions) and interjurisdictional activities (which by definition are not central to any one organization). In the Rogue basin, participants commented that their regional efforts have helped them to identify the key limiting factors to improving watershed health, which allows federal agencies and watershed councils alike to focus on activities that are likely to produce the greatest benefit. But these benefits are hard to quantify and they are shared among all the partners. As one participant remarked, "I view my role down here as to build the partnership that will help us achieve long-term watershed-scale gains for achieving properly functioning conditions. I put my window out there one hundred years and I am encountering a lot of resistance within my agency."[19]

One type of benefit that is easier to describe, but still difficult to quantify, is the savings and economies of scale that happen when activities are carried out together. For example, it can be more cost effective for three organizations to conduct monitoring together across a wide area than for each one to carry out monitoring separately. This was one of the chief benefits that a network of local government environmental planners in South East Queensland could use to sell their regional coordination efforts to elected officials. The group was able to jointly fund several regional habitat and vegetation studies that none of the local governments could afford individually (Margerum and Holland 2000).

Similarly, avoiding duplication can also be a selling point within organizations. When I worked on water integration issues for the Wisconsin DNR, a staff person in a regional office told me a story that I used several times to support calls for coordination. He and a colleague were taking water samples in a stream when they noticed a suspicious pair of men working downstream from them. Putting their "enforcement hat" on, they went downstream to confront the two men, only to discover that they were two staff members from a different DNR division who were also collecting samples in the same creek. With the numerous activities and programs that occur within an agency, this was not an isolated incident.

Another benefit of a network approach is the ability to create an ongoing forum that allows participants to make adjustments, respond to issues more quickly, and anticipate problems. A participant involved in the Rogue River efforts commented that without regular interaction points, stakeholders generally don't come together until there is already a crisis or significant problem. In other words, there is a certain inertia to assembling participants, and therefore people may get together only when they have to respond to something. Participants involved in networks in the Trinity Inlet and Rogue basin mentioned the value of having access to something as simple as the activities that other organizations are doing.

An issue raised in the literature is whether organizational leaders go through a conscious calculation of costs and benefits, or whether they rely on other factors, such as moral dimensions, collective goals, and public goods (Alter and Hage 1993; Etzioni 1988). For example, Gray (1989, 58) observes that "the recognition by stakeholders that their desired outcomes are inextricably linked to the actions of the other stakeholders is the fundamental basis for collaborating."

While my research has not explored this decision calculus, I did find that organizational policies about priorities, job duties, and employee performance affected participation in interorganizational networks. In cases in Wisconsin and Oregon, employees working for government organizations emphasized that their job duties and performance evaluations were important influences. In Wisconsin, an agency employee was told that the work of a network was not part of his job description— even though he could see the long-term benefits it would have for the work that was listed in his job description. Rather than withdrawing from the group, he continued to attend meetings and participate on his own time. In Oregon, a local government employee was under similar pressure to demonstrate the benefits of her work to the city:

I don't have enough time, so I might be interested in the topic professionally or personally, but I need to link it to the work I do for the city. Things need to be linked to accomplishments—it has to be done within a year. That way I can justify my time for the city.[20]

These kinds of cost and benefit calculations mean that the resources to support collaborative activities can be an incentive to participate in a network. Participants involved in coordinating the implementation of several watershed plans in Wisconsin indicated the significance of the funding linkages. For many organizational representatives, this funding made participation in this network an easy sell to their leadership. Integrated management plans prepared for the same regions, in contrast, did not have the same funding linked to it. As one county official remarked sarcastically, "They are nice plans; won't it be nice if someone implements them."[21]

Organizational Dynamics

Why do some organizations work collaboratively, and others do not? This has been a question raised by several researchers examining collaboration efforts (Wondolleck and Yaffee 2000; Thomas 2003; Danter et al. 2000; Cortner and Moote 1999; Clarke and McCool 1996). There are several reasons why organizations may be reluctant to commit to an interorganizational network.

First, many of these researchers refer to "organizational culture" as a key parameter, including the internal reward structures, and whether the norms of the organization support this kind of interaction (Wondolleck and Yaffee 2000; Cortner and Moote 1999). Several researchers also note the importance of organizational flexibility and the willingness to give discretion to lower-level managers (Wondolleck and Yaffee 2000; Thomas 2003). For example, Thomas (2003, 274) describes how Bureau of Reclamation officials "read directly from the agency's multivolume codebook at interagency meetings to delimit what they could not or would not do."

Second, many organizations are evaluated by specific missions or have narrow mandates that they must fulfill, such as commodity production or regulatory responsibility (Wondolleck and Yaffee 2000; Cortner and Moote 1999). This problem seems to be compounded when organizations face significant budget constraints. In the Rouge basin case, the reduced funding for the National Marine Fisheries Service and the Fish and Wildlife Service made it difficult for them to be consistent supporters. As these agencies absorbed funding cuts, an interagency task group such as the Rogue Basin Restoration Technical Team was hard to defend. Jack Williams of the AuCoin Institute explained that as agencies lose funding for staff, "these interagency coordination things look like icing on the cake. It is nice to do, but maybe they are not really critical. . . . They are not viewed as part of the core business."[22] Frank Bird of the National Marine Fisheries Service noted that federal agencies were going through a 10 percent per year budget decrease and administrators raised questions about the cost of the efforts in the Rogue basin: "This is what I call an elective. This is not a requirement, so these things go first. . . . We are fighting right now to continue funding it. The funding and political reality of this stuff happens, but it is really shortsighted, because if you take the long view the basin needs this kind of group."[23] Similarly, a representative of the Fish and Wildlife Service stated:

We have court-ordered mandates of where we need to spend our money. Even though a proactive effort like this is good and everyone supports it . . . sometimes our hands are tied on what we can set down in our priorities. It might be a high priority, but it might be among four or five high priorities, and so therefore the funding is not there on a yearly basis. We can't count on it.[24]

Third, participating in regional coordination networks creates new dependencies with increased complexity and turbulence (Wood and Gray 1991). One of the seldom-mentioned effects of an interorganizational network is the impact that it has on an organization's internal workings and mechanisms. Supporting a network's activities may mean an internal reallocation of priorities, rewards, and job responsibilities. This makes participation in these networks difficult for organizations, particularly large, highly centralized ones. In small organizations, such as a non-profit group, this can be a relatively simple process that happens through meetings with managers. Within large organizations, such as federal and state bureaucracies, this can instead be a significant undertaking. In several studies of federal agencies participating in collaborative efforts, researchers have cited the barrier of these internal procedures (Jones, Martin, and Bartlett 1995; Doppelt, Shinn, and DeWitt 2002; Danter et al. 2000).

Fourth, organizational issues often involve broader interrelated policy concerns that span organizations, their organic acts, and their governing statutes. As a result, there may be more fundamental issues that require higher-level forums to support these efforts. In the Rogue basin case, participants commented that the Provincial Interagency Executive Committee provided an important forum for resolving budget, resource, and policy issues. The executive committee was set up as part of a subnational structure to coordinate the implementation of the Northwest Forest Plan, but its existence in the region offered a venue for solving issues in the Rogue basin. Williams of the AuCoin Institute asserted that the executive committee was the

go-to group where technical people can go . . . and the bosses are there to listen and try to do something about it on behalf of the whole region. . . . It is good to have those people together so you have a venue to discuss these kinds of things. Otherwise you have to go around and talk to these people individually.[25]

Barr from the World Wildlife Fund also indicated that the structure created by the Northwest Forest Plan

forces all those agencies to talk among themselves and see how opportunities like this could help further all of their goals. So the more those agencies talk at those higher levels, the more the spotlight shines on these kinds of projects that can occur with coordination from all of them.[26]

Craig Tuss of the U.S. Fish and Wildlife Service emphasized the practical benefits of the forum:

Without the PIEC, without that forum for interagency discussion, it would have been really tough for me or for Frank Bird or Al Henning [Environmental Protection Agency] to go to the land management agencies in southwest Oregon and say, "Hey guys, let's have a meeting here to talk about river basins." They would have said, "Great, when I have time I'll do that, but right now I have court suits to deal with, forest plans to deal with, I've got this to do, I've got that to do." It would have been really tough to get their attention and have it be directed to this proactive, pilot process.[27]

A final organizational dynamic relates to staff training and guidance. Training and guidance is important, because historically many natural resources degrees did not provide training in skill sets such as communication, consensus building, and conflict resolution. As a result, studies have repeatedly found that staff from agencies and organizations are not well prepared for collaboration efforts (Doppelt, Shinn, and DeWitt 2002; Koontz et al. 2004; Danter et al. 2000)

Likewise, some organizations have not developed adequate information and processes to provide internal guidance for staff participating in collaborative efforts. When I asked Wisconsin DNR staff members about the guidance they received for their project, 42 percent believed it was adequate, while about half (47 percent) thought there had been little guidance (n = 36). Among the latter group, about one-third felt that this limited guidance was appropriate. One coordinator maintained, "I prefer to have more direction in the agency; we were floundering during the first six months."[28] Similar difficulties were revealed when I asked Australians representing organizations (state agencies, local government, and nongovernmental groups) whether they had sufficient guidance from their organization. A majority of the respondents (59 percent) believed they had sufficient guidance, but one-quarter of them said they did not, and an additional 16 percent were not sure.

Conclusions

This chapter describes a range of coordination networks and the factors that can be used to evaluate them. As indicated throughout the chapter, one of the strengths of interorganizational networks is that they provide pathways for ongoing communication and interaction, which in turn can be important for problem prevention and adaptation.

Also critical in many cases is that ongoing interaction results in new efforts, spin-off projects, and continuous commitment to implementation. By simply keeping a set of issues on the front burner, participants are more likely to follow through on activities. This may also include applying peer pressure to get results.

One overarching weakness of interorganizational networks is that they are hard to establish and sustain. Throughout this chapter, there has been an emphasis on developing, specifying, and documenting these networks. Yet this in itself requires time and resources, with few immediate results.

Any analysis of coordination networks also has to take into account that they are part of a broader set of institutional rules governing decision making. As such, interorganizational networks may be affected by an array of forces, rules, and structures not related to collaboration efforts. Conversely, the efforts of collaborative networks may address activities that have much broader implications. The Rogue basin technical team had to keep in mind that they were not just creating a scientific model but rather a management model that was going to affect the management activities of federal agencies and watershed councils. This makes the efforts of these networks more complicated, as illustrated by the technical team's need to seek out the resolution of several issues through a higher-level interagency committee.

Interorganizational networks, in short, are key for many types of collaboratives. They are clearly most relevant to organizational collaboratives, but action collaboratives may utilize these networks to resolve higher-level issues. Moreover, in creating a structure to implement new policies or programs, policy collaboratives and the established implementation agency may utilize interorganizational networks for implementation.

9

Producing Results through Political Networks

During 2008–2009, several prominent collaborative efforts that I had been following faced dramatic turning points. In the Murray Darling basin, continued degradation and drought led to a significant shift in management from a collaborative model to a regional agency with new powers. In the United States, the state-federal effort to address critical ecological issues in the CALFED case was quickly unraveling. At the same time, policy-level efforts in metropolitan San Diego and metropolitan Denver continued to be sustainable, with varying levels of results.

One of the factors important in all these cases was the ability (or inability) of the collaborative to foster a political network to support implementation. This chapter discusses the definition of political networks, and the factors that can be used to assess their effectiveness. It is based on my case study research and secondary analysis of published cases. Nevertheless, of all the topics covered in this book, I have the least data directly related to political networks and their effectiveness. While the topic of political networks is described and researched in the literature, there has been little research about its role relative to collaborative efforts. This chapter thus aims to integrate theories about political action with my research and secondary analysis. As a result, the factors and approaches to assessing political networks are ripe for further evaluation.

What Are Political Networks?

I define political networks as being composed of a set of individuals who occupy political and policy positions along with their sustained relationships with other position holders. Knoke (1990) defines political networks in terms of formal positions, and the connections between those positions. Yet I suggest that political networks are a combination of both the position and the social, intellectual, and political capital that develops among political actors (Innes et al. 1994; Roberts and King 1996). In describing the role of networks in relation to collaboration, I start with several assumptions.

For one, the position holders in a political network may be elected officials, representatives of interest groups, or representatives of organizations with political clout. The stakeholders participating in the CALFED process included elected officials, administrators from state and federal agencies, major interest groups, and industry associations (Little Hoover Commission 2005).

Second, I focus on political networks that develop from collaborative processes, which include a diverse and heterogeneous set of political actors who are willing to work together on joint problem solving. This is in contrast to networks that emerge as coalitions of policy actors with like-minded policy beliefs (Sabatier, Jenkins-Smith, and Lawlor 1996; Sabatier, Jenkins-Smith, and Palumbo 1995; Knoke 1990).

Political networks also include both formal and informal relationships among position holders (Knoke 1990; Roberts and King 1996). Hence, this network may be defined by one's role as a stakeholder in a collaborative project, a member of a legislative committee, or a participant in informal but ongoing groups concerned about an issue.

Finally, political networks are complex, dynamic, and interconnected. The efforts to analyze these networks therefore often reveal complex connections and relationships among participants (Burt 1983; Roberts and King 1996). Like social and interorganizational networks, political networks exist irrespective of collaborative processes and encompass a wide range of political activities. This makes it difficult to describe the boundaries of these networks.

Why Are Political Networks Important?

There are several reasons why political networks are important to support implementation. First, overlapping jurisdictions and contradictory policies may require simultaneous changes to multiple policies, thereby requiring complex and interactive deliberations among political actors. One of the ongoing areas of deliberation in Australia's Murray Darling basin, for example, related to the allocation of water rights across the states in the region. Because the Australian government has very limited environmental management powers, the process involved complex and contentious deliberation among the states.

Then too, a one-time policy change assumes that the solutions to the problems are clear, which is often not the case in complex systems. There may be differences and debate about both the objectives (end points) and the means to achieve those objectives (strategies). This was demonstrated in the CALFED case, where management partners invested billions in a science program to better understand the management of the estuary and river basin (Innes et al. 2006, Little Hoover Commission 2005).

Political networks also allow for a more adaptive approach, which is critical for problems involving dynamic systems, changing information, and variable conditions. The CALFED and particularly Murray Darling cases illustrate these dynamics in terms of climatic variability. In Australia, prolonged drought raised questions about modeling and management assumptions, leading to new deliberations about policy responses (Connell 2007).

Delineating Political Networks

In describing political networks, it is essential to keep in mind that they involve high-level actors engaged in ongoing policy adaptation and implementation. Political networks thus are not required for all adaptive management approaches—just those in which significant *policy* adaptations are involved.

For example, in the Lower Wisconsin River valley, policy-level stakeholders deliberated about the policies to manage recreation and development. These policies were enshrined in new legislation and funding, which resulted in a new organization called the Lower Wisconsin Riverway Board. The implementation of management plans by the Wisconsin DNR and the riverway board has required ongoing monitoring, adaptation, and adjustment through an interorganizational network. But there has not been a need to revisit or adapt the policies, and as such, there has not been an ongoing political network engaged in implementation. In cases like CALFED, the Murray Darling basin, and metropolitan Denver, there was an ongoing need for policy adaptations and adjustment.

It is also important to recognize that political networks may involve implementation tools ranging from completely voluntary approaches to highly regulatory ones. Political network participants are focused on policy-level solutions, which means their efforts center on policy strategies. In the Denver region, for instance, policy has revolved around incentive-based strategies to encourage the local adoption of urban growth boundaries. Local governments impose this policy on themselves with monetary incentives for compliance.

Moreover, when policy collaboratives play an ongoing role in addressing an issue or problem, they become part of a political network. It can be hard, then, to define the boundaries between the collaborative and the other network relations. For example, elected officials from across the Denver and San Diego regions participate on regional boards and committees created by the metropolitan planning organizations. Many of them are board members of the collaborative as well as members of a political network related to transportation and land use. This also means that collaboratives at the action or organizational level seeking to utilize political networks are at a disadvantage relative to policy collaboratives, because they must build their own network or seek out an already-existing one.

Examples of Political Networks

Throughout this chapter, I will refer to several policy collaboratives that I have researched directly and/or analyzed through published research. These cases provide examples of the potential of policy-level collaboration and the weaknesses in producing results. The weaknesses relate to the difficulty of sustaining political networks over the long term.

Denver Metro Vision

The Denver metropolitan region has been growing rapidly for several decades, adding over 550,000 people between 1990 and 2000 alone. These high growth rates along with the accompanying transportation and congestion issues led DRCOG to initiate Metro Vision 2020 to manage growth. DRCOG is a public agency funded primarily by federal grants and contributions from the participating local governments in its eight-county region. As the designated transportation-planning agency, DRCOG is tasked with preparing a six-year capital plan for transportation in the metropolitan region.

DRCOG is governed by a fifty-two-member board of directors, which is composed of elected officials from each of the member local governments in the region and three nonvoting members appointed by the governor. Four officers, elected to one-year terms each February, and an executive director lead the board (DRCOG 2000). Metro Vision 2020 started in 1993 with a forty-member task force, eventually leading to the Metro Vision 2020 Framework to address regional transportation, land use, air quality, water quality, and open space (ibid.). In 1997, the members of DRCOG adopted Metro Vision 2020 on a vote of thirty-seven to two, with one abstention (Katz 1997; Margerum 2005).

The challenge for DRCOG and the Metro Vision plan has been to sustain this agreement over time. As individual jurisdictions are affected by the regional policies, more pressure and criticism has been directed toward the regional plan. Furthermore, as elected officials in the region changed, it has been difficult to sustain the agreements. Elected officials, in particular, are busy with their own local government activities, committees, and issues, and are often reluctant to participate on committees and forums that address regional concerns.

CALFED

In California's Sacramento and San Joaquin river and estuary systems, significant drought and water use conflicts led federal agencies to work collaboratively with the state of California to develop a new management approach. In June 1994, these state and federal partners signed an agreement to coordinate activities in the Delta, particularly for water quality standards, which was the beginning of a

California-federal partnership called CALFED. The planning area for CALFED covered over 40 percent of California, requiring intensive involvement among a wide range of public and private partners. The partners worked for six months to develop a science-based proposal for water quality standards, which then led to an agreement known as the Bay-Delta Accord. The accord along with the accompanying agreements and memorandums of understanding were eventually signed by twenty-five state and federal implementing agencies that agreed to work collaboratively toward achieving balanced improvements in the Delta (California Bay-Delta Program 2008).

The CALFED Bay-Delta Program was charged with implementing a long-range comprehensive plan to reduce water use conflicts while restoring the bay delta ecosystem in northern California, the core of the state's water supply system. The program was overseen by the CDBA, which was composed of interests such as state and federal agency representatives, members of the public, ex officio legislative members, and members at large. The CDBA also maintained a thirty-member Bay-Delta Public Advisory Committee and supported the CDBA Science Program, which included scientific reviews, regional conferences, and the Independent Science Board (Little Hoover Commission 2005).

CALFED has been attempting to restore the ecological integrity of the California bay delta system through an extensive array of policy changes and program shifts. It has spent over three billion dollars to address water quality, water supply, ecosystem restoration, floodplain management, and water storage issues. The road has been a rocky one for CALFED, however, with state and federal partners failing to fully fund the effort, calls for restructuring, and critical reviews of the agreements and management structure (Heikkila and Gerlak 2005; Innes, Connick, and Booher 2007; Little Hoover Commission 2005; Owen 2007). A lack of political support and the California fiscal crisis has effectively ended CALFED (Kallis, Kiparsky, and Norgaard 2010).

Murray Darling River Basin

As noted in chapter 2, the Murray Darling River is the largest in Australia, crossing five states and territories on its journey from Queensland to South Australia. The system drains an area of over 1 million square kilometers (approximately 386,000 square miles), which is one-seventh of Australia's mainland (Pigram 1986). The primary authority for managing water quality and quantity resides with the states, so the commonwealth of Australia has limited environmental management powers. As a result, the basin was managed through a state-federal partnership called the Murray Darling River Basin Initiative.

The initiative was a partnership designed to promote and coordinate the planning and management of water resources in the basin. It was supported by the Murray

Darling Basin Agreement of 1992, which was eventually signed by the Australian government as well as the basin states and territories. There were six formal partner governments in the agreement, with many departments and agencies involved. The initiative's decision-making forum, the Murray Darling Basin Ministerial Council, oversaw the agreement. The forum maintained a community advisory committee with members from communities and interest groups across the basin. The council's work was carried out by the Murray Darling Basin Commission (2009), which had administrative and technical staff to support its implementation programs.

This chapter focuses on the structure prior to 2008. In December 2008, the commonwealth and states created the new Murray Darling Basin Authority, which absorbed all the functions of the former Murray Darling Basin Commission. The new, independent authority has more substantial powers. Most important, it has the power to set limits on water that can be taken from surface and groundwater systems across the basin. To allow the authority to be created, the basin states of Queensland, New South Wales, Victoria, and South Australia all had to pass legislation that allowed the Australian government to amend the Commonwealth Water Act of 2007 (Murray Darling Basin Authority 2009). This change effectively ended the collaborative approach to water *quantity* management in the basin. At this time, it is too early to judge the effectiveness of the new authority to address these issues.

Theory Related to Political Networks

There is a range of literature related to policy-level processes and networks, including contributions from the literature from fields such as public policy, planning, political science, and management.

One major body of work has emerged from the advocacy coalition framework developed by Paul Sabatier, Hank Jenkins-Smith, and their colleagues (Sabatier, Jenkins-Smith, and Lawlor 1996; Sabatier, Jenkins-Smith, and Palumbo 1995). They argue that policymaking occurs primarily among specialists who seek to influence policy within specific subsystems defined by both function (e.g., water) and territory (e.g., California). Another major area has developed around regime theory, which examines how power, interests, knowledge, and context affect the formation of international coalitions to address transboundary problems (Haas 1989; Lindemann 2008; Mostert et al. 2007; Pahl-Wostl 2006). Then there are an array of structural approaches to analyzing political processes that address the issue of political networks, structures, and communication networks (Burt 1982, 1992; Knoke 1990; Granovetter 1982). There is also Ostrom's work (1986a, 1986b, 1990) on institutional analysis and development, which uses a set of evaluative criteria, and applies them to the patterns of interaction formed by participants and the outcomes produced. Finally, there is a range of literature related to theories of collaborative governance from the fields of public policy, urban planning, leadership, and political science (Heikkila and Gerlak 2005; Scholz and Stiftel 2005; Innes and Booher 2010; Chrislip and Larson 1994; Crosby and Bryson 2005, 2010; Huxham and Vangen 2005; Silvia and McGuire 2010).

Based on this literature, there are four themes that are relevant to political networks that emerge in collaborative settings: the costs and benefits of interaction, the effectiveness of competing venues, political actor coalitions and conflict, and leadership.

The Costs and Benefits of Interaction

One theme related to political networks and coalitions is that participants use assessments of costs and benefits in evaluating their participation. Based on concepts from political contracting, Lubell argues that collaboration involves political contracts among actors seeking to minimize the collective action problems associated with common-pool resources. Because it is a voluntary exchange, "the greater the transaction costs of developing and maintaining the partnerships, the less likely partnerships will emerge" (Lubell et al. 2002, 150). Sabatier and others note that this is particularly important during the start-up phase of a collaborative effort, when the transaction costs are the highest (Sabatier, Leach et al. 2005).

As Ostrom (1999) points out, though, the transaction costs are just one aspect of a broader calculation that actors place on the costs and benefits of various strategies as well as their probable outcomes. Many actors are fallible in their analysis, and many of the resource problems they are dealing with are uncertain and complex. People frequently assess processes and outcomes through bounded rationality— meaning that they make rational choices based on limited knowledge:

Individuals, therefore, often must make choices based on incomplete knowledge of all possible alternatives and their likely outcomes. With incomplete information and imperfect information-processing capabilities, all individuals may make mistakes in choosing strategies designed to realize a set of goals. (Ostrom 2007, 256)

This underscores the significance of the costs and benefits of the current problem situation as well as the potential solutions, including uncertainty about the costs and benefits. Thus, participants involved in a political network may not be able to fully evaluate the costs and benefits of participating but instead are more likely to assess their transaction costs. Assessing the costs and benefits of both participation and the policy solutions is also likely to be an ongoing activity.

The Effectiveness of Competing Venues

Another theme from the literature is the idea that policy stakeholders are often evaluating and comparing venues to determine which are most effective for addressing their concerns (Nagel 2006). In comparing the conflict resolution advocacy coalition literature, Sabatier, Leach, Lubell, and Pelkey (2005) maintain that a crucial factor impacting the effectiveness of a collaborative effort is the presence of a stalemate or dissatisfaction with the status quo. Similarly, Crosby and Bryson (2010) propose that failures to address problems through noncollaborative approaches also increase the potential for stakeholders to pursue collaborative venues. In other words, stalemate and failure generally leads policy stakeholders to pursue new venues and consider participation in a network even when they have been in conflict with participants previously.

It is also important for collaborative venues to involve all major stakeholders to ensure the adequate consideration of all perspectives (Sabatier, Jenkins-Smith, and Lawlor 1996). In Roberts and King's (1996) analysis of policy entrepreneurship, they found that a diversity of membership helped avoid groupthink, promoted creativity, and improved the problem-solving capacity of participants. In policy-level deliberation, however, this may create the potential for large stakeholder groups, which can become dysfunctional (Susskind 1985). As a result, Innes (1999) contends that participation is defined by judging who has the ability to block or veto agreements from the group. In Carlson's analysis (1999) of negotiated rule making, he reaches a parallel conclusion, emphasizing the importance of having stakeholders representing interests as opposed to those who may be representative of diffuse interests (e.g., a farmer or community resident).

An effective venue also means that it needs to continue to operate as a venue for communication and consensus building. This requires open communication, consensus decision rules, and often a neutral facilitator (Susskind and Cruikshank 1987; Innes 1998; Sabatier, Leach et al. 2005). In several meta-analyses of collaborative venues, these factors are continually stressed for producing results and a commitment to the decision-making venue (Beierle 2002; Mattessich, Murray-Close, and Monsey 2004; Leach and Pelkey 2001).

Political Actor Coalitions and Conflict

Much of the literature on policy-level interaction underscores that stakeholders form groups or coalitions, even with groups with which they may have previously disagreed, when they believe it will benefit them. The literature on policy subsystems emphasizes the creation of strong power triangles or networks, while others have argued that this appears as more flexible and less rigid political networks, "issue networks," or "advocacy coalitions" (Hajer 1993; Sabatier, Jenkins-Smith, and Lawlor 1996; Weible 2005; Sabatier and Jenkins-Smith 1993; Knoke 1990).

One of the key principles of the advocacy coalition framework is that individual actors are underpinned by normative beliefs that create a set of perceptual filters. At the deepest level are core beliefs that include basic assumptions about human behavior, such as liberty, equality, the welfare of certain groups, and the role of government. At the next level are policy core beliefs, which are the result of deep core beliefs being applied to a policy subsystem. Finally, there are secondary beliefs that are narrower, such as views about rules and budgetary applications within a specific program. The advocacy coalition framework stresses that policy arenas are difficult places to resolve these differences, particularly when the policy differences are rooted in deep core beliefs (Sabatier, Jenkins-Smith, and Lawlor 1996).

The conflict resolution literature also addresses the sources and origins of conflict, but is less pessimistic about its ability to resolve issues. Sabatier, Leach, and their colleagues (2005) note the pessimism of the advocacy coalition framework theory toward consensus-based processes, because they assert that it must overcome the modification of a range of belief systems. Many of the researchers who have studied stakeholder networks suggest that interaction often leads to new information, a new appreciation of different perspectives, and new analyses of existing information. A network that allows open interaction and creative problem solving can often produce win-win scenarios, or identify acceptable ways of compensating losses (Susskind and Cruikshank 1987; Dukes 1996). That said, in an analysis similar to Sabatier, Leach, and their colleagues (2005), Lord (1979) points out that resolution approaches work best when dealing with technical conflicts (debates about information and its interpretation) and interest conflicts (debates about the distribution of gains and losses). Resolution is much more difficult when interaction involves value conflict, claims Lord, because successful agreements ultimately require participants to adjust or reassess their values.

Like the conflict resolution literature, research on political networks and policy entrepreneurship demonstrate the transformational capacity of these forums (Knoke 1990; Roberts and Bradley 1991; Roberts and King 1996). Roberts and King (1996) emphasize how diverse sets of leaders come together through "collective entrepreneurship" to foster policy innovation. These teams are strengthened by the diversity of their membership along with their extended networks of contacts and associations. Yet in Knoke's analysis (1990, 168) of policy change, he remarks on the dynamic nature of these forums, explaining that networks do not seem to be "the bipolar sets of opponents implied by class conflict or power elite theories." Instead, each event attracts a unique set of participants that maintain different portfolios of interests and communications, making it hard to reassemble them as new decisions arise.

Leadership

A final theme relates to the importance of political-level leadership in sustaining momentum on a policy issue. Leadership of political networks shares some common principles with leadership of a collaborative entity (see chapter 6). At the same time, leading a political network is much more complex and involves a much wider array of political actors, including those with no history with the collaborative.

Roberts and King (1996, 165) define this broad role as entrepreneurial leadership, and comment that while this team may be centered on a core of people, it is "not concerned with protecting itself from interference and control." Instead, the team builds a significant network of people involved in various aspects of the policy process, which Roberts and King cite as including policy intellectuals, policy champions, policy administrators, and policy evaluators. Similarly, Innes and Booher (2010) suggest that collaborative governance requires joint learning, building public capacity for problem solving, and generative leadership. They define generative leadership as a process where leaders build collective capacity, and guide interaction to provide opportunities to jointly inquire into problems and solutions.

Similarly, Mary Dengler's analysis (2007, 451) of collaborative governance in the Everglades illustrates the role of "super-agents" who advocate for the "common good" rather than strictly sectional interests:

Super-agents are even more powerful than in a traditional top-down decision-making structure because their power is bolstered through other actors recognizing their central role in facilitating the collaborative environmental governance regime, and also through politicians external to the arena accepting the super-agents as brokers of knowledge in [the] policy-regime.

Assessing Political Networks

This section uses case studies and the literature to identify the factors for assessing the effectiveness of political networks. For the four factors summarized in table 9.1, this section explains each one, discusses one or more examples, explores the research findings from my studies and the literature, and describes some specific measures.

Throughout this section, I refer to the political networks established as a result of consensus-building efforts. There are clearly many political networks that exist independently of these projects, but the question I am asking here is, When a political network is needed to support implementation by a collaborative, how do we assess its potential for effectiveness?

Network Affinity

The first factor includes several elements that I group under the term network affinity. Network affinity refers to the appeal, connections, and feelings of identification that individual political actors have with others who are affiliated with the network. Chapter 3 discusses some of the qualities that support the convening of stakeholder forums, and chapter 6 looks at some of the factors that commit stakeholders to a collaborative on an ongoing basis. Still, the difficulty of

Table 9.1
Assessing a political network strategy

Factors	Measures of factors	Related references
Network affinity: The network is viewed as an appealing forum to discuss issues	• Participants in the network represent diverse perspectives • Participants in the network include key decision makers • Trust and respect develops among network members • Network becomes a key forum	Howlett 2002; Dengler 2007; Roberts and King 1996
Political leadership: Key elected officials and leaders support the political network	• Political leaders publicly support and champion the network • Continued external funding • Legislative and policy support	Heikkila and Gerlak 2005; Roberts and King 1996; Crosby and Bryson 2010; Innes and Booher 2010
Policy relevance: Entity with the capacity to support collective policy goals and sustain the network	• Activity level of political networks • Extent of political attention to implementation responsibility	Roberts and King 1996; Crosby and Bryson 2010
Network revitalization: The collaborative entity works to continuously build, expand, and diversify its political network	• Communication strategies that seek to expand input • Efforts to reach out to broader set of political actors	Roberts and King 1996; Crosby and Bryson 2010; Innes and Booher 2010

maintaining ongoing participation is compounded within political networks for several reasons.

For one, political networks face stiff competition for political actors' time and attention, because there is a vast array of intertwined political networks. As Knoke (1990) notes, individual issues attract a complex set of participants that is hard to reassemble as new decisions arise. A legislator, say, may participate in a political network, serve on a legislative committee related to the topic area, and participate in other political networks with overlapping issues. This high level of involvement and connectedness is what makes these people desirable members of the political network. But this involvement also makes it hard to secure their time and commitment to the process. It also means that policy actors are constantly assessing the benefits of addressing issues through the network versus the other forums in which they may operate. Compared to collaborative social and interorganizational networks, political networks are likely to face the greatest competition from other forums and network opportunities.

Additionally, political networks often don't have the benefit of going through initiation and convening phases. Collaborative groups bring parties together into a process with an intense burst of interaction. Political networks are more likely to evolve organically, adding and losing members at various points in time (Knoke 1990; Roberts and King 1996). This makes some of the group socialization lessons from stakeholder collaboration processes less applicable to political networks.

Assessing Network Affinity

Because of the complexity, dynamic qualities, and informality of network affinity, even describing and defining networks can be difficult. Therefore, assessing network affinity is also hard, but it can be evaluated by examining the network's reputation, and the extent of trust and respect among its participants.

Reputation of Network

One way of assessing network affinity is to look at the diversity and reputation of the participants. Diversity is important, because the strength of the network depends on its ability to bridge political parties and perspectives (Crosby and Bryson 2010). Michael Howlett's analysis (2002) of networks in Canada suggests that those with thin boundaries that are open to new actors are more likely to develop changes in policy goals than those that are more insulated. For example, in San Diego and Denver, the network of participants engaged in ongoing regional planning efforts includes a diverse cross section of political affiliations, city sizes, and types of communities (rural, suburban, and urban).

The reputation of the participants refers to their prestige and influence on decision making. This is parallel to concepts in the conflict resolution literature that emphasize the importance of including participants with the power to block or veto decisions (Innes et al. 1994). Similarly, Kingdon (2003, 180) notes that policy entrepreneurs need to have some "claim to a hearing." This claim comes from expertise, an ability to speak for others such as an interest group, or from holding a decision-making position. The goal of entrepreneurs in a network is not to build an advocacy coalition or support for a particular policy, however, but rather to forge a coalition that includes those with both shared and conflicting views of policy change.

Trust and Respect among Participants

Another way of assessing network affinity is to examine the level of trust, respect, and interpersonal relations that develop across the network (Leach and Pelkey 2001; Leach and Sabatier 2005; Kingdon 2003). Network members often build these relationships from a history of political connections and networking skills (Kingdon

2003). This is similar to the commitment of stakeholders to a policy collaborative, but the informal and ephemeral nature of political networks makes trust and respect more difficult to build (Roberts and King 1996). One way of measuring this trust and respect is to ask the stakeholders themselves, but another way of examining it is to look at stakeholder turnover in the political network. Trust and respect are developed through interaction, so turnover in participants means that this process of trust and respect building must be renewed.

In Dengler's (2007, 448) study of the Florida Everglades, her interviews highlighted the important role that formal and informal interaction play among participants in their process of promoting communication and building trust: "It wasn't just sitting around tables. Being in the same hotel gave all these opportunities to have 'side-bar' conversations with people you would never talk to unless brought together in that environment. In matter of fact, most business got taken care of outside of the room where we met."

Political Leadership

A second factor that can be used to assess political networks is the effectiveness of political leadership. Collaborative leadership has already been noted as a significant factor in sustaining collaboratives (chapter 6), but leadership is compounded in political networks because it requires widespread support across a diverse range of political actors. Some of these actors will have been involved in the consensus-building process, but many will not have been directly involved. The ability of a diverse set of stakeholders to present a consensus approach on a policy direction carries weight, although it often requires broader political support for the financial, legislative, and administrative changes that are necessary (Crosby and Bryson 2010; Roberts and King 1996).

Political leadership is different from external pressures that might come from elected officials or policy-level stakeholders. These external pressures are "push" factors or concerns about problems that keep stakeholders engaged. Leadership of political networks means collective entrepreneurship in which there is a symbiotic relationship between a range of policy entrepreneurs and elected officials (Polsby 1984). Roberts and King (1996) conclude that the complex stakeholder map of policy settings makes it difficult for one person to act as a change agent. Similarly, Innes and Booher (2010) suggest that collaborative governance requires a shift in leadership from a directive approach to a generative one that promotes a collective capacity to learn about problems and create solutions.

The role of political leadership has been noted in several cases. For example, the Murray Darling Basin Commission was criticized for its failure to address some of the fundamental water allocation issues in the region. There was a wide range of proposals to change the institutional arrangements in the basin, but they generally failed to address water reallocation and the array of interlocking policies that influence (or are influenced by) water allocation at the state level. Don Blackmore (2001, 10–11), former chief executive of the commission, noted:

The Murray Darling Basin Initiative is essentially a political initiative. Without active political support it will revert back to a narrow River Murray focus. . . . The current debates on environmental flows . . . vegetation clearing controls, [and water allocation caps] . . . are just a few examples of the issues that tear at the fabric of the political commitment necessary to manage for Basinwide outcomes rather than more narrowly focused state and regional outcomes.

Blackmore concluded by saying:

The Murray Darling Basin Initiative is a testament to the great strength of our Federal system, which has provided the enduring base on which to build. However there will always be tensions in this or any system that must continually be attended to.

Keeping us together and maintaining our vision can only be achieved through shared knowledge, a well-informed and engaged community and *active bipartisan political leadership* [emphasis added]. (ibid, 11)

Political leadership has also been stressed in evaluations and reviews of the CALFED case, as demonstrated by the testimony gathered by the Little Hoover Commission (see table 9.2). Yet the commission decided to embed CALFED in the governor's office—a fairly traditional approach that Giorgos Kallis, Michael Kiparsky, and Richard Norgaard (2010, 640) refer to as the "return to state authority."

Assessing Political Leadership

Indicators of political leadership can be particularly difficult to assess, because much of it takes place behind closed doors and out of the public eye. One theme that emerges from the literature is the presence of champions or entrepreneurs (Crosby and Bryson 2010; Roberts and King 1996; Kingdon 2003). A key distinction is that these people must be champions of the process as opposed to being wedded to any specific problem definition or solution (Crosby and Bryson 2010; Huxham and Vangen 2005). Political actors themselves may be best at assessing political leadership, but other indicators include public positions, funding support, and legislative and policy changes.

Public positions are one way of evaluating political leadership. The office of the U.S. presidency has been described as being important not only for its direct power but also for the president's ability to use the position as a "bully pulpit." Similarly, the extent to which political leaders champion and support the political network in public and political forums is one marker of political leadership. For example, Heikkila and Gerlack (2005) contend that political leadership was critical in policy collaboration efforts in both CALFED and attempts to address policy issues in the Florida Everglades. According to Edward Epstein (2004),

Table 9.2
Political Leadership in CALFED

• Steve Hall, executive director, Association of California Water Agencies: "The most significant point about the formation of CALFED is that it took the leadership of people at the highest levels of state and federal government to overcome the strong gravitational pull that has historically kept the respective state and federal agencies in their own orbits."
• Bill Jones, San Joaquin member, CBDA: "The only reason CALFED worked was because Governor Wilson invested his personal political capital. . . . [U]nless [Governor Schwarzenegger] puts his muscles behind [CALFED], that is the only way it is going to work."
• Pete Wilson, former governor of California: "CALFED has substituted process for leadership."
• Susan Kennedy, former cabinet secretary and chief of staff to Governor Gray Davis: "Political leadership is the main issue, and we are lacking that right now. . . . Without the big personalities that get things done, and without the investment from the state or federal administrations, no one at [the CBDA] has the political permission to institute beneficiary pays. . . . Government happens whether or not political leadership is there."
• Michael Machado, California state senator: "Politically, we are lax on leadership. . . . Leadership has a big role to play. The obstacle is that the entities that have the most resources also have the most political sway."
• Bruce Babbitt, secretary of the interior, Clinton administration: "We have a plan and we have the resources. All we need now is the political will to move forward."
• Marc Holmes, member of the public, CBDA: "Everyone is looking for someone to defer to. Leadership and direction must come from the governor's office. The governor must instruct the secretary of resources to say that we have to make CALFED work."

Source: Little Hoover Commission 2005.

In both cases, federal and state legislative leaders played significant roles in mobilizing legislative support and the necessary authorizations regardless of political party affiliation. Former Senator Dianne Feinstein and Congressman Richard Pombo of California worked tirelessly to ensure federal authorizations for the CALFED Bay-Delta Program.

Political leadership may be assessed through an analysis of public records, news coverage, speeches, and political statements. The extent of political leadership in the legislative realm of government appears in the form of hearings, inquiries, audits, and reviews of the political network. This is not to suggest that political *attention* is a substitute for political *leadership*; it does indicate, though, the extent to which the activities of the political network are "on the radar" of elected officials.

Another sign of political leadership is the trends in funding to support the implementation activities of the political network. For instance, several observers correlate shortcomings in state and federal funding for CALFED with declining political leadership (Little Hoover Commission 2005; Owen 2007). Increased political leadership in Denver around regional planning and public transit, in contrast, helped lead to significant new funding to expand the light-rail system.

Finally, because the implementation activities of the political network often involve legislative and policy changes, the degree to which passage and support for these policies occurs provides an assessment of political support. In the case of CALFED, the passage of legislation by the state of California in 2000 and congressional authorization for federal participation in 2004 demonstrated the political leadership for the effort in its early days. Conversely, the failure by California and Congress to authorize funding evidenced a clear loss of political leadership. Whether state and federal leaders act to reform CALFED and its arrangements will be an important indicator of whether political leadership will increase in the future.

Policy Relevance

A third factor for assessing political networks includes a range of issues related to a collaborative entity, and its relevance to policy and political decision making. As noted in chapter 5, collaborative efforts do not always require ongoing deliberation during implementation, because political actors are able to reach consensus on a policy framework and then delegate implementation. In other cases, there may be a need for ongoing political and policy deliberation, but these deliberations must be relevant to political leaders. I define relevance in terms of discussions that garner the interest, time, and attention of political actors—enough so that it overcomes the transaction costs of participating in the network (Lubell et al. 2002). Although political networks may start out large and robust, they may diminish over time for several reasons.

For starters, change in external pressures to address an issue may lead political actors to reduce their attention (Wondolleck and Yaffee 2000; Weber 2003). After many years of high-profile debate, for example, policy-level activity in Lake Tahoe has garnered much less political and media attention (Imperial and Kauneckis 2003).

Second, as policy issues are resolved over time, there may be less need for a political network. An analysis of the meeting minutes of the Trinity Inlet steering and technical committees revealed fewer policy issues emerging over time. In response, the steering committee began reducing its participation from quarterly to yearly meetings.

Then too, it is possible that political actors seek out other venues when they become dissatisfied with how the network is functioning (Crosby and Bryson 2005, 2010). A parliamentary review of management efforts on the Murray River criticized the procedures of the Murray Darling Basin Commission (bureaucracy) for sending forward only decisions that had been fully resolved rather than allowing political debate within the Ministerial Council. "As a result, the Commission tends to send to the Council only those recommendations it thinks the Council will want to receive" (Connell 2007, 190). This can be problematic, because a political network can cease to become a key forum in which to interact and debate.

Assessing Policy Relevance

Assessing policy relevance is difficult, because political actors ultimately judge whether they find it relevant. Still, based on my case study research and published case studies, I suggest there are two ways of assessing policy relevance.

Policy relevance can be judged by the political network's activity level, for one. The activity level may be assessed by the frequency of meetings and the participation of political leaders at those meetings. It may also be evaluated by the extent, diversity, and amount of participation on committees, forums, and other formal meetings. This includes the array of informal interactions among political actors, which can be assessed and mapped to examine their density and diversity (Khator 1999; Schneider et al. 2003). On the other hand, political activities outside the network may indicate dissatisfaction, such as the decision by environmental groups involved in CALFED to file lawsuits.

Second, policy relevance can be judged by the degree to which joint implementation responsibility garners political attention. The question is whether the collaborative entity has sufficient joint authority or funding to merit the attention of a political network.

The collaborative growth management efforts in South East Queensland and San Diego offer an interesting comparison. In both cases, the decision to manage growth was reached through regional negotiation rather than state law. The authority and funding delegated to the regional supporting agency varied considerably. In South East Queensland, the funding for regional open space acquisition was gutted, and the regional implementation agency had few powers or resources. In contrast, San Diego voters passed a forty-year sales tax in 2004 that will generate more than $14 billion in funding to be allocated by the San Diego Association of Governments, including funding to acquire over three hundred thousand acres of land and $280 million for promoting investment in transit centers. Because of the potential financial incentives and acquisition programs, the deliberations in San Diego have significant relevance for elected officials (Margerum 2005; Barbour and Teitz 2009). This in turn makes elected officials from across the region willing to participate in political networks in both formal and informal ways. In other words, many are engaged because the decisions at the regional level are important.

Network Revitalization

A final factor is the effectiveness of the political network to be revitalized and renewed. As noted above, these networks are dynamic and changing, which means that members come and go on a regular basis (Knoke 1990). While political leadership helps to periodically revitalize a network, the entity charged with supporting the collaboration effort may also play a role in this. For example, while regional agencies in Denver and San Diego devoted considerable time and resources on outreach for elected officials, planning efforts in South East Queensland and CALFED relied mostly on defined committee structures.

In Mark Schneider and his colleagues' analysis (2003) of management activities in U.S. estuaries, they found that the collaborative governance strategies were building more dense and diverse networks of actors than in estuaries that weren't pursuing collaborative approaches. Furthermore, they discovered that these networks developed because there were extensive efforts to encourage broad participation and disseminate information. As discussed above, Howlett (2002) concluded that networks with low insulation (thin boundaries) with the community were more likely to be open to new actors and new ideas.

Assessing Network Revitalization

In the cases where I observed network revitalization efforts, they were being carried out by a collaborative entity or agency. This role often reflected the philosophy of the agency's leaders as much as its leadership board. Communication strategies and political outreach efforts can be used to evaluate network revitalization projects.

Communication strategies are important because they help keep political networks engaged in collaboration attempts. First, communicating findings about implementation progress (outputs) and conditions (outcomes) can focus attention on implementation efforts. Self-imposed evaluations or "report cards" can keep "policy windows open," for example. Regional performance monitoring in South East Queensland ultimately led to a political conclusion that collaborative growth management was not effective (Mayere, Heywood, and Margerum 2008).

Paying attention to communication approaches and strategies is also critical for reaching policy stakeholders with competing demands for time. A city councillor in the Denver region noted that DRCOG's communication "has been very good. If anything, it has been too good—sometimes there is too much information." Similarly, a city planner remarked, "Regional planning has to be presented very simply. The people don't understand the complexity of the issues. DRCOG has come in and presented information and tried to explain the problem, and they lose people." In San Diego, the smaller number of local municipalities has allowed San Diego Association of Governments staff to make regular presentations to each city and county council in the region. As a result, even elected officials who were skeptical of regional planning indicated that they felt well informed.[1]

Another indicator of network revitalization includes efforts to reach a broad range of political actors, including those who are not directly involved in the collaboration effort. In the Denver region, several elected officials commented that committees and working groups were dominated by staff members, and lacked adequate elected official participation:

For example, a lot of people involved on the DRCOG committees don't interact with elected officials. I would say that only 10–20% communicate with their elected officials. A lot of people show up without talking. So, you get a real problem with the issues being discussed in the committees, because they don't match the political direction of the elected officials.[2]

Similarly, in the Little Hoover Commission review of the CALFED case, they noted that the California Bay-Delta Authority (CBDA) created a difficult venue to debate policy issues, because department-level officials were reluctant to debate issues that had not been vetted or cleared by senior officials. Furthermore, the high level policy group that was established during the consensus building phase was not maintained.

A number of officials and stakeholders have advocated a return of the policy group, a mechanism developed during the planning phase of CALFED to encourage cooperation among the departments. Issues that could not be resolved at the staff level were elevated to management and then if necessary senior management. Policy commitments were made by the state and federal secretaries.

The policy group frustrated some stakeholders and legislators who believed too much was decided behind closed doors without adequate public vetting or consultation. However, the CBDA board—because of its makeup, its limited authority, the public setting and its nascent decision-making procedures—has not adequately assumed the role of the policy group. (Little Hoover Commission 2005, 56)

In contrast, the San Diego Association of Governments is able to involve at least three elected officials from each municipality through its set of committees and working groups. This not only creates a dense network of political actors across the region but also means that each city or council has a majority of participants involved in regional policy deliberation.[3]

Discussion

This chapter examines political networks and their role in supporting implementation. Two issues raised by this analysis include the fluidity of political networks and accountability. These concerns also relate to debates about collaborative governance, which are discussed in more detail in chapter 11.

The Fluidity of Political Networks

As noted above, political networks are unique because they bring together policy stakeholders in ongoing forums where personal trust and commitment play influential roles in sustaining implementation efforts. But because many policy stakeholders are elected officials, designers of networks have to prepare for turnover, transition, and a constant rebuilding of networks. Thus, political networks will tend to be fluid.

As Blackmore (2001, 11), the former executive director of the Murray Darling Basin Commission, observed, "At least one election at [the] state or commonwealth level occurs every twelve months within the basin, making stability in membership more difficult." The concern about turnover was even more significant when I evaluated the Denver Metro Vision efforts in 2001 and 2002. Several local government elected officials expressed concern about the new term limits that were going to come into effect. The term limits meant that people who had worked for many years on regional issues—and developed both an understanding of the issues and trust with other local government colleagues—were going to be leaving office. Although about a third of the elected officials who responded to my survey thought that term limits would bring "new blood" into the decision-making process, most raised concerns about the lack of continuity created by this change. A mayor from a medium-size outer suburb asked:

Will newcomers be invested and understand the process? This is still an open question. Already we are seeing newcomers question things. It will be an ongoing struggle to keep them informed. The lack of collegial relationship is also a problem.[4]

A council member from a medium-sized suburb felt that term limits

will hurt. The common perception is that Vision 2020 was top down, but it wasn't. Newly elected officials come in with that misperception. They don't understand what went into it or why, and think it is top down. We are working on developing courses for newly elected board members on issues such as transportation planning, senior issues, water issues, etc. The learning curve is so steep for newly elected officials.[5]

And another council member, from a medium-sized outer suburb, suggested that

in the long-term, though, everything will become staff driven. DRCOG is third priority for new staff people after local and county stuff. Transportation funding is so complicated. Local officials will have a hard time with the steep learning curve.[6]

Because of the high potential for stakeholder turnover, the large size of many political networks, and participants' limited time, political networks will naturally be fluid. This contrasts with interorganizational networks, where there is a need to define the structure and process. This kind of structure is unrealistic for political networks, which will be complex, messy, and hard to either describe or evaluate.

Accountability

A final issue is accountability. While accountability is relevant to all types of network settings, it is most germane to political networks, because they are usually focusing on significant policy decisions and public expenditures. The accountability concerns include political accountability, public accountability, and transparency.

In terms of political accountability, who participates in the network is an important issue, because access is power. The extent to which participants include elected officials defines the degree to which the network is integrated into, or separate from, the political structure and political accountability. As the discussion about the CALFED case demonstrated, the efforts to insulate the management structure from the constant changes of the political system produced concerns about the network's accountability and management organization. Furthermore, Fraser Schilling, Jonathan London, and Raoul Liévanos's analysis (2009) of CALFED's stakeholder process suggests that its privileged access approach to participation marginalized environmental justice perspectives from the process. Kallis, Kiparsky, and Norgaard (2010), however, note that calls for stronger state authority ignore the infallibility of state decision making, and the limited access and political accountability of conventional governance.

Political networks also are still a limited approach to participation in terms of public access. They are clearly networks of decision makers defined by power and influence. Frequently, stakeholder involvement appears to be a substitute for public involvement. There are many indications that effective political networks associated with collaborative governance efforts provide broad and open participation. Smith, Nell, and Prystupa (1997) assert that these participation approaches are not mutually exclusive, and propose models for converging representative and public forms of input. The issue for political networks therefore may be how they engage the broader public, which may mean integrating political network models with broad-based forms of engagement offered by deliberative democracy strategies (Weeks 2000).

A final issue with political networks is the transparency of public governance. While the network involves political actors, these individuals represent a range of public, private, and nonprofit interests. This is key, because the political network may be making decisions on extensive expenditures of public money and the management organization may be making significant decisions on implementing policy. Janet Newman and her colleagues (2004, 207) propose that collaborative governance approaches may be enriched by the concept of a "political opportunity structure," which refers to the degree of openness or closure of political access to social movements and political protest. Like several researchers of collaboration, they argue that the dispersal of power may create new opportunities for access to political networks (ibid.; Weber 2003; Innes and Booher 2010). However, this requires political actors to view these perspectives as being important, which may marginalize less powerful groups (Newman et al. 2004; Lane 1997, 2003).

Conclusions

In interviews and the literature, political networks appear to attract both enthusiasm and criticism, which likely reflects the strengths and weaknesses of these networks. In terms of strengths, they are often applauded because they allow deliberation on complex problems. These forums offer opportunities to communicate among diverse perspectives and concentrate on solving specific problems. They also allow political actors to maintain focus, support, and leadership around key policy concerns. For example, despite all the controversies surrounding regional growth management in Denver, and little support from state agencies or the governor, the political network to address growth has been sustained.

One of the chief weaknesses of political networks is that they appear precarious and prone to failure. There are instances of policy-level collaborations that have achieved substantial policy reform. There are also a limited number of cases where strong and enduring networks have been created to support ongoing work. Why does failure occur? Failure relates to the assessment factors listed above, particularly the difficulty of maintaining political networks.

I suggest that failure is more likely when political networks have difficulty producing tangible results. This does not mean that networks have to completely solve problems; instead, they have to produce successes that garner further confidence and satisfaction. I also contend that political networks will involve periods in which they surge ahead, followed by periods of stagnation or even demise. This seems to fit theories about policy windows, and indicates that these windows open and close on policy collaboratives as well. The interconnections of political networks with the political system may increase the likelihood of failure.

One final conclusion about political networks is that we need to understand more about why they disintegrate, stagnate, and survive. If policy windows are going to close, how does a political network prepare for this? Should stakeholders assume, say, that the network will be short lived and prepare for its demise, or should they look for ways of keeping the policy window open? Moreover, why have certain political networks sustained themselves? There are examples of networks that have lasted for years and even decades, such as the International Joint Commission overseeing the management of the Great Lakes and efforts taking place in Chesapeake Bay. What has allowed these networks to continue, and have they been effective? These questions are complicated not only by the difficulty of measuring effectiveness but also by the difficulty of researching political networks.

IV

Synthesis

10

The Translation to Practice

As a researcher who has often had one foot in academia and another in professional work, I have been interested in the interaction between theory and practice. Theory provides an important perspective that doesn't fully explain practice but instead can supply a critical lens that allows practitioners to critique, analyze, and improve their work. In turn, practice presents new challenges, questions, and issues for theory.

The tidiness of the chapters presented in this book belies the complications describing the many variations and unique conditions that influence the work of collaboratives. These complications frequently create a gap between the theory and experience that makes it hard to translate the findings, lessons, and concepts to new settings. This chapter's goal is to provide more assistance with translating the conceptual ideas of the previous chapters into practice. First, I summarize the major forms of collaboration that usually occur in practice and present some of the crucial questions for interrogating them. I next review some case studies that belie classification to highlight the messiness of practice as well as the challenge for future research. Then I address the significant issue of results, which is one of the key terms in the book's title.

Summary of Collaboration Forms

This book explores a range of different approaches that fit under the name of collaboration, and in particular how these forms translate consensus into results. Figure 10.1 summarizes the factors critical to producing results from collaboration, and integrates them into the figure I introduced in chapter 2. This figure highlights four types of approaches to achieving results: passive, cooperative, adaptive network, and informal approaches. The figure also illustrates that cooperative and adaptive network approaches build on the previous steps. I briefly discuss each of these major approaches, and then the implications of employing them.

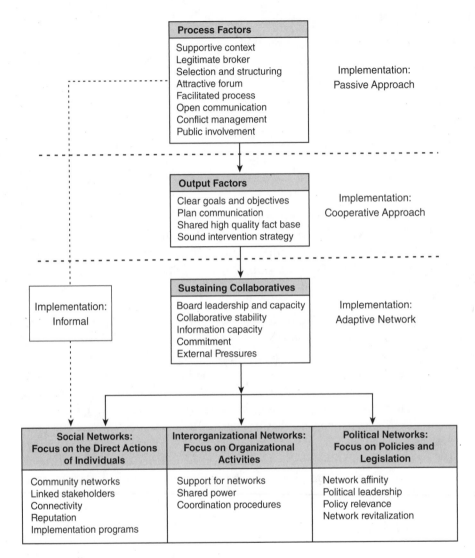

Figure 10.1
Factors affecting results from collaboration

Increased Understanding (Passive Approach)

One approach to implementing a collaborative effort is to view it as an information and exchange process leading to increased understanding among the participants. Gray (1985) refers to this approach as information exchange leading to a shared vision, which often operates as an information forum. Chapters 3 and 4 identify a number of factors with which to evaluate these processes for their effectiveness. In some cases, this may be the intended outcome of the collaborative effort—meaning there is no concerted attempt to develop a plan or an implementation structure. This approach assumes that the process of information sharing and generation can offer important results. Many communities in the United States, for example, are creating neighborhood forums where people can share information about how to reduce energy use and live more sustainably. For some small, community-based collaboratives, increased understanding may be the primary basis for bringing about change.

In the 1990s, Queensland began embarking on a series of nonstatutory, collaborative regional plans around the major urban centers along the coast. In many regions, this was the first time that elected officials, government employees, and the public thought of themselves as a region, or shared information with each other. The result was that local and state governments began recognizing regional issues that they had not acknowledged before, local governments began thinking more regionally, and a number of spin-off projects were spawned by this interaction.[1] In many cases, increased understanding is an intermediate step toward another outcome. This step is also essential to supporting ongoing collaboration efforts and/or the implementation of a collaboratively developed strategy.

I also suggest, however, that "increased understanding" can be an excuse for failure—or at least underperformance. For instance, many of the Queensland regional plans noted above failed to generate adequate state agency support to guide regional development in the way it was intended. An increased understanding result thus should be carefully scrutinized, particularly in light of the transaction costs involved in running a collaborative process. We seldom like to admit mistakes, but processes that don't move beyond a passive approach may be failed cases.

Agreements and Networks (Informal Approach)

A second form that collaboration may take is an informal approach. This refers to a group that does not produce a formal plan or agreement but relies instead on a social network among the participants. Some of the smaller Australian Landcare groups that I met did not prepare plans or reports. Instead, they identified land and water conservation issues, devised a set of actions, and then applied for funding to support conservation efforts. The increased awareness and understanding that they gain through their deliberation process is the basis for an ongoing approach. They also rely on their existing social networks to spread their ideas and influence. This approach generally works well, because it limits the transaction costs and allows the group to focus on undertaking actions. Yet these groups may not incorporate diverse perspectives, tending to reflect the more powerful and connected elites in a community. Furthermore, these kinds of groups are prone to failure if key members leave or decide to shift their volunteer energy elsewhere.

Results as a Plan or Contract (Cooperative Approach)

The third approach is collaboration as a plan, contract, or other type of agreement. As defined in the beginning of this book, this can be considered a cooperative approach in which participants are working independently toward common goals. This means that participants work through an information-sharing and deliberation process that produces common goals, objectives, and actions. This is then documented in a plan or contract. The implementing parties use this plan or contract to guide their implementation activities, but the implementation process does not require sustained, ongoing interaction.

The most important aspect of this kind of approach is that it involves a static document. The document is based on the knowledge, understanding, interpretations, and agreements of the participants at the time it was prepared. When the underlying conditions and participant perspectives are stable, this plan can act as the main driver of implementation.

I have studied several examples where these kinds of contractual approaches have led to significant results. As noted in chapter 6, a city and a state environmental agency produced a joint agreement for Berowra Creek that defined water quality objectives along with cleanup actions. The result of their efforts was a series of discreet actions, such as a wastewater treatment upgrade and new stormwater management policies. These actions were relatively independent, so there was little need for an ongoing structure to coordinate activities.

Participants and researchers can evaluate these plans using the factors listed in chapter 5, with the end goal of quality improvement. It is also essential to recognize that a good-quality process supports a good-quality plan. By this I mean that the better the deliberations, interaction, and communication during the consensus-building process, the greater will be the communication, trust, and commitment to the plan during implementation. This was reinforced by Burby's evaluation (2003, 44) of sixty comprehensive plans in Florida and Washington State, in which he found that "broad stakeholder involvement contributes to both stronger plans and the implementation of proposals in plans."

Ongoing Interaction (Adaptive Network Approach)

In many cases a plan formally documents agreed-on approaches, but implementation requires ongoing interaction and adjustment. This need for interaction may arise due to insufficient knowledge of the system, a dynamic system with changing factors that make it hard to predict, or a changing social or political system that makes it hard to specify management actions. Under these circumstances, producing results from collaboration requires ongoing interaction.

Ongoing interaction as an implementation approach is a major focus in this book, because so many of the issues being addressed through collaboration require adaptive approaches to management. Adaptive management has become an increasingly common concept in environmental management (Webster 2009; Layzer 2008), but the underlying notions have been around for many decades in fields such as planning and public policy (see, for example, Lindblom 1973; Bryson 1988). The general idea is that management requires a baseline understanding, and the identification of gaps in that understanding. Management interventions are approached in terms of experiments with monitoring and feedback to assess progress, and allow adjustment in activities and implementation efforts (Holling and United Nations Environment Programme 1978; Layzer 2008).

The increasing interest in adaptive management for addressing environmental issues has come about for several reasons. The greater availability of data over longer periods of time and the increased ability to compare data and findings on a global scale have made scientists increasingly aware of the complexity and dynamics of ecological systems.

Also, many traditional regulatory frameworks are based around proscriptive end points or targets, such as the goal of "fishable and swimmable waters" enshrined in the U.S. Clean Water Act. For many emerging issues, though, the end points are unclear, complex, or dynamic. We may want to prevent the decline of a species or ecological decline in an estuary, but we are not sure what this means in terms of measuring progress.

There is also a more pragmatic reason for the increased attention on adaptive management. Managers and policymakers often need to develop policy responses or management plans, and they cannot wait for the science to completely predict causes, effects, and the decisions that will support the desired outcomes. Thus, adaptive management offers these decision makers a trial-and-error approach, which can be combined with monitoring and feedback to allow for reassessment and adjustment. Lindblom's historic public policy article (1959) called this kind of approach "the science of muddling through." He argued that comprehensive decision making is frequently not possible, because the systems are too large or complex to fully predict.

As noted in chapter 1, however, adaptive management also requires a structure that allows for monitoring and feedback, and ensures that there will be decision makers learning from the feedback loops (Webster 2009). These structures must also be robust enough to maintain their activity and overcome the likely transition in participants (Layzer 2008). A plan can provide the starting point for this approach, but an ongoing entity is necessary to operate in this role and respond. As mentioned in chapter 6, this entity can take many different forms across the action-organizational-policy spectrum, yet sustaining it is important in all these settings. What figure 10.1 also captures is that an adaptive approach requires supporting networks to respond to this information and make adjustments.

Chapters 7–9 describe the range of networks that can help support implementation. This range mirrors the action-organizational-policy typology, but under several different scenarios the type of collaborative may not line up with these categories.

One scenario is that some collaboratives do not fit neatly into one category. For example, I have suggested that some of Oregon's watershed councils fit between the action and organizational collaborative prototypes. These councils utilize their social connections to work with private landowners on restoration projects, and utilize their organizational partners in working with state and federal agency partners. As such, these groups utilize both social and interorganizational networks.

A second scenario is that collaboratives higher in the action-organizational-policy spectrum may utilize multiple networks during implementation. The Murray Darling Basin Commission represented an approach built around three different network strategies. The political network was central to the workings of the ministerial council, and its efforts to develop and implement new policies. The commission also supported a network of catchment committees that involved a cross section of stakeholders representing community members, local government, and state government. Many of these groups were not involved in the "direct doing" of conservation efforts but rather in helping to align an array of governmental and nongovernmental programs into a more coherent catchment-scale approach (interorganizational networks). The commission and the catchment groups supported locally based, volunteer Landcare groups as well. These groups of local landowners and concerned individuals almost solely concentrated on doing things on the ground, and utilized their social networks of friends, families, and neighbors to influence land management.

A third scenario is that collaboratives may utilize existing networks to address issues that they cannot resolve. The Rogue Basin Coordinating Council confronted several issues related to the inconsistencies in federal legislation. Although each agency participant could have sought out answers within their chains of command, this would have been time-consuming and may not have resolved the inconsistencies. Instead, they were able to access a higher-level network that was set up to support the implementation of the Northwest Forest Plan. The Provincial Interagency Executive Committee was created to coordinate the management of old-growth habitat for the northern spotted owl, but it also provided an established network that the Rogue River participants utilized to answer questions.

Key Questions for Collaboration Options

This discussion emphasizes that collaboration may take many different forms, and there is not one way that is best. Nevertheless, I believe there are some key questions that participants and evaluators can use to identify the approach to collaboration that might be most suitable (see table 10.1).

For a passive approach, it is important for participants to consider whether increased understanding is the intended result or whether there is the potential to develop a specific implementation approach. Participants may not be able to answer this in the early stages of a process, but the intended approach may affect the decision of some individuals whether to participate. It is also essential to identify the concrete ways in which this approach will influence decision making to allow participants and evaluators to judge its effectiveness. Thus, even if a forum on wetlands

Table 10.1
Key questions for collaboration options

Passive approach	• Is increased understanding the intended result of the process?
	• What are the concrete ways increased understanding will influence decision making?
Informal approach	• Are social networks strong enough to support ongoing interaction across the community?
	• Is there adequate current and future leadership to maintain momentum?
Cooperative approach	• Are conditions stable enough for participants to predict necessary actions?
	• Will the plan be good enough to guide action?
Adaptive network approach	• Is the problem complex and dynamic enough to warrant ongoing transaction costs?
	• Is there the commitment and energy to support a sustained effort?
	• Can the supporting networks be developed to facilitate implementation?

leads only to increased understanding among planners about the role and function of wetlands, it may be crucial to know how these participants think this information might affect decision making.

For informal approaches, long-term viability is highly dependent on sustaining the social networks on which collaborations are based. Furthermore, even though participants don't assume formal board leadership roles, the ability of these efforts to maintain leadership and foster future leaders is important. While Australia's Landcare program has been highly successful at nurturing these types of groups, research suggests that an overreliance on a few key people has led to burnout and the dissolution of many groups (Byron and Curtis 2002; Byron, Curtis, and Lockwood 2001).

For cooperative approaches, I believe there are two critical issues for participants and evaluators. First, as pointed out above, a cooperative approach to implementation depends on a stable setting. If participants can assess the stability of the systems from the outset, they can determine whether a cooperative approach is likely to be effective or ineffective. Second, they need to ensure that there is a high-quality plan to guide implementation. It is particularly important for participants to assess whether there is adequate information to accurately identify effective implementation activities.

For an adaptive network approach, the key questions relate to transaction costs. Participants must consider from the outset whether the conditions warrant the transaction costs. This deliberation includes whether the issues are sufficiently complex and dynamic to warrant the additional time as well as resources. It is essential to also determine whether the individuals and organizations will be able to maintain their commitment over time. The tendency in some efforts is for participants to view their role as being over once the plan is produced. Their role is just beginning, in fact, and the expectations for ongoing effort may actually increase. Finally, participants need to evaluate whether they will be able to develop the social, interorganizational, and/or political networks that will provide the ongoing structure to support implementation. As chapters 7–9 highlight, establishing these networks can require significant maintenance, but they are important for translating the consensus to the broader set of decision makers that it aims to influence.

The Messiness of Practice

As noted above, the examples presented throughout this book are used to illustrate how the principles and concepts are applied. Yet there are often cases that don't fit into the framework. In this section, I take apart some of the neatness of the model by examining collaboration through short snapshots of practice. I liken this model to the gak I saw demonstrated at a science show with my two young sons.

Composed of two parts of cornstarch to one part of water, this mixture is rock hard when you slam your fist into it. You can also pick up a ball of gak by shoveling it up and squeezing hard. But as soon as you let go, the mixture liquefies and begins to ooze through your fingers. Models are like this. They are rock hard on the surface, and when you confine them tightly they stay clean and rigid, but as soon as you loosen your grip or let go, they get messy and ooze between your fingers. The following cases from Wisconsin, Lake Tahoe, and Australia depict some of the complexities and messiness of practice.

Lower Wisconsin: Collaboration and New Authority

The Lower Wisconsin River case has been used in several places in this book, but the implementation approach doesn't fit neatly into the frameworks I have described in this text.[2] The planning process was positioned at the organizational and policy levels, with the result being significant changes in DNR organizational policies and new legislation granting powers to a regional planning authority. Implementation efforts clearly involve an ongoing role in management, but the approach is both more formal in some aspects and more informal in others.

One unique aspect of the case is that the interorganizational network that helps support ongoing implementation is centered on a single person—in this case, the riverway coordinator. Two factors are critical to understanding how this works. First, the DNR is a superagency (involves all natural resources, water management, and environmental regulation responsibilities)—meaning that the coordination function is internalized within one large organization. This is not to say there are not coordination issues; it just means that organizational hierarchy is an important power dynamic that does not occur when working across organizational boundaries. Second, the riverway coordinator has traditionally reported directly to top administrators within the DNR. This arrangement provides the coordinator with direct access to the agency hierarchy, which ensures that the coordinator has far more leverage than someone who had to beg, cajole, or entice support.

This structure may be unique because the Wisconsin DNR is unique, but it is not unreasonable to expect other cases in which major ongoing management issues are housed within a single agency. In terms of the interorganizational network factors discussed in chapter 8, the issues of structures and procedures for coordination are still relevant, but most of the pressures, support, and shared power are internal to the organization. These issues are still present, because there can be as much fighting within an agency as between agencies. Nevertheless, hierarchy, internal powers, and agency policies all play a much more significant role.

Another unique aspect of this case is the formal powers and structures given to the riverway board to oversee land use regulations. This is not a collaborative entity designed to support the entire set of management efforts but rather a regulatory body created with limited and specific powers related to aesthetics. In this case, a relatively narrow implementation function has been sliced off and turned over to an organization with the power to implement it. There is nothing collaborative about the implementation. I stress this because it is conceivable that a number of policy and organizational implementation approaches may result in entities with significant authority to address individual issues. In succinct terms, a collaborative process produced top-down, command-and-control implementation for specific functions.

Lake Tahoe: Collaboration and Politics

Lake Tahoe, which straddles the California-Nevada state line, is nestled at 6,225 feet among the peaks of the Sierra Nevada range. "Lake Tahoe is one of the world's few primordially pure large alpine lakes, and is renowned for the unusual clarity of its waters" (Wise 1975, 2). The splendor of Lake Tahoe and its environs, however, has also produced intense pressures for recreation and development, which in turn has resulted in increasing impacts to the watershed, and a decrease of water clarity in the lake of one foot per year between 1968 and 1985 (Turner 1985). The Tahoe basin has had over one hundred years of planning and management activity at the local, state, and federal levels.

From time to time, I have questioned whether Lake Tahoe belongs in my set of case studies about collaboratives. Bill Morgan, the executive director of the Tahoe Regional Planning Agency in the 1980s, clearly oversaw a deliberative and negotiated process involving a wide range of stakeholders. The planning agency is also involved in a complex interorganizational network in managing the region, involving not only local governments and state agencies, but also the federal land management agencies that own most of the land within the basin (Imperial and Kauneckis 2003). I leave this case in the book because it underscores several issues associated with collaboration, and because other researchers have described it as a collaborative governance approach (ibid.).

For one, it shows that policy-level action does not always correspond to scale. By North American standards, the Lake Tahoe basin is not big. Yet because of its iconic status, it has garnered far higher-level attention than we would expect for an equivalent-sized region. It is also interesting to note how political attention, interest group pressures, and public concern have all combined to periodically draw policy-level attention to the basin throughout its history.

Second, the case reveals how the same organization can choose to pursue collaborative and noncollaborative processes at different points in its history. The agreement that led to the new Tahoe Regional Planning Agency plan in the 1980s does not fit the traditional model of a stakeholder roundtable but instead clearly involved intensive consultation, dialogue, and conflict resolution. This approach is in contrast to prior planning efforts that were highly rational-scientific endeavors that assumed science would provide the necessary evidence for resolving competing demands. Some organizations survive and evolve to adjust to these changing expectations of operation, and some do not.

Then too, it demonstrates how policy-level deliberation can produce an implementation approach based on authority and regulation, rather than consultative and voluntary mechanisms. The planning agency has made a concerted attempt to involve the public and stakeholders in planning efforts. In terms of implementation, though, the planning agency wears a regulatory hat that requires it to police activities, monitor conditions, and enforce violators. Similarly, other types of policy collaboratives have been deliberative and interactive during policy development, but the policy implementation may not be deliberative at all.

Australian Natural Resources Management Bodies: Organizations Created to Collaborate

In 1996, a new Australian federal administration announced it would establish the National Heritage Trust, and allocated $1.25 billion Australian dollars ($812 million in 1996 U.S. dollars), to address environmental degradation and sustainable agriculture. The program was built on several community-level participatory approaches that were already in place across many parts of Australia, including the local Landcare groups and regional catchment committees described throughout this book.

A review of the National Heritage Trust program in 2000 revealed many useful outcomes, but called for improved measurement of the outcomes and more stringent federal requirements. The result was funding for new regional, incorporated entities (known as regional bodies) composed of a broad membership (Head 2005). The mandate for the regional bodies has been to integrate natural resources target setting, implementation, monitoring, and reporting at the regional level by working with government agencies and community stakeholders (Robins and Dovers 2007a; Head 2005). The Australian government developed bilateral agreements with each of the eight states and territories on the role, authority, and structure of these regional bodies, resulting in wide variation among the fifty-six regional groups that currently operate.

In a review of these regional bodies along with their structures and capacity, Lisa Robins and Stephen Dovers (2007b) classify the regional bodies into ten different categories. As table 10.2 portrays, there is a wide range of resources and capacity across these organizations. A brief description of three different regional bodies highlights some of the structural differences.

The Mackay Whitsunday Natural Resource Management Group manages an area of eight thousand square kilometers along the tropical coast of Queensland. It

Table 10.2
Regional body comparison

Regional body	State or territory	Budget allocation (millions) 2004	2005	Funding per square kilometer	Funding per person
Swan River	Western Australia	$3.5	$7.3	$953	$2.52
South East	South Australia	$2.2	$5.9	$281	$37.52
Wimmera	Victoria	$4.2	$13.3	$567	$36.30
Cape York	Queensland	$1.1	$1.3	$9	$28.45
Hunter and Central rivers	New South Wales	$3.3	$4.1	$112	$0.75
South West	Queensland	$1.2	$2.0	$12	$135.26
Mackay Whitsunday	Queensland	$1.7	$2.4	$268	$9.99
Terrain (Wet Tropics)	Queensland	$2.2	$3.2	$145	$4.45
Port Phillip and Westernport	Victoria	$2.5	$5.0	$389	$0.27

Note: Funding reported in Australian dollars (2007 $1 Aus = $0.84 US)
Source: Robins and Dovers 2007b; Australian Government 2005.

formed when three existing catchment management committees merged, and it has continued to maintain community involvement through its stakeholder board and support for locally based Landcare groups. The group also works closely with cities and agricultural industries in the region for its water quality improvement planning. It has identified water quality targets for each of the catchments, and assessed the changes in management practices and the costs required to meet those targets.

Terrain (formerly Wet Tropics NRM Group) manages twenty-four thousand square kilometers along the northern coast of Queensland. The city of Cairns and the region are important tourism destinations, with many people coming to enjoy the tropical rain forests and Great Barrier Reef (McDonald et al. 2005). Terrain is a not-for-profit public company funded from community, corporate, and government resources, with a ten-member governing board representing a range of sectors. It has developed a regional plan for managing the region, and works extensively with state and federal agencies, agricultural organizations, and local governments to improve information and analysis about regional issues, enhance management activities on public and private lands, and undertake restoration initiatives. It also reaches individual landowners through its network of Landcare groups, which it supports with funding, information, and technical assistance.

The Port Phillip and Westernport Catchment Management Authority (Port Phillip CMA) covers 30 municipalities in the greater Melbourne region, with a total population of 3.4 million. The urban area represents 18 percent of its jurisdiction, with 40 perent in rural farmland and 42 percent in forest (Port Phillip CMA 2004). As with all Victorian natural resources management groups, the board of the Port Phillip CMA must include people with knowledge or experience across a range of areas, such as land management, water resources, waterway management, agriculture, business planning, and financial management. A state minister, an elected official, appoints the board members (Robins and Dovers 2007a). The Port Phillip CMA works closely with a number of organizations, including cities, forestry agencies, and Melbourne Water. Its restoration efforts in major river corridors are done in conjunction with Melbourne Water, which has the statutory authority for waterway management. Another key component of the Port Phillip CMA approach is its fostering, facilitation, and financial support of community-based groups throughout the region, including Landcare, resident, "friends of," and even school groups. In summary, the CMA is not engaged in direct restoration projects but rather facilitates restoration attempts through a range of agency and community partnerships.

The natural resources management groups in Australia have been developed to integrate management, involve community, and work collaboratively. All three of these organizations fit into the organizational collaborative category in terms of where they focus their activities. They are not engaged directly in on-the-ground action but instead they partner with a range of governmental and nongovernmental organizations to help achieve results on the ground. Like the other cases presented in this section, though, they don't necessarily fit the model of collaboratives.

First, I assert that they have been formed as a policy solution as opposed to a response to a specific resource problem (Zahariadis 1999). Many of the collaboration cases I have examined originated with stakeholders who were confronting problems, stalemates, conflicts, or other conditions that caused them to look at how they could better respond through a collaborative approach. Yet in Australia, national and state government essentially started with a structure based on the need to integrate management around broad national targets, and then left the natural resources management bodies to determine how their regional problems fit into these national targets (Robinson, Taylor, and Margerum 2009).

Second, the boards that govern these organizations are not collaborative in terms of the traditional characteristics. In many groups, members are chosen based more on their organizational and management skills than their substantive perspectives. Many natural resources management groups also lack representatives from state agencies, even though these organizations are key partners in implementation efforts. Finally, elected officials often appoint many governing board members (Robins and Dovers 2007a; Robinson, Taylor, and Margerum 2009), which can leave boards open to political interference. This scenario, as I noted in previous chapters, transpired in New South Wales with the ministerial appointment of catchment committees, thereby severely undermining the legitimacy of these groups to work across the range of people in the community.

This is not to say that natural resources management groups have not accomplished a lot. Researchers have argued that they have produced more coordinated and accountable government along with significant commitment by a range of organizations (Roberts and Bradley 1991; Morrison and Lane 2005). Many groups have also made substantial progress in terms of integrating data, developing strategies, and undertaking efforts to restore and address an array of natural resources issues. At the same time, I believe it remains to be seen where or whether these groups fit the descriptions of collaboratives. In fact, Robins and Dovers (2007a) contend that natural resources management regional bodies are effectively a fourth tier of government.

Discussion

The cases that I list here don't fit neatly into the collaboration approaches or typology. All of them involve collaboration at some point in their history, but it is not clear whether we can describe them as collaboratives. These anomaly cases highlight several issues relevant to collaboration, which may also provide the basis for amending the typology that I present.

One interesting element across all these cases is that they include organizations led by governing boards with significant resources or delegated power. While these governing boards may be required to have diverse representation, they are not equivalent to the collection of autonomous stakeholders described in the definitions of collaboration in chapter 1.

Several of the cases also raise the question of what distinguishes collaboration from organizations that use diverse governing boards and consultative processes to achieve their mission. For example, many of the Australian natural resources management bodies have structures similar to U.S. nonprofit or public corporations. They strive for a range of participants on their boards, and some even have rules governing the types of representatives that should be included. On the other hand, these participants' fundamental role is to govern the organization, set goals and objectives, and oversee its finances. The question that I posed to Australian researchers and participants in natural resources management bodies is whether this fits the collaborative model of management.

Another theme relates to potential tensions during implementation that result from creating organizations with substantial resources and often authority. Their formation through direct government initiatives can lead them to be viewed as an arm of government rather than regional, community-based organizations (Robins and Dovers 2007a). This can make it difficult for them to work through social networks on voluntary programs and activities if this is one of their intended implementation strategies. The regulatory powers of the Lower Wisconsin Riverway Board and the Tahoe Regional Planning Agency, for instance, position these organizations in a way that makes it challenging to build social networks.

The cases also demonstrate that creating new organizations can generate competition and tension with other government agencies because of their overlapping responsibilities. This can make it hard to participate in interorganizational networks to support implementation efforts. In fact, one of the results of establishing the regional natural resources management groups in Australia was the withdrawal of state agency activities in a number of areas (McDonald et al. 2005; Robins and Dovers 2007b). Both the natural resources management and state agency staff in Queensland described how state agency administrators consciously pulled back from a number of management activities, saying, "It's the natural resources management body responsibility now."[3]

In conclusion, I suggest that cases like these raise important questions about the alternative forms and formats that may occur under the topic of collaboration. The goal of future research should be to explore these anomaly cases further and interrogate the differences with current collaboration concepts. These kinds of cases may reveal the weaknesses of the model I present in this book, or may represent instances that don't fit under collaboration at all. Yet we need to understand more about these kinds of case studies that involve elements of collaboration to help explain practice and guide future efforts.

Measuring the Results of Collaboration

The final issue that is essential for translating collaboration into practice is the need to define and measure results. Chapter 2 introduced the concept of evaluating results, and throughout the book I refer to collaboratives achieving results. In this section, I discuss in more detail the reasons for measuring results, and the different approaches to measurement and evaluation. I do not talk about the myriad of specific biophysical and socioeconomic outcomes that collaboratives could measure, however, which are as diverse as the places where they operate.

Reasons for Measuring Collaboratives

Measuring collaboratives and their results is critical to a range of people. For those directly involved in the process, it is important conceptually in terms of the group's mission and goals.

During my involvement with the Long Tom Watershed Council, participants and outside observers would often ask some fundamental results question: Is the water quality improving? Are there more trout or salmon in the watershed? It was not easy to provide a quick answer, but that focus on an end result is what kept stakeholders engaged, gave meaning to long meetings and volunteer efforts, and offered people a sense of mission for what the group was trying to achieve. Conceptually, it was also a crucial filter for the organization to decide whether to participate in partnerships or joint projects. A regional recreation plan thus was an interesting idea that could have produced secondary water quality benefits, but we decided that we should be spending our limited resources on the activities more directly related to water quality and habitat objectives. The plan also did not rule out the use of eminent domain for purchasing key properties, which raised concerns among council members that our association with the plan could damage our ability to promote voluntary conservation to private landowners.

Those who fund collaborative efforts—including governments, nonprofits, foundations, and individuals—are also concerned about results. Grantors want to know whether their funding is producing outcomes. They want to know whether their funds are being spent in efficient and effective ways. They also want to know whether their investment in the collaborative's work is the best way to achieve their own goals and objectives. For elected officials and government agencies, this issue of investment is particularly important as they consider national and state goals along with the options for funding efforts to achieve those goals.

Finally, researchers want to know about effectiveness. Some of them work with collaboratives or funding agencies to evaluate collaboratives. Many researchers, though, are also interested in more basic questions about the effectiveness of collaboration generally, the lessons to improve theories that can inform future practice, and the findings that can be incorporated into educating students who will become future practitioners.

Approaches to Measuring Results

There is a rich body of literature discussing the use, construction, and compilation of indicators (Hezri and Dovers 2006). First, public administration and public policy uses indicators for evidence-based policy analysis. In this approach, indicators are viewed as a way of evaluating the effectiveness of policy interventions so that adjustments can be made to programs and delivery. This is generally much more common in policy areas such as health, social services, and education, where data are more readily available and effects can be observed in a shorter time frame (Elliot and Popay 2000).

Second, in environmental management, indicators are used as models of pressure-state-response systems that are designed to promote adaptive management. These are delivered in a range of forms, such as state of the environment reporting, to monitor ecological conditions for managers and the public (Koontz and Thomas 2006).

Table 10.3
Evaluation approaches

Evaluation approach	Concept	Examples
Input evaluation: Inputs into planning process	• Improving the information basis for decision making will improve the products and lead to better results	• Oregon requirement for watershed councils to prepare a watershed assessment
Process evaluation: Quality of the process	• Improving the process of decision making will produce better products and results	• Self-assessments by collaboratives • Academic case study evaluations • Chapter 4 in this book
Output evaluation: Assesses plan or agreement quality	• Improving outputs will ensure more success in producing results	• Plan approval processes, such as New Jersey cross acceptance • Plan evaluation approaches • Chapter 5 in this book
Performance indicators: Measures of plans or policies	• Improve plans and policies through shorter feedback loop	• Miles of stream restoration • Urban development within growth boundary
Outcome measures: Reports actual conditions	• Monitoring of actual results important for determining success of efforts	• State of environment reports • Community indicators • Ambient monitoring (e.g., air quality)
Program logic: Evaluates outputs to outcomes links	• Assessing the logic of outputs to outcomes will improve quality of collaborative implementation	• Elements of chapters 6, 7, 8, and 9 in this book • Academic case study evaluations

Finally, urban planning indicators have emerged from the community sustainability movement and State of the Environment plans. There is also an increasing focus on indicators for assessing the performance of plans and planning organizations (ibid.; Mayere, Heywood, and Margerum 2008).

In considering the different types of indicators that are used for evaluation, it is important to be clear on the terminology that has emerged around indicators and monitoring (Carmona and Sieh 2004; Koontz and Thomas 2006). Severine Mayere, Phil Heywood, and I (2008) reviewed some of these different approaches as they are applied to urban and regional planning (see table 10.3).

Input indicators measure the quality of the information, data, and analysis that goes into planning and management. For example, Oregon's land use planning system requires local governments to prepare a series of analyses (like population growth, buildable lands, and housing needs) before embarking on any changes to local urban growth boundaries.

Process indicators provide benchmarks for evaluating the planning process and planning steps. In the United Kingdom, for instance, there have been considerable efforts to assess the plan approval and consultation processes of local government planning authorities (Carmona and Sieh 2004).

Output indicators measure the products of the planning process, such as plans, policies, and regulations. To cite one case, researchers undertook an evaluation of the natural hazard elements of 139 plans to determine whether state mandates had an effect on the quality of the plans produced (Berke et al. 1996).

Performance indicators (also called intermediate outcomes) assess the shorter-term performance of specific plans and policies. For example, a quarterly monitoring report prepared for the South East Queensland region listed the number of new residential dwelling approvals in infill or redevelopment areas (as an intermediate indicator of population and density targets) (Queensland Department of Infrastructure and Planning 2008).

Outcome measures (also called long-term outcomes or impact measures) assess the actual on-the-ground changes that result from the combination of policies, plans, and social, economic, and environmental trends. Many state of the environment reports, say, document the changes in water quality or air quality (Hezri and Dovers 2006; Carmona and Sieh 2004; Koontz and Thomas 2006).

Lastly, *program logic* approaches to evaluation assess whether a plan, policy, or program has clearly linked objectives to outcomes through a logical and well-researched set of intervention efforts and mechanisms. For example, Ralph Renger and Carolyn Hurley (2006) describe how a logic model can be evaluated to determine whether a federal program to address nursing shortages will be effective.

As this discussion of the different types of indicators highlights, they have emerged with different purposes in mind, including to discriminate between competing scientific hypotheses, structure understanding and solutions, track management performance, discriminate between policy alternatives, and inform general users or the public (Dovers 1995; Failing and Gregory 2003; Hezri and Dovers 2006). This section's goal is to discuss the types of measures, examples of those measures, and the advantages and disadvantages of using them.

Measuring Inputs

The basic concept behind input evaluation is that better information *in* produces better information *out*, which will lead to better results. These inputs may be defined in general terms. For instance, Oregon watershed councils need to prepare a watershed assessment if they want to apply for operational funding from the OWEB. While OWEB assesses these plans, and provides guidance to councils on sources of information and parties to consult, they are less prescriptive on what these assessments must contain.

As noted above, the Oregon Department of Land Conservation and Development also assesses inputs in local planning decisions, but it is more prescriptive in what local jurisdictions must prepare. State administrative rules, for instance, specify that local governments must prepare studies such as a buildable lands inventory and housing report, and document natural areas and good-quality agricultural lands. Nevertheless, if a local jurisdiction confronts a trade-off of expanding its urban area into agricultural land versus natural areas, the department does not evaluate the trade-off decision. It instead ensures that the local jurisdiction has considered every state and local issue in making that decision, and that it has followed proper processes.

The advantage of the input evaluation is that it lifts the bar of decision making by ensuring some quality control over the information being used in decisions. Thus, one of the reasons that the OWEB requires watershed councils to conduct watershed assessments is to ensure that restoration projects are being undertaken strategically. For example, if a council relies on landowner-initiated projects on a first come, first serve basis, it may not be undertaking projects in the places that are highest priority or have the greatest potential for success.

This approach to evaluation also provides the greatest latitude and flexibility for decision makers. In its pure form it merely says, "You must use this information when making your decisions." It does not say how you must use it or whether there are consequences if you decide the information is not going to influence your decisions.

This latitude and flexibility is also the potential weakness of input evaluation. In simple terms, improving the inputs may not improve either the outputs or outcomes, particularly if the decision-making structures and processes are poor. If a stakeholder group excludes certain perspectives, does not allow for adequate debate of issues, or doesn't accurately analyze and interpret information, for instance, improved inputs may not produce any better results.

This is especially a concern in complex, large, and/or dynamic systems where it can be difficult to interpret or use the information to make decisions. Decision makers may become overwhelmed, and simply fall back on their "gut instinct" or "what their neighbor says" rather than a rational assessment of the information inputs. For this reason, input evaluation approaches are often combined with evaluations of process and/or outputs, which are discussed more below.

The other potential significant weakness of input evaluation is that the quality of the inputs may be poor due to a lack of data. This has been a common issue with regional natural resources management organizations in Australia, many of which have confronted sparse data sets over limited time frames and geographic scopes (Robinson, Taylor, and Margerum 2009). They are confronted with accusations of "garbage in, garbage out" approaches to target setting, but there is little they can do until they have the resources and data to begin making more accurate assessments.

Measuring Process

The idea behind measuring process is that better processes of deliberation and decision making will lead to better outputs and outcomes. As many authors have pointed out, this has been one of the most common ways of evaluating collaboratives (Leach, Pelkey, and Sabatier 2002; Innes and Booher 1999; Koontz and Thomas 2006). This is due, in part, to the interest in collaboratives among researchers in fields such as conflict resolution and public participation—fields that are most interested in the process elements. It is also due to the greater methodological ease of information gathering. A researcher or collaborative can conduct a quick snapshot of its process using survey evaluation tools, self-assessment workshops, or observation by external parties. Chapters 3 and 4 focus on these types of processes factors. There are several excellent compilations of processes qualities, including the work of Gray (1989), Mattessich, Murray-Close, and Monsey (2004), and Dukes and Firehock (2001). There have also been several meta-analyses and studies using larger sample sizes that provide some important insights (Ansell and Gash 2007; Beierle 2002; Frame, Gunton, and Day 2004; Leach and Pelkey 2001; Leach, Pelkey, and Sabatier 2002; Schively 2007). The advantage of process measures is that they offer a good picture of the quality of the interaction occurring among a set of stakeholders, which is hypothesized to lead to better results for several reasons. First, good process is alleged to produce a better compilation of data and analysis, because participants are more open to information sharing (Innes 1998; Ozawa 1991). This means that participants are more likely to share data, work together to assemble information sources, and contribute to the analysis and interpretation of the information. This does not just mean scientific interpretation but implications for management activities too.

Second, information sharing means that the individual participants understand the information and analysis better (Innes 1998; Burby and May 1998; Moreland, Levine, and Cini 1993). They are exposed to information from other participants, and must engage with the material and understand the analysis. Hence, there may be a range of informal or undocumented changes in attitudes and approaches among participants as they incorporate this into their views as well as decision making.

Third, good process can also lead to greater support and commitment to implementation efforts. This means that participants are more likely to act as champions for implementation in their communities, organizations, or networks (Burby 2003; Brody 2003). It also means they are more likely to understand and support implementation efforts, thereby improving the prospect for success. More broadly, effective processes build stakeholder trust, social capital and collective action beliefs (Lubell et al. 2005). This can create a sense of accountability among participants (Weber 2003) or a "realization of collective action" (Innes and Booher 2010, 202).

There are at least three limitations to process evaluations, all of which are methodological. For one, many evaluations are snapshots of process at a specific moment in time. The quality of interaction is always under flux as new problems arise and participants change; therefore, a group may model good process one day, only to have that process degrade quickly the next.

In addition, evaluations are often based on a limited assessment by an external party or a self-assessment by the participants themselves, and both approaches have validity issues. External, short-term evaluations may not accurately characterize the quality of the process (although there are examples of longer-term evaluations). External evaluations require filtering and interpretations by the observer, which can produce biases. Self-evaluation can also produce biases, because participants may have a limited basis for comparison or may censor their responses out of a concern for how the results will be used.

Finally, a process evaluation approach makes a leap of faith assumption that good process will produce good results. Koontz and Thomas (2006) note that some analysts have criticized this basic assumption along with the premise that process can overcome societal factors such as power disparities (Lane 2003; Bidwell and Ryan 2006). In other words, by focusing on the quality of interaction around a stakeholder table, process evaluations may ignore more fundamental assumptions about access and the ability of stakeholders to perform effectively. It may also ignore the larger societal and political forces that are affecting how a system operates.

Measuring Outputs

A third approach to evaluation is to examine the outputs of a collaborative. Outputs often refer to the plans, programs, and policies produced by the collaborative (Koontz and Thomas 2006). The idea behind measuring outputs is that the better the quality of the plan, policy, or agreement, the more likely it will be effective in terms of achieving results. Chapter 5 is an example of output reviews that can be used to judge the quality of plans and agreements produced by collaboratives. In many cases, output evaluations are combined with criteria for process.

There has been considerable effort in both the urban planning and conflict resolution literature to measure the quality of outputs. For example, there have been several attempts to evaluate plan quality as a way of determining whether it will be more likely to lead to effective implementation (Burby, French, and Nelson 1998; Baer 1997). Other evaluations have examined plans against specific substantive criteria, including normative elements such as sustainability (Berke and Conroy 2000), or policy and legislative elements such as the requirements of disaster mitigation legislation (Berke et al. 1996). The conflict resolution literature has also focused on the criteria for evaluating the quality of agreements (Jandt 1985; Innes 1999; Fisher and Ury 1981). Researchers, for instance, have pointed out the importance of a plan that has clear objectives with measurable targets and a transparent delineation of responsibilities. This allows the progress on the plan and implementation steps to be more accurately assessed.

The advantage of outputs is that they are readily measurable by researchers, participants, and funding organizations. This can be especially critical for reporting to elected officials and others who oversee and monitor these efforts. Thus, a team of evaluators can easily assess a large number of plans to provide an oversight organization with an assessment of whether the plans are high quality.

Another advantage of outputs is that they can be compared and aggregated if the evaluation process uses consistent criteria. For example, the U.S. Federal Emergency Management Agency has assessed the quality of hazard mitigation plans nationally, and it could aggregate information on a state or national basis to monitor progress in plan quality. A third advantage of output evaluations is that they supply immediate feedback to those preparing the plan. If the quality of a hazard mitigation plan is poor, say, this feedback can lead to immediate plan improvements and changes, rather than waiting until feedback from an actual disaster provides an indication of what is working or not working.

One of the chief problems with the approach is that outputs may not produce the desired outcomes. The criteria used to evaluate the plan may not accurately reflect the factors important to achieving results, such as local conditions and circumstances. Another problem is that the evaluation process can be time-consuming and subjective. Even if standard criteria are used, it requires time to develop evaluation criteria as well as review the plan or policy. A final limitation of evaluating outputs is that it assumes a standard type of output. If the issues being addressed by a plan or policy are fairly narrow, well understood, and consistent across different places and times, a standard evaluation approach may work well. But the greater the breadth, uniqueness, and complexity, the harder it is to evaluate. Thus, a series of watershed plans that are all trying to reduce nutrient loads in similar types of systems can be more easily evaluated than an integrated ecosystem management plan that may be addressing a range of unique habitats, species, and trends.

Measuring Performance (Interim Outcomes)

A variety of terms have been used to describe performance indicators, and recent increased interest has revolved around the administrative use of key performance indicators (Smith 1990; Carmona and Sieh 2004; Propper and Wilson 2003). Developed originally for business, it has spread to the public administration and public policy literature as a means for assessing agency, policy, and program performance. The rationale behind measuring interim outcomes is that there are shorter-term measures of policy effectiveness that provide an indication of trends toward the final outcome objectives (Smith 1990). Many of the factors listed in chapters 7, 8, and 9 are examples of these kinds of performance measures.

Evaluations of performance are some of the most common approaches to evaluation in collaborative natural resources management approaches. For example, watershed councils in Oregon have been asked to report data on items like how many miles of stream they have restored, how many trees have been planted, and how many acres of wetlands have been restored. Similar types of evaluation approaches have also been used on a national scale to evaluate regional natural resources management efforts in Australia. The Australian government, for instance, has produced a voluminous document that details these kinds of figures for its multibillion-dollar National Heritage Trust expenditures (National Audit Office 2008).

One of the significant advantages of these kinds of interim evaluation approaches is that they offer a shorter-term feedback loop about implementation progress. When monitoring shows that implementation is not proceeding or the targets are unrealistic, the participants can review the program and adjust its implementation strategies.

This shorter-term feedback loop can also be more satisfying for those concerned about progress and results. A collaborative can immediately report the number of stream miles (or kilometers), say, that have been fenced to protect riparian areas. Whether this is doing any good in terms of habitat, water quality, and other benefits may take many more years and much greater efforts to demonstrate.

Like output measures, interim outcome measures also have limitations. First, they are not measuring the desired future condition, so there is always a danger that the cause-and-effect logic is faulty. For example, a watershed program may assume that restoring more streambanks will produce the desired outcomes. In some watersheds, streambank restoration may not be the key limiting factor. Other factors such as upstream water storage, lack of habitat, or poor quality may be the crucial issue for restoration. Streambank restoration thus can produce dramatic results in one watershed and little results in another watershed.

Second, the direct outcome indicators may not capture the sequence of intermediate outcomes critical to produce results. Streambank restoration efforts therefore may need to be followed by ongoing maintenance and changes in management practices for proper ecological functioning.

Finally, documenting outputs on a large scale frequently involves self-reporting. There may be a tendency to intentionally overstate the products or simply overcompensate on estimates of a collaborative's activities. An education and out-reach attempt may generously report the number of people at a meeting, the number of people contacted, or the number of people who received information. This kind of reporting also tells us little about whether the people who received the informa-tion actually viewed it, or more important, made any changes in response to it. For collaboratives that depend on this kind of reporting for their funding, their efforts may concentrate more on the measures being used to evaluate them than the out-comes they are trying to achieve. If an educational effort is being evaluated by the number of people it reaches, for instance, its designers may focus more on getting numbers than on influencing people's behavior.

Measuring Outcomes (Impact Measures)

Measuring outcomes is sometimes considered the holy grail of monitoring and evaluation because it is asking the basic question of whether collaboratives are producing better environmental and social outcomes. For example, for almost forty years, the goal of the U.S. Clean Water Act and its amendments has been to achieve "fishable and swimmable" waterways.

Measuring environmental outcomes usually requires a substantial investment in long-term and extensive monitoring. For environmental settings, this monitoring may include variables like changes in land cover, biological diversity, and biophysical parameters (e.g., water temperature, water nutrient levels, air quality, etc.). In some places this has been popularized in "State of the Environment" reporting as a way of consolidating information from a wide range of sources into a single document or database that can be understood and interpreted by a broad audience.

The chief advantage of outcome measurement is its focus on data related to the core objectives that a collaborative is attempting to achieve. Thus, increases in salmon in a watershed are firm and tangible proof that there is improvement in relation to the goal. Even if the data are demonstrating a worsening condition, this can be important for increasing the pressure to respond. In places like British Columbia's Fraser River basin, for instance, annual indicator reports on the state of the basin provide a check on the goals of the management efforts there. Decreases in a condition can attract media attention, public pressure, and political actions to respond to this kind of trend.

Although there are some significant benefits to outcome measures, there are also some significant drawbacks. One of the chief limitations is the amount of time and data required to accurately detect a trend. In the case of water quality, a significant monitoring network that collects data over long periods of time is necessary to accurately demonstrate a clear tendency. This is due in part to the seasonal and yearly variability in environmental conditions. For example, low flows and hot weather in one year can produce different results than another year that has high flows and cool temperatures. Until there is adequate data to smooth out this variability, it is hard to detect a pattern.

Another limitation relates to cause and effect. For a factor such as water or air quality, identifying changes from diffuse sources usually requires a sustained and significant effort over a fairly long period. Improvements in air quality over time, say, would require widespread improvements in auto emissions or significant decreases in driving over time to detect a trend. If the policy intervention is auto emissions testing, a change may be noted within a few years as the program begins to eliminate high-emitting vehicles from the roads. If the policy intervention is to reduce air pollution levels by increasing public transit through new high-density development near transit stops, the anticipated changes in air quality may take decades to be realized. All of this assumes that this policy is most likely to reduce trips. In many metropolitan areas, factors such as the location of affordable housing and fuel prices have a much greater impact on driving (and thus air quality).

A final limitation of outcome monitoring implied by the factors above is that it requires patience and funding. Patience is necessary because it may take several years of monitoring data to even tell the public or elected officials whether there is a positive or negative trend in an environmental condition. Funding is essential because monitoring is often expensive and hence must be seen as a long-term investment. For example, a review of the results from the Northwest Forest Plan noted that the uncertainty and complexity of the ecological system was far greater than anticipated, making it hard to separate the effects of the plan versus other influences. This was the conclusion *after* twelve years of monitoring that cost over fifty million dollars (Rapp 2008). When budgets and funding gets cut, monitoring is frequently the first thing to get eliminated. Faced with budget constraints, a manager is more likely to cut monitoring than to cut the program that is trying to affect the conditions that are being monitored. Spatial and temporal gaps in data can make monitoring programs more susceptible to variability and inconclusiveness, further increasing criticism of the expense of undertaking the monitoring.

Measuring Program Logic

A final approach to examining progress involves more of a soft systems method. Rather than evaluating the process, outcomes, or outputs of a particular collaborative, the evaluator instead looks at the program logic. A program logic model is defined as a plausible and sensible model of how a program will work under certain conditions to solve identified problems (Bickman 1987). More succinctly, it is described as the basis for a convincing story about a program's expected performance (McLaughlin and Jordan 1999). This means that the evaluator assesses the collaborative's objectives, proposed actions, and intended outcomes, and the logic of the connections between these elements.

One framework designed for use by community-based organizations is the antecedent-targeting-monitoring approach to logic modeling. The antecedent step requires people in the collaborative to study the root causes of or conditions leading to a problem. The targeting step entails a process of identifying the conditions that exist within the mission scope of the collaborative, examining whether the condition can be changed, and exploring evidence about the likely success of proposed actions (Renger and Hurley 2006). Although program logic models are often depicted as maps, Renger and Hurley emphasize that this map is just the output. They also stress that it is important that the model is backed up with research and analysis, which may include not just literature but also interviews with key "experts." They define these experts as anyone who may provide insight into why a problem occurs, including those who are directly affected by the problem (ibid.).

As described in chapter 5, the approach used by the Mackay Whitsunday Natural Resource Management Group to assess its water quality improvement plan incorporated some logic model testing. In developing its management interventions to reduce nutrient and sediment loads, the group identified a range of management practices, and estimated the likely effects that each practice would have on water quality. It then tested these practices with different agricultural communities to explore the amount of effort required to meet the higher-level management practices, the total cost of changing to those practices, and the likely incentives required for those changes to occur. This entire system is based on rough data, estimates, interviews on expected practice, and other data that may lead to errors in terms of actual results. The plan, however, is based on a series of logic steps backed up with several sources of data.

As the Mackay example suggests, program logic is often portrayed in terms of its use as a planning tool for implementing organizations, but it can also be used as an evaluation tool by funding organizations and government bodies (McLaughlin and Jordan 1999). One significant advantage of a program logic approach is that it provides short-term feedback on the implementation program designed by a collaborative or organization. A reviewing body can assess the quality of the data put into the model, the quality of the research done to test the assumptions and implementation mechanisms, and the quality of the effort in terms of testing and ground truthing the model.

Another advantage of this approach is that it requires a more qualitative and subjective methodology. This means more work by the reviewing team and more dependence on expertise, but it also allows more opportunity for feedback and program improvement. In particular, researchers and government bodies that review more than one of these types of efforts can share findings with other groups about data sources, relevant literature, and methods for developing targets as well as intervention efforts.

These qualitative and subjective aspects also underlie the disadvantages of this evaluation approach. Because it is more intensive and subjective, this approach requires more time and resources to complete an evaluation process. Rather than assembling spreadsheetlike facts, the reviewers must delve into a program, analyze its details, and probably interview people involved with the program's design and implementation. If there are further attempts to fact-check or ground truth the models, this requires additional time and resources on behalf of the reviewers. This method also implies some expertise, experience, or multiple reviewer processes for ensuring quality control. If programs are scored or evaluated, for instance, there may need to be a system of multiple reviews with procedures for resolving scores if there are significant differences between them.

The qualitative nature of this evaluation approach also makes it less appealing to the public and elected officials who are often one of the key audiences for these findings. Although a measure like miles of streambank fencing may have little effect on resource conditions, it can appear more meaningful to outsiders than a score or passing grade for a watershed restoration program model.

Finally, the findings from such monitoring still do not answer the crucial issues that many raise about collaboratives: Are they producing better outcomes generally, and in particular, are they producing better outcomes than other approaches to management?

Conclusions

The review above highlights a wide range of approaches to measuring the results from collaboration. This book focuses on the process, outcome, and program logic components of assessing collaboratives, and the hypotheses produced in these chapters are generic ones. To be applied by either a collaborative or an evaluating entity, these approaches must be adapted and tailored to the context and setting. I also suggest that these kinds of evaluation approaches need to be combined with both output and outcome measures that provide both interim and long-term evaluation of progress.

Although some observers emphasize the need to focus on outcome indicators, I am less enthusiastic about relying on these as the sole means of assessment for several reasons. First, in most systems that collaboratives are attempting to manage, it has taken a century of modifications and actions to "stuff it up," and it is unrealistic to expect significant changes in the three- to five-year time frames that are being used to evaluate many collaborative groups. The inconclusive results of ten years of extensive monitoring under the Northwest Forest Plan demonstrate the difficulty of depending solely on this approach.

Second, the scale of changes necessary in many systems to demonstrate significant improvements is often substantial, making even major restoration projects a drop in the bucket compared to the overall need. Many of the problems that collaborative efforts address are diffuse and distributed, which means that they are unlikely to produce rapid results.

Third, collaborative attempts sit within a broader set of societal, economic, and environmental forces that can have a dramatic impact on trends. Water pollution, say, may be affected as much by commodity prices as by conservation efforts. In Oregon's Rogue River basin, endangered species regulations coupled with the expiration of hydroelectric dam licenses is encouraging dam removal. The Rogue Basin Coordinating Council has helped facilitate this process, but a driving force is that the cost of retrofitting the dams exceeds the revenues and benefits of maintaining them.

Ultimately, to achieve results, collaboratives need outcome indicators. They need to establish baseline conditions and collect data that will allow their progress (or lack thereof) to be evaluated. Yet our conclusion from reviewing data collection efforts for Australia's National Heritage Trust program was that regional natural resources management organizations were being expected to report findings that neither the commonwealth nor state governments had ever been able to do previously (Robinson, Taylor, and Margerum 2009). Similarly, Oregon's investment in watershed councils has been great, but so is the scale of the problem. A river basin such as the Umpqua covers over three million acres with a state administrative support investment of approximately $230,000, which works out to 7¢ per acre, $54 dollars per stream mile, or $171 per "water-quality-limited" stream mile.[4]

Therefore, collaboratives also need other ways of measuring their activities that speak to the audiences they are trying to reach and help ensure the quality of their management efforts. When I worked for the Wisconsin DNR in the early 1990s, the nonpoint source control program was spending thousands of dollars monitoring and modeling watersheds before and after a focused set of runoff control projects. The goal was to prove to legislators and others that the program was not only helping farmers but also improving water quality in the nearby stream. The problem was that it took a lot of time, data, and significant effort to demonstrate a clear trend in water quality improvement. Department staff members spoke of briefing legislators, and then getting "glassy-eyed" looks as they explained the inconclusive results in terms of trends, data variability, and statistical significance.

In contrast, when they provided legislators with one-page "glossy" sheets explaining each project, profiling the farmer, and showing before and after photos, "they got it."[5] The legislators understood what the program was trying to do and what it was achieving. Oregon's watershed councils took a similar tact after being frustrated with the monitoring and evaluation approaches undertaken by the OWEB. Coordinators in the Willamette Valley river basin produced a self-published *Accomplishments Atlas* that profiled studies of what each of the councils were doing, how the councils were using state funding, and how each state dollar was leveraging federal and in-kind dollars.

I don't suggest that all monitoring and evaluation should be considered a political or public relations process but rather that they should be viewed with some underlying concepts in mind. First, monitoring and evaluation need to be tailored to the audience they are trying to reach. Scientific, long-term data on resource conditions are critical for program managers and scientists, but such information is not the only way of answering the shorter-term questions that elected officials as well as the public have about how tax dollars are being spent.

Second, using different types of measures is critical for assessing collaboratives and their implementation efforts. None of the frameworks presented here should be considered the sole approach to measuring results. Instead, a suite of evaluation and monitoring information should be collected to analyze process, outputs, and outcomes.

Finally, all of this monitoring and evaluation effort is useless if it is not viewed as a means to improvement as opposed to a final grade. In educational terms, this difference is comparable to formative versus summative assessment. Formative assessment is the interim feedback that the student receives that allows them to improve, while summative assessment is the final grade that a student receives at the end of the term. Feedback from evaluations should be used to make improvements rather than just provide feedback at the end.

I don't mean to suggest that evaluation efforts should never lead to sanctions or consequences. If feedback systems are in place, and time is allowed for adjustment and improvement, it is appropriate to sanction collaboratives that are not producing results. Failure should also always be an option, and it can sometimes be a blessing because it forces reassessment, new approaches, or renewed efforts to achieve results. Ultimately, the goal of collaborative attempts is to achieve results, and if those results are not forthcoming, a collaborative approach may not be the best way to address these problems.

11

The Future of Collaboration

During my year as a visiting researcher in Brisbane, I sat at a desk overlooking a courtyard lined with palm trees. This subtropical climate has been one of the factors leading to more than twenty years of substantial growth in South East Queensland. Yet the climate in the region didn't seem very subtropical during my stay. I was amazed to learn that the region had not had a significant tropical storm since I moved away from Brisbane seven years earlier. Years of drought combined with the addition of thousands of new residents led to dramatic water restrictions. Furthermore, urbanization and recreation increased environmental pressures on the region. The policy response trends typify the kinds of environmental management approaches that are likely to compete with each other in the future.

One approach has been highly collaborative. The South East Queensland Healthy Waterways Partnership has been working for over a decade to improve water quality in the Brisbane River and Moreton Bay. It has produced a partnership among state agencies, local governments, private partners, and the community through a range of actions, including regulations, restoration efforts, infrastructure investments, education and outreach, and volunteer efforts. The work in the basin has been recognized through national awards as it struggles to address increasing demands from population growth along with dramatic cycles of drought and flood.

The other approach involved little collaboration. The extended drought created a water supply crisis. In response, the Queensland Water Commission imposed Level 6 water restrictions that severely limited the use of water for things like landscaping, pools, and car washing. Residents were installing rain tanks, diverting shower water to gardens, and having water trucked in from outside the region. In 2007, the state of Queensland unilaterally announced it would construct a new reservoir on the Mary River north of Brisbane to increase supply for the region. The controversial project would have dammed a free-flowing river that is home to Mary River cod and turtle, which are both listed by the Queensland government as endangered species.[1]

These cases represent two water resource management issues in the same region under the same administration, but with different approaches. They each offer characteristics about the problems, process, and context that may help explain the Queensland government's response. For example, if the government is determined to build a dam *somewhere*, there is little room for a negotiated agreement. Rather than analyzing why the government took this approach, I use this case to illustrate that interactive and discursive approaches to decision making may take place side by side traditional, top-down decision making. This example raises the question of how future pressures such as drought, floods, and catastrophic weather will affect the way we govern environmental issues. It also remains to be seen how complex problems, such as urban sprawl, deforestation, overfishing, and greenhouse gas emissions will play out in terms of governance.

This chapter considers the future of collaboration through several different lenses. It looks at some of the broader trends affecting environmental management and governance. It then reviews the trends specific to action, organizational, and policy collaboratives. Finally, it explores some of the key questions for government, community, and researchers.

Contextual Trends

Collaboration has been described by some as a "movement" or a "new management paradigm," which implies that it is being driven by collective action or management thinking. While these factors have played a part in advancing the role of collaboration, I believe there are also some broader contextual trends that suggest a continued need for some version of a collaborative governance approach.

First, as noted throughout this book, the increased importance of diffuse environmental problems is one reason for the increased use of collaboration. In developed countries like the United States, water pollution control is continuing to shift its focus to runoff from urban and rural areas, thereby requiring many changes in individual behaviors and practices. Similarly, there is increasing attention in air pollution control around travel behavior, urban form, and attitudes toward alternative transportation. This will not replace the need for ongoing regulatory controls on point water and air source pollution. As the incremental benefits of these controls become smaller and increasingly more expensive, however, there will be increasing concentration on diffuse sources.

Second, there is more concern about complex and difficult (or wicked) problems, such as greenhouse gas emissions, climate change, natural hazards, and endangered species. Each of these issues requires significant regulatory components, but regulation alone cannot solve the fundamental changes needed to address some of these problems. Likewise, market-based strategies have been cited as a means for addressing these problems. Many of these issues do not involve easy market mechanisms, though; they entail high transaction costs, involve highly complex interjurisdictional issues, and/or require fundamental changes in human behavior. For example, Thomas Friedman (2008) highlights the scale of change needed to address the impacts from current carbon emissions while accommodating the expected population and economic growth of developing countries like China and India. He claims that to achieve this by 2050, the world has to conserve almost as much energy as we are currently using. Friedman laments the popular media response to the problem with articles such as "205 Easy Ways to Save the Earth." Instead, he suggests that to reduce our carbon emissions by two hundred billion tons while our population continues to grow, we must make at least eight massive changes from a list that includes:

• Drive two billion cars only five thousand miles per year rather than ten thousand miles (at thirty miles per gallon)
• Increase solar power seven-hundredfold to displace all coal-fired power plants
• Halt all cutting and burning of forests
• Adopt conservation tillage (which emits much less carbon dioxide) in all agricultural soils worldwide

In short, these all require massive changes without one clear path, regulatory structure, or implementation responsibility for making them happen.

Third, collaborative efforts will continue to be central to many environmental problems because of the need to link social, economic, and environmental actions. Often described in simplistic terms as the three legs of the sustainability stool, connecting them in practice is difficult and complex. Just integrating efforts focused on environmental systems is difficult and complex, and this is compounded when management efforts are expected to link with social and economic systems. Linking these issues will not occur through just a policy fix but instead will require hard work at a range of levels.

Fourth, these factors highlight that many problems and solutions are interjurisdictional in nature. There are periodic calls for the reorganization of local or even state government along ecological boundaries, but every boundary that is created will confront issues that cross it. Even ecological boundaries such as river basins or climatic zones often do not align with each other, nor do they align with social and economic boundaries. Thus, cross-boundary problem solving should be assumed as a given.

Finally, for all the complexity of the problems presented in this book, none of them touch on the added complexity of working across national boundaries. As recent trends in global warming and the global finance system underscore, we live in an increasingly interconnected world. These interconnections mean increased attention at the global scale with only a limited capacity for international governance systems to guide implementation. While there have been many calls for increased powers to implement and enforce international treaties, these are seldom utilized in practice. For example, the European Union's significant efforts to reform water policy are supported by substantial powers and funding, but implementation is proving to be a difficult task (Newig, Pahl-Wostl, and Sigel 2005). Thus, for many of these global-scale issues, collaborative approaches at an international level may play a key role.

To capture the complexity of all these contextual issues and the role of collaboration, I turn to the example of small-diameter timber utilization in eastern Oregon. This issue pales in comparison to some of the global problems we confront, but it reveals how several of the aforementioned contextual trends conspire to create a complex governance setting.

For many years, western forests have been managed to suppress fire, which is a natural part of the ecological process. Before European settlement, these areas experienced periodic, low-temperature brushfires, which burned the ground cover and small plants, but only scorched the large western ponderosa or lodgepole pines. Furthermore, the fire replenished nutrients in the soil, and encouraged a rich and diverse understory. The advent of modern forestry led to a suppression of this fire regime to preserve the land for timber production. Over time, the small plants and seedlings that historically were burned away have become small trees reaching into the canopy. This buildup in biomass means that when fires ignite, they are far more intense, leading to devastating infernos that destroy all forest cover and can even sterilize the soil. The impact of these fires is compounded by rural sprawl, as private homes, rural estates, and resorts are built on private lands adjacent to public ones (Kelly and Bliss 2009).

One of the solutions to addressing this problem is to remove the small-diameter timber through physical cutting and thinning, because it is too large to burn. Yet this is an expensive process, and the timber removed from the forest has little economic value. Thus, there has been considerable exploration of ways to utilize this small-diameter timber for electric generation, woodstove heating, furniture, building materials, and other uses. In eastern Oregon this has led to collaborative efforts among environmentalists, local government, federal land management agencies, state and local economic agencies, and other stakeholders. Their goal is to invest in economically productive uses of small-diameter timber that will lead to a reduction of biomass on public and private forestlands. This requires new equipment for timber companies, investment in local facilities and industries, changes in land management policies, and training for an array of new workers in the jobs that support the approach. It also necessitates assurances that these activities will restore the landscape and not damage critical habitats.

This is just one story of one regional problem that belies simple regulatory or market solutions. Similar issues surround everything from substance abuse services to natural hazard mitigation to regional growth management. In the absence of a willingness or ability to infuse massive public investment, or create significant new governmental powers, many of these problems will increasingly rely on some type of cross-jurisdictional, collaborative approach.

Trends Affecting Collaboratives

The contextual trends described above can affect all types of collaboratives. This book stresses many differences between collaboratives, though, and the future of collaboration may look different for different types of collaboratives. The following sections review some of the trends that may specifically affect action, organizational, and policy collaboratives.

Action Collaboratives

The underlying need for action-level collaboratives, and their place in many planning and public policy areas, is unlikely to change. In particular, there will continue to be a role for these groups for solving diffuse problems that are difficult to address through traditional government initiatives. Still, I believe there are several macrotrends that may affect the ability of these kinds of groups to operate in the future.

First, the long-term success of action collaboratives will depend in part on the patience of funders and government in relation to the progress that these groups are making. Even if we assume that all of the groups working at this level are completely effective and efficient (which of course is not the case), the scale of the problems they are addressing and the rate at which they are bringing about change means that it will take decades to see substantial change. As a watershed council coordinator remarked at one meeting, "It took us a hundred years to screw up this watershed; we're not going to fix it in five."[2]

For some, this rate may be too slow or other funding priorities may be more important. In Oregon, for example, one of the key reasons that watershed councils have been able to maintain their efforts in the face of state budget cuts has been their lack of reliance on general fund revenue. Their efforts are supported by lottery funding, license plate revenues, and other sources established through a public referendum.[3]

Second, action collaboratives will also be affected by the attitudes toward transaction costs by those who fund these efforts. These funders may be legislatures, agencies, foundations, or individual donors. Many of these funders are motivated by problem solving, so in addition to the impatience that they may exhibit toward collaboratives, they may also have different views about the need to fund the collaborative itself. This is apparent in Oregon, where legislators were commonly heard to say that they wanted to "fund projects, not people." Yet the job of supporting, managing, and carrying out the work of collaboratives requires people. It is not enough to just offer incentives for restoration; there needs to be people to recruit landowners, design the restoration projects, usher the project through the permit process, oversee the restoration project, and check on ongoing maintenance. Any one of these elements—if not done correctly—could result in more environmental harm than good.

Third, long-term success will depend on the capacity of action collaboratives to not only sustain themselves but also to mature in their ability to address problems. Cyclic funding, high turnover, and low levels of training and support will all tend to undermine their capacity. Increased partnerships, more diversified funding sources, more financial security, and more stable organizations will tend to increase their capacity. For this reason, paying attention to sustaining collaboratives (chapter 6) and strengthening social networks (chapter 7) will be critical.

Finally, success will depend on the willingness of communities to continue to support and work with these groups to solve problems. Many action collaboratives are highly dependent on the communities in which they work, whether for volunteer time, support, or financial contributions. This may not be an issue in communities with strong networks and a population base with adequate skills and volunteers. But for collaboratives working in rural and remote areas, with an aging population and a dependence on a few key people, the potential is high for volunteer burnout and the dissolution of the collaborative itself.

The well-documented burnout rates among volunteers and staff members under the Landcare and catchment programs was one of the factors that led the Australian government to create regional, quasi-governmental organizations (see, for example, Byron, Curtis, and Lockwood 2001). Watershed council coordinators in Oregon raised similar concerns, since their groups often suffer from limited board involvement, difficulty in recruiting new members, and heavy workloads on coordinators and a few key volunteers (Parker et al. 2010).

Organizational Collaboratives

Organizational collaboratives are facing the same kind of contextual trends, but they are more susceptible to political and administrative changes. In particular, organizational collaboratives are most likely to be affected by the increased complexity of planning and policy problems, and the increasing importance of diffuse sources underlying the basis for these problems.

The issue of air pollution illustrates this classic shift and the resultant pressures it has placed on a range of organizations to work collaboratively. For roughly the first twenty years of the Clean Air Act, the focus was reducing emissions from point sources (such as factories) and increasing the emission standards for mobile sources (cars and trucks). As these controls have been ratcheted down, however, the incremental cost of each improvement has grown and the significance of many smaller sources has received increased attention.

Nowhere is this more evident than in metropolitan areas, where emissions from transportation have broadened the focus from "end-of-pipe" controls to the generation of trips and miles that vehicles travel. This requires air quality regulators to coordinate with transportation planners, who must in turn coordinate with local governments and their land use policies. It also requires major employers, transit agencies, and school systems to develop strategies to reduce trips and travel. This network of participants will expand even more as attention shifts to the impacts from greenhouse gases. This same story line is being repeated around issues such as ecological habitats, water quality, education, and community health.

With the demand for collaboration by organizations increasing, there is also pressure to reduce costs. Some of this depends on political cycles, but few levels of government are flush with resources, and many are cutting positions and programs. This can lead to two different responses. One is to seek out more collaboration, avoid duplication, pool resources, and develop partnerships. The other is to pull back to "core business." As discussed previously, this means cutting back programs and positions that are not central to the organization's mission. As several participants in the Rogue River basin commented, collaborative efforts are frequently seen as the icing on the cake. The more organizations pull back to core business, the more likely that collaborative efforts will flounder.

The consequence of pulling back to core business is that organizations will be responding more to problems than trying to prevent them. This usually leaves the organization fighting fires rather than trying to be proactive and reduce fires (sometimes literally). This has been highlighted in recent years by the lack of forward planning and preparation for natural disasters. As Hurricane Katrina demonstrated so vividly, the personal and economic costs of reactive management can be devastating.

Policy Collaboratives
Because policy collaboratives are closely intertwined with political systems, their long-term success will depend on political powers and forces, but sustaining them may rely more on the views of the problem. In policy analysis terms, policy collaboratives are more suited to initiatives opened in response to a problem than initiatives opened in response to a political ideology. Attention and concern about the problem will help maintain pressure on the collaborative as a constructive forum, while efforts driven by political ideology will come and go with

administrations. Thus, even significant shifts in ideology—such as that witnessed with the transition from the Bush to the Obama administration—will be tempered by the long time horizons of many collaboratives. When problems draw attention, the collaborative efforts are more likely to span political parties and administrations.

This is not to suggest that political leadership is not important. As suggested in chapter 9, the efforts by political actors are critical for sustaining a political network. Political leaders have also been crucial for putting pressure on these networks to develop solutions. Perhaps most important, elected officials have helped secure funding for these attempts. Thus, the substantial financial commitments of the first Bush administration to Florida everglades restoration have helped sustain these efforts over many years.

Lastly, the future of policy collaboratives will be affected by the willingness of political leaders to create forums for problem solving versus seeking more unilateral solutions or legislative negotiations. The efforts to manage the Great Lakes, Chesapeake Bay, and Sacramento–San Joaquin Delta have all depended on the willingness of elected officials to create these forums and support them with funding over the long term. Likewise, their continued support or lack thereof has paralleled the history of sustaining these efforts.

Summary

As noted above, the action-organizational-policy framework describes a spectrum of collaboratives. The forces affecting collaboratives, furthermore, are overlapping rather than distinct. This means that the array of underlying forces described above may affect all collaboratives, but in different ways. As illustrated in figure 11.1, some of these factors will be more important for some collaboratives than others, but often all of them are key for sustaining a collaborative and supporting its ability to achieve results.

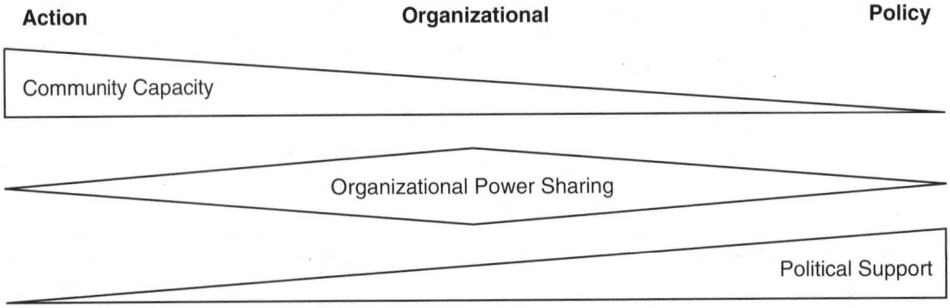

Action	Organizational	Policy

Community Capacity

Organizational Power Sharing

Political Support

Figure 11.1
Key factors affecting the future of collaboratives

Debates Related to the Future of Collaborative Governance

Although collaboration has been practiced in a range of forms and settings for many years, the research and theory of collaboration continues to evolve. Applied scholarship lags behind practice, but it is essential for assessing practice, developing theory to guide practice, and determining the settings where collaboration or alternative approaches are most suitable. The scholarship around collaboration touches on several broader issues related to the future of collaboration, including the relationship with voluntary action, collaborative governance debates, and the alternatives to collaboration.

Collaboration and Voluntary Action

In the literature on collaborative natural resources management, there is a close linkage between collaboration, grassroots efforts, and volunteer approaches. This is in large part due to the explosion of collaborative groups working in local communities to address issues such as watershed management, ecological restoration, and neighborhood revitalization. These action collaboratives have built their efforts on social networks and stakeholders, typically implementing their objectives through education, outreach, volunteer work, and incentive-based programs. As Cass Moseley (1999) notes, they are filling in the gaps of current management approaches by tapping into networks to support voluntary action.

Collaboratives operate at many different levels, though, and the role of collaboration is different at different levels. As many cases in this book demonstrate, organizational- and policy-level collaborations often don't depend on voluntary approaches. They focus on how to improve existing governance through the integration of efforts across jurisdictions and more decision-making input. In the case of policy collaboratives, they may be exploring new roles for governance, changes in policy, or new policy. This recognition of different levels of collaboration leads to two implications related to localism.

For one, the concept of collaboration needs to be decoupled from that of localism (Margerum 2007). Many collaborative efforts cover large regions with large populations. Furthermore, some collaboratives that are local in scope are working with other collaboratives or organizations to address broader-scale issues. Nevertheless, not all collaborative efforts are local or operate at the action level.

Collaboration also needs to be decoupled from the concept of voluntary action. Once again, as the cases throughout this book illustrate, there are many collaboratives that don't rely solely on voluntary efforts to produce results.

Governance Debates

One of the discussions emerging around collaboratives relates to how they are governed. This will be an area of ongoing debate, particularly as monitoring and evaluations provide more performance assessment. The findings I present in this book do not resolve the debate, but three observations help focus and narrow some of the key issues and questions.

First, in settings where policy collaboration leads to a policy resolution, implementation will often shift to an organizational level. This may require interorganizational networks to support crosscutting activities, but it does not require *ongoing* political networks. For example, in earlier chapters I cited the cases of the Lower Wisconsin River and Lake Tahoe. In each instance, a significant policy deliberation led to a new policy or structure, but ongoing activities have mostly centered on management activities and policy implementation under this new policy or structure.

Second, there could be settings where a policy resolution leads directly to an action-level focus supported by social networks. Perhaps the example that comes the closest to this scenario is Australia's National Landcare Program, which emerged from a partnership among political leaders and two peak advocacy organizations—the Australian Conservation Foundation and the National Farmers Federation—that typically found themselves on opposite sides of many debates. Campbell (1994, 31) describes how this "unholy alliance" of two key interest groups that usually disagreed on most issues led to a ministerial task force, a joint seminar, and eventually a joint proposal to foster thousands of community-based conservation groups supported by an original allocation of $340 million Australian dollars ($265 million 1990 U.S. dollars). The implementation of this policy took place through a fairly traditional federal-state agency structure, leading to grants and technical assistance to support the work of locally based, voluntary conservation groups.

Third, collaboration involving ongoing policy debates and deliberation is most likely to raise debates about the governance model. This can be summarized as debate about the role and power of the collaborative entity (chapter 6), and the role and power of the political network (chapter 9). The different views are highlighted by the debate about CALFED. Kallis, Kiparsky, and Norgaard (2010, 638) describe the debate as a question of whether CALFED "should be governed as a program by a dedicated agency [or instead] be more of a voluntary, fluid structure of working group exchange, coordinated by a high level policy group."

The collaborative agency perspective portrays collaborative governance in terms of formalized partnerships that both negotiate management plans and implement actions (Sabatier et al. 2005). Proponents of this model argue that the collaborative agency needs adequate powers over the agencies to manage funds and assure implementation (Bobker 2009; Little Hoover Commission 2005; Kallis, Kiparsky, and Norgaard 2010). The Little Hoover Commission review of CALFED advocated for a structure operating like an advisory group directly accountable to the governor and the secretary of the interior, which Kallis, Kiparsky, and Norgaard (2010) refer as the "return to State" model.

In contrast, Innes and her colleagues (2006, 51) argue that the collaborative agency model is "trying to fit CALFED into a traditional governance box." Innes and Booher (2010, 201) contend that traditional governance relies too much on top-down hierarchy under central control where agencies have closed boundaries; "in collaborative governance by contrast a structure typically involves distributed control, open boundaries, and interdependent, nested network clusters of participants." Similarly, Raul Lejano and Helen Ingram (2010) assert that a centralized implementing body hinders networking and the translation of information between stakeholders.

I offer two observations based on my secondary analysis of CALFED and other cases. First, even with a fluid governance structure, policy-level deliberations require a collaborative agency with significant resources and capacity. A collaboration needs resources, because a fluid political network necessitates maintenance, support, and revitalization. While researchers have documented political and policy reforms led by small groups of loosely affiliated leaders (Roberts and King 1996; Crosby and Bryson 2010), these are typically short-term policy development processes and not ongoing governance approaches. A collaborative agency needs capacity, because political networks are not able to dedicate the time and resources to ongoing management oversight. The political network will remain engaged in monitoring, evaluating, and overseeing the management entity.

Then too, I suggest that it is a mistake for the advocates of either collaborative agencies or fluid structures to treat politics as external to collaborative governance. For example, Innes and her colleagues (2006, 51; emphasis added) observe: "In one sense, the course of events in the last year or two can hardly be blamed on CALFED. Natural factors, *political power*, and agendas *outside* CALFED have been at work." I maintain that when collaboratives are dealing with ongoing policy issues, politics are central to governance, and collaboratives must develop effective political networks to produce results. Importantly, this governance must be tied to a network rather than a specific office or administration if it is to be sustained over time. The recommendation of the Little Hoover Commission that CALFED should be an advisory group to the governor and the Secretary of the Interior thus would have faced significant problems during every election cycle.[4]

The synthesis I draw from these observations is that collaboratives addressing ongoing policy issues need a significant *and* capable collaborative agency. A political network needs the agency to coordinate activities and allocate resources as well as provide the network support functions described above. It also needs an interorganizational network to help implement its activities. Therefore, the collaborative agency serves a crucial implementation coordination role among the set of participating organizations.

Collaboratives addressing ongoing policy issues also need a fluid political network to achieve results. This network is fragile and prone to failure, but as Kallis, Kiparsky, and Norgaard (2010) note, it was the earlier state authority approach in the CALFED region that led to endless rounds of litigation and power plays over water allocation. This final section about governance, then, discusses some principles for comparing collaborative governance to other approaches.

Collaboration and Its Alternatives

This book concentrates on the factors to improve collaboration, but there is the larger question of how collaboration compares to other approaches. It is a difficult question to answer for two methodological reasons. The first reason is that there are only a few settings where we can compare collaborative and noncollaborative approaches that offer similar settings, scope, and conditions. For example, Schneider and his colleagues (2003) compare the densities of management networks in areas participating in the national estuary program to similar estuaries where the programs did not exist. This kind of research allows for more careful comparison, but they note that a more systematic exploration of outputs and outcomes is also required.

The second reason relates to this need for a systematic analysis of outputs and outcomes. As mentioned in the evaluation discussion in chapter 10, these kinds of data are necessary to evaluate whether collaboration—or any governance approach—is achieving results. Yet it takes a substantial level of activity sustained over a long period of time to begin to answer that question.

Chapter 1 reviews many of the reasons why collaboration has emerged. In this section, I draw on some of my research findings to present preliminary propositions for comparing a collaborative approach to three alternatives: new governing bodies, new regulatory authority, and direct incentive mechanisms.

New Governing Bodies

One alternative is to create new government organizations that encompass some of the responsibilities and functions of collaboratives. In essence, the view is that the diverse sets of decision makers need to be combined into a single entity with coordinating responsibility. In New South Wales, the regional bodies created under the recently reformed federal natural resources program have granted them more authority and resources than their predecessor organizations. This is what has led Robins and Dovers (2007a) to suggest that they have become another tier of government.

In the United States, there has been little movement in this direction for natural resources management, but in many parts of the country there continues to be an increasing role among metropolitan planning organizations to address issues such as growth management. In Europe, the European Union has been playing an increasing role in natural resources management, working to create a more unified set of regional water policies and programs (Lindemann 2008; Mostert et al. 2007). Leaving aside the political challenges of creating new governing bodies, I present two conditions under which they may be more effective than collaborative approaches.

For one, new governing bodies can be effective when they have a clear scope and purpose that does not substantially compete with the responsibilities and jurisdictions of other management entities. There will always be some overlap of jurisdictions, but if the issues being addressed are highly interconnected with other entities, it becomes difficult to encompass the boundaries of the problem under one governing body. For example, land use planning, infrastructure investment, and transportation decision making all combine to affect regional growth patterns. In metropolitan Portland, Oregon, a regional elected council has significant powers over planning and land use, but many of the planning and transportation issues that affect its work overlap with the state transportation agency, neighboring counties, adjacent metropolitan planning organizations, and cities and counties across the Columbia River in Washington State.

Second, new governing bodies can be effective when they have substantial resources to allocate to other management entities. If a new governing body has a clear, independent scope and resources, there may not be an interjurisdictional function. If its scope does overlap with other jurisdictions, however, its role in allocating funding can be important for coordinating activities. For instance, when regional management bodies were created in Queensland, some state agencies were pulling away from some of their past activities because they judged them the responsibility of the regional entity. The funding allocated by the Wisconsin DNR, in contrast, brought many other state and local agencies into their management efforts.

New Regulatory Authority

A second alternative is to create new regulatory authority to address management objectives. In the United States, for example, there has been a gradual shift in stormwater management toward more authority and regulation. Early management efforts focused entirely on voluntary actions, but over the years the U.S. Environmental Protection Agency has been requiring more cities to obtain pollution discharge permits for stormwater. To obtain permit approval, cities have had to develop management plans, and some cities are including regulations in their zoning codes (Daniels et al. 2003). New authority also presents political barriers, but putting these aside, there are several conditions under which authority may be a viable alternative to collaboration.

First, regulatory authority is most effective when objectives are clear and measurable. Stormwater management plans have to be linked back to the quality of the receiving water for which there are water quality standards. In contrast, managing ecosystems includes a much more complex set of factors that are often hard to measure.

New authority also can be effective when it can be administered and enforced. The more diffuse an action, the more difficult it is to administer and enforce. Social pressures can supplement enforcement, but it has to be clear and understood when actions are in violation. Activities like littering and smoking in public places are against the law, yet such laws are hard to enforce. Public knowledge of improper activity and social pressure helps reduce violations. In contrast, activities like non-point source pollution and degradation of habitat are hard to identify as well as enforce.

Third, regulatory authority is better for stopping negative action than promoting positive action. For example, regulations may prevent a landowner from disturbing riparian areas, but it can be difficult for regulations to require a landowner to manage a riparian area for habitat benefits. This is not to suggest that stopping action is not a powerful tool—such as stopping a development project, an infrastructure project, a policy, or a management plan; it just has limitations in promoting a positive response.

Finally, regulations can play an important symbolic role—even when they don't meet the conditions listed above. In several earlier chapters I noted that the Endangered Species Act has been an important motivator for voluntary and collaborative activity. The Endangered Species Act authority often does not meet the three conditions mentioned above, but the *threat* of government intervention has been widely cited as a motivator for action. Watershed restoration efforts in Oregon have complex goals, difficult enforcement, and a need for positive action, but a widely acknowledged motivator is the threat of regulation.

Direct Mechanisms

A third approach is to focus on mechanisms that directly affect individual decision making. Economists promote these mechanisms because of their administrative efficiencies as well as reliance on markets and rational choice to influence action. In his book *Earth in a Balance*, for instance, Al Gore argued for a carbon tax to significantly affect the U.S. use of resources (Gore 1992). Similar kinds of strategies could also be applied to other resources and commodities, so that consumers pay the full societal costs of hydropower or corn production. While some of these ideas face substantial political difficulties, they should not be dismissed based on the current political winds. Gore backed away from his proposal during the 2000 election because of criticism, but it is an idea that appears to gain more traction every year. In another example, the Conservation Reserve Program has been paying farmers for over twenty years to take agricultural lands with conservation value out of production. This has led some environmental groups to view the Farm Bill as one of the most important pieces of *environmental* legislation. Direct mechanisms are most likely to be effective under several conditions.

First, direct mechanisms can be effective when the specific actions are known. Agricultural conservation programs are based on an extended history of research on best management practices and guidelines that provide clear prescriptions. But even within these programs there is significant variation in transaction costs. For example, the actions and steps for participation in the wetlands reserve program are more complex, and they involve far higher transaction costs than participation in soil conservation programs.

Direct mechanisms also can be effective when there is a means to administer programs and provide quality assurance for the resulting action. The agricultural conservation programs in the United States are backed up with a wide-ranging system of agricultural extension experts along with state- and county-level conservation staff. A carbon tax would require a less intense infrastructure, but it would necessitate significant public resources to administer and oversee as well, not to mention significant private resources to implement.

Third, there needs to be a clear link between the direct mechanism and the desired action. There is good evidence, say, that dramatic increases in gas prices affected driving behavior, but this effect may be reduced over time as the price shock wears off. Many farmers don't participate in conservation programs because they don't like government programs, are uncomfortable with changing their practices, are concerned about risk, or confront other barriers, such as capital investment, increased labor, more training, or reduced flexibility of operations.

Direct mechanisms have to be significant enough to overcome broader economic forces too. Thus, in some parts of the United States, high commodity prices put lands under conservation reserve programs back into production. Other kinds of economic and external forces, such as droughts, economic expansion, or a recession, may overwhelm government incentives.

Conclusions about Collaborative Governance

One of the most important principles from these discussions about the future of collaborative governance is that contrasting models and approaches are not mutually exclusive. While collaboration is often addressing voluntary action, it may also be addressing management and regulatory action—even within the same collaborative process. Similarly, as noted in the governance debates, collaboration at the policy level frequently needs *both* a significant management entity and strong but fluid political networks. Finally, none of the alternatives explored above are mutually exclusive to collaboration. Even those that contrast collaboration with top-down regulation ignore the importance of regulation in getting participants to the table. They also ignore collaborative efforts that lead to new regulations and top-down policy or management initiatives.

Key Questions for Moving Forward

The future of collaboration will be significantly affected by the people and organizations that fund, support, participate, and evaluate the efforts. The success of a collaborative will depend on many variables, including context, personalities, and history; still, there are some critical questions for governmental and nongovernmental organizations that will affect its success.

Questions for Practice

One essential question relates to the willingness of stakeholders and stakeholding organizations to share power. As has been noted in several places in this book, even sharing information is a form of power sharing. Sharing power becomes more significant as organizations are asked to adjust policies, change priorities, and move resources.

Another question relates to the extent to which organizations and stakeholders focus on problems and overarching missions. This approach directs participants to end goals first, allowing more room for creative solutions and ideas. When stakeholders concentrate too early on the means, they are more likely to get bogged down.

Collaborative processes also require some flexibility when they are applied. This can be particularly problematic for large state and federal agencies, which must consider policy consistency across their jurisdictions as well.

Then too, collaboration demands a more comprehensive view of evaluation. While outcome indicators are important, they must be complemented with other ways of measuring progress. This is critical for making program assessments and improvements, and also important for communicating with elected officials, the public, and other key audiences.

A further question for many collaborative efforts relates to capacity and burnout. This was discussed in some detail in relation to action-level collaboratives, but it is relevant to all types of efforts. Even policy-level groups may have difficulty maintaining high-level involvement as stakeholders and policymakers are drawn to other forums and priorities.

Lastly, collaboration needs pressure, attention, and a willingness to consider alternatives. Because of its high transaction costs, collaboration depends on pressure from the public, elected officials, the media, regulators, and others. Collaboration is most effective when alternatives remain in play, especially the threat of government intervention or top-down regulation.

Questions for Researchers

Throughout this book I have pointed to some specific issues for future research. I believe there are also some key overarching issues that would benefit from more detailed investigations.

For starters, there has been little research on the failure of collaboratives. This may include collaborative efforts that were unable to convene, collaborative groups that were unable to reach consensus, and collaboratives that achieved consensus but disintegrated over time or were unable to achieve results. These kinds of efforts are difficult to research, because they are hard to identify and people are often less interested in discussing failure. Furthermore, the participants involved may be dispersed and difficult to reach. Since most research has focused on groups that have been sustained or have achieved some degree of success, however, more assessment of failed efforts would provide important comparative data.

Second, there is a need to understand more about network functioning in the context of collaboration. Much of the research presented in this book has examined networks in other contexts, and there needs to be a more systematic collection of information to understand the specifics of how they work. I believe this is particularly acute for political networks, because there has been limited research and analysis of how participants in these high-level forums interact, and how their interaction helps sustain or undermine collaboratives.

For collaboratives at the action and organizational level, there are many questions about how they relate to neighboring collaboratives, regions, or activities. This is especially relevant when groups of collaboratives have overlapping responsibilities, as was the case in both the Rogue River and Columbia River basins. These cross-regional collaboration issues begin to raise higher-level issues and problems, for which there are often not forums for addressing and resolving them. In the case of both the Rogue and Columbia rivers, regional structures created to address regional habitat planning (such as the Northwest Forest Plan or the Northwest Power and Conservation Council) have helped support and facilitate cross-regional collaboration. More assessments of the roles of these cross-regional activities would be helpful. In the United States, it would be particularly important to understand their potential role across regions that don't have such a significant federal presence. For example, there are many watershed-based efforts in the midwestern United States that raise cross-regional issues for which there are no readily available forums.

Final Thoughts

In 1995, I arrived in Australia to study the collaborative management of land and water. In the course of my case study travels, I took time off to go scuba diving on the Great Barrier Reef near the Whitsunday Islands. It was a spectacular place—especially for someone who received their diving certification in a rock quarry in Ohio.

Over the succeeding decade, I conducted over twenty dives on the reef, and each time it seemed like there was more bleaching, more die-off, and less reef to see. I wondered whether I was becoming blasé about the scenery; perhaps the scuba diving companies were not choosing their locations as well; perhaps there were too many divers like me affecting the reef.

When I got ready to move from Australia in 2000, the press and the government both focused on recreational impacts along with the discharge of sediments and nutrients from the river basins emptying into the lagoon. It was on my mind when my wife and I took one final diving trip before our move. We spent three days diving on the reef in the Whitsunday Islands, and during that trip the reef's deteriorating condition was a common discussion among the experienced divers.

When I returned to Australia in 2008, I heard a presentation by the Commonwealth Scientific and Industrial Research Organization scientists who were observing significant die-off—caused not just by recreational users and runoff, but also by rising sea temperatures fluctuating beyond the narrow zone at which coral live. These fluctuations were making the coral more susceptible to predators, disease, and the effects of nutrients and sediments. What shocked me about this trend was not that it was occurring but rather the rate at which it was doing so. It dawned on me as I heard these scenarios that the Great Barrier Reef could die off during the lifetime of my two sons.

Ultimately, I'm not interested in collaboration as a concept. I'm interested in collaboration as a way of solving problems, addressing concerns and achieving results. When it is underperforming it needs to be evaluated critically so it can improve, and when it is failing it needs to be replaced by better alternatives. The problem for both researchers and practitioners is that there are few clear alternatives to address complex, interjurisdictional, dispersed, and diffuse problems. Until we find better alternatives, collaboration will continue to play an important role. My hope is that this book will help collaboration proceed better and faster. My hope is that others will come along and improve on the practice as well as implementation of collaboration. But ultimately, my hope is that places like the Great Barrier Reef will be there not just for my sons' generation but also for many generations to come.

Appendix: Research Methods

This appendix reviews the methods used in the research for this book. Much of this work has been published previously, but the typologies of collaboratives and networks are a relatively recent development in my research. Therefore, I reanalyzed previously collected data to explore and test the typology and assessment factors that I present. This included going back through transcripts and examples from recorded transcripts, interview notes, Web sites, and written documents. When I had written permission to attribute quotes, I used names and job titles. Many interviews and surveys were confidential. For others I did not request permission for attribution, so I treated them as confidential. I have made an effort to ensure the accuracy of these quotes, and attempted to present a balance of perspectives when they are available. Any mistakes, misinterpretations, or factual errors contained in the case studies are mine.

Some case information used in this book was based on my personal involvement in collaborative efforts along with exploratory or unpublished research. Between 2003 and 2007, I was a steering committee member for the Long Tom Watershed Council, serving as vice chair and chair. For the past several years, I have been a member of the Lower Willamette Groundwater Management Area Committee. I also helped lead and facilitate a working group charged with examining school facility and management issues for the Eugene 4J school district. Finally, I have undertaken exploratory analysis of several collaboration groups, issues, or data sets that were not developed into full research projects but are referenced in this book. These are described in the "Other Research" section of this appendix.

Major Research Studies

In the following sections, I outline the methods used in a range of research projects over fifteen years. Much of my research entailed case studies, which Yin (2009) notes is a particularly valuable method when seeking to capture the richness and complexities of a setting. It involves an empirical inquiry that investigates a phenomenon within its real-life context and uses multiple sources of evidence. The case studies I list in this book were all based on multiple interviews with participants. In some cases, I also observed collaborative groups in operation and/or collected written survey information from the group.

Several cases also involved more broad-based written or online surveys of participants. This provided an opportunity to test some specific hypotheses, collect a wider range of views, and improve the external validity (transferability) of the findings.

Wisconsin Case Studies (1993–1995 and 1997)

The study of collaborative efforts in Wisconsin was part of my dissertation research conducted over two years (Margerum 1995a). The project was funded by the Wisconsin DNR, which had been undertaking a number of collaborative efforts, and was interested in developing a better model for how to guide and support them. At that time, the concept of collaborative management (referred to as integrated environmental management) was still emerging, and there was little guidance or theory. As a result, my work was exploratory, examining the steps in convening, the process of consensus building, and the ongoing management issues. Rather than conducting experiments or testing hypotheses, I was describing and comparing recognizable patterns to help build a general model and hypotheses of collaboration.

I used two criteria for selecting the case studies. The case had to involve the successful development of a collaborative approach, which was defined in terms of outputs or outcomes. I did not examine failed efforts, yet there were clearly varying levels of success, and several cases experienced previous failures.

Second, the cases had to meet the substantive definition of a collaborative approach, even if they did not use those terms by name. Based on these criteria, I selected seven case studies in cooperation with Wisconsin DNR staff, and one case study outside the state.

For each case, I reviewed published reports and internal DNR background materials to summarize the factual information about the case. I interviewed multiple individuals involved with each project, including participants not employed by the DNR. Interviewees were identified through a snowball sampling process, starting with the lead DNR staff person. At the end of each interview, I listed my interviewees and asked if there were additional names that should be included. This created a fairly comprehensive list of participants for each case.

A total of eighty-two interviews were conducted for the eight case studies, with the number of interviews per case ranging from four to twenty. The confidential interviews usually lasted sixty minutes and covered four topic areas:

- background information that could not be obtained during background research
- perceptions of collaboration and organizational support of the concept
- listings and assessments of techniques and processes that were most effective for exchanging information, resolving conflict, and involving the public
- evaluations of the outcomes and outputs of the case

Each interview was tape-recorded and transcribed into a database that could be queried for analysis. In addition to the interviews, I asked participants to complete a written ranking of the coordination mechanisms used in the cases.

The case study analysis was carried out in three steps. First, a narrative of each case was prepared, and then sent to participants for review and fact-checking. Second, I conducted a cross-case analysis of similarities and differences to identify themes from the cases. This was an iterative process that used both quantitative and qualitative data. These common themes were analyzed using relevant theories from the literature on coordination, conflict resolution, collaboration, planning, and public participation.

I also scrutinized the cases through a more analytic lens. This approach involved describing institutional rule types at different levels of analysis (based on work by Ciriacy-Wantrup 1970; Gregg et al. 1991; Ostrom 1986b, 1990). I examined these rule sets at different points in time to document and compare changes across the cases. The goal of this approach was to systematically analyze interaction in the cases and identify more generalizable findings about coordination during implementation.

In 1997, I had the opportunity to revisit the Lower Wisconsin River and Lake Winnebago cases, and interview two key individuals for each one. These confidential interviews, which were tape-recorded and transcribed, focused on implementation progress and barriers.

Australian Case Studies (1995–2000 and 2007–2008)
In 1995, funded by a postdoctoral Fulbright fellowship, I conducted a yearlong research effort of collaborative management in Australia (Margerum 1996, 1999a, 1999b, 1999d). My research focused primarily on the role of regional catchment committees, but I also interviewed many individuals involved in local Landcare groups. Moreover, I examined several higher-level collaborative efforts: the Murray Darling River basin, a collaborative growth management effort in South East Queensland, and a regional strategy for managing the Mount Lofty Ranges near Adelaide, South Australia. The goals of the research were to further test the model developed from the Wisconsin research, compare and contrast the findings, and investigate the issue of implementation in more detail.

Australia was an ideal location for investigating collaborative efforts, because several states had initiated policies to support them. The age of the groups also varied between states and within states, with some operating for as long as six years at the time I conducted my investigations. This allowed comparison between and within states. Unlike the Wisconsin cases, the Australian ones were chosen in a more random fashion with a wider range of implementation success.

In carrying out the research, I met with catchment coordinators, interviewed ninety-two participants, and observed many catchment committee meetings. I also reviewed past meeting minutes in several cases to gain a better understanding of the issues they were addressing.

To obtain a broader set of perspectives, I conducted a mail survey of committee participants in New South Wales and Queensland. The purpose of this survey was to collect data about collaboration process, support, commitment, roles, and implementation. All catchment coordinators in these two states were contacted and invited to provide their members' contact details. The survey was sent to 550 stakeholder participants, and the response rate was 36 percent ($n = 197$). Of the respondents, 31 percent represented organizations, 69 percent were individuals, and the mean number of years participating on the committee was 2.3 (with a range of 0 to 6 years).

Coordination Network Cases, Australia (1998)

In 1998, I researched coordination networks related to the implementation of collaborative management efforts in Australia (Margerum 1999b, 1999c; Margerum and Born 2000). In my earlier Australian research, two case studies had presented interesting examples of coordination networks that I wanted to analyze and evaluate in more detail. To identify additional cases involving interorganizational networks, I consulted with researchers and state agency officials. I ultimately selected four cases that had networks in place with a sufficient maturity to allow evaluation: the Illawarra Integration Team (New South Wales), the Berowra Creek project (New South Wales), Trinity Inlet (Queensland), and Tully River (Queensland).

Multiple sources of evidence were used to research each case study. I conducted interviews with a range of participants, reviewed reports and project evaluations, and when possible looked at meeting minutes. All of the interviews were tape-recorded and transcribed for accuracy. Summaries of these cases were sent to participants for review and comment. The assessment of the cases followed the institutional analysis framework that I used to scrutinize coordination networks in my dissertation research. For this study, I documented the structures and mechanisms, and examined their effectiveness over time.

Collaborative Growth Management Cases

In addition to my research on watershed collaboratives, I also investigated two collaborative growth management cases: South East Queensland 2001 and Denver Metro Vision 2020.

South East Queensland, Australia (1999–2000)

The fundamental question explored by this research was how a collaborative approach to regional growth management influenced local government planning and management (Margerum and Holland 2000; Margerum 2001b, 2002b). The important and more complex corollary questions were: How influential was South East Queensland 2001 compared to other factors? What factors made South East Queensland 2001 more effective and less effective?

I chose six local governments that reflected the range of the eighteen local governments in the region. All of the six local governments had prepared plans before and after the completion of South East Queensland 2001 in 1994. Due to limited funding, the study focused on the environmental and land use planning aspects of regional planning.

The research project used six sources of information: content analysis of local government plans; interviews with sixteen local government staff members involved in strategic planning; written evaluations by local government staff members; written evaluations by local government elected officials; local government documents, reports, and materials; and interviews with seven state agency staff members involved in open space planning, conservation, and regional planning efforts. Rachael Holland, a graduate student at the Queensland University of Technology, conducted much of the detailed data collection.

For the content analysis, we used the environmental and land use criteria of South East Queensland 2001 to evaluate the six local government plans prepared before and after the regional planning process. The interviews took place between April and August 1999; they were recorded, transcribed, and sent to the interviewees for corrections or comments, and the findings were sent to participants for review and comment. The local government interviewees were also provided with a short questionnaire that asked them to evaluate their organization's environmental performance and the influence of South East Queensland 2001. We mailed a similar written survey to all sixty-four local government councillors (elected officials) from the six local governments included in the study, and twenty-six responded (response rate = 41 percent).

Throughout the project, the research was described as a study of local government environmental planning rather than an exploration of South East Queensland 2001 to avoid bias toward the effects of South East Queensland 2001. In analyzing the data, I made every effort to distinguish between the effects of South East Queensland 2001 and other external factors, but the fuzziness of interpreting indirect effects often made this difficult. Whenever possible, I looked to confirm conclusions with multiple sources of information, particularly when interpreting the small survey samples.

Denver Metro Vision 2020 (2000–2001)

The growth management efforts in Denver offered a second opportunity to investigate collaborative efforts across a wide range of jurisdictions (Margerum 2005). The research for this evaluation was based on a review of secondary documents, a confidential written survey of local government elected officials, and confidential interviews with twenty-five elected officials and planners.

The documents that were reviewed included DRCOG reports, local government plans, research reports, and all *Denver Post* and *Rocky Mountain News* articles on Metro Vision and DRCOG published between 1994 and 2003. A written survey was mailed to all the elected officials from the twenty-nine largest municipalities (cities and counties) in the region. A reminder email notice to 94 individuals with published email addresses, a second survey to 129 nonrespondents, and an additional email reminder followed the mailing. The survey asked elected officials to provide their evaluation of the Metro Vision process and products, and also assess factors such as public support in their region and support of their council. Sixty-two elected officials responded (30 percent response rate). Forty-nine elected officials (24 percent) returned the survey, and thirteen provided written comments but did not complete the survey. While these written statements are not included in the quantitative measures, many of the comments supplied valuable information.

The research included five personal interviews with local government officials and DRCOG staff members, who were interviewed for approximately one hour each. Twenty local government elected officials participated in semistructured phone interviews—conducted by graduate student Melanie Mintz—of approximately thirty minutes each (this represents 10 percent of the elected officials from the major jurisdictions in the metropolitan area). The interviewees were recruited from the returned surveys and were selected based on their range of views about Metro Vision. The purpose of these interviews was to document information that could not be adequately covered in the written survey, including the direct and indirect effects of Metro Vision on local decision making, perceptions of the planning process, the adequacy of the implementation tools, the adequacy of the implementation structure, and the interviewee's opinion about the likely success of the collaborative growth management efforts.

One of the methodological weaknesses of the survey was external validity, for two reasons: the response rate was low, and elected officials not as familiar with

Metro Vision 2020 were potentially less likely to have responded at all. This risk was reduced through several steps. First, the survey and interviews asked respondents to report on both their own personal opinion and the perceptions of their council and residents in their area. When possible, multiple responses from the same jurisdiction were compared to check for their validity. Second, the findings relied on several sources of information, including the interviews, documents, data, and newspaper reports. Finally, a summary of the study was sent to all interviewees, all county commissioners, all planning directors of each major local government in the region, and elected officials who requested a copy of the findings.

In 2010, these collaborative efforts in Denver were again evaluated as part of another project on land use and transportation planning, which is described later in this section.

Other Studies

Rogue Basin Case Study (2002)

A case study of the Rogue Basin Coordinating Council was based on my research and the firsthand involvement of the technical teams's coordinator (Margerum and Whitall 2004). I began researching this case in summer 2002, and interviewed ten governmental and nongovernmental participants in the Rogue River basin. The personal interviews were approximately one hour long, and were tape-recorded and transcribed. The phone interviews were approximately thirty to forty minutes long and documented with written notes. The interviews addressed the issues of the project history, the process of collaborating in the Rogue basin, the factors supporting and constraining collaboration, and the lessons learned from the process.

Debra Whitall, who coauthored the findings on this case study, was the coordinator of the Rogue Basin Restoration Technical Team since its inception in 1999. After discussions about mutual research interests, we decided our internal and external perspectives offered a unique opportunity to document and analyze the efforts taking place in the Rogue River basin. Working separately, we identified the issues based on the case study research and experience, and then compared findings in a series of meetings to develop a draft case study write-up. This draft was sent to the interviewees and other participants to ensure its accuracy as well as obtain additional comments and corrections.

Landowner Watershed Study (2003–2005)

One concern for watershed councils is how to improve their outreach to landowners. The goal of this project was to understand where landowners obtained information, who they trusted, who influenced their decision making, and how they perceived watershed councils. This study was conducted in collaboration with five watershed groups in western Oregon: the Coos Watershed Association, the Coquille Watershed Association, the Siuslaw Watershed Council, the Yamhill Basin Council, and the Marys River Watershed Council. I oversaw the project as a principle investigator, but Stacy Rosenberg (2005; Rosenberg and Margerum 2008) carried out the bulk of the data collection and analysis as part of her PhD dissertation work.

The watershed councils that we worked with varied in size, and their regions ranged from 310 to 1,059 square miles, and included a diversity of land types. Based on discussions with researchers, state agency staff members, and others knowledgeable about watershed groups, these five watersheds were selected because: they have a significant amount of private land; they have a similar cross section of private land uses, including agricultural, small woodlands, and rural residential property; they are in two ecoregions, which each have similar climate, geology, and vegetation; and the groups working in these watersheds have used a range of educational and outreach programs over several years.

A mail-out survey and face-to-face interviews were conducted with private landowners in the five watersheds. The written questionnaire was developed and sent out to nine hundred landowners using a modified version of Don Dillman's tailored design method (2007). Half of the nine hundred landowners were randomly selected from county property records (i.e., a random list), and the other half were selected from watershed group mailing lists (i.e., a watershed group list). Only riparian landowners (i.e., landowners whose property is adjacent or next to a stream) were selected from county property records, and the majority of landowners selected from the watershed group lists owned riparian property.

The study focused on riparian landowners because their properties were the highest-priority lands for improving water quality and habitat. Information from watershed groups, federal agencies, and county property records were utilized to obtain an equitable selection of small woodland, agricultural, and rural residential landowners from each watershed. The random list was obtained by segregating agricultural, small woodland, and rural residential property from zoning data within each watershed, and then randomly selecting thirty landowners (one-third of the random list) from each group. Only landowners who lived on their property were selected, because we wanted to investigate landowners who were actively involved in the management of their property. The watershed group list was developed by overlapping watershed group mailing lists with county property records to select riparian landowners, although the ownership data were sometimes inconclusive and a small number of nonriparian landowners was included. One hundred eighty questionnaires were mailed out to landowners in each watershed (i.e., ninety from each list). The mailings occurred between August and November 2003, and included a prenotification letter, original mailing, reminder postcard, and second mailing to nonrespondents (Rosenberg and Margerum 2008).

Rosenberg conducted eighty semistructured, face-to-face interviews with watershed group members, landowners not involved in watershed group activities, landowners who had implemented watershed restoration practices, and landowners who had not conducted restoration activities. A snowball sample was utilized in the interview process. Key informants and previously interviewed landowners provided the names for potential interviewees. Landowners were then selected from this group of names depending on which of the above categories they were thought to fit into, and interviews continued until there were enough landowners in each category. The interviews focused on gaining a more in-depth understanding of why landowners adopted restoration activities, why they chose not to conduct restoration projects, views on local community groups, personal land ethics, and interpretations of survey questions (ibid.).

Local Government Advisory Committee Survey (2005)

Research on consensus building spans several disciplines, but there are inconsistencies between the findings from experimental research and case study research. Experimental studies have relied heavily on student subjects and onetime scenarios, while collaboration research has relied on limited (small n) case studies. Both approaches make it hard to assess collaboration processes relative to other ones.

This study attempted to overcome some of the methodological shortcomings identified above by examining a large sample of local government advisory committees operating under a range of collaborative and noncollaborative approaches (Margerum 2006). I surveyed local government advisory committees in Oregon about their processes and outcomes. The study focused on committees without direct authority across seven common types of committees: parks and recreation, transportation, arts and entertainment, downtown/redevelopment, economic development, historic preservation, and community facilities (museums and libraries). Letters to city officials led to the participation of nineteen cities by providing the names and contact details for committee members. The result was a list of 695 valid names and addresses. The survey followed a modified approach to Dillman's tailored design method (2007), which generated 488 valid responses (70 percent response rate). The responses, aggregated by committee, produced a database of eighty-three different committees for analysis (each committee had two or more responses).

The survey instrument was based on 164 different measurement descriptors from the literature. To measure consensus, I used evaluation criteria based on descriptions of consensus using three process qualities: discussion, decision making, and agreement.

I grouped the other measures into three broad categories: context (23 descriptors), process (81 descriptors), and outcomes (59 descriptors). The context variables included measures of city support, committee context, the committee's relationship with the city, and the type of facilitation. The process measures were based on a list of fifteen commonly cited process measures grouped under the categories of "Advisory Committee Communication" and "Advisory Committee Process." For each of the following statements, respondents were provided with a scale from one to nine (one = strongly disagree; nine = strongly agree).

I used several approaches to measuring outcomes. First, I asked participants for their overall satisfaction with the committee's accomplishments, and supplied them with a scale from one to nine (one = very unsatisfied; nine = very satisfied). Second, I used the literature to develop a list of ten commonly cited outcome measures. For each of the following statements, respondents were given a scale from one to nine (one = strongly disagree; nine = strongly agree).

Although the study had the advantage of examining a large number of groups with a range of decision-making approaches, there were also some limitations. For one, there are structural differences between advisory committees and collaborative groups that may limit the applicability of the findings. These committees are also overseen by a city or city department, which creates a different dynamic than more independently operating collaboratives. Finally, advisory committees are only advisory—they provide input to city staff and city councils, but they are not the ones making the final decisions nor are they leading the implementation effort.

Oregon Watershed Coordinators Survey (2005–2006)

The goal of this study was to examine the governance of community-based collaboratives by researching the factors affecting coordinator job satisfaction, the roles of coordinators and boards, and the reasons for coordinator turnover (Parker et al. 2010). The study was carried out through a mail survey of current coordinators in Oregon, and interviews with current and former coordinators from a range of Oregon watershed councils. The project was conducted by Kate Parker (formerly Bodane) for her master's thesis, and overseen by myself and two people with watershed coordinator experience: Dana Dedrick (formerly Erickson), the coordinator for the Long Tom Watershed Council; and Jason Dedrick, formerly a coordinator for the Crooked River Watershed Council.

The questions for the survey of coordinators were developed from the literature and the team's experiences with watershed councils. The survey instrument included five sections: the characteristics of the council and coordinator, coordinator job satisfaction, the distribution of responsibility between the staff members and board for twenty common council tasks, and open-ended questions about board and staff member roles. The survey was pretested with five council coordinators before distribution.

Although there are over ninety councils in Oregon, some do not have coordinators, and many have formed umbrella councils with shared staff. As a result we identified seventy-one current coordinators. A modified Dillman (2007) approach was used, which included an initial mailing, a reminder email, a reminder postcard, and a second mailing. The final response rate for the survey was 70 percent (fifty out of seventy-one).

To further explore coordinator and board issues, Parker conducted fifteen interviews with current coordinators and another fifteen with individuals who had left a coordinator position in the past four years. An initial list of potential former coordinators was identified by the team, and then expanded through snowball sampling using information from current and former coordinators. Of the twenty-seven former coordinators identified as having left a council in the prior four years, Parker was able to contact nineteen, and fifteen agreed to participate in the study. The interviews focused on their role as a coordinator, relationship with the board, and reasons for leaving the coordinator position.

We selected a stratified sample of fifteen current coordinators for phone interviews from thirty-nine respondents who nominated themselves on the written survey. These individuals were selected to include a cross section of coordinators based on the data they provided about their previous employment, job tenure, level of job satisfaction, and council nonprofit status along with the location of the watershed in the state. The interviews explored the topics of workload, governance, job commitment, and board development.

There were several limitations to this study. First, there was a potential response bias among those who chose to respond or participate. The high response rate and stratified sampling of interviews reduced this potential bias, however. Second, the findings were all based on self-reporting by coordinators. The responses were confidential to ensure candid answers, but we did not collect information from board members. Lastly, the surveys and interviews were introduced as a study of board-coordinator relationships, which may have prejudiced participants' responses.

Area Commission on Transportation Study (2007–2008)

The objective of this study was to assess Oregon's Area Commissions on Transportation (ACTs), and identify the extent to which they were achieving their goal of improving transportation decision making and collaborating about regional decision making (Brody and Margerum 2008). The study provided me with insights into collaborative practice in transportation and explored interorganizational network arrangements. My coresearchers were Susan Brody (National Policy Consensus Center) and Bob Parker (University of Oregon). We used a range of approaches to examine this issue, including interviews with key individuals, an online survey, and case studies.

We conducted interviews with a total of forty-eight individuals, including local government officials, staff and community members, and Oregon Department of

Transportation policymakers and key staff members. Though interview subjects were not selected using a scientific sampling technique, every effort was made to include a cross section of interests, representing those involved with ACTs and metropolitan planning organizations (MPOs) from geographic areas throughout the state where ACTs have been formed.

To assess the current role and experience of ACTs and MPOs, we administered an online survey to approximately 350 Oregon Department of Transportation, ACT, and MPO officials as well as other appropriate individuals. The primary purpose of the online survey was to understand more about the current roles and experiences of ACTs and MPOs. All respondents were asked to provide information about themselves, assess ACTs effectiveness, judge coordination across different jurisdictions, and offer open-ended comments about ACTs and transportation planning. Respondents associated with an ACT were asked to assess its structures, processes, outputs, and outcomes along with the participants' commitment. For an ACT that contained an MPO within its boundary, respondents were asked questions about ACT-MPO relationships. Most questions used a Likert scale (e.g., ratings on a scale of one to five, or strongly disagree to strongly agree), while others allowed for respondents to write brief comments.

The survey was administered online with the commercial vendor Survey Monkey, using a modified Dillman (2007) survey method. A total of 178 individuals responded (51 percent); however, the sample size varied by question, as some respondents did not answer every question.

To understand the range of structures and approaches to regional transportation planning in Oregon, we prepared summaries of all ten ACTs in Lane County and Portland's metro area as well as all of the Oregon MPOs. Using online documents, meeting minutes, and other information, the research team summarized the geographic extent, membership, structure, priorities, and accomplishments as well as other crucial issues for all eighteen entities. We also conducted a more detailed investigation of three case studies: the Mid-Willamette ACT, the Northeast ACT, and the Rogue Valley ACT. These ACTs were chosen because of their geographic, political, and economic diversity. The investigations included document reviews, interviews with key individuals involved with the ACTs, and focus groups with participants involved in ACTs or familiar with their operation.

Metropolitan Transportation and Land Use Study (2009–2010)
This study focused on the issue of regional efforts to coordinate land use and transportation decision making. As in the study discussed just above, I conducted this project with Brody and Parker along with a team of graduate students from the University of Oregon's Community Planning Workshop (Christina Bond, Adam Erickson, Mark McCaffery, and Claire Otwell). The study was funded by the

Oregon Department of Transportation Research Unit and the Oregon Transportation and Research Education Consortium.

The study's purpose was to examine regional coordination of land use and transportation by exploring governance arrangements, coordination mechanisms, and funding incentives across four metropolitan regions: Portland, Oregon; Puget Sound, Washington; San Diego, California; and Denver, Colorado. These cases also represented a range of land use planning authorities among the regional agencies, ranging from those with direct authority (Portland and Puget Sound) to no direct land use power (San Diego and Denver).

The study involved key stakeholder interviews with approximately 40 individuals, including MPO staff members, local government officials, elected officials, state agency staff members, and other stakeholders. Our research team also conducted group interviews with local planners and public works directors in Puget Sound and Portland. These interviews explored the topics of governance arrangements, coordination arrangements, and implementation outcomes.

The individual and group interviews were supplemented by an online survey sent to 450 individuals in the four regions. The participants were selected because of their involvement in either transportation or land use decision making, and were surveyed using a modified Dillman (2007) method. Approximately 200 people responded to the survey (44 percent response rate), but all respondents did not complete all questions. The survey addressed topics similar to the ones in the interviews, but asked several evaluation questions using a Likert scale.

Other Sources of Data

Ipswich Landowner Survey (1997)

In 1997, I taught a class on landscape planning at Queensland University of Technology. The class worked with Ipswich Shire Council, a regional municipality west of the city of Brisbane. The council contained significant areas of open space in agricultural and rural residential land use, and one of its concerns was landowner management. Council staff members were concerned, in particular, about landowner awareness and perception of landscape condition. As part of the graduate class, students mailed a survey to approximately a hundred residents in one of the watershed areas. The survey provided landowners with pictures of riparian areas that ranged from natural to highly managed.

The high number of invalid addresses and the moderate response rate limited the generalizability of the data, but the written comments about the riparian photos highlighted some interesting issues. In particular, many respondents rated the highly managed landscape (a grassy corridor with no trees) as the most desirable condition and viewed natural corridors (riparian cover and understory) as less desirable. These findings supported the council staff members' observation, which was that some land management practices were based on faulty assumptions about what constituted a desired ecological condition.

Oregon Watershed Council Data (2001–2009)

In the course of my work in Oregon, I have collected information about several watershed councils. These include the Salem Area Councils, Johnson Creek, Umpqua Basin, Coos Bay, and Siuslaw. All of these case investigations involved interviews with the coordinator and at least one other stakeholder, observation of a council meeting, and a review of council strategies and/or reports.

In addition to this information, I have been compiling a range of data across watershed councils in Oregon to examine differences in funding, decision making, partnerships, and outreach. This work has been carried out with the invaluable assistance of several graduate students interested in watershed councils who helped compile a cross section of financial data, survey data, and procedural information. Over the years, these data have been entered into a database that provides comparative financial, procedural, and partnership information for most watershed councils in the state.

There were three sources for this information. First, I obtained financial information on all watershed councils from the OWEB. Sam Fox (a master's student) compiled a database drawing from this information and a review of Web sites to gather information about decision procedures.

Second, in her study of board-coordinator relationships, Kate (Bodane) Parker (then a master's student) surveyed coordinators about partnerships. In one section of the survey, we obtained permission to report their responses by committee (see coordinator study summary for details on the survey methods).

Finally, for her master's thesis, Chu Chen grouped a cross section of watershed councils according to the action-organizational typology. The councils were grouped by percentage of public land, with the assumption that high percentages of public land (>75 percent) were more likely to exhibit characteristics of organizational collaboratives, while those with low percentages of public land (<25 percent) were more likely to exhibit characteristics of action collaboratives. Using council charters, Web sites, and the 2009–2011 OWEB administrative support grant applications, she compared eighteen watershed councils for differences in stakeholder composition, decision-making approaches, and strategies and approaches to outreach.

Because of the variation in structure, scale, and approach among Oregon watershed councils, this case data was especially valuable for testing, evaluating, and refining the typology presented in this book.

Oregon Natural Hazard Plans (2004)

In 2004, I conducted a preliminary investigation of natural hazard mitigation plan quality. The work was based on plan quality assessment criteria developed from the literature, the Oregon Natural Hazards Workgroup, and the Federal Emergency Management Agency. I first collected six plans from local governments and six county plans. Along with graduate student Elliot Shuford, I then independently rated the quality of the plans. We compared our ratings and then mediated score differences based on a review of the plans. From there, I selected four jurisdictions based on the quality of the plans (two rated high quality and two rated low quality). I conducted phone and in-person interviews with individuals working for these organizations to discuss their assessment of plan quality and the implementation success of the planning efforts. The interview notes were recorded in notebooks and transcribed.

Notes

Chapter 1

1. Based on Wisconsin Department of Natural Resources recreation surveys, noted in an unpublished document: *Summary: Lower Wisconsin Riverway: The Proposed Plan and Its Impacts* (Madison: Wisconsin Department of Natural Resources, 1998).

2. Wisconsin DNR staff person, interview with author, recorded and transcribed, November 11, 1992.

Chapter 2

1. Between 2004 and 2007, I was a member of the Long Tom Steering Committee, including as vice chair and chair.

2. This account is reconstructed from participant interviews as well as a case study description by Judith Innes and her colleagues (1994).

3. Imperial's framework was published in 2005, while I first published my framework in 2007. I was not aware of his 2005 publication until we met at a conference in 2009. His application of the levels concept follows the institutional analysis and design framework more closely, but both of our work recognizes that collaboration is occurring at different levels, and the difference between levels is important for understanding collaborative practice.

4. Imperial (2005) refers to this in terms of institutional-level action and collaborative organizations, but I found that collaboratives at this level operate in several different ways, which are outlined throughout this book.

5. Based on an interview and conversations with the Lower Rogue Watershed Council coordinator in September 2001, and Lower Rogue WSC 2007–2009, Oregon Watershed Enhancement Board (OWEB) council-support grant application #210–014.

6. These committees were changed significantly in 2000, and many of the catchment groups were amalgamated into larger natural resources management regions with more substantial funding and responsibilities.

7. The management's role and structure in the Murray Darling Basin was changed substantially in 2008. This description is based on my research on management efforts in the 1990s

through 2008. Catchment committees have been substantially restructured throughout Australia, but many Landcare groups continue to operate.

8. The one potentially significant issue that I have not analyzed is resources, because I have been unable to gather consistent data across the cases I examined. The inconsistencies are due to the lack of data about operating budgets, the complexity of measuring resources like in-kind support, and the difficulty of separating out the project-based work of collaboratives from administrative work.

9. Master Gardeners is a program offered by the University of Oregon's Extension service. People who achieve this designation must go through sixty to seventy hours of training with Extension staff.

10. Even in a state like Oregon, which has committed ongoing resources for these efforts, the 2009–2011 funding for its watershed council program is only 0.16 percent of the state budget.

11. Executive committee members, Lockyer Catchment Management Committee, confidential interview with author, recorded in notebook, May 15–16, 1995.

12. For a more detailed discussion of this case study, see Wondolleck and Yaffee 2000.

Chapter 3

1. Information from McKenzie Watershed Council Web site, available at http://www.mckenziewc.org (accessed October 20, 2009), and the Oregon Watershed Enhancement Board support grant application for 2009–2011 biennium.

2. Unpublished research conducted with Ipswich Shire Council with help from students in my landscape planning class. The study included a survey of landowners in which they were sent photos of different riparian landscapes, and asked to evaluate their condition along with their own interest in undertaking conservation efforts.

3. Bruce Babbitt, remarks at the Community-Based Collaboratives Research Consortium meeting, Sedona, AZ, November 19, 2005.

4. Queensland state agencies were involved directly and indirectly on committees, subcommittees, and ad hoc groups, making it hard to establish a firm number. According to the regional framework for growth management produced by this process in 1994, 22 different state government representatives served on committees and working groups. There were a total of 150 participants on the steering committee and 5 working groups. Other categories included local government (31 representatives), the professional sector (14 representatives), business and industry (11 representatives), and community members (10 representatives). The other major category of participants was "official observers," which mostly consisted of representatives from local government or regional organizations of councils.

5. Agency staff person, interview with author, tape-recorded and transcribed, October 15, 1992.

6. Catchment committee member, phone interview with author, recorded in notebook, August 14, 1997.

7. Written comment on survey from citizen member of a New South Wales committee. Question asked: "Our committee has been inhibited by. . . ." Collected and transcribed into database, October–November 1995.

8. Ibid.

9. Agency staff person, interview with author, tape-recorded and transcribed, November 11, 1992.

10. Agency administrator, interview with author, tape-recorded and transcribed, November 10, 1992.

11. Business representative on committee, interview with author, recorded in notebook, July 11, 1996.

12. Agency regional manager, interview with author, tape-recorded and transcribed, June 11, 1992.

13. Citizen participant, interview with author, tape-recorded and transcribed, November 30, 1992.

14. County planner, interview with author, recorded in notebook, May 8, 2001.

15. Citizen participant, interview with author, recorded in notebook, May 16, 2001.

16. Agency staff members in northern Queensland, interviews with author, recorded in notebook, October 1995.

17. Watershed coordinator, interview with author, recorded in notebook, August 30, 2001.

Chapter 4

1. I was a member of the Southern Willamette Groundwater Management Advisory Committee, as a representative of the Long Tom Watershed Council.

2. Unpublished results from a survey in 1994 of New South Wales catchment coordinators.

3. Participant, personal interview with author, recorded in notes, July 12, 1996.

4. Written comment on survey from citizen member of a New South Wales committee. Question asked: "Our committee has been inhibited by. . . . " Collected and transcribed into database, October–November 1995.

5. Ibid.

6. Agency staff person, interview with author, tape-recorded and transcribed, October 15, 1992.

7. The exact question was: "In a few words, describe what you believe *your* role is on your catchment management committee."

8. Agency regional manager, interview with author, tape-recorded and transcribed, June 11, 1982.

9. Participant, interview with author, recorded in a notebook, July 11, 1996. Innes and her colleagues (1994) also describe this voting system in their study of collaborative growth and environmental management cases.

10. Sam Fox compiled these data in 2005 by reviewing information submitted to the OWEB for council support grants.

11. Written comment on survey from citizen member of a New South Wales committee. Question asked: "Our committee has been inhibited by. . . . " Collected and transcribed into database, October–November 1995.

12. Comment from a farmer to the author during a meeting of the Southern Willamette Valley Groundwater Management Advisory Committee.

13. Confidential written reply from local elected official survey (response no. 217).

14. Denver region local government planner, confidential interview with author, March 21, 2001.

15. This summary of public involvement efforts is based on information and documents from the Envision Utah Web site, available at http://www.envisionutah.org.

16. This is based on meetings that I attended in Queensland and New South Wales between January and December 1995.

17. This section draws extensively from Margerum 2002a.

18. Confidential written reply from citizen on a New South Wales committee (response no. 101).

19. Confidential written reply from citizen on a Queensland committee (response no. 125).

20. The meeting minutes show that the committee argued about the issue at almost every meeting for almost one year. The committee initiated discussions and data collection efforts, but it could not reach consensus on a position.

21. Local citizen, confidential interview with author, tape-recorded and transcribed, November 30, 1992.

Chapter 5

1. State agency planner, interview with author, recorded and transcribed, August 13, 1992.

2. State government planner in northern Queensland, interview with author, October 2, 2008.

3. Quote from a catchment coordinator in the Sydney, recorded in notebook, June 22, 1995.

4. Remark by watershed coordinator at the annual meeting of the watershed council, attended by author on October 19, 2010.

5. I believe that the plans and policies were written to be intentionally vague. The Labour Party government had lost its majority in the Queensland Parliament in part because of its approach to planning in South East Queensland. By maintaining the regional plan, but with vague language, the conservative coalition could indicate that it was supporting regional planning without imposing any new state policies, funding, or expectations.

6. Open-ended comments from survey of local government advisory committees collected September–October, 2005. Question read: "What do you think are the weaknesses of this committee?"

7. Coos Watershed Association coordinator, interview with author, recorded in notebook, August 14, 2001.

8. Sydney area catchment coordinator, interview with author, recorded in notebook, July 12, 1995.

9. This was a preliminary plan review conducted in conjunction with Andre LeDuc of the Oregon Natural Hazards Workgroup (now Partners for Disaster Mitigation). Along with a graduate research assistant, I independently conducted the plan assessment work, and then

compared the evaluation scores across the criteria and resolved score differences. Personal and phone interviews were then conducted with local government emergency managers in four jurisdictions.

10. County emergency management officer, interview with author, recorded in notebook, May 21, 2004.

11. Clackamas County emergency management coordinator, interview with author, recorded in notebook, June 4, 2004.

12. Jack Williams, researcher with Trout Unlimited, interview with author, Ashland, OR, August 2, 2002. At the time of the interview, Williams was working for the AuCoin Institute at Southern Oregon University under a cooperative exchange with the U.S. Forest Service.

13. Again, as noted earlier, I have been a member of the Southern Willamette Valley Groundwater Management Area Committee since its inception in 2004.

14. City of Logan staff person, personal interview by author tape recorded and transcribed, September 16, 1999.

15. City of Ipswich staff person, personal interview by author tape recorded and transcribed, September 23, 1999.

16. Queensland state agency regional planner, interview with author, recorded in notebook, October 2, 2007.

17. New South Wales catchment coordinator, interview with author, recorded in notebook, April 26, 1995.

18. Recorded in research notes during author's visit with a catchment committee in Southern Queensland, October 9, 1995.

Chapter 6

1. Based on information listed on the Southern Gulf catchments from the Queensland Water and Land Careers Web site, available at http://www.qwalc.org.au (accessed May 11, 2010).

2. For several years, OWEB has reviewed and evaluated applications for administrative support. Based on these evaluations, the councils are allocated different levels of funding.

3. This section is based on Margerum and Whitall 2004, and unpublished material written by Debra Whitall and Dr. Jonathan I. Lange, professor of communications at Southern Oregon University.

4. CALFED Web page on program performance and tracking, available at http://calwater .ca.gov/calfed/library/library_archive_PPF.html (accessed on June 4, 2008).

5. This section is based in part on the literature review conducted by Bodane (2006) for her master's thesis.

6. This included my reduced availability due to new administrative duties at the University of Oregon.

7. Farmer, interview with author, recorded in notebook, May 15, 1995.

8. Community member, phone interview with author, recorded in notebook, August 14, 1997.

9. The direct quotes are based on confidential written responses to surveys of Australian catchment committees. The surveys were coded to allow for comparison by committee; seven

responses were received from this committee, and two follow-up phone interviews were conducted with committee members who listed their contact details.

10. A total of 550 surveys were distributed, and 197 were received (response rate = 36 percent). The survey question was: "The committee has accomplished a lot," and possible answers included: strongly agree, agree, disagree, strongly disagree, and not sure. The respective mean scores for these two committees were -0.75 (n = 4) and -0.43 (n = 8).

11. Long Tom Watershed Council Web site, overview of water quality monitoring program, available at http://www.longtom.org/waterquality2.html (accessed June 5, 2008).

12. State agency staff person, interview with author, tape-recorded and transcribed, September 10, 1992.

13. County staff person, interview with author, tape-recorded and transcribed, September 10, 1992.

14. Catchment coordinator, interview with author, recorded in notebook, April 26, 1995.

15. Interestingly, they found that for younger partnerships (less than three years) trust is significant and negatively related to the evaluation of agreements when other variables are held constant. They speculate that crises or problems may encourage young partnerships to forge agreements despite their distrust for other stakeholders. "In older partnerships, this risk is replaced by relative certainty and the detrimental effects of distrust are unfettered" (Leach and Sabatier 2005, 249).

16. State agency regional manager, interview with author, tape-recorded and transcribed, December 15, 1992.

17. State agency administrator, interview with author, tape-recorded and transcribed, August 10, 1992.

18. Coordinator of the Rogue Basin Coordinating Council, interview with author, recorded in notebook, September 5, 2002.

19. Former coordinator of the Trinity Inlet Management Program, interview with author, recorded in notebook, August 3, 1998.

20. Mary Smelcer, district management, Bureau of Land Management, interview with author, Medford, OR, December 16, 2002.

21. Confidential written reply from local elected official survey (response no. 320).

22. Oregon watershed council coordinator, interview with author, recorded in notebook, June 27, 2006.

23. This section draws heavily from Parker et al. 2010.

24. Elected officials and staff members in the San Diego region, interviews with author, written notes were recorded in a notebook, March 17–19, 2010.

25. This was a common phrase used by the OWEB staff members and watershed coordinators in both private interviews and public forums.

26. Craig Tuss, Regional Supervisor, Roseburg District, United States Fish and Wildlife Service. Personal Interview, tape-recorded and transcribed, December 16, 2002.

27. The quote is from an email exchange among board members. The bylaws were eventually found.

Chapter 7

1. This story is based on written notes taken during a field visit on October 9, 2005. The quotes are approximate.

2. Putnam (2000, 356) charts state-level data using a "social capital index" and a composite index based on survey data about attitudes toward racial integration (whites only), civil liberties, and gender equality.

3. Catchment coordinator in north Queensland, confidential interview with author, recorded in notebook, June 15, 1995.

4. Based on Alexander 1995; Campbell 1994; Curtis and De Lacy 1996.

5. Personal communication during a regional groundwater management committee meeting.

6. Farmer, personal communication with author, recorded in notebook, June 9, 2005.

7. Based on information gathered on the Siuslaw, Coos, and Long Tom subwatershed program efforts along with the streambank restoration program developed by the Mary River Catchment Committee. These programs are also documented by several sources, including: Flintcroft et al. 2009; Kelly 1998.

8. Mary River catchment staff members, interviews with author, October 9–10, 1997.

9. Based on notes from interviews with staff members at the Umpqua River Basin Council (now called the Partnership for the Umpqua Rivers) on August 13, 2001. The staff members also noted that the legal issues surrounding this case were so complex that this kind of project was not attempted again.

10. Sources: Rosenberg (2005) dissertation and 2007–09 Siuslaw Watershed Council Administrative Support Grant Application.

11. This summary of public involvement efforts is based on information and documents from the Envision Utah Web site, available at http://www.envisionutah.org.

12. Based on interviews with Port Phillip CMA staff members on January 10, 2008.

Chapter 8

1. At the time, this was referred to by the agency in terms of "integrated management."

2. Wisconsin DNR agricultural/private land specialist, interview with author, tape-recorded and transcribed, July 24, 1992.

3. Wisconsin DNR fisheries manager, interview with author, tape-recorded and transcribed, December 15, 1992.

4. This example also highlights the complexity of these networks, as raised by Huxham and Vangan (2005), and reinforces how the level at which a collaborative operates differs from the network that it utilizes. The Western Gateway team was operating at an action level, but its activities were being implemented through an interorganizational network.

5. My research of both cases was based on participant interviews along with a review of meeting minutes and publications; for the Rogue River basin, I also coauthored a publication

with the coordinator of the regional technical committees. My description of these cases is based on the conditions at the time that I conducted the research.

6. The Cairns and Mulgrave city councils were amalgamated in 1995 into the Cairns City Council. The Department of the Premier Economic and Trade Development was the representative for all Queensland state agencies.

7. Based on a comprehensive review of the TIMP technical team's meeting minutes between March 1992 and October 1997.

8. This section is based on: Margerum and Whitall 2004; unpublished material written by Debra Whitall and Dr. Jonathan I. Lange, professor of communications at Southern Oregon University.

9. Jody Hoffer Gittell and Leigh Weiss (2004, 132) use the term "lasting patterns" in their discussion about coordination in health care; Alexander (1998, 343) bases his analysis of public policy coordination on Anthony Giddens's (1979) concepts of social structures that may be defined by families, organizations, governments, or even the weekly poker game. The concept of social structures is also consistent with Ostrom's (1986a) institutional analysis framework, which Margerum and Born (2000) and Imperial (2005) have used to analyze coordination settings.

10. Frank Gregg and his colleagues (1991) combine Ostrom's framework with the work of S. V. Ciriacy-Wantrup (1970) to describe institutional settings at different levels: operational, organizational, and policy levels. Applying this framework to interorganizational coordination is a significant departure from its intended application in the public choice and institutions literature.

11. Based on an exchange rate of 1 Australian dollar to 0.64 U.S. dollars.

12. Based on an evaluation of six local governments along with the plans prepared before and after the regional planning process. We evaluated the plans for both language and supporting policies related to regional open space. In the western region, the Ipswich City and Beaudesert Shire councils showed significant improvements. In the northern region, Pine Rivers Shire and Maroochy City had more modest improvements. The previous Maroochy plans were moderately strong on *local* environmental issues, but showed limited improvement in addressing regional open space (see Margerum and Holland 2000).

13. Environmental Specialist, United States Environmental Protection Agency, interview with author, tape recorded and transcribed, Eugene, OR, July 30, 2002.

14. State agency and local government staff, interview with author, tape recorded and transcribed, Cairns, Queensland, August 26–28, 1997.

15. World Wildlife Fund staff scientist Brian Barr, interview with author, Ashland, OR, August 2, 2002.

16. Wisconsin DNR staff person, interview with author, tape-recorded and transcribed, November 11, 1992.

17. Two state natural resources agency staff in Queensland, interview with author, October 1, 2007.

18. NSW fisheries representative, interview with author, recorded in notebook, April 24, 1995.

19. Federal agency official, interview with author, recorded on tape and transcribed, August 1, 2002.

20. Local government staff person, phone interview with author, recorded in notebook, August 2, 2002.

21. County conservation officer, interview with author, recorded on tape and transcribed, August 28, 1992.

22. Researcher, U.S. Forest Service and AuCoin Institute, Southern Oregon University, interview with author, tape recorded and transcribed, Ashland, OR, August 2, 2002.

23. National Marine Fisheries Service team leader Frank Bird, interview with author, tape recorded and transcribed, Roseburg, OR, August 1, 2002.

24. U.S. Fish and Wildlife Service regional supervisor Craig Tuss, interview with author, tape recorded and transcribed, Roseburg, OR, December 16, 2002

25. Williams, interview with author.

26. Barr, interview with author.

27. Tuss, interview with author.

28. DNR staff person, interview with author, tape recorded and transcribed, October 16, 1992.

Chapter 9

1. Elected officials in the San Diego region, interviews with author, recorded in notebook, March 18, 2010.

2. County planner, interview with author, recorded in notebook, May 8, 2001.

3. Staff members and elected officials in the San Diego region, interviews with author, recorded in notebook, March 17–19, 2010.

4. Phone interview by Melanie Mintz, recorded in notebook, July 1, 2002.

5. Phone interview by Melanie Mintz, recorded in notebook, June 12, 2002.

6. Phone interview by Melanie Mintz, recorded in notebook, July 23, 2002.

Chapter 10

1. Based on my review of the South East Queensland regional effort in 1999, and interviews with state and local officials in November and December 2007.

2. This example is based on my dissertation, which included the Lower Wisconsin as one of my case studies. I carried out a set of interviews in 1997 to update the case, and reviewed online documents in 2008.

3. State agency and natural resources management group staff, interview with author, Mackay and Townsville, Queensland, October 2–3, 2007.

4. Based on data obtained from the OWEB and the Partnership for the Umpqua Rivers application for administrative support. The OWEB funding for the Umpqua was for the 2003–2005 biennium.

5. Policy staff members from the Bureau of Water Resources, Wisconsin DNR, interviews with author, June 9, 1992.

Chapter 11

1. Commonwealth environment minister Peter Garrett ruled in November 2009 that the Traveston Dam should not go forward due to its environmental impacts. He stated: "My decision requires me to balance environmental, economic and social impacts. The likely economic and social benefits of this proposal do not outweigh the serious environmental impacts on our nationally protected species" (quoted by Australian Broadcasting Corporation, available at http://www.abc.net.au/news/stories/2009/11/11/2739725.htm [accessed June 9, 2010]).

2. Watershed coordinator, comments during watershed council meeting attended by author, recorded in notebook, July 8, 2004.

3. On November 2, 2010, Oregon voters passed Measure 76 by a 69 to 31 percent majority. A previous measure designating 15 percent of lottery funding for the upkeep and restoration of Oregon parks, beaches, watersheds and salmon habitat was due to expire in 2014. The passage of the measure makes the designation a permanent part of the Oregon Constitution.

4. Although I hesitate to call the OWEB a policy collaborative, it has been able to maintain a significant program even as watershed programs in other states have folded. I believe that its sustained role can be attributed to: the move of the agency from the governor's office to a state agency; the use of an oversight board that includes a broad cross section of political and regional leaders; and the success in securing lottery funding that has insulated it from the regular crises of the Oregon state budget.

References

AACM and Centre for Water Policy Research. 1995. *Enhancing effectiveness of catchment management planning*. Adelaide, Australia: Australian Department of Primary Industries and Energy.

Agranoff, Robert. 1990. Responding to human crises: Intergovernmental policy networks. In *Strategies for managing intergovernmental policies and networks*, ed. R. W. Gage and M. P. Mandell. New York: Praeger.

Agranoff, Robert, and Michael McGuire. 1999. Managing in network settings. *Policy Studies Review* 16 (1): 18–41.

Agranoff, Robert, and Michael McGuire. 2003. *Collaborative public management*. Washington, DC: Georgetown University Press.

Alexander, Ernest R. 1984. After rationality, what? A review of response to paradigm breakdown. *Journal of the American Planning Association* 50 (1): 62–67.

Alexander, Ernest R. 1993. Interorganizational coordination: Theory and practice. *Journal of Planning Literature* 7 (4): 328–343.

Alexander, Ernest R. 1995. *How organizations act together: Interorganizational coordination in theory and practice*. Amsterdam: Gordon and Breach Publishers.

Alexander, Ernest R. 1998. A structuration theory of interorganizational coordination: Cases in environmental management. *International Journal of Organizational Analysis* 6 (4): 334–354.

Alexander, Helen. 1995. A framework for change: The state of the community Landcare movement in Australia. National Landcare Facilitator Project Annual Report. Canberra, Australia: National Landcare Program.

Alper, Steve, Dean Tjosvold, and Kenneth S. Law. 1998. Interdependence and controversy in group decision making: Antecedents to effective self-managing teams. *Organizational Behavior and Human Decision Processes* 74 (1): 33–52.

Alter, Catherine, and Jerald Hage. 1993. *Organizations working together*. Newbury Park, CA: Sage.

Altman, John A., and Ed Petkus Jr. 1994. Toward a stakeholder-based policy process: An application of the social marketing perspective to environmental policy development. *Policy Sciences* 27 (1): 37–51.

Amy, Douglas. 1987. *The politics of environmental mediation*. New York: Columbia University Press.

Anderson, Larz T. 1995. *Guidelines for preparing urban plans*. Chicago: Planners Press.

Ansell, Chris, and Allison Gash. 2007. Collaborative governance in theory and practice. *Journal of Public Administration: Research and Theory* 18 (4): 543–571.

Arnstein, Sherry R. 1969. A ladder of citizen participation. *Journal of the American Institute of Planners* 35 (4): 216–224.

Australian Bureau of Statistics. 2004. Measuring social capital: An Australian framework for indicators. Canberra: Australian Bureau of Statistics.

Australian Government. 2005. *Regional Programs Summary Report, 2004–05*. Canberra, Australia: Natural Resources Management Ministerial Council.

Baer, William C. 1997. General plan evaluation criteria: An approach to making better plans. *Journal of the American Planning Association* 63 (3): 329–344.

Bandura, Albert. 1986. *Social foundations of thought and action*. Englewood Cliffs, NJ: Prentice-Hall.

Banfield, Edward C. (1959) 1973. Ends and means in planning. In *A reader in planning theory*, ed. A. Faludi. Oxford: Pergamon Press.

Barbour, Elisa, and Michael B. Teitz. 2009. Blueprint planning in California: An experiment in regional planning for sustainable development. In *Toward sustainable communities: Transition and transformations in environmental policy*, ed. D. A. Mazmanian and M. E. Kraft. Cambridge, MA: MIT Press.

Bardach, Eugene. 1977. *The implementation game*. Cambridge, MA: MIT Press.

Bardach, Eugene. 1998. *Getting agencies to work together*. Washington, DC: Brookings Institution.

Barrett, Brendan F. D. 1995. From environmental auditing to integrated environmental management: Local government experience in the United Kingdom and Japan. *Journal of Environmental Planning and Management* 38 (3): 307–331.

Beatley, Timothy, T. James Fries, and David Braun. 1995. The Balcones Canyonlands Conservation Plan: A regional multi-species approach. In *Collaborative planning for wetlands and wildlife: Issues and examples*, ed. D. R. Porter and D. A. Salvesen. Washington, DC: Island Press.

Beierle, Thomas C. 2002. The quality of stakeholder-based decisions. *Risk Analysis* 22 (4): 739–749.

Beierle, Thomas C., and David M. Konisky. 2000. Values, conflict, and trust in participatory environmental planning. *Journal of Policy Analysis and Management* 19 (4): 16.

Bender, Thomas. 1978. *Community and social change in America*. New Brunswick, NJ: Rutgers University Press.

Berke, Philip R., and Marcia M. Conroy. 2000. Are we planning for sustainable development? An evaluation of 30 comprehensive plans. *Journal of the American Planning Association* 66 (1): 21–33.

Berke, Philip R., Dale Roenigk, Edward Kaiser, and Raymond Burby. 1996. Enhancing plan quality: Evaluating the role of state planning mandates for natural hazard mitigation. *Journal of Environmental Planning and Management* 39 (1): 79–96.

Besadny, C. D. 1991. Integrated management: The "big picture" of what we do. *DNR Digest* (April–May): 2–3.

Bickman, Leonard. 1987. The functions of program theory. In *New directions for program evaluation*, ed. L. Bickman. San Francisco: Jossey-Bass.

Bidwell, Ryan D., and Clare M. Ryan. 2006. Collaborative partnership design: The implications of organizational affiliation for watershed partnerships. *Society and Natural Resources* 19 (9): 827–843.

Bingham, Gail. 1986. *Resolving environmental disputes: A decade of experience.* Washington, DC: Conservation Foundation.

Blackmore, Don. 2001. Water salinity and the politics of mutual obligation. Paper presented at the Deakin Lecture, Melbourne, May 19.

Bobker, Gary. 2009. The means do not justify the ends: A comment on CALFED. *Environmental Science and Policy* 12 (6): 726–728.

Bodane, Kate. 2006. Board-coordinator relationships among Oregon watershed councils. Master's thesis, University of Oregon.

Bonnell, Joseph E., and Tomas M. Koontz. 2007. Stumbling forward: The organizational challenges of building and sustaining collaborative watershed management. *Society and Natural Resources* 20 (2):153–167.

Born, Stephen M., and Kenneth D. Genskow. 1999. Exploring the "watershed approach": Critical dimensions of state-local partnerships. Report no. 99-1. Madison: University of Wisconsin–Extension.

Born, Stephen M., and William Sonzogni. 1995. Towards integrated environmental management: Strengthening the conceptualization. *Environmental Management* 19 (2): 167–183.

Brody, Samuel D. 2003. Measuring the effects of stakeholder participation on the quality of local plans based on the principles of collaborative ecosystem management. *Journal of Planning Education and Research* 22: 407–419.

Brody, Susan, and Richard Margerum. 2008. *Oregon's ACTS, cross-jurisdictional collaboration and improving transportation planning.* Salem: Oregon Department of Transportation and the Federal Highway Administration.

Bryson, John M. 1988. *Strategic planning for public and nonprofit organizations.* San Francisco: Jossey-Bass.

Bryson, John M., and Barbara C. Crosby. 1992. *Leadership for the common good: Tackling public problems in a shared-power world.* 1st ed. San Francisco: Jossey-Bass.

Bryson, John M., and Robert C. Einsweiler. 1991. *Shared power: What is it? How does it work? How can we make it work better?* Lanham, MD: University Press of America.

Buckle, Leonard G., and Suzann R. Thomas-Buckle. 1986. Placing environmental mediation in context: Lessons from "failed" mediations. *Environmental Impact Assessment Review* 6 (1): 55–70.

Bührs, Ton. 1991. Strategies for environmental policy co-ordination: The New Zealand experience. *Political Science* 43 (2): 1–29.

Bunker, Douglas R. 1972. Policy sciences perspectives on implementation process. *Policy Sciences* 3 (1): 71–80.

Buntz, Gregory C., and Beryl A. Radin. 1983. Managing intergovernmental conflict: The case of human services. *Public Administration Review* 43 (5): 403–410.

Burby, Raymond J. 2003. Making plans that matter: Citizen involvement and government action. *Journal of the American Planning Association* 69 (1): 33–49.

Burby, Raymond J., Steven P. French, and Arthur C. Nelson. 1998. Plans, code enforcement, and damage reduction: Evidence from the Northridge earthquake. *Earthquake Spectra: The Professional Journal of the Earthquake Engineering Research Institute* 14 (1): 59–74.

Burby, Raymond J., and Peter J. May. 1998. Intergovernmental environmental planning: Addressing the commitment conundrum. *Journal of Environmental Planning and Management* 41 (1): 95–110.

Burns, James MacGregor. 1978. *Leadership.* 1st ed. New York: Harper and Row.

Burt, Ronald S. 1982. *Toward a structural theory of action: Network models of social structure, perception, and action.* New York: Academic Press.

Burt, Ronald S. 1983. *Applied network analysis: A methodological introduction.* Beverly Hills: Sage.

Burt, Ronald S. 1992. *Structural holes: The social structure of competition.* Cambridge, MA: Harvard University Press.

Burton, John. 1992. Catchment management in Australia: An historical review. Paper presented at the Catchments of Green: A National Conference on Vegetation and Water Management, Adelaide, Australia, March 23–26.

Byron, Ian, and Allan Curtis. 2002. Exploring working conditions and job-related burnout in Queensland Landcare coordinators and facilitators. In *Report No. 165.* Albury, NSW: Johnstone Centre, Charles Sturt University.

Byron, Ian, Allan Curtis, and Michael Lockwood. 2001. Exploring burnout in Australia's Landcare program: A case study in the Shepparton region. *Society and Natural Resources* 14 (10): 901–910.

CALFED. 2007. 2007 annual report. Sacramento: CALFED Bay-Delta Program.

California Bay-Delta Program. 2008. *History of California Bay-Delta Program.* Available at http://calwater.ca.gov/calfed/about/History/Detailed.html (accessed October 6, 2008).

Campbell, Andrew C. 1994. *Landcare: Communities shaping the land and the future.* St Leonards, NSW: Allen and Unwin.

Campbell, Andrew C. 1995. Landcare: Participative Australian approaches to inquiry and learning for sustainability. *Journal of Soil and Water Conservation* 50 (2): 125–131.

Carlson, Chris. 1999. Convening. In *Consensus building handbook*, ed. L. Susskind, S. McKearnon, and S. Carpenter. Thousand Oaks, CA: Sage.

Carmona, Matthew, and Louie Sieh. 2004. *Measuring quality in planning: Managing the performance process.* New York: Spon Press.

Carpenter, Susan L., and W.J.D. Kennedy. 1988. *Managing public disputes: A practical guide to handling conflict and reaching agreements.* San Francisco: Jossey-Bass.

Center for Watershed Protection. 1998. *Rapid watershed planning handbook: A comprehensive guide for managing urbanizing watersheds.* Ellicott City, ND: Center for Watershed Protection.

Cheng, Anthony S., and Steven E. Daniels. 2005. Getting to the "we": Examining the relationship between geographic scale and ingroup emergence in collaborative watershed planning. *Human Ecology Review* 12 (1): 30–43.

Cheng, Anthony S., Linda E. Kruger, and Steven E. Daniels. 2003. "Place" as an integrating concept in natural resource politics: Propositions for a social science research agenda. *Society and Natural Resources* 16 (2): 87–104.

Chisholm, Donald. 1989. *Coordination without hierarchy: Informal structures in multiorganizational systems.* Berkeley: University of California Press.

Chrislip, David D., and Carl E. Larson. 1994. *Collaborative leadership: How citizens and civic leaders can make a difference.* San Francisco: Jossey-Bass.

Ciriacy-Wantrup, S. V. 1970. *Resource conservation: Economics and policies.* Berkeley: University of California Press.

Clark, Alan. 1993. A statewide approach to watershed management: North Carolina's basin-wide water quality management program. Paper presented at Watershed '93, Alexandria, VA, March 21–24.

Clark, Brad T., Nina Burkardt, and M. Dawn King. 2005. Watershed management and organizational dynamics: Nationwide findings and regional variation. *Environmental Management* 36 (2): 297–310.

Clark, Tim W., Elizabeth Dawn Amato, Donald G. Whittemore, and Ann H. Harvey. 1991. Policy and programs for ecosystem management in the greater Yellowstone ecosystem: An analysis. *Conservation Biology* 5 (3): 412–422.

Clarke, Jeanne Nienaber, and Daniel C. McCool. 1996. *Staking out the terrain: Power and performance among natural resource agencies.* 2nd ed. Albany: State University of New York Press.

Colby, Suzanne M., and Wilbert Murrell. 1998. Child welfare and substance abuse services: From barriers to collaboration. In *Substance abuse, family violence, and child welfare: Bridging perspectives*, ed. R. L. Hampton, V. Senatore, and T. P. Gullotta. Thousand Oaks, CA: Sage.

Colosi, Thomas. 1983. Negotiation in the public and private sectors: A core model. *American Behavioral Scientist* 27 (2): 229–253.

Community Planning Workshop. 2006. *Environmental scan and gaps analysis of prevention programs in Multnomah County.* Portland, OR: Mental Health and Addiction Services Division, Multnomah County.

Connell, Daniel. 2007. *Water politics in the Murray Darling Basin.* Annandale, NSW: Federation Press.

Connick, Sarah, and Judith E. Innes. 2003. Outcomes of collaborative water policy making: Applying complexity thinking to evaluation. *Journal of Environmental Planning and Management* 46 (2): 177–197.

Cooks River Catchment Management Committee. 1993. *Cooks River Management Strategy.* Bankstown, New South Wales: Cooks River Catchment Management Committee.

Cornforth, Chris. 2003. Conclusion: Contextualising and managing the paradoxes of governance. In *The governance of public and non-profit organisations: What do boards do?* ed. C. Cornforth. London: Routledge.

Cortner, Hanna J., and Margaret Ann Moote. 1999. *The politics of ecosystem management.* Washington, DC: Island Press.

Cragan, John F., and David W. Wright. 1990. Small group communication in the 1980s: A synthesis and critique of the field. *Communication Studies* 41 (2): 212–236.

Crosby, Barbara C., and John M. Bryson. 2005. *Leadership for the common good: Tackling public problems in a shared-power world.* 2nd ed. San Francisco: Jossey-Bass.

Crosby, Barbara C., and John M. Bryson. 2010. Integrative leadership and the creation and maintenance of cross-sector collaborations. *Leadership Quarterly* 21 (2): 211–230.

Curtis, Allan. 1998. Agency-community partnerships in Landcare: Lessons for state-sponsored resource management. *Environmental Management* 22 (4): 563–574.

Curtis, Allan, and Penny Cooke. 2006. *Landcare groups in Victoria: After twenty years.* Albury, NSW: Institute for Land, Water, and Society.

Curtis, Allan, and Terry De Lacy. 1996. Landcare in Australia: Beyond the expert farmer. *Agriculture and Human Values* 13 (1): 20–31.

Curtis, Allan, and Michael Lockwood. 2000. Landcare and catchment management in Australia: Lessons for state-sponsored community participation. *Society and Natural Resources* 13 (1): 61–73.

Curtis, Allan, Bruce Shindler, and Angela Wright. 2002. Sustaining local watershed initiatives: Lessons from Landcare and watershed councils. *Journal of the American Water Resources Association* 38 (5): 1207–1216.

Daniels, Thomas L., Katherine Daniels, and the American Planning Association. 2003. *The environmental planning handbook for sustainable communities and regions.* Chicago: Planners Press.

Danter, K. Jeffrey, Debra L. Griest, Gary W. Mullins, and Emmalou Norland. 2000. Organizational change as a component of ecosystem management. *Society and Natural Resources* 13 (6): 537–547.

Darlington, Yvonne, Judith A. Feeney, and Kylie Rixon. 2005. Interagency collaboration between child protection and mental health services: Practices, attitudes, and barriers. *Child Abuse and Neglect* 29 (10): 1085–1098.

Dedekorkut, Aysin. 2000. What makes collaboration work? An empirical assessment of determinants of success in interorganizational collaboration. Paper presented at the ACSP, Baltimore. MD Medical Newsmagazine, November.

Dengler, Mary. 2007. Spaces of power for action: Governance of the Everglades restudy process (1992–2000). *Political Geography* 26 (4): 423–454.

Depoe, Stephen P. 2004. Public involvement, civil discovery, and the formation of environmental policy: A comparative analysis of the Fernald Citizens Task Force and the Fernald Health Effects Subcommittee. In *Communication and public participation in environmental decision making*, ed. S. P. Depoe, J. W. Delicath, and M.-F. A. Elensbeer. Albany: State University of New York Press.

Derby, Stephen L., and Ralph L. Keeney. 1981. Risk analysis: Understanding "how safe is safe enough?" *Risk Analysis* 1 (3): 217–224.

Derry, Sharon J., Lori Adams DuRussel, and Angela M. O'Donnell. 1998. Individual and distributed cognitions in interdisciplinary teamwork: A developing case study and emerging theory. *Educational Psychology Review* 10 (1): 25–56.

Dillman, Don A. 2007. *Mail and internet surveys: The tailored design method.* 2nd ed. Hoboken, NJ: Wiley.

Dodge, Douglas P., and Raymond M. Biette. 1992. River protection in Ontario, Canada: A case for holistic catchment management. In *River conservation and management*, ed. P. J. Boon, Peter Calow, and Geoffrey E. Petts. New York: Wiley.

Doppelt, Bob, Craig Shinn, and John DeWitt. 2002. *Review of USDA Forest Service community-based watershed restoration partnerships.* Portland, OR: Mark O. Hatfield School of Government, Portland State University.

Dovers, Stephen. 1995. Information, sustainability and policy. *Australasian Journal of Environmental Management* 2 (3): 142–156.

DRCOG. 2000. *Metro Vision 2020 Plan.* Denver: Denver Regional Council of Governments.

Drewry, John, Will Higham, and Carl Mitchell. 2008. *Water quality improvement plan: Final report for Mackay Whitsunday region.* Mackay: Mackay Whitsunday Natural Resource Management Group.

Dukes, E. Franklin. 1996. *Resolving public conflict: Transforming community and governance.* Manchester: Manchester University Press.

Dukes, E. Franklin, and Karen E. Firehock. 2001. *Collaboration: A guide for environmental advocates.* Charlottesville: University of Virginia.

Dutton, Jane E., Susan J. Ashford, Regina M. O'Neill, and Katherine A. Lawrence. 2001. Moves that matter: Issue selling and organizational change. *Academy of Management Journal* 44 (4): 716–736.

Edelenbos, Jurian, and Erik-Hans Klijn. 2005. Managing stakeholder involvement in decision making: A comparative analysis of six interactive processes in the Netherlands. *Journal of Public Administration: Research and Theory* 16 (3): 417–446.

Edwards, Charles, and Chris Cornforth. 2003. What influences the strategic contribution of boards? In *The governance of public and non-profit organisations: What do boards do?* ed. C. Cornforth. London: Routledge.

Edwards, Jeffrey R. 1991. Person-Job Fit: A Conceptual Integration, Literature Review and Methodological Critique. In *Industrial and Organizational Psychology*, ed. Cary L. Cooper. New York: New York University Press.

Ehrmann, John R., and Barbara L. Stinson. 1999. Joint fact-finding and the use of technical experts. In *Consensus-building handbook: A comprehensive guide to reaching agreement*, ed. L. Susskind, S. McKearnon, and S. Carpenter. Thousand Oaks, CA: Sage.

Elliot, Heather, and Jennie Popay. 2000. How are policy makers using evidence? Models of research utilisation and local NHS policy making. *Journal of Epidemiology and Community Health* 54 (6): 461–468.

Elmore, Richard F. 1982. Backward mapping: Implementation research and policy decisions. In *Studying implementation: Methodological and administrative issues*, ed. W. Williams. Chatham, NJ: Chatham House Publishers.

Epstein, Edward. 2004. "Bipartisan bid to end state's water wars." *San Francisco Chronicle*, May 6, B1.

Erickson, Bonnie H. 1982. Networks, ideologies, and belief systems. In *Social structure and network analysis*, ed. P. V. Marsden and N. Lin. Beverly Hills: Sage.

Etzioni, Amitai. 1988. *The moral dimension: Toward a new economics*. New York: Free Press.

Failing, L., and R. Gregory. 2003. Ten common mistakes in designing biodiversity indicators for forest policy. *Journal of Environmental Management* 68 (2): 121–132.

Failing, Lee, Robin Gregory, and Michael Harstone. 2007. Integrating science and local knowledge in environmental risk management: A decision-focused approach. *Ecological Economics* 64 (1): 47–60.

Fernandez, Sergio, Yook Jik Cho, and James L. Perry. 2010. Exploring the link between integrated leadership and public sector performance. *Leadership Quarterly* 21 (2): 308–323.

Fisher, Roger, and William Ury. 1981. *Getting to yes: Negotiating agreement without giving in*. New York: Penguin Books.

Flitcroft, Rebecca L., Dana C. Dedrick, Courtland L. Smith, Cynthia A. Thieman, and John P. Bolte. 2009. Social infrastructure to integrate science and practice: The experience of the Long Tom Watershed Council. *Ecology and Society* 14 (2): 36.

Forester, John. 1999. *The deliberative practitioner: Encouraging participatory planning processes*. Cambridge, MA: MIT Press.

Frame, Tanis M., Thomas Gunton, and J. C. Day. 2004. The role of collaboration in environmental management: An evaluation of land and resource planning in British Columbia. *Journal of Environmental Planning and Management* 47 (1): 59–82.

Fraser, Evan D. G., Andrew J. Dougill, Warren E. Mabee, Mark Reed, and Patrick McAlpine. 2006. Bottom up and top down: Analysis of participatory processes for sustainability indicator identification as a pathway to community empowerment and sustainable environmental management. *Journal of Environmental Management* 78 (2): 114–127.

Friedman, Thomas L. 2008. *Hot, flat, and crowded: Why we need a green revolution—and how it can renew America*. 1st ed. New York: Farrar.

Giddens, Anthony. 1979. *Central problems in social theory*. London: Macmillan.

Gigone, Daniel, and Reid Hastie. 1993. The common knowledge effect: Information sharing and group judgment. *Journal of Personality and Social Psychology* 65 (5): 959–974.

Gigone, Daniel, and Reid Hastie. 1997. The impact of information on small group choice. *Journal of Personality and Social Psychology* 72 (1): 132–140.

Gittell, Jody Hoffer, and Leigh Weiss. 2004. Coordination networks within and across organizations: A multi-level framework. *Journal of Management Studies* 41 (1): 127–153.

Glass, James. 1979. Citizen participation in planning: The relationship between objectives and techniques. *Journal of the American Planning Association* 45 (2): 180–189.

Gore, Albert. 1992. *Earth in the balance: Forging a new common purpose*. London: Earthscan.

Granovetter, Mark. 1982. The strength of weak ties: A network theory revisited. In *Social structure and network analysis*, ed. P. V. Marsden and N. Lin. Beverly Hills: Sage.

Granovetter, Mark. 1983. The strength of weak ties: A network theory revisited. *Sociological Theory* 1: 201–233.

Gray, Barbara. 1985. Conditions facilitating interorganizational collaboration. *Human Relations* 38 (10): 911–936.

Gray, Barbara. 1989. *Collaborating: Finding common ground for multiparty problems*. San Francisco: Jossey-Bass.

Gray, Barbara, and Donna J. Wood. 1991. Collaborative alliances: Moving from practice to theory. *Journal of Applied Behavioral Science* 27 (1): 3–22.

Gregg, Frank, Stephen M. Born, William B. Lord, and Marvin Waterstone. 1991. *Institutional response to a changing water policy environment*. Tempe: Water Resources Research Center, University of Arizona.

Guerin, Turlough F. 1999. An Australian perspective on the constraints to the transfer and adoption of innovations in land management. *Environmental Conservation* 26 (4): 289–304.

Guetzkow, Harold. 1966. *Relations among organizations, studies on behavior in organizations: A research symposium*. Athens: University of Georgia Press.

Guruswamy, Laksham. 1989. Integrating thoughtways: Re-opening of the environmental mind? *Wisconsin Law Review* 47 (3): 463–537.

Haas, Peter M. 1989. Do regimes matter? Epistemic communities and Mediterranean pollution control. *International Organization* 43 (3): 377–403.

Hage, Jerald, Michael Aiken, and Cora Bagley Marrett. 1972. Organization structure and communications. In *Organizational systems: A text reader in the sociology of organizations*, ed. K. Azumi and J. Hage. Lexington, MA: D. C. Heath and Co.

Hajer, Maarten A. 1993. Discourse coalitions and the institutionalization of practice: The case of acid rain in Britain. In *The argumentative turn in policy analysis and planning*, ed. F. Fischer and J. Forester. Durham, NC: Duke University Press.

Hamilton, Jennifer Duffield. 2004. Competing and converging values of public participation: A case study of participant views in Department of Energy nuclear weapons cleanup. In *Communication and public participation in environmental decision making*, ed. S. P. Depoe, J. W. Delicath, and M.-F. A. Elensbeer. Albany: State University of New York Press.

Hanemann, Michael, and Caitlin Dyckman. 2009. The San Francisco Bay-Delta: A failure in decision-making capacity. *Environmental Science and Policy* 12 (6): 710–725.

Harbin, Gloria, Jane Eckland, James Gallagher, Richard Clifford, and Patricia Place. 1991. Policy development for PL 99–457. University of North Carolina at Chapel Hill.

Harrington, Hugh, and Norman Miller. 1993. Do group motives differ from individual motives? Considerations regarding process distinctiveness. In *Group motivation: Social psychology perspectives*, ed. M. A. Hogg and D. Abrams. New York: Harvester Wheatsheaf.

Head, Brian. 2005. Participation or co-governance? Challenges for regional natural resource management. In *Participation and governance in regional development: Global trends in an Australian context*, ed. R. Eversole and J. Martin. Hampshire, UK: Ashgate.

Heikkila, Tanya, and Andrea K. Gerlak. 2005. The formation of large-scale collaborative resource management institutions: Clarifying the roles of stakeholders, science, and institutions. *Policy Studies Journal* 33 (4): 583–612.

Helling, Amy. 1998. Collaborative visioning: Proceed with caution! Results from evaluating Atlanta's Vision 2020 project. *Journal of the American Planning Association* 64 (3): 335–349.

Herman, Robert D. 1989. Board functions and board-staff relations in nonprofit organizations: An introduction. In *Nonprofit boards of directors: Analyses and applications*, ed. R. D. Herman and J. Van Til. New Brunswick, NJ: Transaction Publishers.

Hezri, Adnan A., and Stephen R. Dovers. 2006. Sustainability indicators, policy, and governance: Issues for ecological economics. *Ecological Economics* 60 (1): 86–99.

Hibbard, Michael, and Jeremy Madsen. 2003. Environmental resistance to place-based collaboration in the U.S. West. *Society and Natural Resources* 16 (8): 703–718.

Hill, Carolyn J., and Laurence E. Lynn Jr. 2003. Producing human services: Why do agencies collaborate? *Public Management Review* 5 (1): 63–81.

Hjern, Benny, and David O. Porter. 1981. Implementation structures: A new unit of administrative analysis. *Organization Studies* 2 (3): 211–227.

Hoch, Charles. 1992. Evaluating plans pragmatically. *Planning Theory* 1 (1): 53–75.

Hoch, Charles, Linda C. Dalton, and Frank S. So. 2000. *The practice of local government planning*. 3rd ed. Washington, DC: International City/County Management Association.

Holling, C. S., and United Nations Environment Programme. 1978. *Adaptive environmental assessment and management*. Chichester, NY: Wiley.

Hooper, Bruce P. 1995. Towards more effective integrated watershed management in Australia: Results of a national survey and implications for catchment management. *Water Resources Update* 100: 28–35.

Howlett, Michael. 2002. Do networks matter? Linking policy network structure to policy outcomes: Evidence from four Canadian policy sectors, 1990–2000. *Canadian Journal of Political Science/Revue canadienne de science politique* 35 (2): 235–267.

Huntingon, Charles W., and Sari Sommarstrom. 2000. An evaluation of selected watershed councils in the Pacific Northwest and northern California. Etna, CA: Sari Sommarstrom and Associates.

Hutchinson, Judy, Avis C. Vidal, Robert Putnam, Ivan Light, Briggs Xavier de Souza, William M. Rohe, Jennifer Gress, and Michael Woolcock. 2004. Symposium: Using social capital to help integrate planning theory, research, and practice. *Journal of the American Planning Association* 70 (2): 142–192.

Huxham, Chris, and Siv Vangen. 2000. Ambiguity, complexity, and dynamics in the membership of collaboration. *Human Relations* 53 (6): 771–806.

Huxham, Chris, and Siv Vangen. 2005. *Managing to collaborate: The theory and practice of collaborative advantage*. London: Routledge.

Imperial, Mark T. 1999. Institutional analysis and ecosystem-based management: The institutional analysis and development framework. *Environmental Management* 24 (4): 449–465.

Imperial, Mark T. 2005. Lessons from six watershed management programs. *Administration and Society* 37 (3): 281–320.

Imperial, Mark T., and Derek Kauneckis. 2003. Moving from conflict to collaboration: Watershed governance in Lake Tahoe. *Natural Resources Journal* 43 (4): 1009–1055.

Independent Scientific Review Panel/Independent Scientific Advisory Board. 2004. *Scientific review of subbasin plans for the Columbia River basin fish and wildlife program*. Portland, OR: Independent Scientific Review Panel/Independent Scientific Advisory Board.

Innes, Judith E. 1991. Implementing state growth management in the U.S.: Strategies for coordination. Institute of Urban and Regional Development, University of California at Berkeley.

Innes, Judith E. 1995. Planning theory's emerging paradigm: Communicative action and interactive practice. *Journal of Planning, Education, and Research* 14:183–189.

Innes, Judith E. 1996. Planning through consensus building: A new perspective on the comprehensive planning ideal. *Journal of the American Planning Association* 62 (4): 460–472.

Innes, Judith E. 1998. Information in communicative planning. *Journal of the American Planning Association* 64 (1): 52–63.

Innes, Judith E. 1999. Evaluating consensus building. In *Consensus-building Handbook: A comprehensive guide to reaching agreement*, ed. L. Susskind, S. McKearnon, and S. Carpenter. Thousand Oaks, CA: Sage.

Innes, Judith E., and David E. Booher. 1999a. Consensus building and complex adaptive systems: A framework for evaluating collaborative planning. *Journal of the American Planning Association* 65 (4): 412–423.

Innes, Judith E., and David E. Booher. 1999b. Consensus building as role playing and bricolage: Toward a theory of collaborative planning. *Journal of the American Planning Association* 65 (1): 9–26.

Innes, Judith E., and David E. Booher. 2010. *Planning with complexity: Introduction to collaborative rationality for public policy*. 1st ed. New York: Routledge.

Innes, Judith E., Sarah Connick, and David Booher. 2007. Informality as a planning strategy: Collaborative water management in the CALFED Bay-Delta Program. *Journal of the American Planning Association* 73 (2): 195–210.

Innes, Judith E., Sarah Connick, Laura Kaplan, and David E. Booher. 2006. Collaborative governance in the CALFED program: Adaptive policy making for California water. Working paper. Institute of Urban and Regional Development, University of California, Berkeley, and Center for Collaborative Policy, California State University, Sacramento.

Innes, Judith E., Judith Gruber, Michael Neuman, and Robert Thompson. 1994. Coordinating growth and environmental management through consensus building. California Policy Seminar report, University of California at Berkeley.

International Joint Commission. 2008. *Who we are*. Available at http://www.ijc.org/en/background/ijc_cmi_nature.htm (accessed October 6, 2008).

Jandt, Fred. 1985. *Win-win negotiating: Turning conflict into agreement*. New York: Wiley.

Johnson, David W. 2000. *Reaching out*. 6th ed. Needham Heights, MA: Allyn and Bacon.

Johnson, David W., and Frank P. Johnson. 2000. *Joining together: Group theory and group skills.* 7th ed. Boston: Allyn and Bacon.

Jones, Jeff R., Roxanne Martin, and E. T. Bartlett. 1995. Ecosystem management: The U.S. Forest Service's response to social conflict. *Society and Natural Resources* 8 (2): 161–168.

Justice, Thomas, David Jamieson, and NetLibrary Inc. 1999. *The facilitator's fieldbook: Step-by-step procedures, checklists and guidelines, samples and templates.* New York: Amacom.

Kallis, Giorgos, Michael Kiparsky, and Richard Norgaard. 2010. Collaborative governance and adaptive management: Lessons from California's CALFED water program. *Environmental Science and Policy* 12 (6): 631–643.

Kaner, Sam. 1996. *Facilitator's guide to participatory decision making.* Gabriola Island, British Columbia: New Society Publishers.

Katz, Alan. 1997. Growth plan for Denver area adopted. *Denver Post*, March 20, 1.

Keeney, Ralph L., and Detlof von Winterfeldt. 1986. Improving risk communication. *Risk Analysis* 6 (4): 417–424.

Kelly, Erin Clover, and John C. Bliss. 2009. Healthy forests, healthy communities: An emerging paradigm for natural resource-dependent communities? *Society and Natural Resources* 22 (6): 519–537.

Kelly, Steve. 1998. Community restoration efforts in the Mary River catchment. Gympie, Queensland: Department of Natural Resources.

Kenney, Douglas S. 2000. *Arguing about consensus: Examining the case against western watershed initiatives and other collaborative groups active in natural resources management.* Boulder: Natural Resources Law Center, University of Colorado.

Kenney, Douglas S., Sean T. McAllister, William H. Caile, and Jason S. Peckman. 2000. *The new watershed source book.* Boulder, CO: Natural Resources Law Center, University of Colorado.

Khator, Renu. 1999. Networking to achieve alternative regulation: Case studies from Florida's national estuary programs. *Policy Studies Review* 16 (1): 21.

Kingdon, John W. 2003. *Agendas, alternatives, and public policies.* 2nd ed. New York: Longman.

Knoke, David. 1990. *Political networks: The structural perspective.* New York: Cambridge University Press.

Koontz, Tomas M., Toddi A. Steelman, JoAnn Carmin, Katrina Smith Korfmacher, Cassandra Moseley, and Craig W. Thomas. 2004. Collaborative environmental management: What roles for government? Washington, DC: Resources for the Future.

Koontz, Tomas M., and Craig W. Thomas. 2006. What do we know and need to know about the environmental outcomes of collaborative management? *Public Administration Review* 66 (supplement).

Lane, Marcus B. 1997. Aboriginal participation in environmental planning. *Australian Geographical Studies* 35 (3): 308–323.

Lane, Marcus B. 2003. Participation, decentralization, and civil society: Indigenous rights and democracy in environmental planning. *Journal of Planning, Education, and Research* 22 (4): 360–373.

Lang, Reg. 1986a. Achieving integration in resource planning. In *Integrated approaches to resource planning and management*, ed. R. Lang. Calgary: Banff Centre.

Lang, Reg. 1986b. Introduction to *Integrated approaches to resource planning and management*, ed. R. Lang. Calgary: Banff Centre.

Laninga, Tamara J. 2005. Collaboration and the Bureau of Land Management: Differential adoption of community-based approaches to public lands planning in the West. Department of Urban and Regional Planning, University of Colorado at Denver.

Lasker, Roz D., Elisa S. Weiss, and Rebecca Miller. 2001. Partnership synergy: A practical framework for studying and strengthening the collaborative advantage. *Milbank Quarterly* 79 (2): 27.

Layzer, Judith A. 2008. *Natural experiments: Ecosystem-based management and the environment, American and comparative environmental policy*. Cambridge, MA: MIT Press.

Leach, William D., and Neil W. Pelkey. 2001. Making watershed partnerships work: A review of the empirical literature. *Journal of Water Resources Planning and Management* 127 (6): 378–385.

Leach, William D., Neil W. Pelkey, and Paul A. Sabatier. 2002. Stakeholder partnerships as collaborative policymaking: Evaluation criteria applied to watershed management in California and Washington. *Journal of Policy Analysis and Management* 21 (4): 645–670.

Leach, William D., and Paul Sabatier. 2005. Are trust and social capital the keys to success? Watershed partnerships in California and Washington. In *Swimming upstream: Collaborative approaches to watershed management*, ed. P. Sabatier, W. Focht, M. Lubell, Z. Trachtenberg, A. Vedlitz, and M. Matlock. Cambridge, MA: MIT Press.

Lejano, Raul P., and Helen Ingram. 2010. Collaborative networks and new ways of knowing. *Environmental Science and Policy* 12 (6): 653–662.

Levy, John M. 1997. *Contemporary urban planning*. Upper Saddle River, NJ: Prentice-Hall.

Libecap, Gary D. 1989. *Contracting for property rights: Political economy of institutions and decisions*. Cambridge: Cambridge University Press.

Lin, Nan. 1982. Social resources and instrumental action. In *Social structure and network analysis*, ed. P. V. Marsden and N. Lin. Beverly Hills: Sage.

Lindblom, Charles E. 1959. The science of "muddling through." *Public Administration Review* 19 (2): 79–88.

Lindblom, Charles E. 1973. Incrementalism and environmentalism. In *Managing the Environment* report. Washington, DC: Environmental Protection Agency.

Lindblom, Charles E. 1979. Still muddling, not yet through. *Public Administration Review* 39 (6): 517–526.

Lindemann, Stefan. 2008. Understanding water regime formation: A research framework with lessons from Europe. *Global Environmental Politics* 8 (4): 117–140.

Linden, Russ. 2008. Collaborating across organizational boundaries. In *The trusted leader: Building the relationships that make government work*, ed. T. Newell, G. Reeher, and P. Ronayne. Washington, DC: CQ Press.

Little Hoover Commission. 2005. *Still imperiled, still important: The Little Hoover Commission's review of the CALFED Bay-Delta Program.* Sacramento, CA: Little Hoover Commission.

Logsdon, Jeanne. 1991. Interest and interdependence in the formation of social problem-solving collaborations. *Journal of Applied Behavioral Science* 27 (1): 23–37.

Long Tom Watershed Council. 2008. *Council history and charter.* Available at http://www .longtom.org/history2.html (accessed October 16, 2008).

Lord, William B. 1979. Conflict in federal water resource planning. *Water Resources Bulletin* 15 (5): 1226–1235.

Lubell, Mark, Paul Sabatier, Arnold Vedlitz, Will Focht, Zev Trachtenberg, and Marty Matlock. 2005. Conclusions and recommendations. In *Swimming upstream: Collaborative approaches to watershed management*, ed. P. Sabatier, W. Focht, M. Lubell, Z. Trachtenberg, A. Vedlitz, and M. Matlock. Cambridge, MA: MIT Press.

Lubell, Mark, Mark Schneider, John T. Scholz, and Mihriye Mete. 2002. Watershed partnerships and the emergence of collective action institutions. *American Journal of Political Science* 46 (1): 148–163.

Lund, Jay, Ellen Hanak, William Fleenor, Richard Howitt, Jeffrey Mount, and Peter Moyle. 2007. *Envisioning futures for the Sacramento–San Joaquin Delta.* San Francisco: Public Policy Institute of California.

Lyons, Thomas F. 1971. Role clarity, need for clarity, satisfaction, tension, and withdrawal. *Organizational Behavior and Human Performance* 6 (1): 99–110.

MacKenzie, Susan Hill. 1991. On the development and implementation of ecosystem management plans for water resources in the Great Lakes: A case study of the RAP initiative. PhD diss., University of Michigan.

MacKenzie, Susan Hill. 1993. Ecosystem management in the Great Lakes: Some observations from three rap sites. *Journal of Great Lakes Research* 19 (1): 136–144.

Mandell, Myrna P. 1999. The impact of collaboratives: Changing the face of public policy through networks and network structures. *Policy Studies Review* 16 (1): 4–17.

Mandell, Myrna P. 2001. Collaboration through network structures for community building efforts. *National Civic Review* 90 (3): 10.

Marans, Steven, and Mark Schaefer. 1998. Community policing, schools, and mental health: The challenge of collaboration. In *Violence in American schools: A new perspective*, ed. D. S. Elliott, B. A. Hamburg, and K. R. Williams. Cambridge: Cambridge University Press.

March, James G., and Herbert A. Simon. 1958. *Organizations.* New York: Wiley.

Margerum, Richard D. 1995a. Examining the practice of integrated environmental management: Towards a conceptual model. PhD diss., University of Wisconsin at Madison.

Margerum, Richard D. 1995b. *Integrated management for the Wisconsin Department of Natural Resources.* Madison: Wisconsin Department of Natural Resources.

Margerum, Richard D. 1996. Integrated environmental management: A framework for practice. Discussion paper no. 6. Armidale, NSW: Centre for Water Policy Research.

Margerum, Richard D. 1999a. Getting past yes: From capital creation to action. *Journal of the American Planning Association* 65 (2): 181–192.

Margerum, Richard D. 1999b. Implementing integrated planning and management: A typology of approaches. *Australian Planner* 36 (3): 155–161.

Margerum, Richard D. 1999c. Integrated environmental management: Lessons from the Trinity Inlet Management Program. *Land Use Policy* 16 (3): 179–190.

Margerum, Richard D. 1999d. Integrated environmental management: The elements critical to success. *Environmental Management* 65 (2): 181–192.

Margerum, Richard D. 2001a. Organizational commitment to integrated environmental management: Matching strategies to constraints. *Environmental Management* 67 (4): 421–431.

Margerum, Richard D. 2001b. South East Queensland 2001: Has it helped improve environmental planning? *Australian Planner* 38 (3–4): 142–150.

Margerum, Richard D. 2002a. Collaborative planning: Building consensus and building a distinct model for practice. *Journal of Planning Education and Research* 21 (2): 237–253.

Margerum, Richard D. 2002b. Evaluating collaborative planning: Implications from an empirical analysis of growth management. *Journal of the American Planning Association* 68 (2): 179–193.

Margerum, Richard D. 2005. Collaborative growth management in metropolitan Denver: Fig leaf or valiant effort? *Land Use Policy* 22 (4): 373–386.

Margerum, Richard D. 2006. Does consensus make a difference? Findings from an empirical investigation of local government advisory committees. Paper presented at the Association of Collegiate Schools of Planning Conference, Arlington, TX.

Margerum, Richard D. 2007. Overcoming locally based collaboration constraints. *Society and Natural Resources* 20 (2): 135–152.

Margerum, Richard D. 2008. A typology of collaboration efforts in environmental management. *Environmental Management* 41 (4): 487–500.

Margerum, Richard D., and Stephen M. Born. 1995. Integrated environmental management: Moving from theory to practice. *Journal of Environmental Planning and Management* 38 (3): 371–391.

Margerum, Richard D., and Stephen M. Born. 2000. Co-ordination for environmental management: A framework for analysis. *Journal of Environmental Planning and Management* 43 (1): 5–21.

Margerum, Richard D., and Rachael Holland. 2000. *Environmental planning in South East Queensland: An evaluation of local government activities and the influence of collaborative growth management.* Brisbane: School of Planning, Landscape Architecture, and Surveying, Queensland University of Technology.

Margerum, Richard D., and Bruce P. Hooper. 2001. Integrated environmental management: Improving implementation through leverage point mapping. *Society and Natural Resources* 14 (1): 1–19.

Margerum, Richard D., and Debra R. Whitall. 2004. The challenges and implications of collaborative management on a river basin scale. *Journal of Environmental Planning and Management* 47 (3): 407–427.

Marshall, Graham R. 2008. Nesting, subsidiarity, and community-based environmental governance beyond the local level. *International Journal of the Commons* 2 (1): 75–97.

Maslach, Christina, Wilmar B. Schaufeli, and Michael P. Leter. 2001. Job burnout. *Annual Review of Psychology* 52: 397–422.

Mattessich, Paul W., Marta Murray-Close, and Barbara R. Monsey. 2004. *Collaboration: What makes it work.* 2nd ed. Saint Paul, MN: Amherst H. Wilder Foundation.

May, Peter J., Raymond J. Burby, Neil J. Ericksen, John W. Handmer, Jennifer E. Dixon, Sarah Michaels, and D. Ingle Smith. 1996. *Environmental management and governance: Intergovernmental approaches to hazards and sustainability.* New York: Routledge.

Mayere, Severine, Phil Heywood, and Richard D. Margerum. 2008. Governance and effectiveness in regional planning: An analysis of North American, European, and Australian practice. Paper presented at the Joint Congress of the Association of Collegiate Schools of Planning and European Association of Planning Schools, Chicago, July 6–11.

Mazmanian, Daniel A., and Paul A. Sabatier. 1983. *Implementation and public policy.* Glenview, IL: Scott Foresman and Company.

McCann, Eugene J. 2001. Collaborative visioning or urban planning as therapy? The politics of public-private policy making. *Professional Geographer* 53 (2): 207–218.

McCarthy, Jane E., and Alice Shorett. 1984. *Negotiating settlements: A guide to environmental mediation.* New York: American Arbitration Association.

McCloskey, Michael. 1996. The skeptic: Collaboration has its limits. *High Country News,* May 13. Available at http://www.hcn.org.

McCloskey, Michael. 2001. Is this the course you want to be on? *Society and Natural Resources* 14 (4): 627–634.

McDonald, Geoff, Bruce Taylor, Jenny Bellamy, Cathy Robinson, Michelle Walker, Tim Smith, Suzanne Hoverman, Clive McAlpine, Ann Peterson, and Steven Dawson. 2005. *Benchmarking regional planning for natural resources management, 2004–05: Progress, constraints, and future directions for regions.* Brisbane: Tropical Savannas Management Cooperative Research Centre.

McKearnon, Sarah, and David Fairman. 1999. Producing consensus. In *Consensus-building handbook: A comprehensive guide to reaching agreement,* ed. L. Susskind, S. McKearnon, and S. Carpenter. Thousand Oaks, CA: Sage.

McKenzie Watershed Council. 2008. *About us 2008.* Available at http://www.mckenziewc .org/about.htm (accessed October 16, 2008).

McLaughlin, John A., and Gretchen B. Jordan. 1999. Logic models: A tool for telling your program's performance story. *Evaluation and Program Planning* 22 (1): 65–72.

Merriam-Webster. 1983. *Webster's ninth new collegiate dictionary.* New York: Merriam-Webster and Co.

Mitchell, Bruce. 1986. The evolution of integrated resource management. In *Integrated approaches to resource planning and management,* ed. Reg Lang. Calgary: The Banff Centre.

Mitchell, Bruce. 1991. Beating conflict and uncertainty in resource management and development. In *Resource Management and Development,* ed. Bruce Mitchell. Toronto: Oxford University Press.

Mitchell, Bruce, and Malcolm Hollick. 1993. Integrated catchment management in western Australia: Transition from concept to implementation. *Environmental Management* 17 (6): 735–743.

Molnar, Joseph J., and David L. Rogers. 1982. Interorganizational coordination in environmental management: Process, strategy, and objective. In *Environmental policy implementation*, ed. D. E. Mann. Lexington, MA: Lexington Books.

Moore, Elizabeth A., and Tomas M. Koontz. 2003. A typology of collaborative watershed groups: Citizen-based, agency-based, and mixed partnerships. *Society and Natural Resources* 16 (5): 451–460.

Moreland, Richard, John Levine, and Marie Cini. 1993. Group socialization: The role of commitment. In *Group motivation: Social psychology perspectives*, ed. M. A. Hogg and D. Abrams. New York: Harvester Wheatsheaf.

Morrison, Tiffany H., and Marcus B. Lane. 2005. What "whole-of-government" means for environmental policy and management: An analysis of the Connecting Government initiative. *Australian Journal of Environmental Management* 12 (1): 47–54.

Morse, Ricardo S. 2010. Integrative public leadership: Catalyzing collaboration to create public value. *Leadership Quarterly* 21 (2): 231–245.

Moseley, Cassandra. 1999. New ideas, old institutions: Environment, community, and state in the Pacific Northwest. PhD diss., Yale University.

Mostert, Erik, Claudia Pahl-Wostl, Yvonne Rees, Brad Searle, David Tàbara, and Joanne Tippett. 2007. Social learning in European river-basin management: Barriers and fostering mechanisms from 10 river basins. *Ecology and Society* 12:1–16.

Murray Darling Basin Authority. 2009. *About the Murray Darling Basin Authority*. Available at http://www.mdba.gov.au/about_the_authority (accessed March 2, 2009).

Murray Darling Basin Commission. 2009. *About the MDBC*. Available at http://www.mdbc.gov.au/about/murraydarling_basin_initiative_overview (accessed March 2, 2009).

Murray Darling Ministerial Council. 2001. *Integrated catchment management in the Murray Darling basin, 2001–2010*. Canberra, Australia: Murray Darling Basin Commission.

Nagel, Peter. 2006. Policy games and venue shopping: Working the stakeholder interface to broker policy change in rehabilitation services. *Australian Journal of Public Administration* 65 (4): 3–16.

Napier, Ted L., Cameron S. Thraen, and Silvana M. Camboni. 1988. Willingness of land operators to participate in government-sponsored soil erosion control programs. *Journal of Rural Studies* 4 (4): 339–347.

Napier, Ted L., Cameron S. Thraen, Akia Gore, and W. Richard Goe. 1984. Factors affecting adoption of conventional and conservation tillage practices in Ohio. *Journal of Soil and Water Conservation* 39 (2): 205–209.

National Audit Office. 2008. Regional delivery model for the Natural Heritage Trust and the National Action Plan for Salinity and Water Quality. Barton: National Audit Office, Australian government.

Newig, Jens, Claudia Pahl-Wostl, and Katja Sigel. 2005. The role of public participation in managing uncertainty in the implementation of the Water Framework Directive. *European Environment* 15: 333–343.

Newman, Janet, Marian Barnes, Helen Sullivan, and Andrew Knops. 2004. Public participation and collaborative governance. *Journal of Social Policy* 33 (2): 203–223.

Northouse, Peter Guy. 2007. *Leadership: Theory and practice.* 4th ed. Thousand Oaks, CA: Sage.

North-West Catchment Management Committee. 1992. *Our plan for the region's natural resources.* Tamworth, New South Wales: North-West Catchment Management Committee.

Nowak, Peter J. 1983. Obstacles to adoption of conservation tillage. *Journal of Soil and Water Conservation* 38 (3): 162–165.

Ospina, Sonia, and Erica Foldy. 2010. Building bridges from the margins: The work of leadership in social change organizations. *Leadership Quarterly* 21 (2): 292–307.

Ostrom, Elinor. 1986a. A method of institutional analysis. In *Guidance, control, and evaluation in the public sector*, ed. F. X. Kaufmann, G. Majone, and V. Ostrom. New York: Walter de Gruyter.

Ostrom, Elinor. 1986b. An agenda for the study of institutions. *Public Choice* 48 (1): 3–25.

Ostrom, Elinor. 1990. *Governing the commons: The evolution of institutions for collective action.* New York: Cambridge University Press.

Ostrom, Elinor. 1999. Institutional rational choice: An assessment of the institutional analysis and development framework. In *Theories of the policy process: Theoretical lenses on public policy*, ed. P. A. Sabatier. Boulder, CO: Westview Press.

Ostrom, Elinor. 2007. Challenges and growth: The development of the interdisciplinary field of institutional analysis. *Journal of Institutional Economics* 3 (3): 239–264.

O'Toole, Laurence J., Jr. 1986. Policy recommendations for multi-actor implementation: An assessment of the field. *Journal of Public Policy* 6 (2): 181–210.

O'Toole, Laurence J., Jr., and Kenneth J. Meier. 2004. Public management in intergovernmental networks: Matching structural networks and managerial networking. *Journal of Public Administration: Research and Theory* 14 (4): 469–494.

O'Toole, Laurence J., Jr., and Robert S. Montjoy. 1984. Interorganizational policy implementation: A theoretical perspective. *Public Administration Review* 44 (6): 491–503.

Otto, Shirley. 2003. Not so very different. In *The governance of public and non-profit organisations: What do boards do?* ed. C. Cornforth. London: Routledge.

ONHW. 2002. *Local natural hazard mitigation plans: An evaluation process.* Eugene, OR: Oregon Natural Hazards Workgroup, Community Service Center, University of Oregon.

OWEB. 2004. *Establishing a watershed council.* Available at http://www.oweb.state.or.us/groups/establishing_councils.shtml (accessed July 2, 2004).

OWEB. 2006. The Oregon plan for salmon and watersheds, 2005–2007 biennial report. Salem: Oregon Watershed Enhancement Board.

OWEB. 2008. Oregon plan biennial report, 2007–2009. Salem: Oregon Watershed Enhancement Board.

Owen, Dave. 2007. Law, environmental dynamism, reliability: The rise and fall of CALFED. *Environmental Law* 37: 1145–1204.

Ozawa, Connie P. 1991. *Recasting science: Consensual procedures in public policy making.* Boulder, CO: Westview Press.

Ozawa, Connie P. 2005. Putting science in its place. In *Adaptive governance and water conflict: New institutions for collaborative planning*, ed. J. T. Scholz and B. Stiftel. Washington, DC: Resources for the Future.

Pahl-Wostl, Claudia. 2002. Participative and stakeholder-based policy design, evaluation, and modeling processes. *Integrated Assessment* 3 (1): 3–14.

Pahl-Wostl, Claudia. 2006. The importance of social learning in restoring the multifunctionality of rivers and floodplains. *Ecology and Society* 11 (1): 1–14.

Parker, Francis H., Thomas E. Peddicord, and Thad L. Beyle. 1975. *Integration and coordination of state environmental programs*. Lexington, KY: Council of State Governments.

Parker, Kate Bodane, Richard D. Margerum, Dana C. Dedrick, and Jason P. Dedrick. 2010. Sustaining watershed councils: The issue of coordinator-board relationships. *Society and Natural Resources* 23 (5): 469–484.

Pasquero, Jean. 1991. Supraorganizational collaboration: The Canadian environmental experiment. *Journal of Applied Behavioral Science* 27 (1): 38–64.

Pearce, Craig, and Henry P. Sims. 2000. Shared leadership: Toward a multi-level theory of leadership. In *Advances in interdisciplinary studies of work teams*, ed. M. Beyerlein, D. Johnson, and S. Beyerlein. Vol. 7. New York: JAI Press.

Pickersgill, Glenda, Steve Burgess, and Brad Wedlock. 2007. Dam threat to a decade of restoration of the Mary River, Queensland. In *Proceedings of the Fifth Australian Stream Management Conference. Australian rivers: Making a difference*, ed. A. L. Wilson, R. L. Dehaan, R. J. Watts, K. J. Page, K. H. Bowmer, and A. Curtis. Thurgoona, NSW: Charles Sturt University.

Pigram, John J. 1986. *Issues in the management of Australia's water resources*. Melbourne: Longman Chesire.

Pigram, John J. 2007. *Australia's water resources: From use to management*. 2nd ed. Collingwood, Victoria: CSIRO Publishing.

Polsby, Nelson W. 1984. *Political innovation in America: The politics of policy initiation*. New Haven, CT: Yale University Press.

Port Phillip CMA. 2004. *Port Phillip and Western Port regional catchment strategy*. Frankston, Victoria: Port Phillip and Western Port Regional Catchment Management Authority.

Poussard, Horrie. 1992. Community Landcare to test government policies and programs. In Proceedings of the Seventh International Soil Conservation Organisation conference: People protecting their land, Sydney, Australia, April 10.

Prell, Christina, Klaus Hubacek, and Mark Reed. 2009. Stakeholder analysis and social network analysis in natural resource management. *Society and Natural Resources* 22 (6): 501–518.

Pressman, Jeffrey L., and Aaron B. Wildavsky. 1973. *Implementation*. Berkeley: University of California Press.

Priem, Richard L., David A. Harrison, and Nan Kanoff Muir. 1995. Structured conflict and consensus outcomes in group decision making. *Journal of Management* 21 (4): 691–710.

Propp, Kathleen M. 1997. Information utilization in small group decision making: A study of the evaluative interaction model. *Small Group Research* 28 (3): 30.

Propper, Carol, and Deborah Wilson. 2003. The use and usefulness of performance measures in the public sector. *Oxford Review of Economic Policy* 19 (2): 250–267.

Putnam, Robert D. 2000. *Bowling alone: The collapse and revival of American community.* New York: Simon and Schuster.

Queensland Department of Infrastructure and Planning. 2008. *Urban development monitoring.* Brisbane. Available at http://www.dip.qld.gov.au/regional-planning/urban-development-monitoring.html (accessed July 3, 2008).

Rapp, Valerie. 2008. *Northwest Forest Plan–The first 10 years: First decade results from the Northwest Forest Plan.* Portland, OR: Pacific Northwest Research Station.

Red Lodge Clearinghouse. 2009. *Stories: Applegate Partnership and Watershed Council.* Available at http://rlch.org/index.php?option=com_content&task=view&id=96&Itemid=36 (accessed January 12, 2009).

Renger, Ralph, and Carolyn Hurley. 2006. From theory to practice: Lessons learned in the application of the ATM approach to developing logic models. *Evaluation and Program Planning* 29 (2): 106–119.

Renz, David O. 2004. Exploring the puzzle of board design: What's your type? *Nonprofit Quarterly* 11 (1): 52–55.

Rittel, Horst W. J., and Melvin M. Webber. 1973. Dilemmas in a general theory of planning. *Policy Sciences* 4 (2): 155–169.

River Federation. 1994. Institutional frameworks for watershed management programs: Profiles and analysis of selected programs. Prepared for the U.S. Environmental Protection Agency.

Roberts, Nancy C., and Raymond Trevor Bradley. 1991. Stakeholder collaboration and innovation: A study of public policy initiation at the state level. *Journal of Applied Behavioral Science* 27 (2): 209–227.

Roberts, Nancy C., and Paula J. King. 1996. *Transforming public policy: Dynamics of policy entrepreneurship and innovation.* 1st ed. San Francisco: Jossey-Bass.

Robins, Lisa, and Stephen Dovers. 2007a. Community-based NRM boards of management: Are they up to the task? *Australian Journal of Environmental Management* 14 (June): 111–122.

Robins, Lisa, and Stephen Dovers. 2007b. NRM regions in Australia: The "Haves" and the "Have Nots." *Geographical Research* 45 (3): 273–290.

Robinson, Catherine, Bruce Taylor, and Richard D. Margerum. 2009. On a learning journey to nowhere? The practice and politics of natural resource management evaluation in northern Queensland regions. In *Contested country*, ed. M. Lane, C. Robinson, and B. Taylor. Canberra, Australia: Commonwealth Scientific and Industrial Research Organisation.

Rochester, Colin. 2003. The role of boards in small voluntary organisations. In *The governance of public and non-profit organisations: What do boards do?* ed. C. Cornforth. London: Routledge.

Rogers, David L. 1974. Towards a scale of interorganizational relations among public agencies. *Sociology and Social Research* 59 (1): 67–70.

Rogers, David L. 1982. Reflections and synthesis: New directions. In *Interorganizational coordination: Theory, research, and implementation*, ed. D. L. Rogers and D. A. Whetten. Ames: Iowa State University Press.

Rogers, Everett M. 2003. *Diffusion of innovations*. 5th ed. New York: Free Press.

Rosenberg, Stacy R. 2005. Watershed restoration in western Oregon: Landowners, watershed groups, and community dynamics. PhD diss., Environmental Studies and Department of Geography, University of Oregon.

Rosenberg, Stacy, and Richard D. Margerum. 2008. Landowner motivations for watershed restoration: Lessons from five watersheds. *Journal of Environmental Planning and Management* 58 (4): 477–496.

Russo, Edward. 2006. Parkway's alternative route could get mayor's support. *Eugene Register-Guard*, B1, B3.

Sabatier, Paul A. 1986. Top-down and bottom-up approaches to implementation research: A critical analysis and suggested synthesis. *Journal of Public Policy* 6 (1): 21–48.

Sabatier, Paul A., Will Focht, Mark Lubell, Zev Trachtenberg, Arnold Vedlitz, and Marty Matlock. 2005. Collaborative approaches to watershed management. In *Swimming upstream: Collaborative approaches to watershed management*, ed. P. A. Sabatier, W. Focht, M. Lubell, Z. Trachtenberg, A. Vedlitz, and M. Matlock. Cambridge, MA: MIT Press.

Sabatier, Paul A., and Hank C. Jenkins-Smith, eds. 1993. *Policy change and learning: An advocacy coalition approach*. Boulder, CO: Westview Press.

Sabatier, Paul, Hank C. Jenkins-Smith, and Edward F. Lawlor. 1996. Policy change and learning: An advocacy coalition approach. *Journal of Policy Analysis and Management* 15 (1): 11.

Sabatier, Paul A., Hank C. Jenkins-Smith, and Dennis J. Palumbo. 1995. Policy change and learning: An advocacy coalition approach. *Journal of Politics* 57 (2): 4.

Sabatier, Paul A., William D. Leach, Mark Lubell, and Neil W. Pelkey. 2005. Theoretical frameworks explaining partnership success. In *Swimming upstream: Collaborative approaches to watershed management*, ed. P. A. Sabatier, W. Focht, M. Lubell, Z. Trachtenberg, A. Vedlitz, and M. Matlock. Cambridge, MA: MIT Press.

Sabatier, Paul A., and Daniel Mazmanian. 1979. The conditions of effective policy implementation. *Policy Analysis* 5 (4): 481–504.

Sanford, Aubrey C., Gary T. Hunt, and Hyler J. Bracey. 1976. *Communication behavior in organizations*. Columbus, OH: Charles E. Merrill.

Schilling, Fraser M., Jonathan K. London, and Raoul S. Liévanos. 2009. Marginalization by collaboration: Environmental justice as a third party in and beyond CALFED. *Environmental Science and Policy* 12 (6): 694–709.

Schively, Carissa. 2007. A quantitative analysis of consensus building in local environmental review. *Journal of Planning Education and Research* 27 (1): 82–98.

Schlager, Edella. 1995. Policy making and collective action: Defining coalitions within the advocacy coalition framework. *Policy Sciences* 28 (3): 243–270.

Schneider, Mark, John Scholz, Mark Lubell, Denisa Mindruta, and Matthew Edwardsen. 2003. Building consensual institutions: Networks and the National Estuary Program. *American Journal of Political Science* 47 (1): 143–158.

Schneider, Mark, Paul Teske, Christine Roch, and Melissa Marschall. 1997. Networks to nowhere: Segregation and stratification in networks of information about schools. *American Journal of Political Science* 41 (4): 1201–1223.

Scholz, John T., and Bruce Stiftel. 2005. *Adaptive governance and water conflict: New institutions for collaborative planning*. Washington, DC: Resources for the Future.

Schulz, Amy J., Barbara A. Israel, and Paula Lantz. 2003. Instrument for evaluating dimensions of group dynamics within community-based participatory research partnerships. *Evaluation and Program Planning* 26 (3): 249–262.

Schwarz, Roger M. 2002. *The skilled facilitator: Practical wisdom for developing effective groups*. San Francisco: Jossey-Bass.

Schwenk, Charles R., and Richard A. Cosier. 1993. Effects of consensus and devil's advocacy on strategic decision-making. *Journal of Applied Social Psychology* 23 (2): 126–139.

Scott, W. Richard. 1998. *Organizations: Rational, natural and open systems*. 4th ed. Upper Saddle River, NJ: Prentice Hall.

Scott, W. Richard, and Gerald Fredrick Davis. 2007. *Organizations and organizing: Rational, natural, and open systems perspectives*. Upper Saddle River, NJ: Pearson Education.

Selin, Steve, and Deborah Chavez. 1995. Developing a collaborative model for environmental planning and management. *Environmental Management* 19 (2): 189–195.

Selin, Steve, Michael A. Schuett, and Debbie Carr. 2000. Modeling stakeholder perceptions of collaborative initiative effectiveness. *Society and Natural Resources* 13 (8): 735–745.

Shaping the Future: Local Control of Growth at Odds with Regional Goals. 2000. *Denver Post*, May 2, 1.

Sharp, Elaine B. 1994. Paradoxes of national antidrug policymaking. In *The politics of problem definition: Shaping the policy agenda*, ed. David A. Rochefort and Roger W. Cobb. Lawrence: University Press of Kansas.

Shrubsole, D. A. 1990. Integrated water management strategies in Canada. In *Integrated water management: International experiences and perspectives*, ed. B. Mitchell. London: Belhaven Press.

Silvia, Chris, and Michael McGuire. 2010. Leading public sector networks: An empirical examination of integrative leadership behaviors. *Leadership Quarterly* 21 (2): 264–277.

Sinclair, Paul Geoffrey. 2001. *The Murray: A river and its people*. Carlton South, Australia: Melbourne University Press.

Sipe, Neil G. 1998. An empirical analysis of environmental mediation. *Journal of the American Planning Association* 64 (3): 275–285.

Sirianni, Carmen. 2007. Neighborhood planning as collaborative democratic design. *Journal of the American Planning Association* 73 (4): 373–387.

Smith, L. Graham, Carla Y. Nell, and Mark V. Prystupa. 1997. The converging dynamics of interest representation in resources management. *Environmental Management* 21 (2): 139–146.

Smith, Peter. 1990. The use of performance indicators in the public sector. *Journal of the Royal Statistical Society* 153 (1): 53–72.

Snape, D., and M. Stewart. 2005. *Keeping up the momentum: Partnership working in Bristol and the West. Report to the Bristol Chamber of Commerce and Initiative.* Bristol: University of the West of England.

Sommarstrom, Sari. 1999. An evaluation of selected watershed councils in the Pacific Northwest and northern California. Etna, CA: Sari Sommarstrom and Associates.

Southwest Oregon Provincial Interagency Executive Committee (SWOPIEC) and South West Interagency Group (SWIG). 1999. Memorandum of understanding for implementing an integrated basin-scale approach to collaborative watershed restoration in southwest Oregon.

Stasser, Garold, Dennis D. Stewart, and Gwen M. Wittenbaum. 1995. Expert roles and information exchange during discussions: The importance of knowing who knows what. *Journal of Experimental Social Psychology* 31 (3): 244–265.

Stasser, Garold, Laurie A. Taylor, and Colleen Hanna. 1989. Information sampling in structured and unstructured discussions of 3-person and 6-person groups. *Journal of Personality and Social Psychology* 57 (1): 67–78.

Stasser, Garold, and William Titus. 1985. Pooling of unshared information in group decision-making: Biased information sampling during discussion. *Journal of Personality and Social Psychology* 48 (6): 1467–1478.

Stasser, Garold, Sandra I. Vaughan, and Dennis D. Stewart. 2000. Pooling unshared information: The benefits of knowing how access to information is distributed among group members. *Organizational Behavior and Human Decision Processes* 82 (1): 102–116.

Steelman, Toddi A. 2010. *Implementing innovation: Fostering enduring change in environmental and natural resource governance.* Washington, DC: Georgetown University Press.

Stone, Melissa M. 2000. Exploring the effects of collaborations on member organizations: Washington County's welfare-to-work partnerships. *Nonprofit and Voluntary Sector Quarterly* 29 (1 supplement): 98–119.

Stone, Wendy. 2001. *Measuring social capital: Towards a theoretically informed measurement framework for researching social capital in family and community life.* Melbourne: Australian Institute for Family Studies.

Sunwolf, and David R. Seibold. 1999. The impacts of formal procedures on group processes, members, and task outcomes. In *The handbook of group communication theory and research*, ed. L. R. Frey, D. S. Gouran, and M. S. Poole. Thousand Oaks, CA: Sage.

Susskind, Lawrence. 1985. Mediating public disputes. *Negotiation Journal* 1 (1): 19–22.

Susskind, Lawrence, and Jeffrey Cruikshank. 1987. *Breaking the impasse: Consensual approaches to resolving public disputes.* New York: Basic Books.

Susskind, Lawrence, Sarah McKearnon, and Susan Carpenter. 1999. *Consensus-building handbook: A comprehensive guide to reaching agreement.* Thousand Oaks, CA: Sage.

Susskind, Lawrence, and Connie Ozawa. 1984. Mediated negotiation in the public sector: The planners as mediator. *Journal of Planning Education and Research* 3 (3): 5–15.

Susskind, Lawrence, and Alan Weinstein. 1980. Towards a theory of environmental dispute resolution. *Boston College Environmental Affairs Law Review* 9 (2): 311–357.

Talbot, Allan R. 1983. *Settling things: Six case studies in environmental mediation.* Washington, DC: Conservation Foundation.

Talen, Emily. 1996. Do plans get implemented? A review of evaluation in planning. *Journal of Planning Literature* 10 (3): 248–259.

Thomas, Craig W. 2003. *Bureaucratic landscapes: Interagency cooperation and the preservation of biodiversity.* Cambridge, MA: MIT Press.

Thomas, Kenneth W., and Ralph H. Kilmann. 1974. *Thomas-Kilmann conflict MODE instrument.* Mountain View, CA: Xicom and CPP, Inc.

Thompson, Don, and Sharon Pepperdine. 2003. Assessing community capacity for riparian restoration. Canberra: Land and Water Australia.

TIMP Steering Committee. 1992. *Trinity Inlet management plan.* Cairns, Queensland: TIMP Steering Committee

TIMP. 1996. *1995–96 annual report.* Cairns, Queensland: Trinity Inlet Management Program.

Turner, Wallace. 1985. Irate property owners fuel attack on Tahoe planning agency, *New York Times*, March 10, section 1, 22.

U.S. Environmental Protection Agency. 1993. *Geographic targeting: Selected state examples.* Washington, DC: U.S. Environmental Protection Agency, Office of Water.

Warner, Jeroen. 2007. *Multi-stakeholder platforms for integrated water management.* Aldershot, England: Ashgate.

Weber, Edward P. 2000. A new vanguard for the environment: Grass-roots ecosystem management as a new environmental movement. *Society and Natural Resources* 13 (3) 237–259.

Weber, Edward P. 2003. *Bringing society back in: Grassroots ecosystem management, accountability, and sustainable communities.* Cambridge, MA: MIT Press.

Weber, Edward P., and Anne M. Khademian. 2008. Managing collaborative processes: Common practices, uncommon circumstances. *Administration and Society* 40 (5): 431–464.

Webster, D. G. 2009. *Adaptive governance: The dynamics of Atlantic fisheries management.* Cambridge, MA: MIT Press.

Weeks, Edward C. 2000. The practice of deliberative democracy: Results from four large-scale trials. *Public Administration Review* 60 (4): 360–372.

Weible, Christopher M. 2005. Beliefs and perceived influence in a natural resource conflict: An advocacy coalition approach to policy networks. *Political Research Quarterly* 58 (3): 461–475.

Weisman, Carol, and Richard I. Goldbaum. 2004. *Losing your executive director without losing your way.* San Francisco: Jossey-Bass.

Weiss, Janet A. 1987. Pathways to cooperation among public agencies. *Journal of Policy Analysis and Management* 7 (1): 94–117.

Wellman, Barry, and Stephen D. Berkowitz. 1988. *Social structures: A network approach. Structural analysis in the social sciences.* Cambridge: Cambridge University Press.

Winer, Michael, and Karen Ray. 1994. *Collaboration handbook: Creating, sustaining, and enjoying the journey.* Saint Paul, MN: Amherst H. Wilder Foundation.

Wise, John. 1975. *The Lake Tahoe study*. Washington, DC: U.S. Environmental Protection Agency.

Wittenbaum, Gwen M. 2000. The bias toward discussing shared information: Why are high-status group members immune? *Communication Research* 27 (3): 379–401.

Wolfred, Timothy, Mike Allison, and Jan Masaoka. 1999. *Leadership lost: A study on executive director tenure and experience*. San Francisco: Support Center for Nonprofit Management.

Wondolleck, Julia M. 1985. The importance of process in resolving environmental disputes. *Environmental Impact Assessment Review* 5 (4):341–356.

Wondolleck, Julia M., and Steven L. Yaffee. 2000. *Making collaboration work: Lessons from innovation in natural resource management*. Washington, DC: Island Press.

Wood, Donna J., and Barbara Gray. 1991. Towards a comprehensive theory of collaboration. *Journal of Applied Behavioral Science* 27 (2): 139–162.

Wood, Miriam M., ed. 1996. *Nonprofit Boards and Leadership*. San Francisco: Jossey-Bass.

Yaffee, Steven L., Ali F. Phillips, Irene C. Frentz, Paul W. Hardy, Sussanne M. Maleki, and Barbara E. Thorpe. 1996. *Ecosystem management in the United States: An assessment of current experience*. Washington, DC: Island Press.

Yin, Robert K. 2009. *Case study research: Design and methods*. 4th ed. Los Angeles: Sage.

Zaccaro, Stephen J., and Richard J. Klimoski. 2001. *The nature of organizational leadership: Understanding the performance imperatives confronting today's leaders*. 1st ed. San Francisco: Jossey-Bass.

Zahariadis, Nikolaos, ed. 1999. Ambiguity, time, and multiple streams. In *Theories of the policy process*, ed. P. A. Sabatier. Boulder, CO: Westview Press.

Index